EXPLORING THE
LITERARY CONTEXTS
OF PATRISTIC
BIBLICAL EXEGESIS

EXPLORING THE LITERARY CONTEXTS OF PATRISTIC BIBLICAL EXEGESIS

EDITED BY

Miriam De Cock and Elizabeth Klein

The Catholic University of America Press
Washington, D.C.

The paper used in this publication meets the minimum requirements of
American National Standards for Information Science—Permanence
of Paper for Printed Library Materials, ANSI Z39.48-1992.
∞

Cataloging-in-Publication Data is available at the Library of Congress
ISBN: 978-0-8132-3741-1
eISBN: 978-0-8132-3692-6

CONTENTS

ACKNOWLEDGEMENTS

The compiling of this collection of essays is occasioned by the retirement of Peter Widdicombe, long-time associate professor of Early Christianity in McMaster University's Department of Religious Studies (Hamilton, ON, Canada). In his work and teaching, Widdicombe always strived to make his students attentive to the patristic authors' own way of understanding the biblical text and to how it gave shape to their world, without attempting to import modern standards of how a text ought and ought not to be read. He always aimed to take the patristic authors as seriously as they took themselves and their own work, and in this mode to discover what was really happening in these sometimes odd and often surprising texts.

OSAR	Oxford Studies in the Abrahamic Religions
OSLA	Oxford Studies in Late Antiquity
OTM	Oxford Theological Monographs
PG	Patrologia Graeca
PL	Patrologia Latina
PS	Patrologia Syriaca
RECM	Routledge Early Church Monographs
RevQ	*Revue De Qumrân*
RIB	Roman Imperial Biographies
RMCS	Routledge Monographs in Classical Studies
SAJEC	Studies in Ancient Judaism and Early Christiaity
SBR	Studies of the Bible and its Reception
SC	Sources Chrétiennes
SECT	Sources of Early Christian Thought
StPatr	Studia Patristica
TCLA	Texts in Christian Late Antiquity
TLG	Thesaurus linguae graecae
TSAJ	Texts and Studies in Ancient Judaism
VC	*Vigiliae Christianae*
VT	*Vetus Testamentum*
VCS	Supplements to Vigiliae Christianae
WSA	Works of Saint Augustine
WUNT	Wissenschaftliche Untersuchungen zum Neuen Testament
ZK	Zeitschrift für Kirchengeschichte

Miriam De Cock and Elizabeth Klein

INTRODUCTION

Scholarly Context

What is patristic exegesis and where is it to be found? In answering these questions scholars have tended to seek to uncover the methodologies, influences, theological assumptions, and rhetorical aims of various patristic writers.[1] Scholars of patristic exegesis thus paid disproportionate attention to the sustained exegesis found in early biblical commentaries and, to a lesser extent, exegetical homilies. As a result, the exegesis found in the multitude of other early Christian literary genres was largely overlooked in discussions of biblical interpretation, despite the fact that the bulk of patristic exegesis is found in these contexts. Moreover, the scholarly focus on exegetical commentaries tended to overlook the fact that the exegesis found in other genres, such as theological treatises and liturgical hymns, undoubtedly informed the exegetical traditions that arise in the biblical commentaries, and vice versa.

The past couple of decades has seen a broadening of perspective on the study of patristic exegesis; the phenomenon is increasingly situated within its various literary contexts and genres, and the definition of what counts as

---

1. The following literature is a representative, though by no means exhaustive, list of scholarship on patristic exegesis: J.-N. Guinot, "La frontière entre allégorie et typologie. École alexandrine, école antiochienne," *RSR* 99 (2011): 207–28; Robert M. Grant and David Tracy, *A Short History of the Interpretation of the Bible*, 2nd ed. (Philadelphia: Fortress Press, 1973); Manlio Simonetti, *Biblical Interpretation in the Early Church*, trans. John A. Hughes (Edinburgh: T&T Clark, 1994); Karlfried Froehlich, *Biblical Interpretation in the Early Church* (SECT Philadelphia: Fortress Press, 1980); Manlio Simonetti, *Lettera e/o allegoria: Un contributo alla storia dell'esegesi patristica* (Rome: IPA, 1985).

patristic exegesis is therefore widened.[2] This volume thus situates itself within this emerging scholarly tradition, which aims not to give an account of exegetical strategies and methodologies as found primarily in exegetical commentaries and homilies, but to demonstrate the highly sophisticated nature of biblical exegesis in other genres, and the manifold uses to which this exegesis was put.

References to and reflection on Scripture can appear in virtually any literary genre of Christian late antiquity for a variety of reasons.[3] Ancient Christian authors lived and breathed Scripture; it served as their primary source of theological and liturgical vocabulary, their way of processing the world, their social ethic, and their mode of constructing self and communal identity. Scripture therefore permeates all ancient Christian literature, regardless of genre, and the various contexts in which interpretation of Scripture took place resulted in a wide variety of uses of the Church's authoritative texts. Accordingly, the volume aims to help the modern person, who is used to hearing the Bible explained in explicitly expository situations (for example, in academic commentaries or religious sermons) to become more habituated to ancient ways of interacting with and expounding the biblical text. These essays attempt to contextualize various types of patristic exegesis, in order for us to glimpse the complex and diverse uses of the Bible in this period.

---

2. In her influential work, *Biblical Exegesis and the Formation of Christian Culture*, Frances M. Young devoted a chapter to the various contexts of patristic exegesis, but given the scope of her larger project, her comments are only suggestive. She examined briefly the exegesis in the related contexts of liturgy and prayer, homilies, hagiography, canons, catechesis, commentaries, letters, apologetics, and doctrinal debates, and all of this in a mere 30 pages. Young, *Biblical Exegesis and the Formation of Christian Culture* (Cambridge: Cambridge University Press, 1997), 217–47. Since Young's pioneering study, see the following selection of scholarly work on our subject: In a different generic mode than the present volume, the *Oxford Handbook of Early Christian Biblical Interpretation* (eds. Peter W. Martens and Paul M. Blowers; Oxford: Oxford University Press, 2019), is a recent example of a growing scholarly recognition that patristic exegesis entails much more than the study of patristic commentaries and exegetical homilies. For example, the handbook contains one section with entries on exegesis in such genres as catechesis and homilies, novels, art, poetry, hagiography, and liturgy. Our volume differs in that we offer thoroughgoing case studies of patristic exegesis in specific literary contexts so as to demonstrate the great variety and rich texture of patristic exegesis.

3. See, for example, a handful of past studies have explored the exegesis found in literary genres other than the commentary and homily. See for example Elizabeth A. Clark's study of monastic exegesis, *Reading Renunciation: Asceticism and Scripture in Early Christianity* (Princeton, NJ: Princeton University Press, 1999), or Derek Krueger's examination of the use of Scripture in the hymnographic tradition, *Liturgical Subjects: Christian Ritual, Biblical Narrative, and the Formation of the Self in Byzantium* (Philadelphia: University of Pennsylvania Press, 2014). In this present volume, we seek to put the study of the various fundamental contexts of patristic exegesis together in one volume, given that they were inextricably linked in the early church.

We examine the exegesis found in the following ten genres[4] of early Christian literature: a martyrdom account; an apocalypse; homilies; paraphrase; argumentative treatises; an encomium; monastic literature (a set of dialogues and a rule text); catenae; and finally, a medieval set of mystical visions.

In the first essay, "The *Passion of Perpetua and Felicity* as Exegesis of the Book of Revelation," Elizabeth Klein illustrates that Perpetua, in her martyrdom and the accounts of her visions, interprets Revelation as teaching that martyrdom is a public, liturgical act, which makes present a cosmic reality and which anticipates and participates in the heavenly liturgy. Klein argues, against much previous scholarship, that the *Passio*'s dreams are not simply a pastiche of biblical images, but that the biblical book of Revelation actually shapes the entire thrust of the authors' lived reality and thus its presentation in the text. As these female figures speak about their experiences in the Bible's terms, they bring the book of Revelation to life by enacting the social order that it envisions. The text thus illustrates the extent to which the author's lived re-presentation of the biblical text constitutes a central form of interpretation.

The second essay, "Congregational Exegesis and Apocalyptic Visions in the Shepherd of Hermas," is by Bronwen Neil, who examines the manner in which the author of the apocalyptic text, *The Shepherd of Hermas*, interprets his ecstatic visions. Despite the fact that the author works within a "biblical" framework in its understanding of prophecy, Neil argues, Hermas does not cite or interpret these authoritative texts. Rather, the author provides his own set of parables, which he seems to privilege above those already available, and seeks to interpret them for the sake of his broader Church community.

Following Neil's are four essays focused on the exegesis of early Christian homilies. As noted above, scholars have paid closer attention to the exegesis found in homilies than in many other early Christian genres, though there nonetheless remains much work to be done to elucidate the nature and content of homiletic exegesis.

---

4. We note, however, the great degree of overlap between many of the genres examined in the volume. For example, the metrical homilies studied by Robert Kitchen are highly poetic, as is the paraphrase examined by Andrew Faulkner. The *Conferences* of Cassian studied by Daniel Opperwall are essentially dialogues, and while we describe them as monastic literature alongside Cassian's *Institutes*, a monastic rule text, we do so with the awareness that the two texts have their own generic complexities. Further, Miriam De Cock's essay on Origen's homilies draws also on his commentaries given her argument that the exegesis found in the two genres is both pastoral and "scholarly." The primary aim of these essays is not to define or redefine the various early Christian literary genres, but rather to highlight the highly exegetical nature of virtually every early Christian text, almost regardless of genre.

The first essay on homiletic exegesis is that of Elizabeth Dively Lauro: "Origen Makes Preachers of Us All: A Collective Analysis of his Nine Extant *Homilies on Judges*." She argues that in the context of the Judges homilies, Origen uses the biblical book's ancient judges, the Israelites' deliverers, to instruct his audience about the soul's journey within the cosmic battle between good and evil spiritual forces. In this context, Origen presents himself variously as angel-savior, overseer, steward, and leader, who delivers his hearers' souls from enemies, instructs them in saving truths, and leads them along the upward path to God. Further, Origen uses the homiletic context to argue that Scripture is calling his hearers not only to enlist as soldiers along the path of ascent, but, with some progress, to effectively perform the preacher's tasks for themselves and for their fellow pilgrims.

The second essay concerned with homiletic exegesis is Miriam DeCock's, "Origen's Exegetical Treatment of Romans 8:15: Spiritual Adoption by the Father, in the Son, through the Holy Spirit." Through a comparative examination of Origen's homilies, this essay highlights the *pastoral* nature of Origen's commentaries, which have long been understood as primarily scholastic. She demonstrates that Origen is remarkably consistent in his exegesis of Rom 8:15 across the commentary and homily genres; in both contexts, Origen is concerned to use the Pauline verse to explain the Christian's trajectory from slave to son, and to exhort his audience, who are at some stage of this journey, to live lives that position them to receive the gift of the "spirit of adoption."

The third essay on exegesis found in the homily is that of Robert Kitchen, "Teaching Lions to Fast: Jacob of Serugh on Daniel 6," in which he analyses one metric homily focused on Daniel in the Lion's Den. Kitchen's essay illustrates the difference the liturgical context makes to the homiletic-poetic treatment of the passage, and how the liturgical poem/homily is representative of Syriac poetic compositions.[5] This *mēmrā*, in which Jacob urges his audience to worship and pray like the devoted ascetic Daniel, is not a scholastic treatment of the biblical text resulting from the classroom; rather, his audience is drawn into the drama of the story, through the performance of the poem, likely within the liturgical celebration of Easter given its resonance with the Gospels' resurrection narratives.

---

5. Exegetical poetry in Greek and Latin, whose performance or reading contexts are less certain and more varied, are not as commonly linked to liturgy.

The final essay on homiletic exegesis is that of Sarah Stewart-Kroeker: "Reading Augustine's Psalm *Sermones* in the Anthropocene." She focuses on Augustine's interest in and use of the verses in the Psalms about animals, natural phenomena, and the non-human world. Stewart-Kroeker demonstrates that, despite the anthropomorphic and anthropocentric framework of Augustine's approach, by attending to his allegorical and "imagistic" approach to the Psalms, one also finds in the *Sermones* "a morally and aesthetically formative site of encounter with the more-than-human world." She argues that in these *Sermones* while the non-human creation lends its behaviors and patterns to Augustine's reflection on the human spiritual life, it is their beauty and sublimity which so inspire praise and awe in the human beholder, an observation that might aid the modern reader of Augustine in her approach to the Anthropocene.

With Andrew Faulkner's "The Late Antique Poet as Scriptural Interpreter: The Case of the *Metaphrasis Psalmorum*," we shift to the genre of the poetic paraphrase. Faulkner examines the highly didactic form of exegesis undertaken by late antique poets. He argues that the author of the *Metaphrasis Psalmorum*—whom he takes to be Apollinaris of Laodicea—engaged exegetically with Scripture, in this case, the Septuagint Psalms, by paraphrasing the psalms in Greek hexameters of classical poetry.[6] Faulkner argues that the poet's programmatic stance in the prologue and the imagery he employs associate him quite closely with the late antique Christian interpreter of Scripture: he makes claims to inspiration, enlightenment, a humble posture before the task, and the appropriate doctrinal credentials. Furthermore, Faulkner demonstrates that the paraphrase reflects the influence of and conscious engagement with the Christian exegetical tradition. Not only is the poet engaged in exegetical paraphrase, but he also engages the exegetical discussions of biblical commentaries proper.

Robin Darling Young next examines the exegesis found within an encomium text of Gregory of Nazianzus, the *Epitaphios Logos*, in which he presents his sister Gorgonia as an exemplary figure whose life embodies the intersection between Scripture and philosophy. In particular, Gorgonia is presented as a scriptural exegete and teacher, a philosophical woman and an

---

6. Faulkner notes that Apollinaris is not unique in doing so amongst the early Christian poets of the fourth and fifth centuries.

ascetic wife, and in order to present her in this light, Gregory makes use of several biblical images and verses, such as patient Job, the wife of Proverbs 31, the generous benefactor to the poor. These two images are augmented by an additional scriptural verse, 1 Cor 4:34, so as to portray Gorgonia as an example of a married, family philosopher who had grown up in a philosophical household and also modelled silence until the very end of her life.

Three essays in the volume examine exegesis within theological treatises. The first is Brian Daley's essay, "'The Beginning of His Ways:' Christ as God's Personified Wisdom in the Early Greek Fathers," which traces the development of the patristic understanding of Wisdom as referring to Christ. Daley provides a characteristically holistic vision of the theological approach and mindset of patristic exegetes, and their attentiveness to biblical modes of expression as he examines the theme of Christ as Wisdom.

The second, Ron Haflidson's essay, "The Differences the Son Makes: The Vocation of the Theologian-Exegete in Augustine's *Confessions* Book 12," demonstrates the complexity and consistency of Augustine's exegesis vis-à-vis the case study of "heaven and earth" (Gn 1:1). Haflidson argues that Augustine joins his contemporaries in producing several interpretations of the verse as he reflects on the Son's work in creation. He argues that for Augustine, just as the Son's work in both creation and the Church is centered on harmonizing differences, so too must the responsible pastoral theologian-exegete offer different scriptural interpretations that will meet the needs of different believers.

The third essay focuses on the exegesis within the genre of the theological treatise is that of Geoffrey Dunn: "Augustine, the Fishermen's Dragnet, the Donatists, and Excommunication." In it, he examines Augustine's exegesis of Mt 13:47–50 in the polemical and conciliar context of the Donatist-Caecilianist sectarian controversy. Dunn demonstrates that Augustine interpreted the parable, in which the kingdom of God is compared to a fisherman's act of separating the good and bad fish from his "full" net, in direct response to the situation in his day. Unlike the Donatists, who took the passage to justify their present excommunication of those they deemed to be "bad fish," for Augustine, the parable meant that there could be bad fish within the Church, and that it was a divine (not a human) task to separate the good fish from the bad, and this at the last judgement. With this interpretation, Augustine joined his Donatist contemporaries in using this passage, among others, to define Christianity from his and his community's vantage point for the imperial commissioner of the controversy.

From theological treatise we move to monastic literature with Daniel Opperwall's essay, "Apocalyptic Imagery and the Transformation of Self: Matthew 24 and the Book of Revelation in John Cassian." Opperwall argues that through his use of the apocalyptic and eschatological passages of Matthew 24 and the book of Revelation in his *Institutes* and *Conferences*, John Cassian deploys Scripture as a spiritual tool in the work of self-transformation, which he models and teaches his fellow ascetics, particularly as it relates to their need to stay the course of asceticism, and the problem of bad spiritual leadership. Surprisingly, Cassian sublimates the eschatological dimension of Revelation almost entirely as he guides his audience in the application of these texts.

Next comes Paul-Hubert Poirier's essay on exegesis of the catenae, "Origen on John 20:25 and on the Name of the Apostle Thomas (*In Iohannem*, Fragment 106)." Poirier offers a translation and examination of the catena fragment, which deals with Thomas' doubt in Jn 20:25. As the title suggests, Poirier argues that we can attribute the fragment to Origen, a case he makes throughout the paper as he demonstrates the author's openness to all useful material. That openness includes traditions already suspect in some early Christian circles, in this case, the Thomasian tradition, the driving force of which was the twinship of Thomas and Christ, based on Thomas' name "Didymus." In the fragment, Thomas' doubt is taken as "accurate" prudence, in a manner that leads the ancient author to take on the questions of his sobriquet, and to makes use of, Poirier argues, material from *The Gospel According to Thomas* so as to explain Thomas' name change, and accordingly, his ability to speak words with double meaning.

In the final essay of the volume, a happy coda if you like, we shift our focus to the medieval period and examine a set of exegetical visions. In Karl Shuve's "Visionary Exegesis: Interpreting Scripture in Hildegard of Bingen's *Scivias*," he demonstrates that Hildegard interprets her own visions *as* scriptural revelation, an indirect claim to their divine source. As she provides a meticulous interpretation of the images of her visions, Hildegard uses the biblical text insofar as it helps her to articulate the meaning of her own visions, rather than to interpret the biblical text itself. Shuve helpfully highlights the paradox of the strict limitations on Hildegard as biblical interpreter due to her gender:

she was free to privilege her own visions of the divine whilst operating on the same interpretive plane as her male counterparts.

The overarching argument of this volume is that early Christian exegesis took place in all of the available literary genres. The form this exegesis took in contexts beyond the sustained biblical commentary ought to be studied further, for each of the ancient authors in focus worked with methods and strategies one might find in a sustained biblical commentary, such as engagement with earlier exegetical traditions, or paraphrases and expansions of the biblical narrative. The exegesis in these contexts is at least as creative and clever as that found in the sustained biblical commentaries of the period, and it is our hope that the essays here will spark further examination along these lines.

EXPLORING THE LITERARY CONTEXTS OF PATRISTIC BIBLICAL EXEGESIS

Elizabeth Klein

1. THE *PASSION OF PERPETUA AND FELICITY* AS EXEGESIS OF THE BOOK OF REVELATION

The *Passion of Perpetua and Felicity,* one of the most well-known martyr-dom accounts of early Christianity, is perhaps most famous for its account of four visions—three of which are purportedly written down by the protagonist Perpetua herself.[1] Sometimes, in summaries of these dreams, the impression can be given that the visions consist largely of a pastiche of biblical images. The dreams seem to pull material from many different biblical sources, which are then recombined in a dizzying and fantastic array. Interpreting these images can be a difficult task. For example, Patricia Cox Miller (following the lead of Peter Dronke) worries that attempting to identify each image with a particu-lar biblical passage runs the risk of reducing the dreams to "biblical common-places" or tropes.[2] The challenge of understanding Perpetua's dream images as

1. It has long been debated whether or not Perpetua herself really wrote or recounted these visions, and to what extent redaction might have changed any words she did relate. Most recently, Ellen Muehl-berger has argued that one ought to approach the text *assuming* that these are not the authentic words of Perpetua—see Ellen Muehlberger. "Perpetual Adjustment: The Passion of Perpetua and Felicity and the Entailments of Authenticity" in *JECS* 30, no. 3 (2022): 313–42. For the purposes of this paper, which treats the literary structure of the visions, it does not much matter to my interpretation whether Perpet-ua or some other author in her community composed or edited the text, and it may in fact strengthen the possible liturgical parallels if the work is a literary composition. Nevertheless, I do not take such a skepti-cal stance as Muehlberger and will use language that suggests access to Perpetua's experience.

2. Patricia Cox Miller, *Dreams in Late Antiquity* (Princeton, NJ: Princeton University Press, 1994),

more than simply a chain of biblical ones seems to be related to the challenge of understanding patristic exegesis more broadly speaking. For us moderns, it can be tempting to view patristic exegesis as fanciful, because early Christian interpreters tend to link many biblical passages in rapid succession, often by theme, common images or word associations, rather than by attending to the particularity of any given passage and its context. Is the *passio* engaging in this same kind of interpretive work? Or, if we read Perpetua's visions as a series of biblical images tenuously joined together, are we in danger of doing the same disservice to her as the early churchmen are accused of doing to the Bible?

Drawing this very broad parallel between the task of interpreting the *passio* and of understanding the nature of patristic exegesis helps to frame our present topic: the *passio* as a work of exegesis. Although we might be accustomed to think of exegesis as an intellectual, expository exercise, for early Christians, exegesis was also an imaginative exercise that took place in a wide variety of contexts.[3] The *passio*, like many ancient Christian texts, interprets reality through the Bible and the Bible through lived reality. For the early Christians, the Bible is not simply a history of Israel or even a handbook of how to live, but it is the text through which one trains oneself to see everything and by which one trains oneself to speak. We might immediately think of Augustine's *Confessions* as a prime example of this type of exegesis, since Augustine speaks in the words of Scripture about his own story, but much of early Christian preaching also follows this pattern of using the Bible as the lens through which to view all other things and as the means by which to synthesize theology, morality, and ritual. Perhaps this fluid interplay between life and text is even more apparent in an early work such as the *passio,* when the canon as such is not yet fixed.

By claiming that Perpetua and her companions interpret their lives through the Bible and vice versa, however, I do not mean to suggest that the ancients favored a kind of purely subjective mode of biblical interpretation. For one thing, they inhabit a world much closer in time and culture to that of the New Testament than we do. But more importantly, the Bible sets the

---

154, and Peter Dronke, *Women Writers of the Middle Ages* (Cambridge: Cambridge University Press, 1984), 6–7.

    3. Reframing biblical exegesis in this broader way also helps us to understand some imaginative modes of later medieval exegesis, such as that of Hildegard von Bingen, as discussed by Karl Shuve in the present volume.

terms for how to discuss, process and proclaim one's own experience of spiritual realities. In turn, those experiences cast light on the meaning of the Bible. Candida Moss notes, for example, that because martyrdom stories are often built on the scaffolding of the gospels, these "passion narratives function like ancient commentaries on Scripture, providing valuable insights into how the earliest Christians interpreted stories about Jesus."[4] In the case of the *passio* in particular, however, one of the key texts that the authors employ to give voice to the truth of the martyrs' deaths is the book of Revelation. In this paper I will argue that Revelation does not simply populate the image world of the *passio*'s visions, but that it supplies a vision of reality that undergirds the martyrs' interpretation of their own experiences and informs the text as a whole. First and foremost, Revelation provides a cultic understanding of history that Perpetua embraces, thus the text of her martyrdom imitates Revelation in its genre and not just in the images upon which it draws. The book of Revelation, moreover, also informs the *passio*'s presentation of the Roman empire and its inversion in the new social order of Christianity (that is, the Church). Perpetua et al. speak about their experiences in the Bible's terms and bring the book of Revelation to life by enacting the social order that it envisions.

The Cultic Vision of the Passio

In the early Christian Church, the key settings for biblical interpretation are communal and liturgical.[5] Justin Martyr, writing around 150 CE, describes the Sunday meeting of Christians as one where the Bible is read and then expounded.[6] For those people with little leisure for intellectual pursuits and who could not read nor afford to own a copy of scriptural texts, communal meetings were the main place where they heard the Scriptures read. It is no surprise, then, that in the *passio* biblical allusions are often woven into the text side-by-side with liturgical ones, and that Revelation, with its cultic imagery and emphasis on martyrdom, would be a particularly resonant text for Perpetua. The

---

4. Candida Moss, *The Other Christs* (Oxford: Oxford University Press, 2010), 45.

5. For more on Perpetua's education, and the likely way in which she learned and remembered the scriptures (and other texts), see Walter Amelig, *"Femina Liberaliter Instituta*—Some Thoughts on a Martyr's Liberal Education," in *Perpetua's Passions: Multidisciplinary Approaches to the* Passio Perpetuae et Felicitas, eds. Jan Bremmer and Marco Formisano (Oxford: Oxford University Press, 2012), 78–102, but especially 95–98.

6. Justin Martyr, *First Apology 67*.

passio, however, has a deeper relationship to the liturgy than simply echoing or referring to liturgical practice alongside biblical texts. It, following the book of Revelation, sees the unfolding of history as a cultic drama. What is experienced in the liturgy is apocalyptic in its proper sense: it is the unveiling of the heavenly order and of the providence of God. To put it more simply: the liturgy reveals what is really going on and where it will end.

In the *passio,* the unveiling of heavenly realities through the liturgy is perhaps most striking in Perpetua's first vision. I (and others) have argued elsewhere that this first vision is like a cosmic rite of initiation,[7] but let me briefly draw out the parallels. Perpetua begins with a kind of renunciation of Satan and adherence to Christ,[8] assuring Saturus (her catechist, who would have prepared her for baptism) that the giant serpent at the bottom of the ladder will not harm her and invoking the name of Jesus as protection (4.6).[9] She then proceeds up a bronze ladder covered in weapons (4.3, 4.7), which upon waking she interprets as martyrdom (4.10). Martyrdom is also understood as a baptism of blood explicitly in the *passio* (18.3 and 21.2)—a common association in this period[10]—and the dream (4.1ff) follows almost immediately after Perpetua's water baptism (3.5). At the top of the ladder, she reaches an "enormous garden" and sees a white-haired shepherd milking sheep (4.8). The man, addressing Perpetua as "child" (in Greek, echoing words used for the newly baptized)[11] gives Perpetua a morsel of cheese (a *bucella,* a rare word found in the Latin New Testament in the context of the last supper),[12] which she receives

7. Elizabeth Klein, "Perpetua, Cheese and Martyrdom as Public Liturgy in the *Passion of Perpetua and Felicity*" in JECS 28, no. 2 (Summer 2020), 175–202. See also Anne Jensen, *God's Self-Confident Daughters: Early Christianity and the Liberation of Women,* trans. O.C. Dean. (Louisville: Knox Press, 1996), 102–08 and Alvyn Pettersen "Perpetua, a Prisoner of Conscience," *VC* 41, no. 2 (Jun. 1987): 147–48.

8. Our earliest evidence for the renunciation of Satan before baptism comes from North Africa; see Tertullian, *Cor.* 3.2 and *Spect.* 4.1.

9. *Passion of Perpetua and Felicity* 4.9. Henceforth references to the *passio* appear in the main body of the text, with Latin text and translation drawn from Thomas Heffernan, *The Passion of Perpetua and Felicity* (Oxford: Oxford University Press, 2012).

10. For example, Tertullian, *Bapt.* 16.2.

11. The word is *tegnon*—a Latin transliteration of τέκνον. Other evidence for referring to the baptized as children (*infantes* or *parvuli*) in the West comes later than the *passio*; see Zeno of Verona, *s.* 1.24, and Augustine, *s.* 226. There is early evidence for calling the newly baptized "children" in the East, however; see Clement of Alexandria, *Paed.* 1.6.25 and perhaps *Barn.* 6.11. More generally, Greek words in a Latin text suggest a liturgical setting. See Jensen, *God's Daughters,* 284, n. 140 and Heffernan, *Passion,* 182, where he mentions that Greek was seen as prestigious among the clergy.

12. For a full discussion of the use of this word and its eucharistic connotations, see Klein, "Perpetua, Cheese and Martyrdom," 190–92.

with cupped hands. The saints dressed in white surrounding her respond with an "amen" (4.9). This eucharistic scene (the reverently accepted cheese) naturally follows the baptismal one (stepping on the dragon and climbing the ladder), as the reception of the Eucharist along with a cup of milk and honey followed water baptism in North Africa at this time, and was the climactic moment of Christian initiation.[13] When Perpetua awakes, she is still chewing something sweet and knows that she will die as a martyr (4.10). In sum, although this vision is not a kind of cipher for baptism, through these liturgical parallels, martyrdom is revealed to be the rite of initiation into heaven (for which Perpetua's water baptism has prepared her),[14] a heaven which is also experienced in strongly cultic terms. This dream, heavily laden with liturgical imagery, is apocalyptic. It reveals the deeper reality of water baptism (itself a combat with the devil,[15] promise of salvation[16] and preparation for martyrdom[17]) as well as Perpetua's fate and its true meaning: martyrdom, her second baptism, which is not defeat, but a victory over Satan and entry into heaven. Heaven (the garden) is seen as a liturgical setting and as the place where current and future events are disclosed.

This first vision also draws heavily on images from the book of Revelation: the dragon and the woman who escapes him (Revelation 12), the white-haired man (Rev 1:14), the saints in white before the throne (Rev 6:9; 7:9, 13–14), who are described in language readily applicable to baptism (they are worshipping and well-fed, having been led to living waters by the shepherd; Rev 7:15–17), and they are identified as martyrs (Rev 7:19). But more significantly, the *passio* takes on the worldview of Revelation—its use of Revelation's specific

13. See Tertullian, *Cor.* 3.3, but this practice is attested elsewhere as well. For a comparative summary of early Christian rites of initiation see Maxwell Johnson, *The Rites of Christian Initiation* (Collegeville, MN: Liturgical Press, 1999), 111.

14. She asks that in baptism she receive the grace for perseverance in martyrdom (3.5). For a more in-depth discussion of the relationship between water baptism and martyrdom in this period, see Klein, "Perpetua, Cheese and Martyrdom," 184–85.

15. An idea found in Tertullian (*Bapt.* 9.1), where baptism is described as drowning of the devil, but the idea is ubiquitous among early Christian writers.

16. Robin Jensen and Patout Burns write that at this time baptism is the "cosmic division between the saved and the damned;" see *Christianity in Roman North Africa* (Grand Rapids, MI: Eerdmans, 2014), 165.

17. Tertullian links water baptism and martyrdom so closely that he includes "exhortation to martyrdom" as part of a summary of the rite of initiation (*Praescr.* 36.5). The mention of this exhortation may indicate an actual practice of exhorting the newly baptized to martyrdom, or it may imply that he saw the whole rite as that exhortation.

imagery should signal to us that this is the case, and it helps us to understand the parallels between Perpetua's vision and John's, but it does not imply that Perpetua's dream is simply a collage, a hasty cut-and-paste job from the Scriptures. Rather, the cultic vision of reality that Perpetua takes on is a hallmark of the book of Revelation. In John's visions, the unveiling of the true history of the world happens frequently in cultic terms. Revelation expresses the battle for this world and the ongoing struggle of Christians as liturgical[18]—e.g., prayers offered like incense (Rev 4:8) at a heavenly altar (Rev 8:3–5), the reading from a scroll (Rev 4:9) and the sacrifice of the lamb (Rev 5:6), the measuring of the temple as prophetic (Rev 11:1–3), judgment coming forth from the altar (Rev 14:18) and plagues from the sanctuary (Rev 15:.8). It also envisions the activity of heaven, and future hope, as that of the heavenly liturgy—e.g., eternal songs of praise offered before the throne of God (Rev 4:.11–14; 7:11), the consummation of history as the wedding feast of the lamb (Rev 19:6–9; 21:2), and heaven as the new Jerusalem, in which God himself is the temple (Rev 21:22–23). Indeed, Crispin Fletcher-Louis has argued that the most common link between various apocalyptic texts is that of cultic imagery—all texts identified in the Jewish apocalyptic genre are the "product of a priestly and cultic milieu."[19] Of Jewish apocalypses, he writes that "temple cosmology—the belief that cultic space and time is a sacramental model of the universe—facilitates the experiences of transcendence, especially ascent to heaven, that so define apocalyptic literature."[20] It is also this character of Revelation, its genre we might say, that the *passio* takes on along with its specific images.

This adoption of genre is apparent in the fact that the first vision is by no means the only place in the *passio* where we see liturgical action as apocalyptic—i.e., as disclosing the true meaning of the events taking place. The worldview of Revelation is present throughout the text even if Revelation is not being cited or echoed explicitly (although both Revelation and other Johannine texts contribute significantly to the language of the *passio* as a whole). One of the most dramatic liturgical moments occurs right before the martyrs die. In the account, the martyrs whom the beasts fail to kill are brought to

18. Of course, these images do not belong to Revelation exclusively and many rely in turn on the prophetic books, and in this case, Ezekiel in particular.

19. Crispin Fletcher-Louis, "Jewish Apocalyptic and Apocalypticism" in *The Handbook for the Study of the Historical Jesus*, eds. Tom Holmén and Stanley E. Porter, vol. 3 (Leiden: Brill, 2010), 1593.

20. Fletcher-Louis, "Jewish Apocalyptic and Apocalypticism," 1594.

the middle of the arena to be executed. Before they meet their final end, the martyrs "kissed each other with the ritual kiss of peace so that the ritual of peace would seal their martyrdom" (21.7). As early as Justin Martyr, the kiss of peace is attested to have occurred just prior to reception of the Eucharist.[21] Although we cannot be absolutely sure that this was the case in North Africa, the kiss of peace was certainly tied to communal prayer.[22] A eucharistic parallel could perhaps be strengthened by the language used of Perpetua tasting (*gustaret*) the pain of the sword after the ritual kiss (21.9). In either case, this scandalous and public performance of a private liturgical act discloses the true meaning of the event. Although from a human perspective the martyrs are about to suffer a humiliating death, from a heavenly perspective, the martyrs are about to offer an efficacious oblation to God for their immediate translation into heaven, which is also effective here on earth (for example, in the conversion of Pudens the jailer and many in the crowd). If the kiss of peace is indeed to be linked specifically to the Eucharist, then the martyrs are conformed to Christ in his death by a liturgical enactment of it, they become "other Christs" not only by imitation, but somehow by sacramental participation.[23] Perpetua tastes martyrdom (or, perhaps it is better to say that she becomes the eucharistic offering) and gains heaven, just as one gains entry to the Church by baptism and Eucharist. We find a similar identification of the martyr with the Eucharist in both the writings of Ignatius of Antioch and the *Martyrdom of Polycarp.*[24] This liturgical conclusion to Perpetua's story is especially poignant, because she vehemently refuses to play-act as a priestess of Ceres before she and the others are brought into the arena (17.4). The worship of the true God prevails in the martyr's seeming defeat, a death brought on by

21. Justin Martyr, *First Apology* 65.

22. Tertullian mentions the kiss of peace at the conclusion of a prayer (*de or.* 18), but the evidence for its exact context is ambiguous. See also Paul Bradshaw, *Eucharistic Origins* (London: SPCK, 2004), 102–03. Bradshaw does not argue against the kiss of peace being performed in a eucharistic context in North Africa, but rather that it was unlikely that in Tertullian's time it was exclusive to that context.

23. A concept discussed at length in by Moss in *Other Christs.* I think we could say of the *passio,* as she does of the *Martyrdom of Fructuosus* that "the martyr's death acquires a sacramental quality even as various ways of imitating Christ—martyrdom, prayer, and the Eucharistic liturgy—are layered upon one another, multiplying their imitative quality" (*Other Christs,* 65).

24. Ignatius famously likens himself to the Eucharist when he writes that "I am God's wheat, and I am being ground by the teeth of the wild beasts so that I may prove to be pure bread" (*To the Romans* 4.1, ed. and trans. Michael Holmes, *The Apostolic Fathers* [Grand Rapids, MI: Baker Academic, 2007], 228). Similarly, in the *Martyrdom of Polycarp* the martyr prays a kind of anaphora before his martyrdom (14) and the appearance of the martyr burning is likened to that of bread baking (15).

refusal to worship the Roman gods; the battle is cast in terms of opposing cult, and true worship translates to true victory.

Another instance where liturgical action reveals a deeper meaning to the events in the *passio* is in the martyrs' choice to celebrate a "love-feast" (*agapem*) rather than a prisoner's "last meal" (*cenam ultimam* 17.1). This heavenly banquet, which occurs the night before the contest in the arena, also suggests, like Perpetua's first vision, that the celebration of the Eucharist prepares one for and pledges one to martyrdom.[25] The last meal is not a last meal at all, but a foretaste of heaven. There are many other examples of the liturgy breaking in and explaining the cosmic significance of events, for example: the procession to the amphitheater is like a procession to heaven (18.1), the crowd's words "a saving bath, a saving bath" (*salvum lotum*) to describe the soaking of Saturus in blood (21.2), which discloses the meaning of martyrdom as second baptism, and Perpetua singing a hymn as she enters into the arena shows that she is already trampling on the Egyptian (again, by adhering to true worship rather than false, 18.7).

In sum, Revelation and its understanding of the liturgy as the place where the meaning of history is unveiled is taken on *in toto* by the authors of the *passio,* as evidenced by the use of the images from Revelation and the frequent references to liturgical action as revealing to us the cosmic significance of the martyrs' death.

The Church as New Society

The book of Revelation is also evoked strongly in the fourth vision of the *passio,* that of Saturus (11.1–13.8).[26] In the vision, the martyrs are carried east

25. Some scholars argue that *agape* is a term used to describe the wider meal context of the Eucharist (i.e., food distributed before, after or alongside any ritual elements), or even a different meal. Tertullian, who is the most pertinent witness in this context, refers to the *agape* meal in *Apol.* 39.16–19; it is debated whether he is referring to a Eucharistic meal, but prayer and other Christian ritual is certainly involved. See also Heffernan, *Passion,* 322. Nevertheless, the martyrs celebrated the meal only "as far as it was possible" (17.1), which may imply that some elements of the ritual, or at least the proper solemnity, was lacking.

26. Many commentators have noticed Saturus' use of Revelation; Heffernan, *Passion* 82, characterizes Saturus' biblical allusions as "intentionally transparent." R. Petraglio, however, argues that only chapter 12 is clearly influenced by the Apocalypse, whereas references in 11 and 13 are dubious; see "des influences de l'Apocalyse dans la 'Passio Perpetuae'" in *L'Apocalypse de Jean: traditions exégétiques et iconographiques, IIIe–XIIIe siècles* (Geneva: Librarie Droz, 1979), 15–31. His argument is based on a textual

by four angels into a garden, where they encounter other martyrs and four even more glorious angels. They are clothed in white and beckoned into "a place whose walls seemed to be made of light" (12.1) guarded by four other angels. They hear the "holy, holy, holy" chanted and meet a man with white hair along with the elders. They are lifted up to kiss the man, the elders say "let us stand" (12.6) and they all offer the sign of peace. Perpetua expresses her great joy. When they leave the assembly, they meet Optatus (a bishop) and Aspasius (a priest), who ask Saturus and Perpetua to make peace between them, and they throw themselves at the martyrs' feet. The martyrs are moved but ask how "our father and our priest" (13.3) could throw themselves down. Perpetua speaks with them and the angels admonish them to forgive one another, and they advise Optatus to rebuke his people. The vision ends with the many martyrs in heaven being nourished by an indescribable fragrance.

The individual images drawn from Revelation are many—again, as in Perpetua's first vision, the white-haired man (Rev 1:14) and the martyrs dressed in robes of white (Rev 3:18, 6:11), but also the four living creatures singing "holy, holy, holy" (Rev 4.8) and the four angels at the four corners of the earth (Rev 7:1). In general, both Revelation (Rev 4:6, 5:7, 5:14, 7:1, 9:15, 14:3, 15:7) and this vision in the *passio* (11.1, 11.7, 12.1) repeatedly mention the number of four in association with heavenly creatures. The *passio* also has four elders (12.4). The martyrs, at the beginning of the vision ask for the others to join them, and at the end are told to rest, reminiscent of Rev 6:11 ("And each was given a white robe and told to rest still a short time until the number would be complete of their fellow servants and of their brothers, who afterwards would be killed according to their own example.").[27]

Other images in Saturus' vision have parallels in Revelation as well, and although they are too commonplace to be tied specifically to the apocalypse, we can see perhaps a shared imagination—such as the radiance of heaven (Rev 1:16, 4:5, 21:22, 22:5; *passio* 12.1),[28] ever-bearing trees (Rev 22:2; the *passio* also

---

analysis comparing the Greek New Testament to the Greek version of the *passio*. The weight of scholarly opinion now falls in the direction of Latin as the original language of composition of the *passio*, although there is still some doubt about Saturus' vision in particular (see Heffernan, *Passion*, 81–82). Petraglio's method may not, therefore, be particularly helpful. However, even if specific linguistic parallels are lacking in some sections of the vision, it stands to reason that Revelation is in the forefront of the martyr's mind and should not be hermetically sealed in chapter 12.

27. Author's translation of the *Vetus Latina*.

28. Heffernan comments that, because of the imagery of walls of light, the "residence of the Lord

specifically mentions leaves in 11.6), the city with open gates (Rev 21:25; *passio* 13.1, 7) and incense / fragrance (Rev 8:3–4; *passio* 13.8). As in the case of the first vision of the *passio*, however, the fourth vision does not merely borrow this or that image from Revelation in a haphazard way, rather, it both takes on its language and adopts its worldview. The cultic nature of heaven which directly relies, in part, on Revelation, is obvious (especially in the hearing of the angelic hymn and in the words of the elders which are highly reminiscent of a liturgical celebration). Saturus' vision, however, also reproduces the societal vision of Revelation, to which we will now turn.

To see how the societal structure of Saturus' vision parallels that of Revelation, we may first note that the way in which the martyrs proceed through their heavenly visitation has many parallels to Revelation 4. They enter the place of light summoned by an angel—presumably, given the activity, the heavenly temple—(*passio* 12.1 matching with Rev 4:1) and the first thing the martyr records seeing is the throne and the one seated on it (*passio* 12.3), as in Rev 4:2. The next group seen in both cases are the elders surrounding the throne (*passio* 12.4, Rev 4:4). The "holy, holy, holy" heard by the martyrs comes first in the *passio* before the throne is seen (*passio* 12.2), but the song is also heard uniquely in this chapter of Revelation (Rev 4:8). Both in the *passio* and in Revelation 4, the angels and the elders speak, but not the Lord directly. The angels in Saturus' vision perform the same kinds of duties as they do in Revelation (and, of course, in the early Christian worldview generally)—they are gatekeepers, and thus those who convey and/or invite people to heaven (*passio* 11.1, Rev 4:1),[29] as well as heralds or messengers (which is what their name means—but see, for example, *passio* 11.7, 11.10 and Rev 14:6–9, 18:2).

We can see by these specific parallels that the roles of various actors in Revelation are reproduced by Saturus, and this is true for the vision as a whole. For example, many scholars have argued that Perpetua, in this vision, shows forth the particular power of the martyr over and against the institutional hierarchy of the Church,[30] but that reading actually goes against the grain of the

[in the *passio*] is a Johannine locus, existing outside time and space, whose dimensionality is bounded by the photons;" see *Passion,* 284.

29. See also Heffernan, *Passion,* 284.

30. For example, Heffernan, *Passion,* 295: "The martyr, depicted as superior to these administrative officials, is able to bring harmony out of discord. Charismatic leadership is superior to bureaucratic." Rex Butler sees the scene as revealing Montanist power dynamics, writing of Optatus and Aspesius that "their prostration before the confessors and their exclusion from the heavenly inner court fitted the Montanist's

text. Certainly it is a reversal to have Optatus and Aspesius falling down before the martyrs, but does the text approve of it? Perpetua explicitly denies that she has authority over the bishop and priest in the vision: "are you not our father and our priest? How can you throw yourselves at our feet?" (12.3). Here, Perpetua might be echoing the angel of Revelation who warns John not to fall down at his feet (Rev 19:10, 22:8). It may also be reminiscent of John the Baptist's hesitation to baptize Jesus (Mt 3:14)—and although John clearly has a pivotal role to play in Jesus' ministry (as Perpetua does in the vision), the gospels portray him as refusing to usurp Jesus. To read the *passio* otherwise is to impute to Perpetua (or to Saturus' and/or to the redactor's Perpetua, anyway) false modesty or irony; it implies that she asks the question in order to prove to the audience that the martyrs do, in fact, have authority or status over the priest and bishop. But it seems that Saturus or his redactor may have had the exact opposite aim in mind, that is, to show the martyrs as being powerful *without* disrupting the social hierarchy, vouchsafed by Perpetua's own words in the vision. In Revelation, the structure of heaven, so to speak, is that angels are the ones who carry out the mediation of prayers and the judgments of God. That structure is reproduced in Saturus' vision generally (as above), but also specifically in the case of Optatus and Aspesius. It is the angels, and not Perpetua or Saturus, who explicitly effect the reconciliation and advise Optatus on how to deal with his congregation (12.6). Likewise, although it is John who writes letters to the Churches in Revelation, it seems that it is the angels of those Churches who are still accountable for the reception of and execution of the letters, that is, the mediation of God's will to the Churches (see Rev 2:1, 2:12, etc.)

Just as the *passio* takes on Revelation's cultic view of reality beyond Perpetua's first vision, so also does it take on Revelation's view of the power structures of the world beyond Saturus' vision. The predominant theme of Revelation is the overthrow of the devil and Babylon (read: Rome) by God, aided

---

elevation of martyrs over clergy… Saturus believed … that the confessor/martyr possessed the power of the keys to mediate peace between Christian factions, even when represented by ecclesiastical hierarchy;" see *The New Prophecy and "New Visions:" Evidence of Montanism in the Passion of the Perpetua and Felicity* (Washington, DC: Catholic University of America Press, 2006), 83. Christine Trevett, however, notes that the scene is complex and is not to be construed, even in the Montanist version of the *passio*, as anticlerical. Montanus himself was a presbyter, but a prophetic one—the disputes over true authority are difficult to classify simply in terms of the prophetic versus priestly. See *Montanism: Gender, Authority and the New Prophecy* (Cambridge: Cambridge University Press 2002[1996]), 189–90.

by his angels and saints. The martyrs help accomplish this feat by their refusal to worship the dragon and his beasts and to ingratiate themselves with the whore of Babylon; by bowing down before the throne of God, and sending up their prayers, the martyrs contribute to the overthrow of evil and secure themselves on the victor's side. This narrative, in a rough way, maps on to the *passio,* where Perpetua identifies her enemy as Satan—in the arguments with her father (3.3), in the first vision (4.4) and above all in her interpretation of the third vision: "I knew that I was going to fight with the devil and not with the beasts, and I knew that the victory was to be mine" (10.14). The victory is won by refusing to sacrifice to the emperor and persisting unto death. As in Revelation, the cosmic picture is one where God and his servants (angelic and human) bring about the overthrow of the devil and his servants (both angelic and human), despite the seeming defeat of the martyrs and the seeming glory of Babylon up until the moment of its final downfall (see Rev 18:10–19). These broad parallels are not meant to undermine the particularity of Perpetua's story nor to imply that it is formulaic, but rather to show that Revelation allows her to interpret the world correctly, to understand her role and that of others, as well as to give expression to her triumph and that of her fellow martyrs. In part because of Revelation, they know who is on the "right side of history" and what the true social order looks like against the false.

Furthermore, as in Revelation, there is a strong communal dimension to the *passio.* Although John is the narrator of Revelation, his visions pertain to the entire community, so also in the *passio* Perpetua clearly has special status and yet her visions and experiences mediate that of the community. Even the visions which center on Perpetua are ecclesial. It is on the request of one of her brethren that she asks for the first vision (4.1), Saturus the catechist appears in it, and heaven is populated with saints welcoming her (as in Revelation). The first part of the second vision happens after an ecstatic outburst during communal prayer (7.1) and concerns the salvation of someone else, her brother Dinocrates. The third vision features Pomponius, who escorts her into the arena (10.1). The combat scene that ensues includes a crowd on both sides—Perpetua's supporters singing hymns while the crowd jeers (10.12).[31]

Revelation, therefore, sets the stage for understanding the hierarchy and

31. For more on the ritual and communal setting for prophecy, see Katharina Waldner, "Visions, Prophecy and Authority in the *Passio Perpetuae*," in *Perpetua's Passions,* 214–15.

power structure of the cosmos. As in Revelation, martyrs are in a privileged position but do not usurp the ministry of angels (nor disrupt the earthly hierarchy). Martyrs in both texts subvert the power structure of Rome and take their hard-won place in heaven. By placing John so frequently in the company of the saints, Revelation invites this reading, i.e. it invites the reader to stand in a well-populated heaven and to witness events that affect a great multitude in heaven and on earth. This ecclesial character has also left its mark on the *passio*—all that takes place, including the prophetic visions, has a communal character and significance for the community, even in a text with such a clear and powerful protagonist.

Conclusion

Having seen that the *passio* relies on Revelation's images and its worldview, how then can we characterize it as a work of *biblical interpretation*? In one way, this essay aims to contribute to the effort of many scholars, including those in the present volume, to expand the definition of biblical interpretation—the authors of the *passio* use Revelation to express and interpret their experiences. Perpetua's current suffering is one where she is facing off against the devil, and what better words to give voice to that experience than those of Revelation? We should not reject the identification of biblical images with particular passages in the *passio* on the grounds that it overdetermines the meaning of the text or flattens our reading, but we can use them to see how the biblical text forms the *passio's* imagination and its view of reality.

But the *passio* can also be seen as biblical interpretation in a more traditional sense, because it not only uses Revelation to give voice to the meaning of martyrdom, but also uses martyrdom and the experience of it to show forth the meaning of Revelation. What, after all, is Revelation about? Its protagonists are those who survive the great trial (Rev 7:14), and how could their heroism be displayed more vividly than in the account of a martyr who consciously follows in their path? We can, if nothing else, see the kind of imagination, determination and faith shared by the author(s) of the book of Revelation and the authors of the *passio*. For an early Christian, Revelation's meaning is not one that resides solely in the past nor is it determined strictly by some past referent, but its meaning continues to be disclosed in the present, where

Perpetua in some fashion lives out the cosmic drama described in John's apocalypse. This understanding of prophecy as that which continues to unfold is not foreign to the text of Revelation (not eisegesis, we might say), but integral to it. Perpetua, in her actual martyrdom and in the accounts of her visions, interprets Revelation as teaching that martyrdom is a kind of public liturgical act,[32] which like other liturgical acts, makes present a cosmic reality, and which is the prelude to the true liturgy of heaven. If we take the *passio* as an authentic piece of biblical interpretation on this score, for example, we might be more inclined to read certain passages of Revelation (to take the same example above, washing robes in the blood of the lamb, Rev 7:14) as referring to baptism or as having baptismal significance.

To return to the questions with which we began: what can this examination of the *passio* say about early biblical interpretation in general? Is the linking of images fanciful, because it removes passages from Revelation from their proper contexts, and does our attention to these images distance us from the character of Perpetua's experiences? Even in the light of this brief reflection on how some of Revelation's images are deployed, I think we can answer no. The linking of images allows the authors of the *passio* to apply Revelation to their own situation and reflect back on the kind of situation and mentality in which the book of Revelation itself was written. Frances Young, using Athanasius as her primary test case, has characterized patristic exegesis as interpretation that aims to get at the "mind of scripture."[33] Young is speaking here about Athanasius' interpretation by way of deduction, that is, she argues that Athanasius interprets a passage by parsing the meaning of biblical words and identifying logical patterns throughout the Scriptures, rather than by having recourse to allegory; he aims to deduce a biblical idiom. I think, however, that a similar analysis can also be suitably applied to the *passio*. The visions in the *passio* are not simply allegories, wherein the biblical images stand for something else. Rather, to understand the situation of the fellow martyrs, and in order to understand the Bible, the authors of the *passio* adopt a biblical idiom, putting on the "mind of scripture," and speaking with its voice.

---

32. For more on this concept in a wide variety of martyrdom stories, see Robin Darling Young, *In Procession Before the World: Martyrdom as Public Liturgy in Early Christianity* (Milwaukee: Marquette University Press, 2001).

33. Frances Young, *Biblical Exegesis and the Formation of Christian Culture* (Hendrickson Publishers: Peabody, MA 2002 [1997]), 29–49.

Bibliography

Amelig, Walter. "*Femina Liberaliter Instituta*—Some Thoughts on a Martyr's Liberal Education," in *Perpetua's Passions: Multidisciplinary Approaches to the* Passio Perpetuae et Felicitas, eds. Jan Bremmer and Marco Formisano. Oxford: Oxford University Press, 2012.

Bradshaw, Paul. *Eucharistic Origins.* London: SPCK, 2004.

Burns, Patout and Jensen, Robin. *Christianity in Roman North Africa.* Grand Rapids, MI: Eerdmans, 2014.

Butler, Rex. *The New Prophecy and "New Visions:" Evidence of Montanism in the Passion of the Perpetua and Felicity.* Washington, DC: Catholic University of America Press, 2006.

Cox Miller, Patricia. *Dreams in Late Antiquity.* Princeton, NJ: Princeton University Press, 1994.

Dronke, Peter. *Women Writers of the Middle Ages.* Cambridge: Cambridge University Press, 1984.

Fletcher-Louis, Crispin. "Jewish Apocalyptic and Apocalypticism" in *The Handbook for the Study of the Historical Jesus*, eds. Tom Holmén and Stanley E. Porter, vol. 3. Leiden: Brill, 2010.

Heffernan, Thomas. *The Passion of Perpetua and Felicity.* Oxford: Oxford University Press, 2012.

Jensen, Anne. *God's Self-Confident Daughters: Early Christianity and the Liberation of Women*, trans. O. C. Dean. Louisville, KY: Knox Press, 1999.

Johnson, Maxwell. *The Rites of Christian Initiation.* Collegeville, MN: Liturgical Press, 1999.

Klein, Elizabeth. "Perpetua, Cheese and Martyrdom as Public Liturgy in the *Passion of Perpetua and Felicity" JECS* 28, no. 2 (Summer 2020): 175–202.

Moss, Candida. *The Other Christs.* Oxford: Oxford University Press, 2010.

Muehlberger, Ellen. "Perpetual Adjustment: The Passion of Perpetua and Felicity and the Entailments of Authenticity" in *JECS* 30, no. 3 (2022): 313–42

Petraglio, R. "Des influences de l'Apocalyse dans la 'Passio Perpetuae'" in *L'Apocalypse de Jean: traditions exégétiques et iconographiques, IIIe–XIIIe siècles.* Geneva: Librarie Droz, 1979.

Pettersen, Alvyn. "Perpetua, a Prisoner of Conscience," *VC* 41, no. 2 (Jun 1987): 139–53.

Trevett, Christine. *Montanism: Gender, Authority and the New Prophecy.* Cambridge: Cambridge University Press [1996] 2002.

Waldner, Katharina. "Visions, Prophecy and Authority in the Passio Perpetuae" in *Perpetua's Passions: Multidisciplinary Approaches to the* Passio Perpetuae et Felicitas, eds. Jan Bremmer and Marco Formisano. Oxford: Oxford University Press, 2012.

Young, Robin Darling. *In Procession Before the World: Martyrdom as Public Liturgy in Early Christianity* Milwaukee: Marquette University Press, 2001.
Young, Frances. *Biblical Exegesis and the Formation of Christian Culture.* Hendrickson Publishers: Peabody, MA 2002 orig., Cambridge University Press, 1997.

Bronwen Neil

2. CONGREGATIONAL EXEGESIS AND APOCALYPTIC VISIONS IN THE *SHEPHERD OF HERMAS*

An important written source on early Roman Christian prophecy and spiritual exegesis is the *Shepherd of Hermas* (*CPG* 1052),[1] a second-century text whose canonicity was debated up to the sixth century.[2] The *Shepherd* presents a novel form of exegesis applied to a series of dreams or visions, rather than to

---

1. Recent editions of the Greek text with translation include: Bart D. Ehrman, ed. *The Apostolic Fathers II*, LCL 25 (Cambridge, MA: Harvard University Press, 2003); Molly Whittacker, ed. *Die Apostolischen Väter I, Der Hirt des Hermas*, GCS 48 (2nd ed., Berlin: de Gruyter, 1967); Robert Joly, ed. *Hermas, Le Pasteur*, SC 53bis (2nd ed. Paris: Éditions de CERF, 1968); Ulrich H. J. Hörtner and Martin Leutzsch, eds., *Papiasfragmente. Hirt des Hermas*, Schriften des Urchristentums 3 (Darmstadt: Wissenschaftliche Buchgesellschaft, 1998), 105–510.

2. For overviews of the issues of dating, context, and authorship surrounding the Greek text, see Robert Joly, "Le milieu complexe du 'Pasteur d'Hermas,'" in *ANRW* 2.27.1, ed. Wolfgang Haase and Hildegard Temporini (Berlin: De Gruyter, 1992), 525–51; Carolyn Osiek and Helmut Koester, *Shepherd of Hermas: A Commentary*, in *Hermeneia: A Critical and Historical Commentary on the Bible* 83 (Minneapolis MN: Fortress Press, 1999); Jorg Rüpke, "Der Hirte des Hermas: Plausibilisierungs- und Legitimierungs strategien im Übergang von Antike und Christentum," *Zeitschrift für antikes Christentum* 7 (2003): 362–84; Joseph Verheyden, "The Shepherd of Hermas," in *Writings of the Apostolic Fathers*, ed. Paul Foster (London: T & T Clark, 2007), 63–71; the monograph of Christian J. Wilson, *Five Problems in the Interpretation of the Shepherd of Hermas: Authorship, Genre, Canonicity, Apocalyptic, and the Absence of the Name 'Jesus Christ,'* Mellen Biblical Press Series 34 (Lewiston, NY: Mellen Biblical Press, 1995); and Alexander Weiss, "Hermas' 'Biography:' Social Upward and Downward Mobility of an Independent Freedman," *AncSoc* 39 (2009): 185–202 consider the hermeneutical challenges of the text and its social context, respectively.

passages of Hebrew or Christian Scripture per se, although scriptural idioms are woven through the text as sources of authority. Canonical Scriptures are rarely cited, though the text is saturated with Scripture-like language, especially from the letter of James, as we shall see. The work stands out in early Christian literature as a bold literary experiment with the fantastic—defined by Marco Frenschkowski as the "deconstruction of reality through the medium of art"—along similar lines as the *Book of Revelation*, whose canonicity was debated until at least the fourth century, and the *Passion of Saints Perpetua and Felicity*.[3] I argue that this collection of texts from the mid-second century CE offers a novel form of exegesis that eschews scriptural sources in favour of new revelations, even though it is grounded in the Hebrew prophetic tradition and New Testament understandings of prophecy. The texts demonstrate the less common technique congregational exegesis. The author's reasons for adopting this form of exegesis, along with the reasons that his promotion of personal revelation was not generally accepted in later Christian centuries, give us new insights into the purpose and reception of this intriguing work.

I have adopted the use of the term 'congregational exegesis' to describe the author's approach to exegeting Scripture in this apocryphal text. This term has been applied to the prophecy in another apocryphal text from the late first to the early second century, *The Odes of Solomon*.[4] The focus of Hermas' prophecy is on groups of people, from Christian families and households to the Church as a whole, rather than individuals.

I focus on the extended allegories in *Vision* 3 and the identity of the female messenger who personifies the Church. I then turn to Mandate 11, one of twelve commandments appended to *Vision* 5. This mandate admonishes its readers and hearers to discern true prophets from the false ones whom Hermas sees proliferating around him. I ask whether Hermas sees himself as a true prophet or as something else. How does he defend his claim to be the

3. "Die Phantastische ist jene Dekonstruktion von Wirklichkeit im Medium von Kunst:" Marco Frenschkowski, "Vision als Imagination. Beobachtungen zum differenzierten Wirklichkeitsanspruch frühchristlicher Visionsliteratur," in *Fremde Wirklichkeiten: Literarische Phantastik und antike Literatur*, ed. Nicola Hömke and Manuel Baumbach, Studien zur griechischen und lateinischen Poesie 6 (Heidelberg: Universitätsverlag Winter), 339–66, at 341. Frenschkowski explores the similarities of these three texts and the *Story of Zosimus*. Elizabeth Klein in this volume treats the visions of Perpetua and Felicity.

4. Before this ascription to the Odes of Solomon, congregational prophecy was limited to 1 Corinthians 12–14, Didache 10–13, and Mandate 11: see David E. Aune, *Apocalypticism, Prophecy and Magic in Early Christianity: Collected Essays*, WUNT 199 (Tübingen: Mohr Siebeck, 2006), 335.

recipient and announcer of visions and their spiritual meaning, as mediated to him by the Church herself in *Visions* 1, 2, and 3?

Authorship and early Alexandrian reception

The *Shepherd* was composed over some 60 years, being completed ca. 140 CE. Apart from Revelation, written in Asia Minor at the end of the first century, the *Shepherd* is the only early Christian text that claims to have been delivered to its author in a series of ecstatic visions. It is somewhat similar to the Corpus Hermeticum's *Shepherd* (*Poimandres*) but no direct dependency has been established.[5] It is no coincidence that both Revelation and the *Shepherd* were ascribed to identifiable authorities. John the Elder, the author of Revelation, was said to have received his apocalyptic vision on the Greek island of Patmos and was identified as the gospel-writer of the same name.[6] In a similar vein, Hermas describes himself as a former slave writing in Rome while his brother Pius occupied the seat of the Church of Rome.[7] His narrative of visions is addressed to an otherwise unknown woman called Grapte, who would relay its message to widows and orphans, and to Clement, whose office was to communicate with other churches. The latter is usually identified as Pope Clement I (ca. 88–99 CE), author of the letter known as *First Clement* and addressed to the early Christian community of Corinth.[8]

I suggest that the debate over *Shepherd's* canonical status was motivated at least in part by the novelty of its genre and its claim to deliver a new kind of spiritual exegesis, one based on visions received by an individual rather than Scripture. Exegesis of Scripture in the second and third centuries was normally delivered in biblical commentaries, sermons, letters, or tractates, but this text contained a series of visions and some new parables and commandments. While it makes many allusions to Scripture, there is only one direct citation, from a scriptural work that is no longer extant. The *Book of Eldad and Modad* is named for two prophets mentioned in the book of Numbers (Num 11:26–27)

---

5. Charles Kannengiesser, *A Handbook of Patristic Exegesis: The Bible in Ancient Christianity* (Leiden: Brill, 2006), vol. 1, 425.

6. Clement and Grapte are named as the destined recipients of the work in *Vis.* 2.4.3.

7. Pius I was bishop of Rome ca. 142 to ca. 155.

8. *First Letter to the Church of Corinth*, edited and translated by Michael W. Holmes, *The Apostolic Fathers: Greek Texts and English Translations*, 3rd ed. Grand Rapids, MI: Baker Academic, 2007), 33–131.

as prophesying in the Hebrews' camp. Hermas writes: 'But say to Maximus …
"'The Lord is near to them who return to Him,' as it is written in *Eldad and
Modat* [*sic*], who prophesied to the people in the wilderness."[9] This citation and
the knowledge of hortatory Jewish preaching in the *Shepherd* and the letter of
James[10] has been noted as suggesting a Roman Jewish heritage for the author
of the *Shepherd*.[11] Unlike other Christian works of a similar era also written in
Greek, it does not quote from standard Hebrew Scriptures.[12]

The relationship between the *Shepherd* and the Epistle of James in particular has vexed scholars for over a century.[13] Up to thirty-eight passages of
Shepherd have been identified as relating to nineteen verses of James in the
form of verbal echoes. Brox has investigated these instances in detail.[14] To take
just one example, the adjective 'double-minded' (Greek δίψυχος), used by Hermas nineteen times and in the letters of I Clement and the pseudonymous
II Clement, is one of several lexical echoes of the letter of James (cf. 1:8; 4:8).[15]
The concept of double-mindedness or duplicity is not necessarily original to
James, however. Seitz has shown that the Greek term is linked with the concept of double-heartedness, which was probably taken from the otherwise
known apocryphal writing or 'Scripture' to which the epistle of James refers
("Or do you think Scripture says without reason that he jealously longs for the

9. *Vis.* 2.3.4, edited and translated by Holmes, 466–7. Cf. '*Targum Pseudo-Jonathan* on Num 11.26:
'The Lord is near to those in distress.' On the Old Testament apocryphal book of Eldad and Modad,
known only from this quotation, see James H. Charlesworth, *The Old Testament Epigrapha* (Peabody,
MA: Hendrickson, 2010), vol. 1, xxii; David Hellholm, *Das Visionenbuch des Hermas als Apokalypse:
Formgeschichtliche und texttheoretische Studien zu einer literarischen Gattung. I. Methodologische Vorüberlegungen und makrostrukturelle Textanalyse* (Lund: C. W. K. Gleerup, 1980), 197, remarked on the use of
the citation at the deepest level of functional communication to authorize Hermas' message.

10. Oscar J. F. Seitz, "Relationship of the Shepherd of Hermas to the Epistle of James," *JBL* 63 no. 2
(1944): 132.

11. See the overview by Josephine Massingberd Ford, "A possible liturgical background to the Shepherd of Hermas," *RevQ* 6, no. 4 (24), (1969): 531–51; and David Hellholm, "The Shepherd of Hermas,"
in *The Apostolic Fathers: An Introduction*, ed. Wilhelm Pratscher (Waco, TX: Baylor University Press,
2010), 215–42.

12. Cf. I Clement's use of *circa* 75 quotations from the Hebrew Scriptures, according to the study of
Donald A. Hagner, *The Use of the Old and New Testaments in Clement of Rome* (Novum Testamentum,
Supplementum 34; Leiden: Brill, 1973), 22.

13. Seitz, "Relationship," 131.

14. Brox, *Der Hirt des Hermas*, 46–47.

15. I Clement 23.3 and II Clement 11.2: "'Let this scripture be far from us where it says: Wretched
are the double-minded, those who doubt in their soul and say, 'We heard these things in the days of our
fathers, and look, we have grown old, and none of these things have happened to us.'" Holmes, 78–79.
Cf. note 23 below on this citation in I and II Clement.

spirit he has caused to dwell in us" Jas 4:5).[16] Hermas' reference to the indwelling spirit in Mandate 11, to be discussed below, may also be an echo of Jas 4:5. Another example of an idiom from Scripture is found in the stones that are rejected for building the tower are those who "apostatize from the living God" (cf. Heb 3:12). In *Vision* 2, he may also be echoing Matthew's gospel: "For the Lord has sworn by His Son, that those who denied their Lord have abandoned their life in despair, for even now these are to deny Him in the days that are coming" (*Vis.* 2.2).[17] There is another possible reference to Mt 26:24 in the expression "Woe to them who hear these words and scorn them: better it were for them had they not been born." (*Vis.* 4.2). A final allusion to the Book of Revelation (whose authoritative status is still quite unclear at this date) is to the "book of life," in which the name of the saints will be written, along with the names of Hermas' sons if they repent.[18]

In the broader second-century context of Christian thought, the role of the intellect in receiving ecstatic visions to explain aspects of Scripture and to elucidate the spiritual life of the Church, seemed problematic to many commentators, including Tertullian.[19] While some Platonist thinkers like the Jewish Hellenist exegete Philo accepted that visions could be a medium of allegorical exegesis, more often this was seen as exceeding the bounds of the intellect and was therefore suspect.

It is not surprising, therefore, that the text found the most support among early advocates of spiritual exegesis, the neo-Platonist philosophers and theologians Clement of Alexandria (ca. 150–211 or 215) and Origen of Alexandria. While the distinction between canonical and non-canonical was foreign to Christians of the period of *Shepherd*'s composition, its scriptural status and reception were endorsed early on by Clement of Alexandria. Clement accepted it as canonical, calling it "a gnostic unfolding of the Scriptures, when faith has already reached an advanced state."[20] In the mid-third century, Origen identified the author of *Shepherd* with the Hermas of Rom 16:14, a member of the original Christian community in Rome. Origen judged *Shepherd* to be "a

---

16. Seitz, "Relationship," 138–40.

17. Cf. Mt 10:33.

18. *Vis.* 1.3; cf. Phil 4:3, where Clement is one of the fellow-workers named, and Rev 20:15.

19. See Tertullian, *De anima* 45.

20. Clement, *Stromateis* 6. Here "gnostic" is used in the sense of secret knowledge (gnosis) rather than in association with the Gnostic sects that proliferated in the first and second centuries.

scripture that seems to me very useful, and in my opinion, divinely inspired,"[21] while also noting that "the little book of the Shepherd … where Hermas is commanded to write two little books [one for Grapte and one for Clement] … seems to be despised by some."[22]

The directive to Hermas to deliver his message to the bishop of Rome is also no accident. Second-century Rome was home to a visionary and eschatological Church community, as described in Clement's *Letter to the Church of Corinth*.[23] The Montanists, who appeared in the late-second century and allowed even women to announce prophecies, were rejected by mainstream churches except in Rome, where bishops took the position that they would not argue with Montanists about true or false prophecy,[24] nor debate about rational versus ecstatic prophecy.[25] It even seems likely that Pope Eleutheros or his successor Victor even briefly endorsed Montanism.[26] However, this was the exception, not the norm, and self-proclaimed prophets like Hermas remained suspect to most Christian communities from the second century onwards.

21. Origen, *Comm. in Rom.* 10.5.5, trans. Thomas P. Scheck, *Commentary on the Epistle to the Romans, Books 6–10*, Fathers of the Church 104 (Washington, D.C.: Catholic University of America Press, 2002), 296.

22. Origen, *De princ.* 4.11, ed. and trans. Henri Crouzel and Manlio Simonetti, *Origène. Traité des principes. Livres III et IV*, SC 268 bis (Paris : Éditions de Cerf, 2006), 312.

23. 1 Clement 23.3 cites a scripture which is now lost, "We heard all these things even in the days of our fathers, and though we have waited day after day, we have seen none of them." Edited and translated by Holmes, 78–79. The pseudonymous, anti-gnostic sermon known as II Clement also cites this text in an extended version at II Clement 11.2–4, edited and translated by Holmes, 150–51. Lightfoot speculated that this is an allusion to the lost apocryphal book of *Eldad and Modad*, cited in *Vis.* 2.3.4 by Hermas. See J. B. Lightfoot, *The Apostolic Fathers Clement, Ignatius, and Polycarp*, Part One: *Clement*, vol. 2, edited by J. R. Harmer (2nd ed. London, New York: Macmillan, 1899), 80–81, with arguments accepted and amplified by Dale C. Allison, "Eldad and Modad," *Journal for the Study of the Pseudepigrapha* 21, no. 2 (2011): 99–131, at 107–12.

24. Christine Trevett, *Montanism: Gender, Authority and the New Prophecy* (rev. ed.; Cambridge: Cambridge University Press, 2002), 56–59.

25. Later Roman bishops flatly refused to grant the possibility of any post-apostolic prophecy by rejecting the apocryphal books in which it appeared, such as the works of Priscilla, Montanus and Maximilla, the *Apocalypse of Paul*, and the separate revelations of Stephen and Thomas: e.g. Gelasius I, *Ep.* 42.7–8, ed. Andreas Thiel, *Epistulae Romanorum Pontificium genuinae et quae ad eos scriptae sunt a S. Hilaro usque ad Pelagium II* (Leipzig: Braunsberg, 1867), 454–71; repeated almost verbatim by Hormisdas of Rome (514–21) in *ep.* 125, ed. Thiel, *Epistulae Romanorum Pontificium*, 931–38.

26. Paul McKechnie, *Christianizing Asia Minor: Conversion, Communities, and Social Change in the Pre-Constantinian Era* (Cambridge: Cambridge University Press, 2019), 96–122.

The decline of ecclesial prophecy in the Church

Although there were some exceptions to the decline and eventual cessation of Christian prophecy from the mid-first century, such as the letter of Ignatius to the Church of Rome, the interpretive trend of 'mainstream' Christianity vis a vis prophets was indisputable: the age of the prophets had come to a close with John the Baptist.[27] Hermas, then, may have wished to communicate through visions while at the same time distancing himself from the title of 'prophet,' with its connotations of an isolated individual operating outside an ecclesial context. While Hebrew prophets had flourished in less structured settings, the number of Christian prophets decreased as the early Church found difficulty in fitting them into the emerging ecclesiastical structure.[28] It has been suggested that the rise in numbers of false prophets contributed to the decline as it became more difficult for the Church to distinguish between the two.[29] The condemnation of false prophets in *Didache* 11 seems to support this, but it offers new criteria for identifying false prophecy, thus addressing the problem.

Unlike *Shepherd*, Hebrew and New Testament prophets did not usually represent their divine revelations as intentionally adding to the body of Scripture. The Spirit sometimes spoke through Christians to give guidance to their communities, but their prophetic utterances could be contested. These secondary prophets were considered pneumatics, who functioned in ways that were similar to the Hebrew prophets but whose range of prophetic activities was limited by comparison. Perhaps only the twelve apostles could be called the true successors of the Hebrew prophets, and their functional equivalents.

Jorg Rüpke argues persuasively that the condemnation of false prophecy in *Mandate* 11 is likely evidence of the continued strength of divinatory practice in Rome in the author's day.[30] Hermas reported that he was on his way to Cumae when the Spirit abducted him and gave him the first and second

27. Stephen L. Cook. *On the Question of the "Cessation of Prophecy" in Ancient Judaism.* TSAJ 145 (Tübingen: Mohr Siebeck, 2011); Christopher Forbes, *Prophecy and Inspired Speech in Early Christianity and Its Hellenistic Environment* (Tübingen: JBC Mohr, 1995).

28. David E. Aune, *Prophecy in Early Christianity and the Ancient Mediterranean World* (Grand Rapids, MI: Eerdmans, 1983), 7–8.

29. David Hill, *New Testament Prophecy*, rev. ed. (Atlanta, GA: Society of Biblical Literature, 1985), 186–92.

30. Jorg Rüpke, "Fighting for Differences," 326.

visions.[31] He was thinking about the vision he had received on the same journey a year before when he received the second one. He at first believed that the female figure who appeared to him was the Sybil, rather than the personified Church.[32] These references indicate that the author wished to locate his account in the cultural context of the oracles given by the Sibyl at this ancient shrine. Such oracles were still taken seriously in Italy in the second century. Like the utterances of the Sibyl, however, prophecies could mislead, deliberately or otherwise.

False prophecy or true?

Prophetic dream-visions played a significant role in the contemplative life of Hellenistic Jews, just as they had done in the pre-Christian Greco-Roman world.[33] Such dreams could be used to convey scriptural exegesis. For example, the earliest known Jewish contemplatives in Egypt, the Therapeutae, are described by Philo (d. ca. 50 CE) as allegorizing Scripture in their dreams.[34]

Following Leo Oppenheim's distinction between message and symbolic dreams,[35] the five visions in the *Shepherd* are message dreams, containing a message that comes unequivocally from a god or divine figure and demands action from the dreamer. Symbolic dreams, by contrast, are those made up of a series of impersonal signs or images, and usually offer a simple prediction of an unavoidable fate rather than containing a direct call to action. In the Christian tradition, message dreams could be clear or opaque, depending on the piety of the recipient. In the case of Hermas, who admitted that he had been guilty of lust, his visions needed interpretation. His visions are unusual in that each provided an interpretation, by a divine messenger, of a vision received earlier. This sort of exegesis of a vision within a vision is not well attested in

---

31. *Herm.* 1:3 and 1[5]:1. See David P. O'Brien, "The Cumaean Sibyl as the Revelation-bearer in the Shepherd of Hermas," *JECS* 5, no. 4 (1997): 473–96.

32. *Herm.* 4[8]:1.

33. On the continuities between them, see especially John S. Hanson, "Dreams and Visions in the Graeco-Roman World and Early Christianity," in *ANRW,* 2.23.2, ed. Wolfgang Haase (Berlin : W. de Gruyter, 1980), 1395–1427.

34. Philo, *De vita contemplativa* 26, ed. and trans. Francis H. Colson, *On the Contemplative Life or Suppliants,* in *Philo,* vol. 9, LCL 363 (Cambridge, MA: Harvard University Press, 1941; repr. 1985), 126–27.

35. Leo Oppenheim, "The Interpretation of Dreams in the Ancient Near East," *Transactions of the American Philosophical Society, New Series* 46, no. 3 (1956): 179–373.

the ancient world. Harrisson has observed that the *Shepherd* resembles imaginative Roman literary genres more than historical genres, the normal venue for vision-narratives in the second century.[36] The relative paucity of Christian novels, epics, and plays may account for the rarity of such visionary exegesis in Christian circles.

The issue for the audience of *Shepherd* was how to tell whether Hermas' visions were true prophecy, false prophecy, or simply made up. False prophets could be distinguished from true prophets by the fulfilment of their prophecies. While a false prophecy could have elements of truth, it did not come true in the same way as a true prophet's message. As Jesus warned in the Gospels (Mt 24:24; Mk 13:22), even false prophets could perform signs. The intentions—pure or otherwise—of the dreamer and his mode of life were further criteria for distinguishing a true prophet from a false one.

Hermas' Visions

Hermas sought to give weight to the practice of visionary exegesis through divine revelation in a series of five dream-visions concerning different but overlapping themes. The first two visions concern discipline and virtue, in both the household of Hermas and the greater household of God, the Church. *Visions* 1 and 2, delivered by an old woman representing the Church, were directed against impure and proud thoughts and criticised Hermas' failure to discipline his sons and his wife. The sins that are singled out in Hermas' family (his son's lustfulness; his wife's talkativeness and general disobedience) represented challenges to the authority of elders in the Church, from both young persons and women. In this respect, *Visions* 1 and 2 resemble the admonitions to the young men who had rebelled against the elders in the Church of Corinth in I *Clement* but he does not compare himself or them with Old Testament types or prophets, as Clement does.[37]

The third vision fulfils God's promise to provide more secret knowledge

---

36. Juliette Harrisson, *Dreams and Dreaming in the Roman Empire: Cultural Memory and Imagination* (London: Bloomsbury, 2013), 148; see also Bronwen Neil, *Dreams and Divination from Byzantium to Baghdad (400–1000 CE)*, OSAR (Oxford University Press: Oxford, 2021), 38–41.

37. I Clement is full of admonitions to the Corinthian community: e.g., to repent (7:1–5), and to take his advice (58:2). He likens himself to Old Testament prophets Noah and Jonah (7:6–7); and calls the Corinthians to be obedient like Enoch and Noah (9:1–4) and Abraham (10:1–7).

via the agency of the woman who symbolises the Church. With frequent fasting, Hermas entreats the Lord "to declare to me the revelation which He promised to show me by the mouth of the aged woman" (*Vis.* 3.1). Hermas had asked for the meaning of the vision so that he could relay it to his community, so that they might be more joyful and know the Lord in his great glory (*Vis.* 3.1). The emphasis is on community benefit, not individual aggrandisement, again pointing to its congregational focus.

The same night, the aged woman appeared to him, saying: "Seeing that you are so importunate and eager to know everything, come into the country where you live, and about the fifth hour I will appear and will show you what you ought to see" (*Vis.* 3.2). *Vision* 3 reveals the building of the victorious Church and the various categories of sinner. The Lady, now appearing more youthful and beautiful, explained that the apostles, bishops, deacons, and readers, are the first of the stones that went into the building of a shining tower on the water (*Vis.* 3.5.1). This tower, the Lady explained, represented the Church. It was being constructed by six young men out of stone drawn from the deep sea and the land. Hermas observed that the best materials were the white, regular stones taken from the sea, which fitted together without visible joins. The Lady explained that these represented apostles, bishops, teachers, and deacons—all who had lived a holy life. (Perhaps they can also be identified with Clement of Alexandria's advanced faithful who would benefit from reading the *Shepherd*).[38] Another group of stones had to be cut to fit. These, she explained, were the struggling believers. The stones that were broken into pieces and thrown far from the tower were those who have turned away from the living God.[39] We also find an echo of the Man of Lawlessness of 2 Thes 2:3 in her pronouncement that these are the Sons of Lawlessness who received the faith in hypocrisy. Finally, those stones that are useless for building the Tower of the Church are thrown into the fire: these are the ones to whom it does not even occur to repent. Ford points to Jewish exegesis, specifically the *Midrash on Isaiah* 54, as the source of some of these allegorical symbols, a plausible argument.[40]

The purpose of Hermas' third vision and the Lady's explanation was to

38. Clement, *Stromateis* 6. See note 20 above.
39. *Vis.* 3.7; cf. Heb 3:12.
40. Ford, "A possible liturgical background," 544.

glorify God and removed doubt from the double-minded (τοὺς διψύχους), who wonder whether these things are true or not (*Vis.* 3.4). She commands Hermas to reveal the truth to all, another sign that this prophecy was meant for a congregational audience.

But observe that it is not for your own sake only that these revelations have been made to you, but they have been given you that you may show them to all. For after three days—this you will take care to remember—I command you to speak all the words which I am to say to you into the ears of the saints, that hearing them and doing them, they may be cleansed from their iniquities, and you along with them.[41]

In *Vision* 4, a radiant young man—the angel of repentance—shows him the approaching trial of humanity and how it will be delivered. This apocalyptic foreshadowing was later identified as the persecution of Christians that took place under Trajan (98–117 CE). There is a strong element of eschatological expectation in this vision, as in Revelation. He relates a vision of a terrifying beast that recalls the beasts of the sea and land in Revelation (cf. Rev 11:7; 12:3; 13:1; 17:8). It is only in *Vision* 4 that Hermas is told the identity of the woman who delivered the previous three visions. The Lady is not the Sibyl, as he had thought, but the Church, established before the beginning of creation.[42] She does not give her message to important individuals, like the Sibyl, but to a community of believers.

Vision 5 is delivered by an angel of repentance in charge of Christians. He is the Shepherd after whom the book is named. This vision is concerned with prophets who produced false teachings, an obvious concern also in the New Testament (e.g., Mt 7:15; 24:11; 1 Jn 4:1; 2 Pt 2: 2:1; Rev 20:10).[43] Hermas closes his fifth vision with a series of twelve mandates and ten similes. The similes concern aspects of Christian practice like fasting, repentance, purity of the

---

41. *Vis.* 3.8, trans. F. Crombie, *The Shepherd of Hermas*, in *Fathers of the Second Century: Hermes, Tatian, Athenagoras, Theophilus, and Clement of Alexandria (Entire)*, ANF 2, ed. Philip Schaff (Edinburgh: T&T Clark, 1885), 25. All translations of this work are taken from Crombie, 9–58 unless otherwise specified. A more recent edition and translation appears in Holmes, *Apostolic Fathers*, 442–685.

42. Hermas, *Vis.* 4.1, trans. Crombie, 27–28.

43. See J. Reiling, *Hermas and Christian Prophecy: A Study of the Eleventh Mandate*. NovTSup 37 (Leiden: Brill, 1973), 58–59, on four kinds of false apocalyptic prophet mentioned in the New Testament, including false apocalyptic prophets in Rev 16:30, 19:20, and 20:10, which Reiling identifies as an eschatological *topos*, like the Beast, rather than a reference to actual prophets. Vision 4 of Hermas is also full of imagery reminiscent of the *Book of Revelation*.

body and almsgiving, and are more like those appearing in the prophetic book I Enoch than the New Testament parables.[44]

Shepherd, therefore, was a new genre for Christian Scriptures and had as its main purpose the unfolding of the Scriptures through a series of extended allegories. This novel, congregational approach to exegesis had a mixed reception from the start with some second- and third-century bishops classing it as unacceptable reading for most Christians, in the same way as they rejected the Odes of Solomon as apocryphal.[45] Hermas may have anticipated a lukewarm reception and thus sought to anticipate it in Mandate 11 on distinguishing true prophecy from false.

The Mandate on True Prophecy

One of twelve injunctions on how to live according to Christian values and the importance of repentance, *Mandate* 11, offers valuable evidence for the fluctuating status of ecstatic visions which required spiritual exegesis. Its position at the end of the work serves to underline its importance. The focus of the *Shepherd's Mandate* 11 is the problem of distinguishing true prophecy from false. In the context of the ongoing controversy in the first two centuries of Christianity over prophecy as a gift of the Spirit, how could a Christian discern between true and false prophets? Hermas sought to answer this question by providing examples of each in *Mandate* 11. He starts with a description of the false prophet, who takes money for his services and sets himself apart from the faithful while filling the doubters' minds with predictions that are simply what they want to hear. This is worth quoting at length:

These doubters then go to him as to a soothsayer, and inquire of him what will happen to them; and he, the false prophet, not having the power of a Divine Spirit in him, answers them according to their inquiries, and according to their wicked desires, and fills their souls with expectations, according to their own wishes. For being himself empty, he gives empty answers to empty inquirers; for every answer is made to the emptiness of man. Some true words he does occasionally utter; for the devil fills him

---

44. Cf. 1 Enoch 2:37–71, translated by Charlesworth, *Old Testament Epigrapha*, vol. 1, 29–50.

45. See Christian Tornau and Paolo Cecconi, eds., *The Shepherd of Hermas in Latin: Critical Edition of the Oldest Translation Vulgata* (Berlin: W. de Gruyter, 2014), 4–5; Ulrich Neymeyr, *Die christlichen Lehrer im zweiten Jahrhundert. Ihre Lehrtätigkeit, ihr Selbsverständnis und ihre Geschichte*, VCS 4 (Leiden: Brill, 1989): 9–15.

with his own spirit, in the hope that he may be able to overcome some of the righteous.[46]

The faithful will keep away from such false prophets, whose powers come from the enemy of humankind.[47] The angelic young man who represents Jesus tells Hermas that by looking at the prophet's way of life and by examining his willingness to associate with the righteous, one can discern whether a prophetic message is true or false:

Then it never approaches an assembly of righteous men but shuns them. And it associates with doubters and the vain, and prophesies to them in a corner, and deceives them, speaking to them, according to their desires, mere empty words: for they are empty to whom it gives its answers.[48]

The focus on the non-congregational settings of false prophecies is made explicit here, which bolsters the argument for *Shepherd*'s congregational understanding of prophecy. True prophecy in congregations is marked by the Holy Spirit; false prophets are possessed by the Devil,[49] a common understanding in early Christianity of extra-biblical revelation, including pagan and Jewish oracles, as we see in Acts 13:10, in the condemnation of a false Jewish magus who practised divination in the Roman proconsul's court (cf. Acts 13:6–12).

Hermas' simile for the infilling of the Holy Spirit in true prophecy, in the assemblies of the righteous at prayer, takes its inspiration from a familiar household activity of clearing out jars of wine or oil in a storehouse. True prophets are filled with the divine spirit, while false prophets, filled with an earthly spirit, are like empty vessels beside men who have the spirit of divinity.[50] Hermas implies that he was filled with the divine spirit.

There is, therefore, no transformation in the life of the empty prophet

---

46. *Mand.* 11, trans. Crombie, 28.

47. *Mand.* 11, trans. Crombie, 27: "For he who inquires of a false prophet in regard to any action is an idolater, and devoid of the truth, and foolish."

48. *Mand.* 11, trans. Crombie, 28.

49. *Mand.* 11, trans. Crombie, 28: "Try by his deeds and his life the man who says that he is inspired. But as for you, trust the Spirit which comes from God, and has power; but the spirit which is earthly and empty trust not at all, for there is no power in it: it comes from the devil."

50. *Mand.* 11, trans. Crombie, 28: "For if you pack closely a storehouse with wine or oil, and put an empty jar in the midst of the vessels of wine or oil, you will find that jar empty as when you placed it, if you should wish to clear the storehouse. So also the empty prophets, when they come to the spirits of the righteous, are found [on leaving] to be such as they were when they came. This, then, is the mode of life of both prophets."

as the result of his false prophecy or his contact with the spirits of the righteous. Even the earthly spirit then abandons the false prophet out of fear and leaves him empty and deprived of speech. The earthly spirit is compared with a stone thrown into the sky, or a jet of water squirted upwards: neither can ever reach the heights of heaven. The authority of those who have the heavenly spirit allows them to interpret visions correctly and for the benefit of their faith communities.

Two more similes in *Mandate* 11 concern prophecy, the first comparing the divine spirit with hail: that which falls from heaven packs a powerful punch even in small doses. The other simile compares the force of true prophecy with that of a single drop of water repeated over time. A constant drip of water from a pitcher held aloft can eventually hollow out a stone. The homespun wisdom of the similes reflects the level of the target audience of the *Mandates*: they are meant for a general Christian congregation who have prophets in their midst. Prophecy is firmly rooted in an ecclesial context and Hermas has to negotiate the space between isolated prophet and congregational visionary interpreter. He addresses above all issues of family discipline: fidelity in marriage, and the appropriate behaviour of wives and children. He critiques the lone fortune-teller who takes money for his trade and eschews others. How then did this work come to be relegated among "books not to be read?"

Conclusion

As we have seen, Hermas' inspired visionary exegesis was not just a charismatic gift for the benefit of the individual but was also received for the good of his congregation in Rome and beyond. After he received his second vision, Hermas advised Clement to circulate his work to the "cities abroad … but in this city [Rome] you will read it yourself with the elders who are in charge of the church."[51] The public reading of the text would perhaps encourage or validate further congregational prophecy. Hermas advises that any prophecy in ecclesial gatherings should be preceded by a group prayer of intercession when "a man who has the Divine Spirit" comes before "an assembly of righteous men who have the faith of the Divine Spirit."[52] Hermas regards himself

---

51. *Vis.* 2.4.3. Aune, in *Apocalypticism*, 181, discusses this passage.

52. *Mand.* 11.9. On congregational prophecy in Hermas and the *Odes of Solomon*, see Aune, *Apocalypticism*, 320–35, especially 335 where this passage is discussed.

as someone who has the divine spirit and undertakes to give his congregational exegesis to the Christian community of Rome, through the agency of its leader Clement. He is not a prophet in the Hebrew sense of one who speaks out against foreign kings and domestic tyrants. Rather, he delivers his message before a congregation of like-minded righteous Christians. The proof of his prophethood lies in the community of elders' acceptance of his message.

In light of the flourishing of Montanism in the late second to early third centuries, the validity of Hermas as a prophetic visionary had to be reassessed by patristic commentators. We can compare their ambivalence to the *Shepherd* with the churches' widespread reservations toward the canonical status of Revelation, not accepted in the East until 367 CE. Unlike John the Elder's apocalypse, Hermas' use of apocalyptic visions to present exegesis to his congregation in Rome and beyond did not find general acceptance. It broke the rule of no prophecy after John the Baptist and could not be accepted as Scripture itself.

The *Shepherd* was repeatedly relegated to apocryphal status in the fourth, fifth, and sixth centuries by Roman critics like the author of the *Muratorian Fragment*, and Popes Gelasius and Hormisdas, who were convinced that it should not be read by catholics. The genre of personal apocalypses such as *Shepherd* and the *Vision of Paul* continued to enjoy popularity in the Christian West, however, as evidenced by the production of a second Latin translation of the *Shepherd* in the fifth century.[53]

The *Shepherd* shows us that the early Church of Rome had its own homegrown, charismatic visionaries. Although congregational exegesis was controversial, Hermas' five recorded visions constituted for some readers an authoritative revelation. His work posed a question that challenged the foundations of the relatively new Christian faith: how should one define what constitutes Scripture? Reading *Mandate* 11 in this context alerts us to the problems that the author—or a later interpolator—faced. His visions claimed to elucidate what it meant to be a faithful Christian, and even to add to Israel's Scriptures well after the age of the Jewish prophets had ended, and several decades before the New Prophecy movement had begun. This novel, Roman form of exegesis was a bold experiment that was not to last beyond the second century in the mainstream Christian churches, but it bears witness to a period in

---

53. The *Palatina* version, ed. Anna Vezzoni, *Il Pastore di Erma Versione Palatina* (Florence: Le lettere, 1994).

which conceptions of Scripture and revelation were still contested. Like the Hebrew prophets Eldad and Modad, Hermas offered a vision of a congregational context in which true prophecy could flourish. His visions and parables did not find favour in the second- and third-century Church, and like the *Book of Eldad and Modad, Shepherd* was regarded with suspicion and eventually dropped from the canon.

Bibliography

Primary Sources

Clement of Rome. *First Letter to the Church of Corinth*, edited and translated by Michael W. Holmes, *The Apostolic Fathers: Greek Texts and English Translations*, 3rd ed. 33–131. Grand Rapids, MI: Baker Academic, 2007.

Clement of Rome. *First Letter to the Church of Corinth*, translated by J. B. Lightfoot, *The Apostolic Fathers Clement, Ignatius, and Polycarp*, Part One: *Clement*, vol. 2, edited by J. R. Harmer. 2nd ed. London, New York: Macmillan, 1899.

Fragmentum Muratori. Edited by Samuel P. Tregelles, *Canon Muratorianus: The Earliest Catalogue of the Books of the New Testament*, 17–21. Oxford: Clarendon, 1867.

Gelasius I of Rome. *Epistula* 42, edited by Andreas Thiel, *Epistulae Romanorum Pontificium genuinae et quae ad eos scriptae sunt a S. Hilaro usque ad Pelagium II*, 454–71. Leipzig: Braunsberg, 1867.

Hermas. *Pastor*. Translated by F. Crombie, *The Shepherd of Hermas*, in *Fathers of the Second Century: Hermes, Tatian, Athenagoras, Theophilus, and Clement of Alexandria* (Entire), edited by Alexander Roberts and James Donaldson, *ANF* 2: 9–58. Edinburgh: T & T Clark, 1885.

Hermas. *Pastor*. Translated by Bart D. Ehrman, *The Shepherd*, in *The Apostolic Fathers II*, LCL 25. Cambridge, MA: Harvard University Press, 2003.

Hermas. *Pastor*. Edited by Molly Whittacker, *Die Apostolischen Väter I, Der Hirt des Hermas*, GCS 48. 2nd ed. Berlin: de Gruyter, 1967.

Hermas. *Pastor*. Edited by Robert Joly, *Hermas: Le Pasteur*, SC 53bis. 2nd ed. Paris: Éditions de Cerf, 1997; reprint, 2011.

Hermas. *Pastor Vulgata*. Edited by Christian Tornau and Paolo Cecconi, *The* Shepherd *of Hermas in Latin: Critical Edition of the Oldest Translation Vulgata*. Berlin: W. de Gruyter, 2014.

Hermas. *Pastor. Versio Palatina*. Edited by Anna Vezzoni (ed.), *Il Pastore di Erma Versione Palatina*, with introduction by Antonio Carlini. Florence: Le lettere, 1994.

Hormisdas of Rome. *Epistula* 125. Edited by Andreas Thiel, *Epistulae Romanorum Pontificium genuinae et quae ad eos scriptae sunt a S. Hilaro usque ad Pelagium II*, 931–38. Leipzig: Braunsberg, 1867.

Origen of Alexandria. *Commentarii in Epistulam ad Romanos*. Translated by Thomas P.

Scheck, *Commentary on the Epistle to the Romans, Books 6–10*, Fathers of the Church
   104. Washington: Catholic University of America Press, 2002.
Origen of Alexandria. *Commentarii in Epistulam ad Romanos. Livres I–II.* Edited by
   C. P. Hammond Bammel and Luc Brésard, *Commentaire sur l'Épître aux Romains /
   Origène.* SC 502. Paris: Éditions de Cerf, 2009.
Origen of Alexandria. *Contra Celsum.* Edited by Marcel Borret, *Contre Celse.* SC 132bis, 136,
   147, 150, and 277. Paris: Éditions de Cerf, 1968–2000.
Origen of Alexandria. *De principiis.* Edited by Henri Crouzel and Manlio Simonetti,
   Origène. Traité des principes. Livres III et IV. SC 268 bis. Paris: Éditions
   de Cerf, 2006.
Papiasfragmente. Edited by Ulrich H. J. Hörtner and Martin Leutzsch, *Hirt des Hermas,*
   Schriften des Urchristentums 3. Darmstadt: Wissenschaftliche Buchgesellschaft, 1998.
Philo of Alexandria. *De vita contemplativa,* translated by Francis H. Colson, *On the Contem-
   plative Life or Suppliants,* in *Philo,* vol. 9, LCL 363. Cambridge, MA: Harvard Universi-
   ty Press, 1941; reprint 1985.

Secondary Sources

Allison, Dale C. "Eldad and Modad." *Journal for the Study of the Pseudepigrapha* 21 no. 2
   (2011): 99–131.
Aune, David E. *Prophecy in Early Christianity and the Ancient Mediterranean World.* Grand
   Rapids MI: Eerdmans, 1983.
———. *Apocalypticism, Prophecy and Magic in Early Christianity: Collected Essays.* WUNT
   199. Tübingen: Mohr Siebeck, 2006.
Brox, Norbert. *Der Hirt des Hermas.* Kommentar zu den apostolischen Vätern,
   Ergänzungsreihe zum kritisch-Exegetischen Kommentar über das Neue Testament 7.
   Göttingen: Vandenhoeck und Ruprecht, 1991.
Charlesworth, James H. *The Old Testament Epigrapha,* 2 vols, Peabody, MA: Hendrickson,
   2010.
Cook, L. Stephen. *On the Question of the "Cessation of Prophecy" in Ancient Judaism.*
   TSAJ 145. Tübingen: Mohr Siebeck, 2011.
Forbes, Christopher. *Prophecy and Inspired Speech in Early Christianity and Its Hellenistic
   Environment.* Tübingen: JBC Mohr, 1995.
Ford, Josephine Massingberd. "A possible liturgical background to the Shepherd of Her-
   mas." *RevQ* 6, no. 4 (24), (1969): 531–51.
Frenschkowski, Marco. "Vision als Imagination. Beobachtungen zum differenzierten
   Wirklichkeitsanspruch frühchristlicher Visionsliteratur." In *Fremde Wirklichkeiten:
   Literarische Phantastik und antike Literatur,* edited by Nicola Hömke und Manuel
   Baumbach, 339–66. Studien zur griechischen und lateinischen Poesie 6. Heidelberg:
   Universitätsverlag Winter, 2006.
Hagner, Donald A. *The Use of the Old and New Testaments in Clement of Rome.*
   NovTSup 34. Leiden: Brill, 1973.

Hanson, John S. "Dreams and Visions in the Graeco-Roman World and Early Christianity." In *ANRW,* 2.23.2, edited by Wolfgang Haase, 1395–427. Berlin: W. de Gruyter, 1980.

Harrisson, Juliette. *Dreams and Dreaming in the Roman Empire: Cultural Memory and Imagination.* London: Bloomsbury, 2013.

Hellholm, David. "The Shepherd of Hermas." In *The Apostolic Fathers: An Introduction.* Edited by Wilhelm Pratscher, 215–42. Waco, TX: Baylor University Press, 2010.

Hellholm, David. *Das Visionenbuch des Hermas als Apokalypse: Formgeschichtliche und text-theoretische Studien zu einer literarischen Gattung. I. Methodologische Vorüberlegungen und makrostrukturelle Textanalyse.* Lund: C. W. K. Gleerup, 1980.

Hill, David. *New Testament Prophecy,* rev. ed. Atlanta: Society for Biblical Literature, 1985.

Joly, Robert. "Le milieu complexe du 'Pasteur d'Hermas.'" In *ANRW,* 2.27.1, edited by Wolfgang Haase and Hildegard Temporini, 525–51. Berlin: De Gruyter, 1992.

Kannengiesser, Charles. *A Handbook of Patristic Exegesis: The Bible in Ancient Christianity.* 2 vols. Leiden: Brill, 2006.

McKechnie, Paul. *Christianizing Asia Minor: Conversion, Communities, and Social Change in the Pre-Constantinian Era.* Cambridge: Cambridge University Press, 2019.

Neil, Bronwen. *Dreams and Divination from Byzantium to Baghdad (400–1000 CE).* OSAR. Oxford: Oxford University Press, 2021.

Neymeyr, Ulrich. *Die christlichen Lehrer im zweiten Jahrhundert. Ihre Lehrtätigkeit, ihr Selbsverständnis und ihre Geschichte.* VCS 4. Leiden: Brill, 1989.

Oppenheim, Leo. "The Interpretation of Dreams in the Ancient Near East." *Transactions of the American Philosophical Society, New Series* 46, no. 3 (1956): 179–373.

O'Brien, David P. "The Cumaean Sibyl as the Revelation-bearer in the Shepherd of Hermas," *JECS,* 5, no. 4 (1997): 473–96.

Osiek, Carolyn and Helmut Koester. *Shepherd of Hermas. A Commentary.* Hermeneia: a Critical and Historical Commentary on the Bible 83. Minneapolis MN: Fortress Press, 1999.

Reiling, J. *Hermas and Christian Prophecy: A Study of the Eleventh Mandate.* NovTSup 37. Leiden: Brill, 1973.

Rüpke, Jorg. "Der Hirte des Hermas: Plausibilisierungs- und Legitimierungs strategien im Übergang von Antike und Christentum." *Zeitschrift für antikes Christentum* 7 (2003): 362–84.

"Fighting for Differences: Forms and Limits of Religious Individuality in the 'Shepherd of Hermas.'" In *The Individual in the Religions of the Ancient Mediterranean,* edited by Jorg Rüpke, 315–41. Oxford: Oxford University Press, 2013.

Seitz, Oscar J. F. "Relationship of the Shepherd of Hermas to the Epistle of James." *JBL* 63, no. 2 (1944): 131–40.

Trevett, Christine. *Montanism: Gender, Authority and the New Prophecy.* Rev. ed. Cambridge: Cambridge University Press, 2002.

Verheyden, Joseph. "The Shepherd of Hermas." In *Writings of the Apostolic Fathers,* edited by Paul Foster, 63–71. T & T Clark Biblical Studies. London: T&T Clark, 2007.

Weiss, Alexander. "Hermas' 'Biography:' Social Upward and Downward Mobility of an Independent Freedman." *AncSoc* 39 (2009): 185–202.

Wilson, Christian J. *Five Problems in the Interpretation of the Shepherd of Hermas: Authorship, Genre, Canonicity, Apocalyptic, and the Absence of the Name "Jesus Christ."* Mellen Biblical Press Series 34. Lewiston, NY: Mellen Biblical Press, 1995.

Elizabeth Ann Dively Lauro

3. ORIGEN MAKES PREACHERS OF US ALL

A Collective Analysis of his Nine Extant *Homilies on Judges*

Throughout his homilies on Judges, Origen draws out of Scripture his familiar theme of the soul's journey to God as an ascent through growth in knowledge and virtue.[1] Yet, he takes advantage of the scriptural focus on the ancient judges as the Israelites' deliverers from recurrent falls into captivity to enemy nations, by placing the soul's journey within the context of a cosmic battle between good and evil spiritual forces in constant, even repetitive competition for possession of the soul.[2] This battle theme drives his exegesis, as

1. For these familiar themes, see the breakthrough work of Rowan A. Greer on the spiritual drama of the soul's ascent to God, in *Origen: An Exhortation to Martyrdom, Prayer and Selected Works*, CWS (New York: Paulist Press, 1979), 1–37. See also Karen Jo Torjesen on the soul's journey of salvation, in *Hermeneutical Procedure and Theological Method in Origen's Exegesis*, Patristische Texte und Studien 28 (Berlin and New York: Walter de Gruyter, 1986), 70–107; Elizabeth Ann Dively Lauro on the higher senses of Scripture as markers for the soul's ascent to God, in *The Soul and Spirit of Scripture within Origen's Exegesis*, BAC 3 (Leiden, The Netherlands, and Boston: Brill Academic Publishers, Inc., 2005), 195–237; and Peter W. Martens on the soul's journey as the structure of the salvation drama and the ideal interpreter's part in this drama, in *Origen and Scripture: The Contours of the Exegetical Life*, OECS (Oxford University Press, 2012), 193–242. See also Origen's treatment of the soul's journey in *Hom. in Num.* 27 as a double trajectory, with one path in this life and one after this life.

2. See Henri de Lubac's discussion of Origen's use of Old Testament motifs of combat and the sin-deliverance cycle in *History and Spirit: The Understanding of Scripture According to Origen*, trans. Anne Englund Nash (San Francisco: Ignatius Press, 2007), 204–22. Arguably, Origen's joinder of the

he likens his homiletic audience to the people of Israel, the evil powers of sin, Satan, and his demons to the enemy nations, the Church to the foreign woman Jael, the preacher to the judges of old and the angelic forces, and Scripture to Gideon's war-trumpet. Within this context, he paints the portrait of the preacher as an angel-savior, overseer, steward, and leader, who plays many roles. He delivers souls from enemies, instructs them in saving truths, protects them from further harm, and leads them to willingly engage their enemies in battle as they progress along the upward path to God. These roles of the preacher are recurrent and simultaneous as well as successive. As he uncovers the full drama of the spiritual war for his audience, Origen reveals that Scripture is calling his hearers not only to enlist as soldiers by entering and persevering along the path of ascent, but, with some progress, to effectively perform these preacher's tasks for themselves and for their fellow journeyers.

Close analysis of these homilies, then, reveals why Origen is preaching about the role and tasks of the preacher to a general homiletic audience rather than reserving it solely for an audience of presbyters in training. He does not view the preacher's role as suited to only a few superior souls within the Church. Rather, he expects every hearer, at some point along the journey to God, to perform the preacher's tasks for both himself and others. The pulpit is not the only place where a preacher is needed. For Origen, the mission of the preacher is to make lead-soldiers, or preachers, of everyone.[3] In this homiletic context, Origen not only explains the preacher's tasks for assisting souls along

---

battle motif (reading the enemies of Israel as spiritual enemies) with the Israelite's repetitive cycle of sin to deliverance is an example of what Frances M. Young referred to as a "process of assembling collages" as a "characteristic of early Christian *paraenesis.*" See *Biblical Exegesis and the Formation of Christian Culture* (Peabody, MA: Hendrickson Publishers, 2002), 224, 234. Origen also arguably exemplifies here Young's observation that early Church Fathers used Scripture to "create" or explain the Church community's "identity," as here Origen likens the Church in general and his audience in particular to the Israelites in the Hebrew Scriptures in order to identify them as the chosen people of God, also using "mimesis" to exhort his audience to behave as the repentant Israelites and the preacher to behave as the deliverers in their spiritualized representation. See Young, *Biblical Exegesis,* 220–35, 263.

3. Origen's humble stance toward his role as preacher is interesting given his historically hard-won title of presbyter, carrying with it the privilege of preaching. Only after his home bishop, Demetrius of Alexandria, consistently refused to give him this honor, did his travels bring him to supporters, Bishops Alexander of Jerusalem and Theoctistus of Caesarea, who ordained him a presbyter, allowing him to preach eventually in front of a congregation in Caesarea of Palestine. See Eusebius, *Church History* 6.8. These homilies on Judges seem to clarify that Origen viewed his title of presbyter as a formality and the heart of his task as a responsibility to which all believers should aspire in an essential though not always titular sense.

the journey but simultaneously performs them in front of his audience as well as upon them so that they have a model of how to act as preachers for themselves and each other.

In these homilies on Judges, Origen employs Scripture both to describe and to model the preacher's tasks through five main exhortatory addresses to his audience. First, he uses stark battle language to shock his audience into paying attention to the fact that their souls are in constant threat by enemy forces. Second, Origen calls his audience to join the Church, where they will find the path of ascent. Third, he urges them to trust and follow him as a preacher charged with leading them away from enemies and toward God. Fourth, he exhorts them to pay heed to the real guide, Scripture, for which he, as preacher, is but a channel, and to study the various ways in which Scripture meets the needs of a soul in battle. Only after having described and modelled the first four tasks of the preacher, does Origen, as his final exhortation, call his hearers to become, like him, channels of Scripture's saving powers both for themselves and others. Close examination of each of these hortatory addresses reveals how Origen uses both Scripture's text and the process of preaching Scripture to form his hearers into fellow soldier-preachers. As a result, these homilies on Judges provide a bird's eye view of an early Church homilist employing Scripture not only as a call-to-arms but also as a call to leadership. Origen exegetes Scripture from the pulpit in order to make preachers of us all.

The Cosmic Battle as the Context of the Journey

Origen begins with the preacher's first and most pressing task of bringing his audience's attention to the cosmic battle for possession of their souls in which they are under ever-present, constant attack. Whether they know it or not, all souls are in a "struggle and spiritual battle" against the Devil[4] and his demons.[5] He points out Paul's precedent in Ephesians 6 for calling it a battle, for "'it is not a battle against flesh and blood'" but "'against principalities

---

4. *HomJud* 9.2; *Origen: Homilies on Judges*, trans. Elizabeth Ann Dively Lauro, The Fathers of the Church, 119 (Washington, D. C.: Catholic University of America Press, 2010), 116; *Origène: Homélies sur Les Juges,* eds. and trans. Pierre Messié, Louis Neyrand, and Marcel Borret, SCs, 389 (Paris: Le Éditions du Cerf, 1993), 216. See also *HomJud* 2.5; FOTC 119:59; SC 398:90. All biblical quotations are translated from the edition of Origen's work, and all biblical references are understood to be in alignment with LXX's chapter and verse.

5. *HomJud* 9.2; FOTC 119:118; SC 389:220. See also *HomJud* 2.3; FOTC 119:57; SC 398:84. Origen

and powers and against the rulers of this world of darkness and against spirits of wickedness.'"[6] These evil spirits are enemies and they have declared war on human souls.[7]

Origen's underlying belief that many in his homiletic audiences live unaware of this battle for their souls receives more explicit articulation in other homilies. In *HomLev* 9, he points out that many in his audience are willingly distracted by the amusements of this world and drawn into preoccupations with their own fleshly passions, and thoroughly uninterested in being rested from their complacencies.[8] In *HomGn* 10, Origen expresses frustrated anger at them for either failing to heed Scripture's instruction, or, worse, sitting in church and blatantly failing to listen.[9] In *HomEx* 12, he even calls out those audience members who leave church either before or directly after the Scripture is read aloud, not waiting to hear the preacher's explanation of its salvific meanings.[10]

In these homilies on Judges, Origen tries to shock his audience into listening to Scripture's call to engage in the battle by impressing upon them the binary nature of the soul's choice at any moment. He wants them to understand

---

also refers to the demons as "contrary powers." See *HomJud* 3.4; FOTC 119:66–67; SC 389:106–8 and *HomJud* 3.3; FOTC 119:64–65; SC 389:102.

6. *HomJud* 6.5–6, referring to Jgs 5:11–13 and quoting Eph 6:12; FOTC 119:92–93; SC 389:164–66.

7. *HomJud* 9.2; FOTC 119:118; SC 389:220–22.

8. Famously, in *Hom. in Lev.* 9, Origen accuses his audience of indulging in the "circus" and "contest" of the "horses" and "athletes," while at the same time indulging their "wrath," "love of the flesh," and "disgraceful passions." *Hom. in Lev.* 9.9.7; *Origen: Homilies on Leviticus 1–16*, trans. Gary Wayne Barkley, Fathers of the Church, 83 (Washington, D.C.: Catholic University of America Press, 1990), 198–99; *Origène: Homélies sur Le Lévitique, Tome 2*, ed. and trans. Marcel Borret, SCs, 287 (Paris: Le Éditions du Cerf, 1981), 120.

9. Origen angrily addresses his audience with these words: "What, then, shall I do?… You spend most of this time, no rather almost all of it, in mundane occupations; you pass some of it in the marketplace, some in business; one has time for the country, another for lawsuits, and no one or very few have time to hear the word of God… Even when you are present and placed in the Church you are not attentive, but you waste your time on common everyday stories; you turn your backs to the word of God or to the divine readings… What, then, shall I do, to whom the ministry of the word is entrusted? The words which have been read are mystical. They must be explained in allegorical secrets. Can I throw 'the pearls' of the word of God to your deaf and averted ears?" *HomGn* 10.1, referring to Mt 7:6; *Origen: Homilies on Genesis and Exodus*, trans. Ronald E. Heine, Fathers of the Church, 71 (Washington, D.C.: Catholic University of America Press, 1982), 158; *Origène: Homélies sur la Genèse*, ed. and trans. Louis Doutreleau, SC, 7 bis (Paris: Le Éditions du Cerf, 1985) 256. See also *HomGn* 11.3; FOTC 71:174; SC 7:288–90

10. See *Hom. in Exod.* 12.2 and 13.3, FOTC 71:368–69, 378–79; *Origène: Homélies sur L'Exode*, ed. and trans., Marcel Borret, SC, 321 (Paris: Le Éditions du Cerf, 1985) 356–58 and 380–82. In this homily, as in *Hom. In Lev.* 9 above, Origen also reprimands others in his audience for sitting in the back of the church occupied with their own thoughts, oblivious to what is transpiring at the pulpit.

that at each moment a person either chooses the allurements of sin, becoming captive to its purveyors, Satan and the demons, or chooses to strive for virtue, becoming more like Christ and thus more ready for heaven; there is no other option.[11] When a person chooses sin or virtue, he determines whether Satan or Christ resides within his soul, for both cannot coexist in the same space. Satan is invited in not only when a person performs sinful actions, but also when he merely desires to sin or feels passion for sinful things.[12] All these demonic weapons weaken both the hearer's clarity that there is a life-or-death battle and his resolve to fight for his rightful *telos* of union with God. When someone sins or harbors desires or passions, he holds within himself "bad days" or "days of the wicked,"[13] because to serve the vices is to serve the devil[14] and allow him to reside within the soul.[15] Here, Origen is drawing out meaning from Jgs 2:7: "the people feared the Lord all the days of Jesus."[16] To avoid or reverse the bad days that mark the devil's presence in his soul, the person must strive to hold within himself "good days" or "days of the just," also called "days of Jesus."[17] Origen explains that each time he plants and nourishes a virtue within himself,[18] the person holds a day of Jesus, which suggests what Origen makes explicit elsewhere, that Jesus is simultaneously each of the virtues and all of the virtues together.[19] When a person grows in and practices virtue, he

11. In *De Principiis* 3.4, esp. 3.4.2, Origen suggests that the human will is always in movement, choosing in the direction of the Christ-like tendencies of the spirit or of the body's fleshly tendencies. See *Origen: On First Principles*, trans. G. W. Butterworth (Gloucester, MA: Peter Smith, 1973), 230–236, esp. 233; *Origène: Traité Des Principes*, Tome 3, eds. and trans. Henri Crouzel and Manlio Simonetti, SC, 268 (Paris: Le Éditions du Cerf, 1980), 198–216, esp. 206.

12. For this distinction between sins, desires to sin, and passions, as separate but similar sources of meeting with captivity to Satan and the demons, see generally *HomJud* 1.1 and 2.2, 2.3 and 2.5.

13. *HomJud* 1.1–1.2; FOTC 11:39 and 45; SC 389:50 and 58–60.

14. *HomJud* 1.1; FOTC 11:44–5; SC 389:58.

15. *HomJud* 2.1 and 2.5, quoting Mt 12:43–5; FOTC 119:51–2, 59–60; SC 389:74, 88–92. Specific vices which Origen lists here are "when out of greed you plan and desire to lay waste to another's goods, … plan debauchery, … are excited by anger … are inflamed with envy, … are spurred on by jealousy, … revel in drunkenness, … are puffed up with pride, … act with cruelty."

16. *HomJud* 1.1, quoting Jgs 2:7; FOTC 119:44; SC 389:58.

17. *HomJud* 1.1–1.2, referring to Jgs 2:7; FOTC 119:44–46; SC 389:58–62.

18. *HomJud* 1.1 and 1.3; FOTC 119:41 and 47–8; SC 389:52–4 and 64. The fuller passages list out the numerous virtues: "days 'of justice' and 'peace' … and sanctification, … prudence, … mercy, and likewise … every single good quality of the virtues," such as also "patience … gentleness and piety and goodness, and everything that pertains to a virtue."

19. For Origen's notion that each and all the virtues are Christ, see *ComCt* 1.5, as well as *ComJn* 32.127, *ComRm* 9.34 and others listed by Martens, in *Origen and Scripture*, 230 n. 17. For discussion, see Dively Lauro, *The Soul and Spirit*, 230–31, and Henri Crouzel, *Origen: The Life and Thought of the First*

"serves the Lord,"[20] and Jesus resides in him.[21] Again, Origen stresses the binary nature of human choice: at each given moment his hearer holds within his soul either the good days of Jesus or the bad, wicked days of Satan.[22] And if the hearer chooses sin and Satan, Jesus is not only dead in him, but, with each sin, he actually "mocks Christ" and "crucifies" him all over again within his soul.[23] By merely desiring to sin, a person "suffocates and kills" Jesus within himself.[24] Not only is the human person limited to two choices in response to the cosmic battle, but he faces only two possible results: freedom and life with Christ or captivity to sin and Satan and the continual death of Jesus within his soul.

Origen also stresses that the hearer, by choosing sin, will experience abandonment by God, as did the Israelites, because sin is a form of idolatry. Just as the Israelites, when "taken captive under the law of sin," "bow down" to gods such as the Baals and "worship images," so the sinful person in Origen's audience makes sin his idol and thereby bows down before his enemy, Satan.[25] Whatever a person "admires and loves above all other things, this is God to him."[26] Like the Israelites, the sinner, by choice, "abandons the Lord."[27] By choosing passions over God, he makes himself unworthy of God, and God withdraws from his mind and heart, leaving him "an empty house."[28] God retreats and allows him to be held captive by the enemy because God honors the sinner's free choice, and so hands him over to his chosen passion and to the evil powers who then can and will "plunder" his soul.[29] Origen wants his hearers to understand the consequences of the battle, and, to that end, he both

Great Theologian, trans. A. S. Worrall (San Francisco: Harper & Row, 1989) 98, 190. See also _Hom. in Isa._ 3.2–3 where Origen states that the virtues "admired" Christ "while he was ascending." See _Origen: Homilies on Isaiah_, trans., Dively Lauro, Fathers of the Church, 142 (Washington, DC: Catholic University of America Press, 2021), 63–66. See specifically _Hom. in Isa._ 3.3 in which Origen discusses the seven women, representing the seven gifts of the Spirit, who adorn themselves with these gifts as qualities of Christ.

20. _HomJud_ 1.1, referring to Jgs 2:7; FOTC 12:44–45; SC 389:58.

21. _HomJud_ 2.1; FOTC 119:51–52; SC 389:72–76.

22. _HomJud_ 1.1; FOTC 11:39–40; SC 389:50–52.

23. _HomJud_ 2.1, referring to Heb 6:6; FOTC 119:51–52; SC 389:74.

24. _HomJud_ 2.2; FOTC 119:53; SC 389:76.

25. _HomJud_ 2.3, quoting Jgs 2:11–12 and Rom 7:23; FOTC 119:54–55; SC 389:78–80.

26. _HomJud_ 2.3; FOTC 119:55–56; SC 389:80–82. Also, the human person "worship[s] an image" whenever he is so dedicated to some vices that he "love[s] them with the whole heart and the whole soul and all strength." See _HomJud_ 2.3, referring to Dt 6:5; FOTC 119:55; SC 389:82.

27. _Hom. in Judg_ 2.4, referring to Jgs 2:12–14; FOTC 119:58; SC 389:88.

28. _HomJud_ 2.5, referring to Mt 12:44; FOTC 119:60; SC 389:90–92.

29. _HomJud_ 2.5, quoting Jgs 2:13–14, and referring to Rom 1:26, 28; FOTC 119:58–59, 60; SC 389:88–92.

describes and performs on them the first task of shocking them into acknowledging the battle and its inevitable effects.

The Church as the Setting for the Journey

This first exhortation for hearers to admit the ever-present spiritual battle for their souls leads naturally to the preacher's second task of calling his audience to *begin* the journey of ascent to God, which is also a call to join the Church. For, Origen states, "there is no other ascent by which one may be raised up to heaven except 'through the Church.'"[30] He explains that the Church herself is always "ascending from bodily to spiritual things and from earthly to heavenly things,"[31] for she is the collective Bride of Christ moving toward the heavenly banquet as the aggregate of believers.[32] Because the Church houses the path of ascent, when Origen calls his audience to begin the journey, he is essentially urging them to come to church, hear Scripture, and engage in liturgy and worship.

To illustrate that the Church is the essential locus of *all* aspects of the journey to God, including deliverance from captivity to sin, reversal of God's abandonment, reform through growth in the virtues, and the ascent upward toward God, Origen presents as a type of the Church the "foreign" woman, Jael.[33] In several ways, he likens the Church to this woman who protected the Israelites by killing Sisera, the commander of the Canaanite army under King Jabin, giving him sleep-inducing milk, then covering him with skins, and then driving a stake through his jaw with a hammer. First, Origen points out that she is a fitting "figure of the Church," both because her name means "ascent" and her foreign status relates to the fact that the Church, God's true chosen

---

30. *HomJud* 5.5, quoting Eph 3:10; FOTC 119:80; SC 389:140.

31. *HomJud* 5.5; FOTC 119:80; SC 389:140. After this statement, Origen explains in the rest of *HomJud* 5.5 that the Church is the first to receive salvation, but Israel will be saved also, citing Rom 11:25–26 as well as the story of Esau and Jacob at Gn 27:5–29 and the hemorrhaging woman in Mt 9:20–22 (parallel to Mk 5:25–34 and Lk 8:43–48). *HomJud* 5.5; FOTC 119:81; SC 389:140–42. Further research into Origen's ecclesiology should consider whether Origen is suggesting that the Church ascends as an independent entity as well as in its capacity as the collective body of individual souls.

32. Origen describes the Church, as the aggregate of souls, as well as the individual soul, to be the Bride of Christ, the Bridegroom, and salvation at the end of time to be the heavenly wedding feast, in *ComCt* Prol. 2 and Book 1, treating Sg 1:2–4. For analysis, see Dively Lauro, *The Soul and Spirit*, 195–237.

33. *HomJud* 5.4–5, referring to Jgs 4:14–22; FOTC 119:78–81; SC 389:136–42. See also *HomJos* 3.4–5, where Origen refers to Rahab, the prostitute of Jericho, as a type of the Church and emphasizes that salvation takes place within the Church.

people, "was assembled together from foreign peoples,"[34] that is, people foreign to the Israelites. Moreover, the way in which Jael killed Sisera speaks to the role the Church plays within a world full of false philosophies. Origen explains that Jael targeted Sisera's "mouth," which figuratively represents the Epicurean doctrine of pleasure that "deceives humankind with the flattery of excess."[35] She stabbed this worldly mouth with "the wood of the cross," to show that, in contrast to the "broad and wide" Epicurean "road of pleasure," Christ stands ready to lead souls on the "narrow and confined" "road of salvation."[36] This road of salvation is the journey of ascent, and it is found within the Church, where the believer can be safe from the entanglements of false, worldly wisdom and receive the necessary aid to begin and continue the ascent to God.[37] The Church is a safe ship surrounded by the storm of the cosmic battle that rages on without reprieve.[38] By emphasizing that the path of ascent is housed safely within the Church, Origen not only explains but also performs through his treatment of Scripture this second exhortation of the preacher, calling his hearers to come to and remain within the Church as imperative for salvation.

34. *HomJud* 5.5; FOTC 119:80; SC 389:140.

35. *HomJud* 5.5; FOTC 119:80; SC 389:140. Origen also describes Sisera as "the animal man," a "prince of vices," representing the "sages of this age" who promote "the philosophy ... of pleasure" [the Epicurean philosophy] who "was destroyed by the teaching of the Church, which he did not receive in faith." See *HomJud* 5.6, referring to 1 Cor 2:14; FOTC 119:82–83; SC 389:142–46. Note that, for Origen, the Epicurean philosophy was a prevalent thought system that he considered to be antithetical to the teachings of Scripture.

36. *HomJud* 5.5, referring to Mt 7:13–14; FOTC 119:80–81; SC 389:140. Also, though Origen does not elaborate further on the details of Sisera's death at the hands of Jael, one might surmise that Origen, if he had had more time, would have explained that the hammer represents Scripture, which the Church uses to send false teachings to their "eternal slumber." See *HomJud* 5.5; FOTC 119:81; SC 389:140.

37. Elsewhere in these homilies on Judges, Origen again stresses that the worthy preacher uses Scripture, as the complete text of instruction, to pierce and expose the false teachings of the age, "extinguish[ing] every 'meaning' of a depraved philosophical doctrine and crass understanding, 'which meaning elevates itself and raises itself up against the spiritual knowledge of Christ.'" By "fighting by means of the word of God, every single judge of the Church" makes himself "a praiseworthy Ehud." *HomJud* 4.1, referring to Jgs 3:17–22, Heb 4:12, and 2 Cor 10:5; FOTC 119:71; SC 389:118–20. Origen explains Ehud to be ambidextrous and "right" all the way around while Satan and his powers are ambi-left, or always "wholly perverse." Also, in *HomJud* 3.5; FOTC 119:67–68; SC 389:108–10, Origen states that Ehud's faith and deeds are "right" and in him nothing is iniquitous, and Origen observes, "I think that, according to a spiritual understanding, all the saints also should be called 'ambidextrous.'"

38. Note that in *HomGn* 2 Origen reads Noah's ark pneumatically/spiritually to represent the Church (and additionally reads the ark psychically/morally to represent the individual soul when it cultivates virtue and Christ within).

The Preacher's Role as "Savior-Angel"

Origen's next, logical instruction for his audience is that they recognize and trust him, their preacher, as a lead-soldier in the cosmic battle who will fight off the enemies and point the way toward God. If the Church houses the path of ascent, then Church leaders, or preachers, are guides for that journey. Origen likens the preacher to the judges of old who delivered repentant Israelites from their cyclical captivities to enemy nations. For Origen, the judges both represent the angelic forces who defend the soul in battle against the demons as well as prefigure the Christian preacher. As Cushanrishathaim, the Mesopotamian captor of the Israelites, spiritually represents the enemy powers, so the delivering judge Othniel represents the angelic powers that God sends to fight the evil spirits in the cosmic battle. For God raised up Othniel to liberate his people from their "humiliating enslavement" under Cushanrishathaim after they finally "cried out to the Lord."[39] As God sent to the repentant Israelites Othniel, Shamgar, Ehud, and Gideon[40] as "savior-angels," so God sends to the repentant sinners "the present leaders and judges of the Church" as "savior-angels" to deliver them from sin and Satan.[41] When describing how the angelic hosts help souls in the battle, Origen explains that the preacher-judges, as savior-angels, are also "angel-overseers," "angel-stewards," and "angel-leaders."[42] They have been sent not only to deliver, but also, like the angels, to instruct, protect, and guide "every least person in the Church."[43] They preach to hearers the need for deliverance, and, to those who are repentant, they teach the ways of virtue, fortify their souls with the truths of Scripture, and guide them on the path of ascent.

---

39. *HomJud* 3.2–3, referring to Jgs 3:9, Eph 2:2, Lk 2:13, and Heb 1:14; FOTC 119:64–65; SC 389:102–04. In a subsequent passage Origen again stresses that the Israelites' judges can be images of the angelic powers whom God sends to aid people when they cry out in a spirit of true repentance. See *HomJud* 3.6, referring to Lk 2:13; FOTC 119:68–69; SC 389:110–12. As for angels protecting the Israelites, note that here Origen cites Moses and the destroyer angel in Ex 12:21–30, as well as an angel sent to free the Israelites from King Sennacherib of the Assyrians, reported at 4 Kgdms (2 Kgs) 19:35. For Origen on angels, see "Angels," Johan Leemans, *The Westminster Handbook to Origen*, ed. John Anthony McGuckin (London and Louisville: Westminster John Knox Press, 2004). See also *De Princ.* 1.8.1 and *HomNum.* 11:4–5.

40. For each judge, see the following passages in *HomJud*: Othniel, *HomJud* 3.3–4; Ehud, *HomJud* 3.3–6; Shamgar, *HomJud* 4.1–3; and Gideon, *HomJud* 8.3–4 and 9.1–2.

41. *HomJud* 3.3, referring to Jgs 3:10; FOTC 119:64–65; SC 389:102–04. See also *HomJud* 4.2; FOTC 119:71–72; SC 389:120–22.

42. *HomJud* 6.2, loosely referring to Gal 4:2 and 3:23–26; FOTC 119:87; SC 389:156.

43. *HomJud* 6.2; FOTC 119:85; SC 389:152–54.

The preacher serves *all* these roles each time he teaches, because he addresses an audience not only varied in levels of advancement but also in frequently shifting places along the sin, captivity, repentance, and deliverance trajectory.[44] Like the Israelites in Judges, the human soul does not pass from sin to deliverance only once. Instead, in a cyclical fashion, souls on the journey of ascent during this life regress back into sin and progress again into repentance and growth many times.[45] After the initial deliverance or calling that starts the soul on the journey of ascent to God, the soul trying to grow in virtue and likeness to Christ will lapse like the Israelites, and the preacher is there to deliver the soul back onto the journey's path again as many times as needed. By constantly teaching Scripture's truths about God's love and Christ's virtues, the preacher effectively makes the soul's repeated sliding back and moving forward a progressively upward spiral toward God so that successive deliverances teach and strengthen the soul until it will remain in God and no longer lapse or struggle. By presenting the cycle of the Israelites as relevant to his audience, Origen makes them aware of what he does for them each time he presents Scripture's meanings to them: he conveys the lessons of Scripture that fortify them for the journey and prepare them ultimately for union with God.

Scripture as the Ultimate Guide on the Journey

Once Origen establishes that the audience should trust him as preacher to navigate them through the battle and upward journey toward God, he explains the various, specific ways in which he is commissioned to bring Scripture's beneficial effects to them. All the tasks by which the preacher helps souls

44. Throughout the homilies Origen relates the soul journeying upward to the Israelites having recurrent falls back into sin. As the analysis that follows clarifies, only someone who abandons God completely loses all the progress he has made before falling back into sin. See n. 81 and the text around it. The journeying soul, as the Israelites, is on the repetitive cycle of sin, captivity, repentance and deliverance, but it is a spiral up the path of ascent with gradual progress over time. Sometimes the setback is so drastic that the soul must start the journey anew, but other times the fall back into sin is quickly caught and the soul resumes the upward climb, though perhaps lower than where it was on the ascending path before sinning again. Note the platforms Origen uses to read spiritually the Israelites' falls back into sin and relay their relevance to his homiletic audience: (1) when a judge or leader died (as a direct result of the people sinning again), *HomJud* 2.1 (Joshua), 3.4 (Othniel), 4.3 (Ehud and then Shamgar); (2) when the Israelites did evil again, *HomJud* 3.1; (3) when they were in need of a judge, *HomJud* 4.2 (Shamgar); and (4) when they were handed over to an enemy, *HomJud* 7.1 (the Midianites).

45. By positing this cycle as the path of ascent, Origen identifies the Church generally and his audience specifically as God's chosen people playing out salvation history in the present age.

through the battle and along the journey to God occur through his multiple uses of Scripture as "the apostolic war-trumpet."[46] As savior-angel deliverer, he uses Scripture to teach each willing soul how to "recognize" and "fight the battles of the Lord."[47] As angel-overseer, he presents the "Divine Word"[48] to teach the redemptive "knowledge of Christ and the mysteries of his cross"[49] and how growing in the virtues will make one more like Christ. As angel-steward, he calls hearers to the safe harbor of baptism, which is "the beginning of the struggle and spiritual battle" "against the Devil,"[50] and then through Scripture's lessons instructs the willing, baptized hearer to put on the virtues, which serve as "the armor of God," so that he may "stand firm against the tricks of the Devil."[51] As angel-leader, the preacher marches ahead, leading the way for souls to persevere along the battle-worn path of ascent to God by both preaching and modelling Scripture's lessons so that they ever deepen their knowledge of Christ and grow stronger in the virtues. The preacher plays each of these roles of bringing Scripture to the hearer both simultaneously and recurrently, as well as successively. As Gideon armed his troops for battle against the Midianites with "jugs and lamps and horned war-trumpets,"[52] so the preacher, as Christ's lead-soldier, causes the demons to flee by equipping his audience with the "power of knowledge" and "light of works" supplied by Scripture's trumpet blow.[53]

While the preacher facilitates interaction with Scripture, Scripture does the work of reforming the willing hearer, all the time employing the preacher in the process as a teacher, model, farmer and healer of the soul. Scripture, as Christ's own word,[54] is the ultimate guide for the soul's journey to God. Since interacting with Scripture is equivalent to interacting with Christ, the hearer, when

---

46. *HomJud* 6.2, referring to Jgs 7:16, 19–22 and Ps 111 (112):9; FOTC 119:87; SC 389:156.

47. *HomJud* 6.2; FOTC 119:86–87; SC 389:154–56.

48. *HomJud* 9.2; FOTC 119:118; SC 389:222.

49. *HomJud* 9.2; FOTC 119:118; SC 389:220.

50. See *HomJud* 9.2; FOTC 119:116; SC 389:216.

51. *HomJud* 6.2, quoting Eph 6:11; FOTC 119:87–88; SC 389:156–58.

52. *HomJud* 9.2, referring to Jgs 7:16; FOTC 119:117; SC 389:218–20.

53. *HomJud* 9.2, referring to Jgs 7:19–22; FOTC 119:117–18; SC 389:220–22.

54. For Origen's understanding that Scripture is Christ, see Dively Lauro, *The Soul and Spirit*, 26–31 and 43–44; Torjesen, *Hermeneutical Procedure*, 108–47, esp. 119–20; Henri de Lubac, *History and Spirit*, 385–426; Crouzel, *Origen*, 70; and Jean Daniélou, *Origen*, trans., Walter Mitchell (Sheed & Ward: London and New York, 1955) 160, 172, 265, and 314. For Origen's corollary understanding that consuming Scripture is consuming Christ, see Dively Lauro, *The Eschatological Significance of Scripture According to Origen*, StPatr (2013) 56:83–102. For Origen's notion of clothing the self with Christ, see *Hom. in Isa.* 3; FOTC 142:59–66.

he consumes Scripture, clothes his soul with the virtues and thus with Christ.[55] The first task is for the hearer to align his will and desires so that he *freely* chooses Christ and the virtues.[56] Acquiring the virtues becomes more and more natural to the hearer as he reorders the parts of his human nature into alignment with God's Spirit. In *De Principiis* 4, Origen explains that Scripture conveys its lessons through its anthropological, tripartite structure of meanings that mirrors the parts of human nature in their right order: body (somatic sense), soul (psychic sense), and spirit (pneumatic sense).[57] Through interaction with Scripture's meanings, the hearer experiences over time, at his own pace, a reordering of his own body, soul, and spirit. The right order will fortify and make consistent his choice to align himself with Christ and virtue and to reject the lure of the evil spirits and their weapons of sin and desire. In *De Principiis* 3, Origen explains that the soul, as the seat of the will, can choose *either* the leadership of the body, with its tendency to the wayward flesh, *or* the spirit, which is the image of God's Spirit, with its natural inclination for God and Godly things.[58] If the body leads, then the soul falls into fleshly tendencies and the spirit lies dormant. If the spirit leads, the body is properly subdued, and the soul chooses the things of God and becomes aligned with Christ's virtuous ways. Then, as Origen declares in *HomJud* 6, "Christ reigns in you," and you have become "king over all things" pertaining to your spiritual welfare, and "deservedly you will be called king," after "the King of kings," Christ, because you have been "made new to rule yourself rightly."[59] When rightly ordered, the person will become more deeply able to hear Scripture and be formed by its lessons into a true likeness to Christ,[60] and he will be participating willingly and directly in his own formation, ruling himself rightly as does Christ.

55. For Origen's understanding that Christ is each and all of the virtues, see sources listed in n. 19 above.

56. Recall Origen's earlier exhortation to his audience that they put into their souls "the days of Jesus" and his explanation that each of the virtues is such a day, clarifying that filling the soul with the virtues causes Jesus to reside within that soul. See *HomJud* 1.1 and 1.3. See ns. 16–21 above.

57. For Origen's understanding of Scripture as containing a threefold, anthropological structure of meaning, see *De Princ.* 4.2.4. For analysis and distinguishing definitions of the three meanings, somatic, psychic, and pneumatic, see Dively Lauro, *The Soul and Spirit*, generally, and for definitions, 2.

58. See Origen's tripartite anthropology and his explanation of its right ordering in *De Princ.* 3.4, as well as *Hom. in Lev.* 2.2.7 and *Hom. in Luke* 11.3. For discussion, see Dively Lauro, *The Soul and Spirit*, 86–91; Dively Lauro, "The Meaning and Significance of Scripture's Sacramental Nature," StPatr (2017) 94:153–85, esp. 168–69; and Crouzel, *Origen*, 87–98.

59. *HomJud* 6.3, referring to Jgs 5:3, 1 Pet 2:9, and Rev 19:16; FOTC 119:88–89; SC 389:158–60.

60. *HomJud* 6.3; FOTC 119:88–89; SC 389:158–60.

Since each person fulfills this reordering in his own time, each lesson of Scripture that the preacher presents simultaneously aids the differing needs of each audience member. Scripture can effect this diverse benefit each time it is preached, because, as "the sweet honeycombs of heavenly teaching" holding the "honey of the Divine Word,"[61] it effectively contains in *all* its parts at *all* times *all* the truth needed for each soul's ascent to God. Though Scripture effects the transformation in the hearer, the preacher is the channel of Scripture's powers. So Origen can declare that no soul makes progress by his "own labor" alone, but all advancement occurs "through the leaders" or "angels" of the Church[62] who are trained to perform the preacher's tasks.

Indeed, the preacher is needed at all stages of a soul's progress in understanding Scripture and taking in its lessons. For the hearer who has only begun to display an "intention of advancing toward the good,"[63] Scripture is "the milk of the Church (*ecclesiae lac*)" which the preacher feeds to young journeyers as the "first moral instruction"[64] or "first principles of Christ."[65] Only after the hearer becomes proficient in the moral lessons directing him to shun vice and grow in virtue is he ready to receive through the preacher "the profound and more hidden mysteries"[66] of salvation in Scripture which are "the more

61. *HomJud* 5.2, referring to Ps 118 (119):103 and Ps 18:10–11 (19:9–10); FOTC 119:77; SC 389:134. See also Origen's treatment of Scripture as the honeycomb providing honey for the nourishment of the soul in *Hom. in Isa.* 2.2.

62. *HomJud* 6.2, referring to Ex 14:19; FOTC 119:86; SC 389:154.

63. *HomJud* 5.6; FOTC 119:82; SC 389:144.

64. *HomJud* 5.6, referring to 1 Cor 3:1–2; FOTC 119:82; SC 389:144. Origen also refers to this "milk of the Church" as the "evangelical and apostolic milk." This milk teaches the "beginner" soul "the correction of morals, the amendment of discipline, and the first elements of religious life and simple faith." See *HomJud* 5.5–6, referring to Col 3:5 and the Epicurean philosophy; FOTC 119:80–83; SC 389:140–46. See also *Hom. in Isa.* 7.1 for another discussion by Origen of how Jesus starts out teaching souls as children.

65. *HomJud* 6.2; FOTC 119:85–87; SC 389:152–56.

66. *HomJud* 5.6; FOTC 119:82; SC 389:142–44. Note that soon after this passage, Origen arguably makes reference to the celebration of the Eucharist and the catechumens who are not yet ready for it, when he states: Because, at first, we are "as 'babes'" in spiritual matters, we must be "nourished 'with milk' and hold to discourse about the first principles of Christ ... 'under the angel-'overseers' and angel-'stewards,'" before we can "obtain the ... 'heavenly bread' and ... be satisfied by the flesh 'of the unblemished lamb' ... [and] become intoxicated with the blood of the 'true vine.'" *HomJud* 6.2, referring loosely to Gal 4:2 and 3:23–26, and to Jn 6:51, 1 Pet 1:19, Jn 15:1, and 1 Cor 3:1–2 and Heb 5:12–6.1; FOTC 119:87; SC 389:156. For an in-depth study of Origen's view of the Eucharist as a sacrament conveying the real body and blood of Christ and as a figure of the eschatological wedding feast, see Dively Lauro, "The Eschatological Significance of Scripture," StPatr (2013) 56:83–102, and Dively Lauro, "The Meaning and Significance of Scripture's Sacramental Nature," StPatr (2017) 94:153–85.

perfect lessons of the Teacher [Christ] himself."[67] Once the hearer, through hearing Scripture preached, becomes good at imitating Christ's virtues *voluntarily*,[68] Christ, already residing within him, will make *himself* stronger within the hearer, which will increase the hearer's fortitude in the battle for his soul.[69]

Because the preacher applies Scripture to a collective audience of different souls at varying levels of progress, his application of the Word at any given moment will act as a sword to some and a plough to others. It will fall on some as a "sharp reproof," a "harsh word,"[70] such as when Origen delivers the sharp battle language to shock hearers into acknowledging the reality of the cosmic battle and rouse them to action. In this case, he spiritually resembles Ehud who used a sword to deliver Israel.[71] A more advanced hearer may receive the same preached Scripture as a "gentle admonition,"[72] receiving Origen's words about the battle as encouragement to continue progressing on the ascent through an increased cultivation of the virtues. In this case, Origen spiritually resembles Shamgar who delivered Israel with a farming "plough."[73] In both cases, according to Origen, the preacher acts as a "farmer" who is "breaking open" "the land of the soul," "driving away vices and sins" and "killing the enemies," so that the soul may receive the seeds of Christ's virtue as conveyed through Scripture.[74] Origen acts as a farmer of the soul when he brings forth Scripture's call to shun vice and grow in virtue. Even by explaining this preacher's task, Origen exhorts the hearer to choose to shun vice and to grow in the virtues. For the hearer not yet so fully re-ordered internally toward his spirit as to be eager, the application feels harsh and painful, while for the hearer already more rightly ordered and stronger in his resolve to choose virtue and Christ, it is welcome correction.[75]

Origen explains that he, as preacher, is also ready to lead back the hearer

67. *HomJud* 6.2; FOTC 119:85–86; SC 389:152–54.

68. *HomJud* 6.2; FOTC 119:86; SC 389:154.

69. *HomJud* 6.6, referring to Phil 4:13; FOTC 119:93; SC 389:168.

70. *HomJud* 4.2; FOTC 119:71; SC 389:120–22.

71. See also in *HomGn* 3.6 and *HomJos* 26.2 Origen's description of Scripture as a sword that cuts away sin from the hearer's soul (in the former case concerning a spiritual circumcision and in the latter case a spiritual second circumcision).

72. *HomJud* 4.2; FOTC 119:72; SC 389:120–22.

73. *HomJud* 4.2, quoting Jgs 3:31; FOTC 119:71–72; SC 389:120–22.

74. *HomJud* 4.2; FOTC 119:72; SC 389:120–22.

75. *HomJud* 4.2; FOTC 119:72; SC 389:120–22. Note that in *Hom. in Jer.* 5.13, Origen calls his hearers to cultivate their own souls as farmers, tearing away the thorns of sin and growing seeds of Scripture.

who, though he has made some progress on the journey, has allowed himself to be lured again into sin. Origen explains that the preacher is a healer to the sinner who slides backwards when he presents Scripture as a medicine of opposites.[76] Origen explains that God handed over the Israelites into captivity to powers such as King Cushanrishathaim of Mesopotamia, whose name means "their humiliation,"[77] so that they would experience humiliation as the "salutary medical practice of 'opposites by means of opposites'" that brings "providential health."[78] God also does the same for Christian believers on the journey of ascent. When the hearer, through pride, "rushes toward the powers and dignified ranks of the age," he "despises the humility of Christ" and so is handed over into humiliation so that he may earn through "reproof" the humility of Christ taught in Scripture.[79] Origen urges his audience to thwart such pride by remembering the words of the credal hymn in Philippians 2: "Christ, who for us, 'although he was God, became man and humbled himself all the way to death.'"[80] By recalling Christ's example of lowliness on the cross, Origen demonstrates how to apply Scripture so that the hearer will be humbled and return to the path of ascent.

Such temporary slides backwards cannot destroy the seeds of virtue that the preacher has already helped to sow in hearers who have applied the lessons of Scripture, unless the hearer makes a *complete* turn away from God.[81] If he has not completely abandoned God, the "seeds" of Scripture's truth that the preacher has "'sown in the spirit" during the hearer's repentant phases cannot be destroyed by spiritual enemies.[82] The preacher carefully and slowly presents the higher, "mystical and allegorical" meanings of Scripture[83] to help

76. See *HomJud* 3.1; FOTC 119:61; SC 389:96–98. Note also Origen's discussion in *Hom. In Jer.* 14.1–2 of the prophet, and by corollary the preacher, as a physician or healer of souls. Also, in *Hom. in Lev* 8.1.1–3, Origen discusses how Jesus is the physician in the Scriptures.

77. *HomJud* 3.1–2, referring to Jgs 3:7–10; FOTC 110:61–64; SC 389:96–102. Cushanrishathaim is only known to history from his mention in Jgs 3:7–10. Jgs 3:7 explains that God allowed this captivity of the Israelites after they had settled in Canaan because they had turned away from God and instead took to worshipping Baal and Asheroth. (LXX mentions Baal and "the groves," perhaps the place of worship of the goddess. Asheroth as a goddess is mentioned again in 3 Kgdms [1 Kgs] 11:5 as belonging to the Sidonians and again in Jgs 10:6 as the god of Sidon alongside Baal, the god of the Syrians.)

78. *HomJud* 3.1; FOTC 119:61; SC 389:96–98.

79. *HomJud* 3.1–2; FOTC 119:62–63; SC 389:98–100.

80. *HomJud* 3.1, referring to Phil 2:5–8; FOTC 119:62; SC 389:98.

81. *HomJud* 7.2, referring to Prv 4:23 and Gal 5:22–23; FOTC 119:96; SC 389:176. See n. 44.

82. *HomJud* 7.2, quoting Gal 6:8, and referring to Jer 4:3, Hos 10:12, and Mt 13:22–23; FOTC 119:95; SC 389:174–76.

83. *HomJud* 5.6; FOTC 119:82; SC 389:142–144.

the hearer "ascend from the lowness of the letter to the heights of the spirit," so that, while he is striving for "the highest summit of spiritual understanding," the evil spirits cannot "tear away anything" or "plunder" the land of his soul as the seeds of God's truth take root over time.[84] Eventually, at the end of time, the willing hearer will finally be free from the lure of pride and the threat of "satanic slavery" and, instead, will be solidly and permanently planted on the "true way," Christ himself.[85] As the savior-deliverers to the Israelites in their cycles of sin, captivity, repentance, and deliverance, the preacher stands ready to assist the Christian believer in his cyclical regressions and progressions along the path of ascent, all the time equipped with Scripture's steady guidance under which spiritual progression ultimately wins out. Origen, as preacher, facilitates this incremental fortification of the soul each time he conveys the higher, allegorical meanings of Scripture to his hearers.

The Communal Dimensions of the Journey and the Preacher's Role

The preacher's ever-present aids are evidence of salvation's communal nature. Not only is the journey of ascent housed within the community of the Church, but Origen explains to his audience that he and they together are, ultimately, co-journeyers on that path to salvation. Origen emphasizes the preacher's and audience's common pursuit by discussing Gideon's tests of God's faithfulness by means of the dew and the fleece together with Jesus' preparations for washing the feet of his disciples.[86] Origen explains that, allegorically, by wringing the dew out of the various books of Scripture, the preacher washes the soul of both himself and his audience members so that it is "cleansed" from the filth and impurity of sins.[87] When he interprets Scripture before his Church audience, both he and his hearers together benefit from its transforming powers.

As a co-beneficiary of Scripture's effects, Origen prays in front of his audience that Christ come and cleanse the feet of his own soul.[88] In this act of

---

84. *HomJud* 8.2, referring to 1 Cor 2:14–16; FOTC 119:102–103; SC 389:190.

85. *HomJud* 3.6, referring to Mt 7:13 and Jn 14:6; FOTC 119:69; SC 386:112–114.

86. *HomJud* 8.5, referring to Jgs 6:36–40, quoting Jn 13:4–5, and referring to Jn 15:3; FOTC 119:107–10; SC 389:198–202.

87. *HomJud* 8.5, referring to Is 12:3 and Ps 67:27 (68:26), and Ez 24:13; FOTC 119:109; SC 389:202.

88. *HomJud* 8.5, referring to Jn 13:4–5; FOTC 119:108–9; SC 389:200–202. Origen's prayer reads

humility, Origen effectively places himself within his audience, revealing that he, like his hearers, is still in progress on the ascent and needs Christ to place Scripture's rich truths within *his own soul*. Origen, though at the head of the congregation, is a hearer along with them before the true Preacher, Christ, indeed, the true Soldier-Leader, Teacher, and Savior.[89] It is ultimately Christ who brings Scripture's transforming powers to the soul in need, albeit through willing human channels. Origen, then, is as much a hearer as a preacher.

Next, Origen reveals that his hearers are, in turn, to become preachers as much as hearers. He announces that only after applying Scripture's cleansing dew to his own soul, does he then apply it to "wash the feet of his brothers" in the audience so that the feet of their souls may also be "cleansed from the filth of sin" and "advance" with him "toward the preparation of the Gospel of peace."[90] He exhorts them to follow his example, stressing that they must, as they advance in the ascent, also become channels of Scripture's powers to cleanse themselves and then their fellow believers. First, Origen urges his audience to pray for Christ "to wash the feet" of *their own souls* so that they too will be cleansed with Scripture's "heavenly dew," specifically, "the grace of the Holy Spirit" and "the word of knowledge."[91] Next, he exhorts his audience to cleanse *each other's souls* as Jesus called his disciples to cleanse one another: "If … I, Lord and Teacher, have washed your feet, then wash also one another's feet.'"[92] Here, Origen, as preacher, addresses his audience as "brothers" and "co-disciples."[93] Not only is Origen, along with his audience, a disciple of the ultimate Teacher,[94] Christ, but he and his audience members are brothers precisely because they

---

as follows: "Come, I pray, Lord Jesus, Son of God, 'strip yourself of garments,' which because of me you wore, and be girded on account of me, and 'put water into a basin and wash the feet' of your servants, wash away the filth from your sons and daughters. 'Wash the feet' of our soul, so that, imitating you and following you, 'we may strip ourselves of the old 'garments.'" See *Hom. in Isa.* 5.2 and 6.3 for similar prayers by Origen for Christ to cleanse the feet of his soul and the souls of his audience with the spiritual water of Scripture figured in the water Jesus used to wash the feet of his disciples. Note that in *Hom. in Isa.* 4.3 Origen states that if he is truly humble and repentant, God will send him, a preacher, his own "deliverer" (*liberatorem*). See *ComJn* 32.4–18 for another spiritualized reading by Origen of Jesus washing the feet of his disciples. Note too that here in *HomJud* 8.5 Origen calls his audience to wash their own and each other's soul's as well, which is discussed further in the text below.

89. Recall that Origen refers to Christ as the "Teacher" among teachers. See *HomJud* 6.2; FOTC 119:85–86; SC 389:152–54. See n. 67 above.

90. *HomJud* 8.5, referring to Ez 24:13 and Eph 6:15; FOTC 119:109–10; SC 389:202.

91. *HomJud* 8.5; FOTC 119:108; SC 389:200.

92. *HomJud* 8.5, quoting Jn 13:13–14; FOTC 119:109; SC 389:200–02.

93. *HomJud* 8.5; FOTC 119:109; SC 389:202.

94. See ns. 67 and 89 above.

are all fellow soldiers in Christ's army. Together they fight the spiritual battle against the demons to secure salvation for their own and each other's souls. Origen effectively assures his audience that when they, by his guidance and example as preacher, do the same, they also become co-savior-angels for themselves and others. As co-savior-angels, overseers, stewards, and leaders, they too help to deliver, instruct, protect, and guide both themselves and their fellow journeyers. All souls on the ascending path to God, then, are called to take on the role of preacher and lift up the community.

The pulpit is only one vantage point, for Christ calls his savior-angel-soldiers in every position within the Church to bring all souls to himself. To this end, Origen encourages his audience members to feel a greater companionship with him and each other on the journey to God. The person making the soul's ascent is not alone but indeed is becoming a preacher to himself and his fellow journeyers, a helpmate, who in this role is making himself and his comrades increasingly fit for union with God. Origen declares that "every single person is called 'horned,'" because, whenever someone relays the "spiritual" truths in Scripture and thereby reveals "the mysteries of the kingdom of heaven," he "sounds the horned war-trumpet" of Christ's word.[95] With this in mind, Origen finishes these homilies by calling his audience to join forces, stressing that together,

being soldiers with this "war-trumpet" and fighting with it, we conquer foreigners and put enemies to flight, ... singing together in "hymns and psalms and spiritual songs" and "calling out to God," so that we may be worthy to obtain victory in Christ Jesus our Lord *from him himself.*[96]

By this declaration of common purpose and submission before Christ, Origen informs his audience that the soul's journey is communal precisely because this victory in Christ is the communal goal or *telos* of union with God. All souls are on a journey to arrive eventually at the heavenly "wedding banquet."[97]

95. *HomJud* 9.2, referring to Jgs 7:19–22, Mt 13:11 and Ps 111 (112):9b ; FOTC 119:118; SC 389:220. Note that the word for "sounds" in Latin here, *concino*, can mean to "sing prophetically." See FOTC 119:118 n. 63.

96. *HomJud* 9.2, referring to Col 3:16 and Jgs 6:7; FOTC 119:118; SC 389:220–22.

97. For this theme of the heavenly wedding banquet in Origen, see *HomJud* 8.5, referring to Mt 22:1–14 and Lk 14:16–24; FOTC 119:109–10; SC 389:202, and the discussion directly below. See also *ComCt* 1, to Sgs 1:2–4. For discussion, see Dively Lauro, *The Soul and Spirit*, 195–237; Crouzel, *Origen*, 121–26 and 220, quoting *ComMt* 17.33 on the spiritual wedding and marriage after the resurrection; and Torjesen, *Hermeneutical Procedure*, 93–96.

None are fully ready during this life, not even the preacher. All are called to help each other in the ascent, not only the preacher. All stand before Christ, who is not only the final reward but also the one who delivers his Bride to himself. This common end, or *telos*, as Origen describes it, is

that all of us, purified together in Christ through the word, may not be cast away from the marriage chamber of the Bridegroom on account of dirty clothes, but with dazzling white garments, washed feet, a "clean heart," may recline at the wedding banquet of the Bridegroom, of our Lord Jesus Christ himself.[98]

At the Eschaton, all souls fully "washed and made clean" will "have a part with Christ."[99] Indeed, they will all, having been led ultimately by Christ, arrive together to final union with Christ himself. The individual Bride-souls will together comprise the Bride-Church, finally fully worthy to arrive as one "at the consummation of all things" and receive the "one reward of victory," which is Jesus Christ himself,[100] our true and ultimate Deliverer.

Conclusion

In these homilies on Judges, Origen presents a battle motif to explain and guide his hearers through the obstacles along the soul's journey to God. He relates his audience members to the Israelites in their recurrent cycle of sin, captivity, repentance and deliverance; sin and Satan's army to the enemy nations; the Church to the woman Jael who kills the enemy to free the Israelites; the preacher to the judges of old who delivered the Israelites from their captivities; and Scripture to Gideon's war-trumpet. The temporal organizing center of this battle drama for Origen is the role of the preacher, which he presents both by describing and modelling it. Close examination has shown that he concentrates his audience's attention on the preacher because he considers the preacher's tasks to be the eventual objective of all souls on the journey to God.

As a preacher, Origen attends to souls within a cosmic battle where the devil's forces fight to make the soul captive to sin while angelic forces strive to keep them free and fortify them against these enemies. Origen stands with the

---

98. *HomJud* 8.5, quoting Mt 22:1–14 and Zec 3:3–5, and Mt 5:8; FOTC 119:110; SC 389:202.

99. *HomJud* 8.5, referring to Jn 13:8; FOTC 119:108; SC 389:200.

100. *HomJud* 5.6; FOTC 119:83; SC 389:146. Origen here also refers to the "consummation of all things" as "the end of the age." See also *HomJud* 9.2; FOTC 119:118; SC 389:222. For Origen's treatment of the Bride as both the individual soul and the Church, see *ComCt* Prol. 2 and Book 1.

angels in this battle, but also with the judges of the Israelites, reinforcing the fact that the Church is God's chosen people. Like the angels and the judges, Origen, as preacher, is an angel-savior delivering, overseer instructing, steward protecting, and leader guiding his hearers as needed. Origen sounds the war-trumpet of Scripture hoping that sinners will recognize their captivity and humbly cry out to God in repentance, and he then stands ready to deliver them from captivity and lead them on the path upward to God by mining the words of Scripture for its exhortatory benefits. He brings Scripture's healing truths to them so that those words can cleanse them and help them to grow in the virtues, which will make them like Christ. Origen presents himself as available to each advancing soul as it may slide back and lose some progress. He applies the medicine of Scripture to bring them back as many times as necessary until they ultimately become resistant to further retreat.

Because of the exegetical context of the homily, Origen can both describe and model the preacher's tasks of using Scripture to lead his audiences on the soul's journey to God through the dangerous terrain of the cosmic battle. By so doing, he calls them to embrace this role of preacher for themselves and each other. Through the homiletic context, he can stress the communal nature of the soul's journey, placing both himself and his audience members on equal footing as co-disciples who are to share the preacher's tasks. Together, they will free fellow souls from the grip of sin and Satan, lead them to the safe harbor of the Church, teach them Christ's truths and how to reach likeness to Christ through growth in virtues, and lead them upward to God until final victory is reached.

Origen presents himself to his audience as a soul equally in need of Scripture's transforming power and, ultimately, as no more highly called to the tasks of the preacher than are all journeyers. The battle rages against each person with equal and non-discriminating force. The preacher is most successful in his efforts when other audience members take on the same savior-angel tasks toward their fellow journeyers that he has exhibited for them. Salvation is a communal journey that occurs within the Church, through constant interaction with Scripture, guided at first by designated leaders but ultimately by every soldier in Christ's army. Origen gives his audience and himself the identity of a community striving for salvation together. The journey is communal because its end is communal, when all souls together will meet the ultimate Deliverer and Teacher, Christ, and finally be received together as Christ's Bride at the eternal wedding feast.

This collective analysis of these nine extant homilies on Judges offers us insight into what motives a homilist such as Origen would have applied to his interpretation of Scripture before hearers at varying levels of spiritual advancement. Knowing that each hearer would take what he could depending on his own level of spiritual growth, Origen held nothing back. He interpreted Scripture in order to describe the soul's journey to God as the common task of all people. Simultaneously, his interpretations of Scripture modelled how one can effectively preach Scripture for the soul's advancement along the path of ascent. What results is a clear understanding of the Christian task and a model of how to apply Scripture's transforming powers to oneself and to others along the journey. Origen's goal is for all to become doers of the preacher's tasks, molding themselves as channels of Scripture's effects, all under the leadership of the true Teacher, Christ. Origen presents his homiletic treatments of biblical texts as examples for others to follow as much as lessons to be learned for one's own edification. By calling all to the preacher's role, he reminds us that we are all equally in a battle for the salvation of our souls, and we march together to the common *telos* of union with our Bridegroom, Christ.

Bibliography

Primary Sources

Origen: Homilies on Genesis and Exodus. Trans. Ronald E. Heine. *Fathers of the Church,* 71. Washington, DC: Catholic University of America Press, 1982.

Origène: Homélies sur la Genèse. Ed. and trans. Louis Doutreleau. SC, 7 bis. Paris: Le Éditions du Cerf, 1985.

Origène: Homélies sur L'Exode. Ed. and trans. Marcel Borret. SC, 321. Paris: Le Éditions du Cerf, 1985.

Origen: Homilies on Leviticus 1–16. Trans. Gary Wayne Barkley. FOTC, 83. Washington, DC: Catholic University of America Press, 1990.

Origène: Homélies sur Le Lévitique, Tome 2. Ed. and trans. Marcel Borret. SC, 287. Paris: Le Éditions du Cerf, 1981.

Origen: Homilies on Judges. Trans. Elizabeth Ann Dively Lauro. FOTC, 119. Washington, DC: Catholic University of America Press, 2010.

Origène: Homélies sur Les Juges. Eds. and trans. Pierre Messié, Louis Neyrand, and Marcel Borret. SC, 389. Paris: Le Éditions du Cerf, 1993.

Origen: Homilies on Isaiah. Trans. Elizabeth Ann Dively Lauro. FOTC, 142. Washington, DC: Catholic University of America Press, 2021.
Origen: On First Principles. Trans. G. W. Butterworth. Gloucester, MA: Peter Smith, 1973.
Origène: Traité Des Principes, Tome 3. Eds. and trans. Henri Crouzel and Manlio Simonetti. SC, 268. Paris: Le Éditions du Cerf, 1980.

Additional Primary Sources

Eusebius. *Church History.*   *Origen: HomJer.*   Origen: *CommMt*
Origen: HomNum.   *Origen: HomLc*   Origen: *CommJn*
Origen: HomJos   *Origen: CommCt*   Origen: *CommRm*

Secondary Sources

Crouzel, Henri. *Origen: The Life and Thought of the First Great Theologian.* Trans. A. S. Worrall. San Francisco: Harper & Row, 1989.
Daniélou, Jean. *Origen.* Trans. Walter Mitchell. Sheed & Ward: London and New York, 1955.
Dively Lauro, Elizabeth Ann. *The Soul and Spirit of Scripture within Origen's Exegesis* (BAC 3). Leiden, The Netherlands, and Boston: Brill Academic Publishers, Inc., 2005.
______. "The Meaning and Significance of Scripture's Sacramental Nature." StPatr (2017) 94:153–185.
______. "The Eschatological Significance of Scripture According to Origen." StPatr (2013) 56:83–102.
de Lubac, Henri. *History and Spirit: The Understanding of Scripture According to Origen.* Trans. Anne Englund Nash. San Francisco: Ignatius Press, 2007.
Greer, Rowan A. *Origen: An Exhortation to Martyrdom, Prayer and Selected Works.* CWS. New York: Paulist Press, 1979.
Leemans, Johan. "Angels." *The Westminster Handbook to Origen.* Ed. John Anthony McGuckin. London and Louisville: Westminster John Knox Press, 2004.
Martens, Peter W. *Origen and Scripture: The Contours of the Exegetical Life* (OECS). Oxford University Press, 2012.
Torjesen, Karen Jo. *Hermeneutical Procedure and Theological Method in Origen's Exegesis* (Patristische Texte und Studien, 28). Berlin and New York: Walter de Gruyter, 1986.
Young, Frances M. *Biblical Exegesis and the Formation of Christian Culture.* Peabody, MA: Hendrickson Publishers, 2002.

Miriam De Cock

4. ORIGEN'S EXEGETICAL TREATMENT OF ROMANS 8:15

Spiritual Adoption by the Father, in the Son, through the Holy Spirit

Throughout his extant writings, Origen draws repeatedly on Paul's words in Rom 8:15,[1] "you did not receive a spirit of slavery to fall back into fear, but a spirit of adoption, by which we cry, 'Abba! Father!'"[2] In this paper, I shall examine how Origen understood and used the verse—one of the scriptural building blocks of his theological program—throughout his corpus.[3] This examination will provide direct entry into what are arguably some of the most central themes of the Alexandrian's thought, such as spiritual sonship,[4] the

---

1. The verse was widely used by early Christians generally. According to Jennifer Strawbridge's recent quantification study of early Christian authors' use of Paul, the verse appears 227 times in the Christian literature of the first three centuries. See Strawbridge, *The Pauline Effect: The Use of the Pauline Epistles by Early Christian Writers* (SBR 5; Berlin: de Gruyter, 2015), 11 n.38. In my estimation, at least a fourth of these citations can be found in Origen's writings.

2. This English translation is from the NRSV, as are all those that follow, unless otherwise specified.

3. Peter Widdicombe notes this in *The Fatherhood of God from Origen to Athanasius* (revised edition; Oxford: Oxford University Press, 2000), 118. He observes that Origen weaves this Pauline verse together with the Johannine Father-Son terminology and themes throughout his corpus.

4. I will use the terms Father and Son, and therefore also, "sonship," simply because these are Origen's, and indeed, the early Church's terms. They were absolutely key terms, provided by the biblical text itself, by which early Christian thinkers articulated their essential understanding of the character of God, and by extension, humanity's relationship to God. See Widdicombe's helpful discussion in *Fatherhood*, 259. I do

freedom of the will, and the Christian soul's ascent to the divine. I will examine here representative examples of broader patterns of Origen's use of the verse, focusing primarily on Origen's treatment of it in the context of his *Commentary on Romans* itself, and on a selection of passages from other texts, such as the newly-translated *Homilies on the Psalms*, the *Commentary on the Gospel of John*, the *Commentary on the Gospel of Matthew*, the *Homilies on Jeremiah*, and the *Homilies on Joshua*.[5] This selection allows us to compare Origen's use of the verse in two distinct exegetical genres: commentary and homily, thus providing a case study of the extent to which genre impacts the exegesis of a given text.

In what follows, I will begin with Origen's comments on Rom 8:15 as he encounters it in his verse-by-verse treatment of the book of Romans in the commentary dedicated to the Pauline letter. I will then provide an account of Origen's use of the verse throughout his corpus as it contributes to his presentation of the Christian soul's ascent to the divine—from spiritual immaturity to maturity, imperfection to perfection. We will see that the verse provides the framework and the vocabulary[6] for Origen to articulate his well-known hierarchy of believers, in which the initiate, who remains under the "spirit of slavery," will eventually mature in the faith, as a result of both divine guidance and just actions, at which point she can receive the "spirit of adoption," and thus "share in the eternal relationship between the Father and the Son."[7] I will then examine several passages in which Origen discusses the spiritual benefits experienced by the Christian who reaches spiritual maturity and is therefore governed by the "spirit of adoption." Finally, I will discuss Origen's treatment of

---

not deny the problems the terms present to the contemporary Church, which has seen and experienced the beneficial developments of the various feminist movements. In any case, "sonship," for Origen, and for me, certainly also includes the female-identifying believer.

5. With the exception of the first 5 books of Origen's *ComJn* all of these texts are dated to the late stage of Origen's career (ca. 245–50). It is therefore certainly not my aim to trace some kind of development in his thought from one text to the next.

6. As I mention in n. 3 above, he certainly made use of the language and terminology provided by other scriptural texts as well.

7. Widdicombe, *Fatherhood*, 93. The reader who knows Origen well will note that I have not mentioned the second group of believers in his schema, namely, that intermediate group who has made some progress in their spiritual ascent. With respect to the verse's two spirits, those of slavery and adoption, the believers who find themselves between the initiates and the perfect remain under the "spirit of slavery" until they reach the stage of perfection. This will become clearer in my discussion of Origen's treatment of John 13 below.

Rom 8:15 in relationship to the two exegetical genres in which his treatments appear (i.e., commentary and homily).

Rom 8:15 in the Commentary on the Epistle to the Romans

Origen's dedicated treatment of the verse is to be found in Book 7 of the Romans commentary, which is extant primarily in Latin translation.[8] By way of a preface to his explanation of the verse, Origen first identifies both the "spirit of God," mentioned in Rom 8:14, "For all who are led by the Spirit of God are children of God," and the "spirit of adoption" of 8:15 with the Holy Spirit. He claims: "In this Paul makes known that the Spirit of adoption (*spiritum adoptionis*) is identical (*ipsum esse*) with him whom he had above called the Spirit of God,"[9] who is, he goes on to say, the same as the Spirit of Christ.[10] Origen is consistent in this identification throughout his corpus as he deals with this aspect of the verse.

Having defined his terms, Origen can then provide some extended comments on Rom 8:15. He begins by explaining the difference between the "spirit of slavery" and the "spirit of adoption." Unlike his predecessors, specifically

---

8. Unfortunately for me, none of the Greek fragments found in the Tura discovery contains Book 7, nor is it preserved in the *Philocalia*. As Thomas Scheck, the English translator of the *ComRm*, says, we have in this text, "Rufinus' Origen," Scheck, *Origen and the History of Justification: The Legacy of Origen's Commentary on Romans* (Notre Dame, IN: University of Notre Dame Press, 2008), 3. As Rufinus himself tells us in the prologue to his translation, his patron has asked him to "produce an abbreviation (*produxit abreviem*) of this entire 15 volume work, a Greek text, which has reached the length of some 40,000 lines or more, and, if possible, compress it to half the space," Rufinus, preface to *ComRm*. Scheck (trans.), *Origen: Commentary on the Epistle to the Romans Books 1–5* (FOTC 103; Washington, DC: Catholic University of America Press), 52. Origenes, *Der Römerbriefkommentar des Origenes: Kritische Ausgabe der Übersetzung Rufins.* Buch 1–3 (ed. C. P. Hammond Bammel; *AGLB* 16; Freiburg im Breisgau: Herder, 1990), 1:36. In addition to ostensibly excising half of the commentary, Rufinus tells us in his epilogue to the translation that, in order not to frustrate the Latin reader, he has also sought to "supply things that were discussed by Origen extemporaneously in the lecture hall in the church … to fill in things that were missing." Rufinus, epilogue to *ComRm*, Scheck, *Origen: Commentary on the Epistle to the Romans Books 6–10* (FOTC 104; Washington, DC: Catholic University of America Press, 2002), 311. (Bammel, 3:860). Despite all this, I am inclined to agree with what seems to me to be an emerging consensus about the overall trustworthiness of Rufinus as a translator, even if his understanding of "literal" does not match our own. In any case, in the material of my focus at least, we will see that Rufinus' Origen does seem to resemble the Origen we encounter in the Greek material. Therefore, as I proceed, I will approach this text as though we have access here to the third-century author's thought, though of course I do so with an awareness of all of these issues.

9. Origen, *ComRm* 7.1.1 (Bammel, 3:553; Scheck, 2:60).

10. Origen, *ComRm* 7.1.2 (Bammel, 3:554; Scheck, 2:61).

Irenaeus and Clement of Alexandria, for whom Rom 8:14–15 proved useful primarily in polemical contexts, Origen's usage of the verses reflects a decidedly internal concern.[11] That is, rather than finding in the Pauline dichotomy a distinction between the members of the Church and the heretical other, in which the "spirit of slavery" governs those outside the Church and the "spirit of adoption" governs those inside, Origen finds language to express an important distinction between Christians in the initial stages of faith; that is, the "simple" majority, and those of the advanced minority, who had already reached spiritual maturity.

The "spirit of slavery" and the "spirit of adoption" are, according to Origen, both spirits from God. He claims, "Now it is certain that a person becomes a son of God through the Spirit of adoption, but a slave of God through a spirit of slavery."[12] He continues, drawing on the biblical wisdom tradition, which claims that, "the fear of the Lord is the beginning of wisdom," and therefore, one begins by serving God as one is filled with the "spirit of fear."[13] In this initial stage, fear serves as a pedagogue (*paedagogus*), says Origen, alluding to Gal 4:2.[14] Allusion turns to direct quotation as Origen continues to describe the "spirit of slavery," and he claims explicitly that it is Paul's insights about fear as a pedagogue that have guided his thinking. He quotes Gal 4:1–3 nearly in full, and I produce it here:

As long as the heir is a child, he does not differ at all from a slave, though he is the lord of everything; but he is under tutors and guardians (ὑπὸ ἐπιτρόπους ἐστὶν καὶ οἰκονόμους) until the date established beforehand by the father. So it is with us, while we were children we were under the elements of this world, being enslaved (Gal 4:1–3).[15]

Based on the verbal connection of the word slave in both Pauline contexts, the Christian in the initial stages, that is, the child according to the inner person, is governed by the divinely authorized "spirit of slavery" until she comes to the spiritual age that merits the deposit of the "spirit of adoption."

---

11. See, for example, Clement of Alexandria, *Stromata* 3.10; *Ex Graec* 9; Irenaeus, *Adv. Haer.* 5.9–13.

12. Origen, *ComRm* 7.2.1 (Bammel, 3:556; Scheck, 2:62–3).

13. Origen, *ComRm* 7.2.1 (Bammel, 3:556; Scheck, 2:62–3). See a fuller treatment of Origen's use of the wisdom tradition in Brian Daley's contribution, "'The Beginning of His Ways:' Christ as God's Personified Wisdom in the Early Greek Fathers," to this volume.

14. Origen, *ComRm* 7.2.1 (Bammel, 3:556; Scheck, 2:63).

15. This English translation is Scheck's translation of the Latin in Origen's *ComRm* (Scheck, 2:63).

Human and Divine Initiative
and the "Spirit of Adoption"

This explanation of the distinction between the two spirits, those of slavery and adoption, is found in most instances in which Origen makes use of Rom 8:15.[16] In some instances, however, Origen also articulates just *how* one advances in spiritual age to receive the "spirit of adoption." For example, in his tenth homily on Joshua, he says:

Let us do what is good and work at correcting ourselves so that, by our actions and way of life and even habits, we may deserve to be ennobled and become worthy to receive 'the spirit of adoption' so that, preferably, we may be considered among the sons of God through his unique and true son, Jesus Christ our Lord.[17]

In this and other such instances, Origen presents spiritual sonship through the "spirit of adoption" as something one must work to earn through one's actions and way of life.[18]

And yet, of course it is not quite so simple, for, according to Origen, the conditions for the Christian's attainment of spiritual sonship have already been made possible by God's loving initiative in sending his Son in the incarnation.[19] Said another way, Origen "is inclined to think that the transition from a knowledge of God as Lord to the knowledge of God as Father is brought about specifically by the incarnation."[20] This function of the incarnation is clear in his discussion of the prayers of the Old Testament, concerning which Origen observes that they do not address God as "Father," for, he explains, they awaited "the one who pours out 'the spirit of adoption' on them … after his coming."[21] Origen addresses the issue again in his treatise *On*

16. In fact, a similar discussion to this one also occurs frequently throughout Origen's corpus, although not always in as much detail. See these representative examples: *ComRm* 4.9.11; 7.3.2; *HomPs* 80 1.1; *On Prayer* 16; *ComCt* 3.10; *Contra Celsus* [*CCels*] 1.57.

17. *HomJos* 10.3. Ed. A. Jaubert, Origène : Homélies sur Josué (Sources Crétiennes 71; Paris : Éditions du Cerf, 2000 réimpr. de la 1re éd. rev. et corr., 1960), 280; trans. Barbara J. Bruce, *Origen: Homilies on Joshua* (FOTC 105; Washington, DC: CUA Press, 2002), 113–14. Cf. *HomJer* 9.4.5; *HomGn* 7.4.

18. This is implied, for example, in his brief discussion of Christ's titles in *ComJn* 1.201, or his treatment of the one who is "of God" in Jn 8:47, in *ComJn* 20.289.

19. As Widdicombe notes, in other places in Origen's corpus it is the resurrection that ushers in the conditions for a supernatural capacity to alter the categories of human existence. See his discussion of these passages in *Fatherhood*, 113–14.

20. Widdicombe, *Fatherhood*, 110. Though Widdicombe rightly points to the tension in Origen's thought concerning the knowledge of God in the Old and New Testaments.

21. Ed. Blanc, *Origène : Commentaire sur saint Jean, Livres XIX–XX* (SC 290 ; Paris : Éditions du

Prayer, where he claims that among the ancients, one is not able to find "the concept of positive and unalterable sonship," but that, "the fullness of time" (Gal 4:4), which "consists in the coming amongst us of our Lord Jesus Christ," ushers in an age in which "those who wish it receive adoption as sons."[22] Notably, this discussion concludes with the quotation of our verse of focus, along with several others that the Alexandrian typically associates with it.[23]

According to Origen, not only does God provide the conditions under which spiritual sonship is made available to "the one who wishes it," but divine assistance is also provided for the striving believer along the way. Therefore, in a few instances throughout his corpus, Origen seems to suggest that the attainment of spiritual sonship is the result of a combination of one's own efforts and various modes of divine guidance and grace. For example, in Book 13 of his *Commentary on Matthew*, when Origen comes to assign the referent of the "little ones" of Mt 18:10 ("see that you not despise one of these little ones"), he discusses the spiritual growth of souls, saying initially that, "in the case of souls, it is what is in our power, namely the quality of our actions and character, that is the cause of someone becoming great, small or in between."[24] It is (again) Paul who provides Origen with the authorization for this argument, for the Apostle presents the spiritual life as one in which a person begins as a child and then finally reaches adulthood and maturity in Christ.[25] In light of such instruction from Paul, Origen concludes that "we must assume there is some measure of spiritual stature which the fully mature soul can attain."[26] The little ones of Matthew 18, then, are, according to Origen, to be thought of as these children in the faith, and, he continues, they are "no different from 'a slave,'" for they have the "the spirit of slavery leading to fear."[27] So

---

Cerf, [2006] ; 1re éd., 1982) 62. Trans. Ronald E. Heine, *Commentary on the Gospel according to John* (FOTC 89; Washington, DC: The Catholic University of America Press, 1993), 174. Although Origen does also leave open the possibility that the figures of the Old Testament had knowledge of God as Father, and thus also prayed to God as Father. We shall address this question in more detail below.

22. *On Prayer* 22.2. Ed. Paul Koetschau, *CCels V–VIII, De oratione* (OW II; GCS 9; Leipzig: J. C. Hinrichs'sche, 1899), 347; trans. John J. O'Meara, *Origen: Prayer. Exhortation to Martyrdom* (ACW 19; New York: Newman Press, 1954), 73.

23. It is typical that Origen cites Jn 1:12 and 1 Jn 3:9 along with Rom 8:15.

24. *ComMt* 13.26. Ed. E. Klostermann, *Origenes: Matthäuserklärung* (GCS 40; Leipzig: J. C.' Hinrichs'sche Buchhandlung, 1935), 250; trans. Ronald E. Heine, *The Commentary of Origen on the Gospel of St. Matthew* (Vol. 1; ECT; Oxford: Oxford University Press, 2018), 151.

25. Here Origen draws on a combination of Pauline verses for this vocabulary and argumentation, such as Eph 4:13; Rom 7:11; 1 Cor 13:11.

26. *ComMt* 13.26 (GCS 40:251; Heine 152).

27. *ComMt* 13.26 (GCS 40:253; Heine, 152).

far, then, this account sounds rather like my previous example of his presentation of one's acquisition of the "spirit of adoption," that is, acquisition through one's own moral striving.

However, it becomes evident as he continues his treatment of the Matthean verse, that Origen also thinks that one requires divine grace in order to attain spiritual sonship. He goes on to identify with more precision the referent of the "spirit of slavery" as an angelic power, a conclusion he reaches with the help of Ps 33:8, "the angel of the Lord encamps around those who fear him and delivers them."[28] Such a verse is the perfect candidate for this argument, given its mention of both an angelic being and the fear of God possessed by the person assisted by the angelic being.[29] This God-given angelic spirit provides assistance to the imperfect child (or slave) and delivers her from evils. This form of divine assistance, however, does not continue once a person reaches a certain point of maturity. This Origen explains as he concludes his discussion of the angelic "spirit of slavery" by saying, "When we have been perfected and have passed through the stage of being under 'foster-fathers, nurses, governors, and trustees,' (all of whom, by the way, he suspects are angels), we are now capable of being provided for by the Lord himself."[30] That is, once one has received the "spirit of adoption," she no longer has need for angelic assistance, i.e., the "spirit of slavery."[31]

Christ's Particular Assistance
on the Journey to Sonship

In addition to that which is provided by angelic beings, Origen envisions other modes of divine grace and assistance for the child-slave in the initial stages of ascent, the most important of which is that given by the Logos

28. *ComMt* 13.26 (GCS 40:253; Heine, 152).

29. Origen goes on to cite various other scriptural texts in this connection, such as Ex 32:34; 33:14–15; Ps 90:15; Gn 48:16.

30. *ComMt* 13.26 (GCS 40:254; Heine, 153).

31. There is an interesting parallel here between Origen's understanding of the angels' management of the initiate believer and his view that the angels also oversaw the Old Testament economy. Perhaps he discerned here a continuity between the Old Testament figures and the "simple" believers, though he is not explicit about this. For a discussion of the Fathers' understanding that the Old Testament economy was managed by angels, see for example, Jean Daniélou's, *The Angels and their Mission: According to the Fathers of the Church* (Westminster, MD: Christian Classics, 1957), 3–23. Cf. Elizabeth Klein, *Augustine's Theology of Angels* (Cambridge: Cambridge University Press, 2018), 110–21.

himself. To the one who is still under the spirit of slavery, the Logos provides cleansing teachings or doctrines as a kind of preparation for the reception of the "spirit of adoption." This he argues in his *Commentary on John* as he interprets Jesus' washing of the disciples' feet in John 13, to which we will turn shortly.

Before examining this passage, however, we must briefly comment on Origen's well-known notion of the "titles" or "aspects" (*epinoiai*) of Christ, which he articulates perhaps most clearly in Book 1 of the *Commentary on John*.[32] We will see in what follows that this notion becomes relevant for his understanding of Christ's provision of assistance to the believer seeking the "spirit of adoption." For Origen, the believer who is in the initial stages of faith relates to Christ as the Good Shepherd, or as Physician, or as Lord and Master, whereas those who have made some progress in the ascent relate to him as Teacher. The perfected ones, however, can relate to Christ as Wisdom, as Truth, as Logos, and through this direct access to the mediating Logos, they can then relate to God as Father.

With this in mind we can return to the second mode of divine assistance in the Christian journey to the attainment of the "spirit of adoption," which is provided by Jesus himself. In John 13, according to Origen, Jesus washes the disciples' feet, relating to them as Teacher, "cleansing the dust from the earth and from worldly things," and providing them with the sufficiency (ἀρκετόν) to be like their teacher.[33] According to Origen, it is the goal of the teacher to make the disciple as he is, so that the disciple no longer needs Jesus as Teacher. However, before the disciples can become like Christ their teacher, Origen tells us, "they need to have their feet washed because they are deficient (ἐνδεεῖς) disciples and they still possess the spirit of bondage to fear."[34] By washing the disciples' feet, Jesus, as Teacher, produced in them "the state of being as their Lord (τὸ γενέσθαι ὡς ὁ κύριος αὐτῶν)," so that they would no longer be under the "spirit of slavery," but under the "spirit of adoption," by whom they cry, "Abba, Father."[35]

---

32. See in particular *ComJn* 1.118; cf. *ComCt* 2.4.3.

33. *ComJn* 32.117. Ed. V. C. Blanc, *Origène: Commentaire sur saint Jean, Livres XXVIII et XXXII* (SC 385; Paris : Éditions du Cerf, 1992), 238 (Heine, 364). The notion of sufficiency Origen finds in Mt 10.25, "it is sufficient for the disciple to be like the teacher."

34. *ComJn* 32.122 (SC 385:240; Heine, 365). It should be noted, then, that for Origen, even though the person who has made some progress, exemplified here by Jesus' disciples, can relate to Christ as teacher, he or she is still under the "spirit of slavery."

35. *ComJn* 32.121 (SC 385:240; Heine, 365).

Thus, the disciples here provide Origen and his readers with models of those who have received the "spirit of adoption," in this case, as a result of Christ's cleansing teachings. To be sure, for Origen, the disciples were those who lived virtuous lives, a fact that accounts for their being chosen as disciples in the first place.[36] However, I think it clear from this and the previous example, that the Alexandrian envisions the Christian's attainment of the "spirit of adoption" to be the result of the combination of both human and divine action and initiative, and the opportunity for both is provided by the conditions set in motion by the incarnation of the Logos. In cooperation with the initiate's good works and upright manner of life, God supplies both the governing "spirit of slavery," i.e., angelic assistance, and the purifying teachings from Christ in his capacity as the mediating Teacher, through whom,[37] finally, one receives the "spirit of adoption."[38]

The Resulting Benefits of the Believer's Reception of the "Spirit of Adoption"

Now, in several instances throughout his corpus, Origen articulates the nature of the benefits experienced by the person who has received the spirit of adoption, and he discusses three in particular: one's participatory eternal begottenness; restoration to the body of Christ in the Church; and freedom of speech in prayer to God the Father.

Let us begin with the first, namely, eternal begottenness, which Origen discusses in the conclusion of his ninth homily on Jeremiah. These comments appear in light of a discussion of two kinds of fathers, the inferior father (i.e.,

36. For example, see Origen's discussion of the evangelist John, who was "considered worthy of this privilege because he was judged worthy of remarkable love from the teacher." *ComJn* 32.263 (SC 385:298; Heine, 391). The privilege referred to is the opportunity to lean on Jesus' breast.

37. Indeed, later authors favoured the latter option. For example, many understood Christ to be *the* ladder of Jacob in Gn 28:12. See for example, Augustine, *Jo. ev. tr.* 7.23. To my knowledge, Origen himself does not make this interpretive move.

38. As Widdicombe has rightly argued: "Origen's perception of the place of moral decision-making in the transition from servitude to sonship must be seen against the background of his adamant opposition to the Gnostic belief that one's spiritual and moral status is predetermined by one's nature." *Fatherhood of God*, 101. However, such a stark anti-gnostic thrust is not always discernible when this theme arises, and I suspect that Origen is more comfortable with the tension between human and divine initiative vis-à-vis the reception of the "spirit of adoption" than we might be. See Widdicombe's lucid discussion of this critical aspect of Origen's articulation of the dynamic between divine and human initiative in his chapter entitled, "The Knowledge of God as Father and Adoption as Sons," 93–118.

the devil) and the superior, God the father, sparked by Jer 11:10, "They have turned back to the wrongdoings of their forefathers."[39] There, Origen says: "The Savior is always begotten by the Father, and likewise also if you have the 'spirit of adoption,' God always begets you in him according to each work, according to each thought. And may one so begotten always be a begotten son of God in Christ Jesus."[40] Therefore, one's reception of the Spirit of adoption results in one's union with the eternally begotten Son, and thus it also results, so to speak, in one's own eternal begottenness, and one's ability to live in accordance with the divine "spirit of adoption."

Now to the other two results of the reception of the "spirit of adoption," namely, restoration to the body of Christ in the Church; and freedom of speech in prayer to God the Father. In the *Commentary on Romans*, as he deals with Rom 10:13, particularly the words, "everyone who calls on the name of the Lord shall be saved," the distinction we have been laying out between those with and without the "spirit of adoption" surfaces again. The words, "calling on the name of the Lord" elicit the comparison, for those simply "calling on the name of the Lord" are the children in the faith, or they are slaves, for they can only call on Jesus, the Lord, whereas the perfected ones are those who can call on God as Father, for they are sons who have received the "spirit of adoption."[41] Here Origen mentions the two interconnected results of one's reception of the "spirit of adoption," both of which are produced by the cooperation of God the Father, the Son, and the Holy Spirit. First, one is "restored in the solidarity and perfection of the whole body" (of Christ in the Church); through Christ's offering of them to the Father, the Holy Spirit sanctifies them and establishes them as members "of the heavenly church."[42] Second, the level of perfection resulting from this allows one to call on God as Father in prayer,[43]

---

39. *HomJer.* 9.4.5. Alfons Fürst and Huracio E. Lona, editors, *Die Homilien zum Buch Jeremia* (Origenes 11; Berlin: de Gruyter, 2018), 260; trans. John Clark Smith, *Origen: Homilies on Jeremiah, Homily on 1 Kings 28* (FOTC 97; Washington, DC: The Catholic University of America Press, 1998), 91.

40. *HomJer.* 9.4.5 (Fürst and Lona, 264; Smith, 93).

41. *ComRm* 8.5.2 (Bammel, 3:654; Scheck 2:144).

42. *ComRm* 8.5.2 (Bammel, 3:654; Scheck 2:143).

43. *ComRm* 8.5.2 (Bammel, 3:654; Scheck 2:143–44). I have not included Origen's full discussion of the issue of praying to Christ here, because he seems to contradict his presentation of the issue elsewhere in his corpus. That is, here, after making the distinction between those who call on the name of the Lord (i.e. the simple or immature majority) and those who call on God as Father (i.e., the elite perfected minority), he claims, "… and if to call upon the name of the Lord and to pray to the Lord are one and the same thing, just as Christ is called upon, Christ must also be prayed to; and just as we offer prayers to

for, the "Spirit of God" coming into their hearts teaches them to call upon the
Father, a devotional act, which, prior to their mature participation in Christ,
had been the distinct activity of the Son.[44]

Origen deals with the mature Christian's capacity to join the Son in calling on the Father in prayer in Book 19 of his *Commentary on John*, a topic
which arises as he discusses Jesus' words in Jn 8:19: "'You know neither me nor
my Father; if you knew me you would know my Father also.'" This is a recurrent topic throughout Origen's writings,[45] and here Origen discusses it in relation to the concrete example of the prayers of the Old Testament patriarchs:

In fact, although there are countless prayers recorded in the Psalms and the prophets,
indeed in the law as well, we have not found a single person who has prayed and addressed God as 'Father.' Perhaps it is because they did not know the Father. They pray
to him as God and Lord, awaiting the one who pours out the spirit of adoption on
them no less than on those who believe in God through him after his coming.[46]

Origen appears here to liken the patriarchs to all believers in the Christian Church with respect to their need to possess the "spirit of adoption" in
order to address God as Father; like the immature Christians, they are simply
unable to do so. However, upon further reflection, Origen will go on to suggest an alternative reading of the Old Testament authors' capacity to pray to
God as Father, saying, "Perhaps Christ had sojourned in them spiritually, and
they had the spirit of adoption because they had been perfected at some time,
but spoke about God as Father only in secret."[47] This second reading arises, of
course, both from a reverence for the Old Testament saints, as well as a desire
to distance himself from the likes of Marcion. Origen does not seem to think
it necessary to choose definitively between one of these two options concerning whether or not the Old Testament authors had already received the "spirit

____

God the Father, to the one who is first of all, so also to the Lord Jesus Christ; and just as we offer requests
to the Father, so we offer requests also to the Son." Perhaps, then, this is one instance in which Rufinus
has smoothed over an issue that by his time is straightforward: of course, one prays to Christ. This was
not self-evident for Origen and he is clear elsewhere (e.g., *On Prayer* 10.2, 15.1; *HomPs* 15 1.3–9; *CCels* 5.4,
11) that one does not pray to Christ, and that one only prays to the Father through Christ. Henry Chadwick made such an argument concerning Rufinus' interjection in his *Alexandrian Christianity: Selected
Translations of Clement and Origen* (Philadelphia: Westminster Press, 1954), 347.

44. See Widdicombe's discussion in *Fatherhood of God*, 105–6.

45. For example, see *On Prayer* 5.27; 22.3; *CCels* 7.43; *HomLc* Frag. 34; *ComMt* 17.36.

46. *ComJn* 19.28 (SC 290 :62; Heine, 174).

47. *ComJn* 19.28. (SC 290:62–64; Heine 2:174).

of adoption." In any case, it is clear for our purposes that he thought one required the Spirit's indwelling, brought about by Christ, in order to pray to God as Father, and it is the lack of such evidence in the Old Testament prayers that leads him to question whether these figures possessed it.

Origen addresses this theme vis-à-vis Rom 8:15 again in his recently discovered *Homilies on the Psalms*. In his first homily on Psalm 67 [LXX], Origen addresses the theme of "freedom of speech" in prayer to God the Father while he deals with the words of the psalm, Ps 67:1, "Let God arise," which presents a problem due to the verse's use of the imperative, for, as we will see below, according to Origen, no one gives God orders.[48] However, it seems that according to Origen, one of the most significant results of receiving the 'spirit of adoption' is the freedom it gives the Christian to pray to the Father, even in the imperative mood. As Origen seeks to teach his hearers how they can come to speak the words of this psalm verse, Origen provides two solutions to this potential problem. First, he informs his readers that "it is the custom (ἔθος) in Scripture often to use imperatives (προστακτικοῖς) instead of optatives (εὐκτικῶν)."[49] He proceeds to provide his hearers with similar examples from the Gospels, and he draws in particular on the example of Christ teaching his disciples to pray the Lord's prayer, in which he prays, "hallowed (ἁγιασθήτω) be your name," and "let (ἐλθέτω) your kingdom come," and "your will be (γενηθήτω) done," not "may (ἁγιασθείη) your name be hallowed," or "may (ἔλθοι) your kingdom come," or "may (γένοιτο) your will be done."[50] However, Origen explains, even if Scripture says these things as imperatives, "we hear optatives instead," for, he continues, "no one gives orders to God."[51]

Origen draws on our verse of focus in his second solution to the problem,

<hr>

48. *HomPs* 67 1.2. Ed. Lorenzo Perrone, *Die neuen Psalmenhomilien: Eine kritische Edition des Codex Monacensis Graecus 314* (Origenes 13; GCS 19; Berlin: de Gruyter, 2015), 175. See also the recently completed English translation of Joseph W. Trigg, *Origen: Homilies on the Psalms: Codex Monacensis Graecus 314* (FOTC 141; Washington, DC: The Catholic University of America Press, 2020). That humans should give orders to God presents a (rhetorical) problem because, as Mark Randall James argues convincingly in his monograph on the new Psalm material, *Learning the Language of Scripture: Origen, Wisdom, and the Logic of Interpretation* (SST 24; Leiden: Brill, 2021), Origen seeks to "deify" the speech of his audience or readers by teaching them how to speak the words of the Psalms themselves.

49. *HomPs* 67 1.2 (Perrone, 175; Trigg, 140). discussion of Scripture's custom of imperatives vs. optatives is much longer than my presentation of it here, and I have presented only the most relevant aspects of it for my purposes. Note also that Trigg translates εὐκτικῶν as "conditional statements."

50. *HomPs* 67 1.2 (Perrone, 175; Trigg, 140).

51. *HomPs* 67 1.2 (Perrone, 175; Trigg, 140).

which he presents by way of a rhetorical "someone" (τις), whom he claims is "bolder" than him, and who suggests that "these things may even be spoken as imperatives."[52] We will see that as this argument unfolds, the rhetorical "someone's" voice fades, and Origen's own voice seems to take over.[53] First, Origen makes an argument based on Paul's presentation of Christ's command that masters treat their slaves as equals, which he extends to God's relationship with the Christian in prayer, saying:

For if masters have received a command from Christ speaking in Paul, "to allow yourselves fairness and equality toward slaves (Col 4:1)" and the good master allows equality with slaves, why is it inappropriate for someone who has been ordered by God and has received orders, to be confident about observing those orders with a certain freedom of speech (μετά τινος παρρησίας), by giving an order reciprocally when praying to God?[54]

In other words, if God gives us commands, and if we are to be treated by God as equals, just as Christ commanded masters to treat their slaves as equals, then it follows that we are to reciprocate and give commands to God. For, he continues, "commanding God is not a greater thing than becoming his heir," and "becoming a joint heir with Christ" (Rom 8:17).[55] Such a privilege is not the result of the Christian's worthiness, Origen tells his hearers, but a result of God's charity, as the apostle John writes, "Beloved, if the heart does not condemn, we have freedom of speech with God and whatever we ask, we receive from him" (1 Jn 3:21).[56] Here enters our verse in an extremely powerful section in which Origen reflects on the significance of this "freedom of speech:" "And it is in accord with 'the spirit of adoption' and 'you are no longer a slave, but a son' (Gal 4:7), and your father is God and your brother is the Lord who said 'I shall pass your name to your brothers' or rather 'my brothers, in the midst of the Church I shall hymn you'" (Ps 21:23).[57] This reflection he concludes by remarking on how astonishing it is for a son of God to have this freedom to command the Father, "not being ashamed of the 'spirit of adoption' when he is

---

52. *HomPs* 67 1.2 (Perrone, 175; Trigg, 141).

53. For example, after presenting this argument, he says: "And so that we might be still more persuaded about freedom of speech … (Καὶ ἵνα ἔτι μᾶλλον πεισθῶμεν περὶ τῆς παρρησίας);" (Perrone, 178; Trigg, 142).

54. *HomPs* 67 1.2 (Perrone, 175–76; Trigg, 141).

55. *HomPs* 67 1.2 (Perrone, 177; Trigg, 142).

56. *HomPs* 67 1.2 (Perrone, 177; Trigg, 142).

57. Ps 21:23.

commanded by the Father to command the Father in return."[58] According to Origen, then, the reception of the 'spirit of adoption' results in the freedom to pray to the Father, even in the imperative mood!

Before I conclude, I will return once more to Origen's *Commentary on Romans*, for in it he also explains what he understands to be the present limits to the mature, perfected Christian's possession of the "spirit of adoption" and its resulting freedom. As he deals with Rom 8:23–25, particularly the words, "in hope we were saved" of 8:24, Origen claims that spiritual sonship "consists in hope," for, as Paul says elsewhere, "now we see through a mirror in a riddle" (1 Cor 13:12).[59] Thus, even adoption and redemption are accepted by the perfect one "through a mirror in a riddle," until such a time when "the perfect things come," at which point the adoption through the spirit shall be attained "face to face" (1 Cor 13:10).[60] For, Origen asks rhetorically, "Who is there placed in the flesh who is able to attain such complete freedom that he no longer serves the flesh in any respect whatsoever? In the same way it is not possible for someone who has been placed in a body to possess the adoption of sons completely."[61] The Christian must wait for the restoration of all things, at which point, as a result of the Word within them, they "will have the contemplation of God (ἡ τοῦ κατανοεῖν τὸν θεόν) as their only activity."[62]

Conclusion

In conclusion, we saw that Rom 8:15 provides Origen one particularly important way of expressing his well-known distinction between the immature majority and the mature minority of elite Christians, granted with much assistance from elsewhere in the Apostle's corpus along the way. Unlike the prior tradition, which had used the Romans verse primarily as a way to distinguish members of the Church from those outside its boundaries, for Origen, both the 'spirit of slavery' and the 'spirit of adoption' were governed by God and were possessed by those within the walls of the Church. As the child or slave under the spirit of slavery progressed—again, as a result of both her own

58. *HomPs* 67 1.2 (Perrone, 179; Trigg, 143).
59. *CommRm* 7.5.9 (Bammel, 3:575; Scheck, 2:77).
60. *ComRm* 7.5.9 (Bammel, 3:575; Scheck, 2:77).
61. *ComRm* 1.1.4 (Bammel, 1:48; Scheck, 1:62).
62. *CommJn* 1.92. (SC 120:104; Heine, 52).

good manner of life and divine aid—she found herself in the position to receive the spirit of adoption, a position in which her relationship with God
was characterized no longer by fear, but by love. She was now united with the
eternally begotten Son, and could now address God as Father in prayer. This
adoption provided yet another happy result, as Origen assures his hearers of
his first homily on Psalm 36, again of the new psalm material: "if you reveal to
the Lord your road and hope in him[63] ... he will make his boast of you and say,
'the justice is the light of my son who has received 'the spirit of adoption.'"[64]
That is, not only can the adopted child of God now speak freely to God as Father, but, according to Origen, God will in turn speak proudly in his assembly
of his adopted child. Thus, Origen expresses the significance of the believer's
reception of the 'spirit of adoption' by placing our Pauline words of focus in
the very mouth of God.

Concerning the contexts in which Origen's exegesis of Rom 8:15 is found,
in my estimation this examination reveals no discernible distinction between
the Alexandrian's use of the verse in his two primary exegetical genres, homily
and commentary. Not only does this demonstrate Origen's interpretive consistency, but that it also provides evidence that ought to deter us from making
too sharp a distinction between his exegetical goals in the two genres. While
we might have expected a more speculative or theoretical approach to the
verse in the commentaries than in the homilies, such a distinction is difficult
to identify.[65] His concern in both contexts is to explain the Christian's trajec-

63. The psalm verse of focus is "Reveal to the Lord your road and hope in him" (LXX Ps. 36:5). This
English translation is Trigg's translation of Origen's Greek homilies.

64. *HomPs* 36 1.6. (Perrone, 125; Trigg, 89).

65. Origen scholars tend to distinguish between the commentaries and the homilies in this manner. Whereas the commentaries are described as Origen's exhaustive and speculative explanation of the
biblical text for his elite readership, the homilies are often presented as records of an oral event, in which
Origen explains the biblical text selectively, with the aim of edifying his hearers, who are at varying levels of spiritual and intellectual maturity. In this construal, then, the homilies differ decidedly from the
commentaries in tone, content, and intended audience. See for example, Ronald E. Heine, *Origen: Scholarship in the Service of the Church* (Oxford: Oxford University Press, 2010), 86, 171, 179–84; Éric Junod,
"Wodurch unterscheiden sich die Homilien des Origenes von seinen Kommentaren?" in *Predigt in der
Alten Kirche* (ed. Herausgegeben von Mühlenberg und J. van Oort; Kampen: Kok Pharos, 1994), 54–81;
Christ—The Teacher of Salvation: A Study on Origen's Christology and Soteriology (Adamantiana 6; Münster: Aschendorf Verlag, 2015), 47–49, 51–53; Joseph W. Trigg, *Origen: The Bible and Philosophy in the
Third-century Church* (Atlanta: John Knox Press, 1983), 178; John A. McGuckin, "The Scholarly Works
of Origen," in *The Westminster Handbook to Origen* (Louisville: Westminster John Knox Press, 2004),
28–29; Christoph Markschies, "Erwägungen zu Absicht und Wirkung der Predigten des Origenes,"
in *Origenes und sein Erbe: Gesammelte Studien* (ed. Markschies; Berlin: de Gruyter, 2007), 35, 60–62,

tory from slave to son, and to exhort his audience, who are at some stage of this journey, to live lives that position them to receive the gift of the "spirit of adoption." I therefore suggest that the two exegetical genres present overlapping exegetical and pastoral concerns. In other words, Origen's interpretive concern is no less pastoral in his *commentaries* on Romans and Matthew than it is in his *homilies* on Jeremiah and the Psalms and vice versa. A much larger study would be required to make the claim that there is little difference between Origen's interpretive commentaries and homilies, though I suspect that my observations based on the details of this small case study are suggestive.[66] Such an observation should caution us against an unreflective imposition of our modern understanding of the biblical commentary genre onto the commentaries of ancient Christians; the biblical commentary resulting from modern historical-critical biblical scholarship takes its form but little else from the ancient Christian commentary.

Bibliography

Primary Sources

Hammond Bammel, C. P. *Der Römerbriefkommentar des Origenes: Kritische Ausgabe der Übersetzung Rufins.* Buch 1–3. *AGLB* 16. Freiburg im Breisgau: Herder, 1990.

Blanc, V. C. *Origène : Commentaire sur saint Jean, Livres XIX–XX.* SC 290. Paris: Éditions du Cerf, [2006] ; 1re éd., 1982.

———. *Origène: Commentaire sur saint Jean, Livres XXVIII et XXXII.* SC 385. Paris: Éditions du Cerf, 1992.

Fürst, Alfons and Huracio E. Lona. *Die Homilien zum Buch Jeremia.* Origenes 11. Berlin: de Gruyter, 2018.

Jaubert, A. *Origène : Homélies sur Josué.* SC 71. Paris: Éditions du Cerf, 2000 réimpr. de la 1re éd. rev. et corr., 1960.

Klostermann, E. *Origenes: Matthäuserklärung.* GCS 40. Leipzig: J. C. Hinrichs'sche Buchhandlung, 1935.

Koetschau, Paul. *Contra Celsum V–VIII, De oratione.* OW II; GCS 9. Leipzig: J. C. Hinrichs, 1899.

67–68; Karen Jo Torjesen, *Hermeneutical Procedure and Exegetical Event in Origen's Exegesis* (Berlin: de Gruyter, 1986), 49, 59–62; Frances Young, *Biblical Exegesis and the Formation of Christian Culture* (Cambridge: Cambridge University Press, 1998), 243.

66. Such a study I recently conducted at Aarhus University with the aid of a Marie Curie Individual Postdoctoral Fellowship. It will result in a monograph preliminarily titled, *Reading Scripture with Origen: A Study of the Greek Exegetical-Homiletic Material.*

Perrone, Lorenzo. *Die neuen Psalmenhomilien: Eine kritische Edition des Codex Monacensis Graecus 314*. Origenes 13. GCS 19. Berlin: de Gruyter, 2015.

Translations

Bruce, Barbara J. *Origen: Homilies on Joshua*. FOTC 105. Washington, DC: The Catholic University of America Press, 2002.

Heine, Ronald E. *The Commentary of Origen on the Gospel of St. Matthew*. Vol. 1. ECT. Oxford: Oxford University Press, 2018.

———. *Origen: Commentary on the Gospel of John Books 13–32*. FOTC 89. Washington, DC; The Catholic University of America Press, 1993.

O'Meara, John J. *Origen: Prayer. Exhortation to Martyrdom. ACW* 19. New York: Newman Press, 1954.

Scheck, Thomas. *Origen: Commentary on the Epistle to the Romans Books 1–5*. FOTC 103. Washington, DC: The Catholic University of America Press.

———. *Origen: Commentary on the Epistle to the Romans Books 6–10*. FOTC 104. Washington, DC: The Catholic University of America Press, 2002.

Smith, John Clark. *Origen: Homilies on Jeremiah, Homily on 1 Kings 28*. FOTC 97. Washington, DC: The Catholic University of America Press, 1998.

Trigg, Joseph W. *Origen: Homilies on the Psalms: Codex* Monacensis Graecus 314. FOTC 141. Washington, DC: The Catholic University of America Press, 2020.

Secondary Sources

Chadwick, Henry. *Alexandrian Christianity: Selected Translations of Clement and Origen*. Philadelphia: Westminster Press, 1954.

Daniélou, Jean. *The Angels and their Mission: According to the Fathers of the Church*. Westminster, MD: Christian Classics, 1957.

Heine, Ronald E. *Origen: Scholarship in the Service of the Church*. Oxford: Oxford University Press, 2010.

Jacobsen, Anders-Christian. *Christ—The Teacher of Salvation: A Study on Origen's Christology and Soteriology*. Adamantiana 6. Münster: Aschendorf Verlag, 2015.

James, Mark Randall. *Learning the Language of Scripture: Origen, Wisdom, and the Logic of Interpretation*. SST 24. Leiden: Brill, 2021.

Junod, Éric. "Wodurch unterscheiden sich die Homilien des Origenes von seinen Kommentaren?" Pages 50–81 in *Predigt in der Alten Kirche*. Edited by Herausgegeben von Mühlenberg und J. van Oort. Kampen: Kok Pharos, 1994.

Klein, Elizabeth. *Augustine's Theology of Angels*. Cambridge: Cambridge University Press, 2018.

Markschies, Christoph. "Erwägungen zu Absicht und Wirkung der Predigten des Origenes." Pages 35–62 in *Origenes und sein Erbe: Gesammelte Studien*. Edited by Christoph Markschies. Berlin: de Gruyter, 2007.

McGuckin, John A. "The Scholarly Works of Origen." Pages 28–29 in *The Westminster*

Handbook to Origen. Edited by John A. McGuckin. Louisville: Westminster John Knox Press, 2004.

Scheck, Thomas. *Origen and the History of Justification: The Legacy of Origen's Commentary on Romans*. Notre Dame, IN: The University of Notre Dame Press, 2008.

Strawbridge, Jennifer. *The Pauline Effect: The Use of the Pauline Epistles by Early Christian Writers*. SBR 5. Berlin: de Gruyter, 2015.

Torjesen, Karen Jo. *Hermeneutical Procedure and Exegetical Event in Origen's Exegesis*. Berlin: de Gruyter, 1986.

Trigg, Joseph W. *Origen: The Bible and Philosophy in the Third-century Church*. Atlanta: John Knox Press, 1983.

Widdicombe, Peter. *The Fatherhood of God from Origen to Athanasius*. Revised edition. Oxford: Oxford University Press, 2000.

Robert A. Kitchen

5. TEACHING LIONS TO FAST

Jacob of Serugh on Daniel 6

Many students of early Christianity are familiar with the biblical interpretations, casual and formal, by Greek and Latin writers in the first three centuries of the faith—Ignatius of Antioch, Clement of Alexandria, Origen, and more. Not as familiar for many is the large corpus of biblical commentary and interpretation by authors of what Sebastian Brock has termed, "the Third Lung" of early Christianity, that is, the Syriac heritage alongside the other two Lungs, the Latin West and Greek East.[1] A brief introduction and overview can help establish the context.

Syriac is an Aramaic dialect which developed in the 2nd century around the Mesopotamian center of Edessa (modern Urfa in southeast Turkey) and became the lingua franca outside Greek- and Latin-speaking regions in Syria, Iraq, Iran, Lebanon, eventually compiling a corpus of literature rivalling that of the western languages. Most of Syriac's linguistic territory fell under Islamic rule, resulting in the West largely forgetting or ignoring its existence and vibrancy. In the last half-century, the influence and impact of Syriac Christianity is being gradually realized as a major player in the early Church.

The standard Syriac biblical version, the Peshiṭta, or "the simple one," emerged in the 2nd and 3rd centuries C.E., first with the Old Testament

---

1. Sebastian P. Brock, "The Syriac Orient: A Third "Lung" for the Church?," *OCP* 71:1 (2005): 5–20.

translated from the Hebrew. While the debate is not finished, the consensus is that this translation was initially the work of Jewish or Jewish Christian scholars, knowledgeable in Hebrew, utilizing the Aramaic dialect of Syriac in Edessa.[2]

The Gospels appeared in the harmonized or "mixed" Diatessaron, reputedly translated into Greek and Syriac versions by Tatian, a Mesopotamian educated in Rome.[3] This melded and unified narrative of the Gospel story, "one Gospel through four," flavoured with ascetical themes, was used in Syriac-speaking churches for over two centuries into the early 5th-century, when it was replaced by more literal translations of the four "separated" Gospels from the Greek. Along with the Old Testament recension, the Gospels, and gradually the remaining books and letters of the New Testament, the entire Syriac Bible retained the title of the Peshiṭta.

Ephrem of Nisibis and the Beginning of Syriac Biblical Exegesis

Formal, intentional Syriac exegesis did not commence until the 4th century.[4] There are several early philosophical, ascetical and foundational narratives—Bardaisan's *The Laws of the Countries* (3rd c.),[5] *The Acts of Thomas* (3rd c.),[6] and *the Teaching of Addai* (early 5th c.)[7]—which retell and reshape

2. Michael P. Weitzman, "The Interpretative Character of the Syriac Old Testament," in *Hebrew Bible / Old Testament: The History of Interpretation. Vol. I: From the Beginnings to the Middle Ages (Until 1300). Part 1: Antiquity*, ed. Magne Sæbø, (Göttingen: Vandenhoeck & Ruprecht, 1996), 587–611; idem., *The Syriac Version of the Old Testament: An Introduction*, University of Cambridge Oriental Publications 56 (Cambridge / New York: Cambridge University Press, 1999).

3. William L. Petersen, *Tatian's Diatessaron: Its Creation, Dissemination, Significance, and History in Scholarship*, Supplements to *VC* 25 (Leiden: E. J. Brill, 1994).

4. General introductions to Syriac biblical exegesis: Sebastian P. Brock, "Poetry and Hymnography (3): Syriac" in *The Oxford Handbook of Early Christian Studies*, eds. Susan Ashbrook Harvey and David G. Hunter (Oxford: Oxford University Press, 2008), 657–71; J. F. Coakley, "Syriac Exegesis" in *The New Cambridge History of the Bible. Volume 1: From the Beginnings to 600*, eds. James Carleton Paget and Joachim Schaper (Cambridge: Cambridge University Press, 2013), 697–713; Jonathan Loopstra, "Syriac Bible" in *The Syriac World*, ed. Daniel King (London: Routledge, 2019), 293–308.

5. H. J. W. Drijvers, *Bardaisan of Edessa* (Assen: Van Gorcum, 1966); idem., *The Book of the Laws of the Countries: Dialogue on Fate of Bardaisan of Edessa* (Assen: Van Gorcum, 1965).

6. A. F. J Klijn, *The Acts of Thomas: Introduction, Text, and Commentary*, 2nd revised edition (Leiden: Brill, 2003).

7. George Howard, *The Teaching of Addai* (SBL Texts and Translations 16; Chico, CA: Scholars Press, 1981).

the Gospel stories, relocating the geographical context to different locations (India and Edessa). Two 4th century collections of discourses, The *Demonstrations of Aphrahat* (337–46)[8] and the anonymous *Book of Steps* (early or late 4th century)[9] are saturated with biblical citations and longer exegeses of biblical narratives, demonstrating theological and ascetical principles addressed to local faith communities in Sasanian Persia.

Ephrem of Nisibis and Edessa (ca. 306–73) provided the first formal Syriac biblical exegesis and commentary. Ephrem's commentaries on Genesis and Exodus survive,[10] along with most of his *Commentary on the Diatessaron*.[11] Ephrem did not examine every verse, but selected the sections he considered to be important upon which to comment.

A deacon in the Syriac, post-Nicene Church, a century before Ephesus and Chalcedon and the ensuing Christological controversies, Ephrem's primary concern was situated in the local congregation and its worship rather than in the classroom. Prose does not always capture the congregant's imagination and is harder to remember. Ephrem preferred poetry, so that worship was filled with song and chant, bringing to life the biblical narratives and images.

Ephrem was not the innovator of this poetical and musical approach to worship, however. Deep in the indigenous roots of Mesopotamian culture were the Sumerian and Akkadian "precedence and dispute poems," in which two personified natural forces—Body and Soul, Gold and Wheat, Months of the Year—are juxtaposed in public debate.[12] In the 4th–5th centuries, Syriac

8. *Aphraatis Sapientis Persae Demonstrationes*, ed. J. Parisot (PS, vol. 1 and 2; Paris, 1894/1907); English translation by Adam Lehto, *The Demonstrations of Aphrahat, the Persian Sage* (Piscataway, NJ: Gorgias Press, 2010).

9. *Liber Graduum*, ed. M. Kmosko (PS, vol. 3; Paris, 1926); English translation by R. Kitchen and M. Parmentier, *The Book of Steps: The Syriac Liber Graduum* (Kalamazoo, MI: Cistercian Publications, 2004).

10. E. G. Mathews and J. Amar, *St. Ephrem the Syrian. Selected Prose Works: Commentary on Genesis, Commentary on Exodus, Homily on Our Lord, Letter to Publius* (Washington, D.C.: The Catholic University of America Press, 1994); Alison Salvesen, *The Exodus Commentary of St. Ephrem*, in the series Mōrān 'Eth'ō, vol. 8 (Kottayam, India: St. Ephrem Ecumenical Research Institute, 1995).

11. Carmel McCarthy, *Saint Ephrem's Commentary on Tatian's Diatessaron: An English Translation of Chester Beatty Syriac MS 709 with Introduction and Notes* (Oxford: Oxford University Press, 1993). The Chester Beatty manuscripts are missing sections of the Syriac text, which McCarthy fills in with the Armenian version of the same work.

12. Sebastian P. Brock, "The Dispute Poem: From Sumer to Syriac," *JCSSS* 1 (2001): 3–10; Robert Murray, "Aramaic and Syriac Dispute-Poems and Their Connections," in *Studia Aramaica: New Sources*

Christians adapted this traditional genre with their own themes, most composed anonymously—the Cherub and the Thief,[13] Abraham and Isaac with Sarah in the Aqedah,[14] Mary and the Angel Gabriel,[15] and Joseph's discovery of his fiancée's pregnancy[16]—performed in the liturgy or during festivals for both education and entertainment.[17] Ephrem used this dialogue motif in his poems, along with images and symbols depicting the ineffable nature and character of God at which one should marvel, not attempt to investigate and dissect. Ephrem's perennial targets were the Greek theologians who in the post-Nicene Christological controversies were seemingly intent on analysing and defining God and Christ.[18]

These metrical homilies were of two principal genres: *madrāshē* which were sung, according to a prescribed melody identified at the beginning, and in varying syllabic meter, as "teaching songs" of biblical content and theological issues; and *mēmrē* which were chanted in a rhythmic isosyllabic meter. *The Odes of Solomon* (late 2nd century) as hymns in a heterodox Syriac-speaking Christian community,[19] and Bardaisan's hymns which were reputedly set to tavern melodies, were closer relatives to Ephrem's initiatives.

From the 4th century through the early 6th, the metrical homily was the mainstay of Syriac exegetical and theological literature, not in the classroom,

---

and New Approaches, eds. Mark J. Geller, Jonas C. Greenfield and Michael P. Weitzman, Journal of Semitic Studies Supplement 4, (Oxford / New York: Oxford University Press, 1995), 157–87.

13. Sebastian P. Brock, "The Dispute between the Cherub and the Thief," *Hugoye: Journal of Syriac Studies* 5:2 (2002): 169–93.

14. S. P. Brock, "Two Verse Homilies on the Binding of Isaac," *Le Muséon* 99 (1986): 61–129.

15. S. P. Brock, trans. *Mary, Joseph, and Other Dialogue Poems on Mary* (TCLA; Piscataway, NJ: Gorgias Press, 2011) 9–30.

16. Brock, trans. *Mary, Joseph, and Other Dialogue Poems on Mary*, 31–48.

17. S. P. Brock, "Dramatic Dialogue Poems" in *IV Symposium Syriacum 1984*, eds. H. J. W. Drijvers, R. Lavenant, C. Molenberg and G. J. Reinink, OrChrAn 229 (Rome: Pontificium Institutum Orientalium Studiorum, 1987), 135–47.

18. Peter Bruns argued that Ephrem's anti-Arian polemic derived from "a deep aversion to everything Greek in theology." P. Bruns, "Arius hellenizans—Ephräm der Syrer und die neoarianischen Kontroversies seiner Zeit," *ZK* 101 (1990): 21–57, esp. 47. See, Jeffrey T. Wickes, *St. Ephrem the Syrian. The Hymns on Faith* (The Fathers of the Church; Washington, DC: The Catholic University of America Press, 2015). Hymn 2.24 (p. 67): "Blessed is the one who has not tasted the bitterness of the wisdom of the Greeks;" Hymn 87.4 (p. 399): "The evil custom of the evil calf … the hidden worm of the Greeks."

19. James H. Charlesworth, ed. *The Odes of Solomon* (Oxford: Clarendon Press, 1973); Michael Lattke, *Odes of Solomon: A Commentary*. Hermeneia 86. Trans. by Marianne Ehrhardt (Minneapolis: Fortress Press, 2009).

but in worship. The majority of Ephrem's corpus was in poetry, while the writings of other principal authors, Cyrillona (early 5th c.),[20] Isaac of Antioch (late 5th c.)[21] and Narsai (d. 500),[22] survive only in poetry.

Whether this Syriac use of metrical homilies in liturgical practice for the purpose of biblical and theological education was unique during the 4th–6th centuries is not yet discernible. Beginning with Ephrem, however, it was imitated in a number of other linguistic and ecclesiastical traditions.

Ephrem's *madrāshē* or "teaching songs" began to be translated into Greek in the early 5th century. There is a large corpus of Ephremic Greek *madrāshē* extant, although it is not certain how many were directly translated from the Syriac.[23] Many imitated Ephrem's use of syllabic meter, while others used a more traditional Greek emphasis on stress. Eventually, many pseudo-Ephremic Greek poems were written, mirroring Ephrem's content and style.[24]

Romanos the Melodist, a citizen of Emesa, a city straddling the linguistic borders of Greek and Syriac in southeast Turkey, has been shown to be under the influence and heritage of Ephrem, developing the Greek *kontakion* poems for use in the liturgy, which flourished through the sixth century.[25] The biblical subjects Romanos explores reflect similar kinds of symbolism and storytelling as Ephrem.[26]

20. Carl W. Griffin, *Cyrillona: A Critical Study and Commentary* (GECS 46; Piscataway, NJ: Gorgias Press, 2016); idem., *The Works of Cyrillona*, TCLA 48, (Piscataway, NJ: Gorgias Press, 2016).

21. Mathews, Edward George, Jr., "A Bibliographical Clavis to the Corpus of Works Attributed to Isaac of Antioch," *Hugoye: Journal of Syriac Studies* 5:1 (2002): 3–14; idem., "The Works Attributed to Isaac of Antioch: A[nother] Preliminary Checklist," *Hugoye: Journal of Syriac Studies* 6:1 (2003): 51–76; *Homiliae S. Isaac Syri Antiocheni*, ed. Paul Bedjan (Paris/Leipzig: Harrassowitz, 1903).

22. A. Mingana, ed. *Narsai doctoris syri homiliae et carmina*, 2 vol. (Mosul, 1905); *Narsai: Rethinking His Work and His World*, ed. A. M. Butts, K. S. Heal, R. A. Kitchen (Tübigen: Mohr-Siebeck, 2020).

23. David G. K. Taylor, "St. Ephraim's Influence on the Greeks," *Hugoye: Journal of Syriac Studies* 1:2 (1998): 185–96; Andrey V. Gusev, "The Sermon of "the Greek Ephrem" on the Feast of Encaenia: Translation and Preliminary Observations," *Bulletin of the Ekaterinburg Theological Seminary* 2 [6] (2013): 179–209.

24. Emanuele Zimbardi, "Translation from Syriac into Greek: The Case of Ephrem the Syrian and the Sermon on Jonah and the Repentance of the Ninivites," *ARAM* 30:1–2 (2018): 295–306.

25. *Kontakia: On the Life of Christ*, St. Romanos the Melodist, trans. Archimandrite Ephrem Lash (New Haven/London: Yale University Press, 2014).

26. William L. Petersen, *The Diatessaron and Ephrem Syrus as Sources of Romanos the Melodist* (CSCO 475, Subs. 74; Louvain: Peeters 1985); Manolis Papoutsakis, "The Making of a Syriac Fable: From Ephrem to Romanos," *Le Muséon* 120:1–2 (2007): 29–75; Demetrios Alibertis, "East Meets East in the Chaldean Furnace: A Comparative Analysis of Romanos's Hymns and Jacob of Serugh's Homily on the Three Children," *JCSSS* 18 (2018): 24–41.

Jacob of Serugh: The Flute of the Holy Spirit

In order to demonstrate and experience the dynamic imagination of this approach to biblical exegesis, let us examine closely a metrical homily on the familiar story of Daniel in the Lions' Den (Dan 6:1–28). The author is the most prolific of Syriac metrical homilists, Jacob of Serugh (d. 521).

Jacob's poetic signature was not rhyme, but a 12-syllable meter, presented in two-line strophes (12+12 syllables) as a meaning unit, which are rhythmically laced throughout Syriac liturgies of all confessions. The majority of Jacob's homilies are now found in two large collections: the first compiled in the first decade of the 20th century by Paul Bedjan,[27] and the recent collection of the Syriac Orthodox Patriarchal Library, edited by Roger Akhrass and Imad Syryany.[28] Both collections contain critical editions of the Syriac texts, but no translations into another language.

There are several 'lives/*vitas*' of Jacob extant, both in prose and as metrical homilies.[29] While a hagiographical tone persists, these do retain some reliable biographical information. *The Vita of Jacob of Serugh* by Saʿid bar Ṣabuni (ca. 1095)[30] is an 1106-line metrical homily in 12-syllable meter, composed and performed for the commemoration of Jacob of Serugh on his death day (November 29). The *Vita* tells of remarkable accomplishments by the three-year-old Jacob. Other biographies tell versions of these stories, but the persistent impression created is that Jacob was a prodigy in the writing of metrical homilies. His reputed first homily was "When Ezekiel Saw the Chariot,"[31]

27. Paul Bedjan, ed. *Homiliae selectae Mar-Jacobi Serugensis*, 5 vols. (Paris: Harrassowitz, 1905–10); Paul Bedjan and Sebastian P. Brock, eds. *Homilies of Mar Jacob of Sarug*, 6 vols. (Piscataway, NJ: Gorgias Press, 2006). Note that this more recent collection is a new transcription of Bedjan's five volumes, plus a sixth volume of Jacob's homilies scattered in other publications.

28. Roger Akhrass and Imad Syryany, eds., *160 Unpublished Homilies of Jacob of Serugh*, 2 vols. (Damascus: Bab Touma Press, 2017). Note that the title infers that these homilies were previously unpublished, but of course now they are indeed published.

29. *Mēmrā* by Ḥabib of Edessa, "On Jacob of Serugh"—CFMM 00130: 211vb7–216vb39, CFMM 00144: 22517–24314; Mēmrā on Jacob of Serugh, CFMM 00256: 001va–005rb. Prose *mēmrā*, anonymous, ed. Paul Krüger in *Oriens Christianus* 56 (1972):80–111.

30. A critical edition and translation are in preparation. The base manuscript is: Church of the Forty Martyrs Mardin (Turkey) CFMM 00162, viewable online at Hill Museum and Manuscript Library (*vhmml.org*).

31. *Jacob of Serug's Homily on the Chariot that Prophet Ezekiel Saw*, ed. and trans. Alexander Golitzin, TCLA 3, *The Metrical Homilies of Mar Jacob of Sarug* 14 (Piscataway, NJ: Gorgias Press, 2016).

composed in his early 20's. As a *periodeutes*, an itinerant teacher and preacher, Jacob traveled among the churches composing and delivering these homilies. He was appointed bishop of Batnan, the major city in his native province of Serugh in northeast Syria, but served only two years before he died in 521.

Jacob's subject matter for this manner of preaching was diverse and wideranging in order to meet the needs of the Church's worship: metrical homilies that narrated and instructed how to perform the liturgy; occasional homilies that addressed secular events, wars and natural disasters; theological expositions of traditional Christian doctrines: Mary and the Virgin Birth, the Crucifixion and Resurrection, death and the departed, along with numerous biographies of saints, holy men and women; and exegetical homilies of biblical narratives which spanned the liturgical year's lectionary.

A series of *mēmrē* were given during funerals which were only 60–80 lines, in some cases referring specifically to the deceased, but more generally a meditation on the Christian understanding of death.[32] At the opposite end of the scale is the 2544-line recital and commentary on the Book of Jonah, which was performed during the Rogation of the Ninevites, a three-day period of fasting observed three weeks before the beginning of the Great Lent.[33] Jacob begins his homily at Jon 1:1 and proceeds in canonical sequence through each verse of the biblical book. Along the way, Jacob not only relates the well-known story, but inserts non-canonical dialogues of what the characters and natural forces were really meaning to say and do, in particular when their words and actions pre-figured New Testament events.

The theme that connects the majority of Jacob's homiletic endeavours is that they all point towards Christ, as seemingly every event or character is interpreted as a type of the Gospel and Christ.[34] As will be seen in the homily on Daniel in the Lions' Den, Jacob seldom distinguishes between the Old and New Testaments, for both are treated as Christian testaments.

---

32. Bedjan, ed. *Homiliae selectae Mar-Jacobi Serugensis*, vol. 5 (Paris, 1910), 183–91, "On the Departed and On Death," 781–836; R. A. Kitchen, "The Pearl of Virginity: Death as the Reward of Asceticism in *Mēmrā* 191 of Jacob of Serug," *Hugoye: Journal of Syriac Studies* 7:2 (2004): 147–56.

33. Robert A. Kitchen, "Jonah's Oar: Christian Typology in Jacob of Serug's *Mēmrā* 122 on Jonah," *Hugoye: Journal of Syriac Studies* 11:1 (2008): 29–62; idem., "On the Road to Nineveh: Dramatic Narrative in Jacob of Serug's *Mēmrā* on Jonah," in *Malphono w-Rabo d-Malphone: Studies in Honor of Sebastian P. Brock*, ed. George A. Kiraz, GECS 3, (Piscataway, NJ: Gorgias Press, 2008), 365–81.

34. See for a comprehensive analysis of Jacob's poetic Christology in Philip Michael Forness, *Preaching Christology in the Roman Near East: A Study of Jacob of Serugh* (Oxford: Oxford University Press, 2018).

Within the Oriental Orthodox Churches, Jacob of Serugh was much admired for his Christological biblical interpretation, with homilies circulating under his name in Coptic,[35] Armenian,[36] Geʿez/Ethiopic,[37] Georgian[38] and Arabic.[39]

A Metrical Homily on Daniel in the Lions' Den

A superb demonstration of how Jacob of Serugh's biblical exegesis and poetic artistry functions is in the recently published edition of his metrical homily on Daniel in the Lions' Den. From volume 2 of the new collection noted above edited by Akhrass and Syryany, homily No. 91, with Church of the Forty Martyrs Mardin (Turkey) Manuscript 00137 (18th c.) as the base text,[40] this *mēmrā* contains 272 strophes/544 lines. This is a relatively late manuscript, but in their introduction the editors have confirmed this as a genuine *mēmrā* of Jacob.

The story of Daniel 6 is retold in its canonical sequence, with references back to previous episodes of the Book of Daniel (Daniel 3—the Three Young Men in the Fiery Furnace), and forward to the Gospel Passion narratives. Depending upon the lectionary cycle, different portions of Daniel 6 are read in the Syriac Orthodox Church on Easter Sunday,[41] indicating that the drama and symbolism of Daniel 6 was perceived to align with the Resurrection narrative.

Jacob's strategy was to envelop the congregation in the narration of the story with its pathos and humour, scriptural instruction, and dramatic highs and lows, by means of the mounting rhythm of his 12-syllable meter and shifts in focus. More than a recitation, Jacob's structuring of the story encouraged

35. Alin Suciu, "The Sahidic Version of Jacob of Serugh's Mēmrā on the Ascension of Christ," *Le Muséon* 128:1–2 (2015): 49–83.

36. Andy Hilkens, "The Armenian Reception of the Homilies of Jacob of Serugh: New Findings," in *Caught in Translation: Studies on Versions of Late Antique Christian Literature*, eds. Madalina Toca and Dan Batovici, Texts and Studies in Eastern Christianity 17 (Leiden: Brill, 2020), 64–84.

37. Witold Witakowski, "Jacob of Serug," in *Encyclopaedia Aethiopica*, ed. Siegbert Uhlig, (Wiesbaden: Harrassowitz Verlag, 2007), 262–63.

38. Tamara Pataridze, "La version géorgienne d'une homélie de Jaques de Saroug Sur la Nativité. Étude et traduction," *Le Muséon* 121:3–4 (2008): 373–402.

39. Aaron M. Butts, "The Christian Arabic Transmission of Jacob of Serugh (d. 521): The Sammlungen," *JCSSS* 16 (2016): 39–59.

40. Akhrass and Syryany, eds. *160 Unpublished Homilies of Jacob of Serugh*, volume 2: 228–37.

41. Two lectionaries—British Library Additional 14445 and BL Add. 14528—read Dan 6:25–28 on Easter Sunday. BL Add 14686 reads Dan 6:19–25 on Easter Sunday.

the congregation to discover themselves living in the midst of this biblical world, praying alone with Daniel, being thrown into the terrible pit full of vicious lions, and being pulled out victorious, resurrected even, at the last verse. The drama of the *mēmrā* oscillates between the beauty of personal virtue, the depth of contemplation, the despair of injustice and cruel death, and then the joy of resurrection. Biblical interpretation for the early Syriac fathers is not a matter of academic analysis, but an event of spiritual absorption and osmosis into the biblical story.

Philip Forness' recent monograph on the Christological preaching of Jacob of Serugh illustrates how Jacob persistently employs the typologies of suffering and miracles with respect to Christ and other actors in the biblical journey.[42] Suffering demonstrates the reality of Jesus' full humanity, while the miracles which he performs proclaim his divinity, and the power it unleashes. This typological dichotomy does not explicitly appear in every metrical homily of Jacob, but certainly does in this homily on Daniel.

Outline of the Mēmrā on Daniel in the Lions' Den

While the manuscripts for this edition of the homily do not indicate section divisions in the poem, this *mēmrā* may be divided into 27 sections of varying length according to the subject and theme. These sections, moreover, may be subdivided into 11 dramatic junctures in the performance of the *mēmrā*, shifting the momentum and tensions of the story.

On Daniel in the Lion's Den (Akhrass & Syryany, 228–237)
   I. Introduction
      [1] (strophes/couplets 1–14) Proemion: Ode and Overture to Daniel

   II. Pastoral Virtues of Daniel
      [2] (15–26) Daniel as Trusted Administrator (Dan 6:1–3)
      [3] (27–32) The Virtue of Daniel to God and King

   III. Jealousy Towards Virtue
      [4] (33–40) The Ambush of Jealousy (Dan 6:4–5)
      [5] (41–49) The Praise of Enemies

---

42. Philip Michael Forness, *Preaching Christology in the Roman Near East: A Study of Jacob of Serugh*, OECS (Oxford/New York: Oxford University Press, 2018). See especially, Chapter 2: "The Christological Debates and the Miracles and Sufferings of Christ," 56–88.

I. *Introduction and Proemion*

Jacob and other Syriac metrical homilists typically begin a *mēmrā* with a *proemion* or introduction. This opening section offers effulgent praise to God and Christ, and declares the author's wretched inadequacy to describe and explain the holy events and people involved in the story he is about to narrate. The author prays then for assistance, by which he hopes to proceed and somehow manage to do a decent job. Seldom do the *proemia* make actual reference to the principal topic of the homily. In this homily, however, Jacob offers an ode to Daniel and an overture of this scriptural chapter in Daniel's story.

In the first two couplets, Jacob employs a rhetorical strategy he frequently uses in other *mēmrē* to dramatically capture the attention of the congregation. He tells them he is not alone.

> Continuing with [the story of] Daniel—Look, he is signaling me to speak
> about him,
> My Lord, give me a word that attains to his praises.
> That virtuous one induces me by his story to speak about him,
> O Lord of virtues, speak through me about him (lines 1–2).

Jacob immediately shows that this is not a treatise *about* Daniel, but an encounter *with* Daniel to be shared by the gathered believers. It is, in fact, initiated by Daniel himself who urges that his story be told again, and Jacob confesses openly that he cannot do so with his own words, but through the Lord who channels the divine drama through Jacob. Jacob's nickname was "the Flute of the Holy Spirit." That is, God used Jacob as an instrument through which the Word is expressed and proclaimed, and the music and song are broadcast. Jacob subtly observes that he is not the creative author of these homilies, but simply, humbly, the means by which God speaks in a human voice. A periodic trope of Jacob is to personify certain figures and personalities who are guiding his writing, especially the *mēmrā* itself, which tells him when to stop or keep going.[43]

A few couplets into the homily, God declares through Jacob his intention to speak about "the faster who taught fasting to the lions" (line 7).

II. Daniel the Model in Government and at Prayer

The teaching segment of the liturgy commences as Jacob narrates the story of Daniel 6, beginning with the description of the virtuous character and competence of Daniel which the king Darius has come to recognize and

---

43. See, R. A. Kitchen, "I, Mēmrā: This Is the Story Talking. Personification of Literary Genre in Jacob of Sarug" in Emidio Vergani & Sabino Chiala, eds, *Atti Symposium Syriacum XII, Roma August 2016*. OrChrAn 311 (2022) 319–327.

appreciate. Appointed a governor in the empire, there was nothing Daniel could not do well and this was acknowledged by all, even by those who were burning with envy and jealousy against his position. They praised him too, and to use a modern expression, it was "killing them," so they busied themselves looking for some possible fault or weakness in Daniel.

> All the tasks of that kingdom were easy for him,
> for there was no sin in his soul to trip him up (27).

> If one is praised by his friends, it is not praise;
> but if his despisers recite his virtues, now look, [those are] praises (40).

Jacob extends the details and discipline of Daniel's life of prayer through many couplets, over one-third of the *mēmrā*, imbedding Daniel's practices into the minds of the congregants listening. The people know where this story is going and how it will end, so Jacob takes the time to impress upon them that if they imitate Daniel in his religious devotion and commitment, the lions will not threaten them either.

III. The Fault of Faith

Jacob did not forget in his summary of Daniel's administrative skills to observe that in addition to competent devotion to the king's service, he devoted himself as well to the service and worship of God. The jealous Medean officials knew that, and thus intuited that in his virtue lay his fault. Daniel is pejoratively labeled a "captive,"[44] betraying the base prejudice of the Medean officials against the Jewish exiles. They concoct a ruse to trap him in his piety, but to accomplish this they had to make up a new religious law, one that both flattered and cornered Darius. For thirty days, they proposed, worship should only be of the King. Obeisance to any other 'deity' would be criminally sacrilegious prayer, punishable by a cruel death. Darius is initially flattered and seduced, but Jacob does not indicate any great enthusiasm on Darius' part, who clearly is naïve and unaware of the trap he has fallen into. He will realize the deception only once the new law has to be enforced.

Jacob goes back to Daniel who does not apparently acknowledge the new law. Daniel returns to his home and prays to God out through his window that faces Jerusalem, so while Jacob does not project defiance on the part of

---

44. Literally, 'a son of the captives' (28).

Daniel, the constancy of his devotion and prayer marks his character. Daniel's calm and persistent prayers are being whispered quietly among the congregants as a model of behaviour.

IV. Daniel as the Pearl

Twice (lines 110 & 158) in his description of the Medean officials' attempts to sully Daniel's reputation, Jacob refers to Daniel and his gifts as "a pearl" (*marganīthā*). The pearl is Syriac Christianity's most cherished symbol, a physical as well as verbal icon. The biblical reference is to "the pearl of great price" (Mt 13:45–46), for which one would sell all else that he owns to possess. The pearl, mysteriously created at the bottom of the sea,[45] is pure and dazzling white, a perfect and simple sphere—indivisible in one piece—for to break the pearl into pieces is to destroy it. The pearl exists as a single, simple whole, like God.

The attention to pearls lies in the revered and dangerous occupation of pearl divers on the Persian Gulf. The hagiographical vita of Mar Augin, the reputed first Syriac ascetic and founder of Syriac monasticism, portrays him originally as a pearl-diver.[46] The *Hymn of the Pearl* included in the *Acts of Judas Thomas*,[47] and the cycle of five hymns "On the Pearl" at the close of Ephrem of Nisibis' *Hymns on Faith*[48] both amplify this imagery and symbolism. Jacob reports about Daniel:

> That one blemish which they found in him is **a pearl**,
> For they caught him praying to the Lord, as if it were a fault. (110)
> The **great pearl of the King** fell into the pit,
> and he signed the seal because he was afraid of thieves. (158)

45. Syriac and Greek literature refer to the myth of lightning striking the oyster and creating the pearl, which symbolizes the birth of Christ through lightning-fire-Holy Spirit from Mary, "the watery flesh." Cf. Sebastian P. Brock, *The Luminous Eye: The Spiritual World Vision of Saint Ephrem the Syrian*, CSS 124 (Kalamazoo, MI: Cistercian Publications, 1985), 106–8. David Taylor notes that this theory was also recorded by Aelianus (d. ca. 235), *De natura animalium*, X.13.

46. *The Life Story of Mor Augin*. Syriac text and English translation by Abgar Garis Gulten (Glane, The Netherlands: Bar Hebraeus Verlag, 2012).

47. *The Acts of Thomas: Introduction, Text and Commentary*, 2nd revised edition, A. F. J. Klijn (Leiden: Brill, 2003) Chapters 108–13, 182–87.

48. St. Ephrem the Syrian, *Hymns on Faith*, transl. and introduction, Jeffrey T. Wickes (The Fathers of the Church: Washington, DC: The Catholic University of America Press, 2015) Hymns 81–85, 372–92. Hymn 85:6 refers to the naked divers who fetched the pearls. "Naked" (*shliḥe*) is also the Syriac word for the Apostles, "those who are sent."

The blemish of Daniel, which is only in the eyes of his jealous enemies, reveals virtue's strength through weakness. With the words "the great pearl of the King," Jacob acknowledges Darius' deep respect for Daniel. Now realizing the subterfuge at play, Darius protests. But Daniel's accusers have thought ahead and remind the King that if he does not obey his own law, he is no longer king.

V. Biblical Images

(a) Daniel as the Image of Christ

At the instant of Darius' anguished consent to Daniel's sentence, Jacob transforms the Old Testament narrative into the prefiguration of the Gospel.

> Here Daniel put on the image of the Son of God,
> by the iniquitous judgment which was stirred up against him by the wicked ones.
> He concealed the beauty from Christ and hid it in his person,
> and made it so that it might be enviable as it is virtuous. (120–121)

The context has shifted from a historical tale in Babylon to the location of its recital—the Christian sanctuary where now Christ has been donned by the doomed Daniel.

(b) Darius as Pontius Pilate

Darius, too, is transformed into the forerunner of Pontius Pilate, although there is a distinct difference. Pilate was not impressed by the flimsy evidence submitted against Jesus, but he had no other knowledge or feeling for him. Darius knew Daniel well and his virtue and competence. Both faced the pressures of the mob (a much smaller one, but just as lethal for Darius) and were not able or allowed to release the accused. The malicious connivance of government is laid bare before the congregations. Scripture may have been more subtle, but during the worship of the Church, Jacob does not pretend it was legal.

Jacob once more expands the biblical verses which witness to Darius' regret and mourning, and inserts Darius' prayer for a miracle from the God he only knows through the virtue and devotion of Daniel. In the ruse of the jealous officials, Darius is supposed to be the god, but he knows he cannot pray to himself, so he turns to God who alone is real. The congregation knows his prayer is genuine, even though he is neither Jew nor Christian, so hearing Darius' desperation, the silent question is asked, can our prayers too be answered?

As much as he was able, the King fought to rescue him,
and when he weakened, he called upon God to assist.
While there was hope, the king laboured on behalf of Daniel,
but after it resulted in despair, he called upon God.
The king prepared his friend for burial, being distraught for him,
and called upon the one who resurrects the dead to raise him up before him.
   (177–179)

Darius himself goes to seal the lions' den shut, parallel to Pilate's ordering Jesus'
      tomb sealed and guarded, lest someone rob the body (Mt 27: 62–66).
The King sealed the stone of the pit so that it might depict the mysteries,
for the stone of the grave of the one who makes all live was sealed. (166)

The pit was sealed and the grave was closed, here and beyond,
for through Daniel the mystery of our Lord was being shown. (168)

Again, these two rationales for sealing the stone of the lions' den illustrate
Jacob's typological imagery, by which he interprets Darius' actions by their
analogy with the Gospel events which the congregants recall.[49] The Christians
who listen again to this favourite story now comprehend how the One
God had begun this story long ago, completed it in the Gospel, yet even now
God is unveiling the sufferings and miracles of Christ among them.

VI. The Descent into Sheol

Descending into the pit (*gūbbā*) or lions' den is a famous feature of Sunday
school lore, but in Jacob's depiction, it becomes more—a universal drama.
Daniel descends into Sheol, re-enacting this non-biblical narrative that
had become virtually canonical in Greek and Russian Orthodox theology,[50]
whereby a still living person enters the realm of death, a premonition of
Christ's descent into Sheol. The theological question remains whether Jesus
was alive or dead when he entered Sheol, but for certain Daniel was alive.

The descent into Sheol is a frequent theme of Jacob. Here he parallels

---

49. Jacob had positively portrayed another pagan ruler who participates in righteous mourning—
the King of Nineveh in his *mēmrā* on Jonah. The King is intimidated and struck to the heart by Jonah
and his preaching. He leads his people in genuine mourning for forty days, not merely overnight like
Darius. The King is surprised by salvation on the fortieth day, and he and the Ninevites are new people.
But Jonah is angry and disappointed with God, as the King unwittingly, but authentically, becomes the
type of Christ who suffers with his people, and cattle.

50. Metropolitan Hilarion Alfeyev, *Christ the Conqueror of Hell: The Descent unto Hades from an
Orthodox Perspective* (Crestwood, NY: St. Vladimir's Seminary Press, 2009).

Daniel in the lions' den with Jonah in the belly of the great fish, as well as the three young men descending into the fiery furnace, three chapters prior in the Book of Daniel (chapter 3). All six—Jesus, Daniel, Jonah, Meschach, Shadrach and Abednego—were in the darkness of death while alive and transformed the environment into one of light.

As Daniel entered the den of cruel death and Sheol, Jacob draws attention to the fact that Daniel was not alone, similar to the fourth person/angel in the fiery furnace (Dan 3:24–25).

> In the dreadful place a good companion was sent to him,
> a watcher of fire (an angel) who shut the mouths of the lions. (185)

The Lord God is also present and does not abandon Daniel, and "sprinkled resurrection" on him to protect him from destruction (183)—an unusual expression implying that the divine power of resurrection is a distinct force and blessing that can be administered prior to death, in the lions' den, in Sheol, and where the congregation is now standing in worship.[51]

VII. Daniel the Ascetic

Down in the lions' den, Daniel becomes the ascetical athlete, the prototype of the monk. While monks were possibly among the congregations, the fundamental role of asceticism in the character of the Syriac Church in the late 5th-early 6th centuries is underlined. Not only are ascetical disciplines fundamental for Christian disciples, but Daniel extends these disciplines to non-rational beings, the lions, whom God has also created.

> That faster had been a wayfarer/passer-by to the lions,
> and taught them to fast discerningly with him. (190)
> The gluttons dwelt with the ascetic and learned from him,
> lest they hasten upon food rashly. (191)
> The smell of fasting spread from him to the lions,
> and they were afraid of him, the fearful ones who had never been
> subjugated. (194)

51. There is little surviving concerning Syriac liturgy in the 5th–6th c. In the Syriac Orthodox Church, sprinkling the congregation with water occurs only at Pentecost. Jacob's idiom, "sprinkling resurrection," may imply a form of divine action in liturgy. The images are close, since water is life, and resurrection is new, revived life.

VIII. The Resurrection of Daniel

The long night's unrest for the King, distraught for his friend, is again expanded by Jacob to show his genuine compassion, which through his penance and prayers has almost made him an acceptable Christian (195–204). Hope against hope, at the dawn's early light, Darius gets up from his bed and goes to the pit, and calls out Daniel's name. Like Jonah answering from the belly of the great fish, Daniel calls back.

From there on, Jacob interprets the whole event as Christological.

> Daniel defeated the lions in the pit in order to depict
> the type of the Son who trampled death at the door of Sheol. (229)
> The king rejoiced at that resurrection he saw there,
> just like that company of the house of John on account of Jesus
>   (Jn 20:20–21). (231)

> The climactic moment occurs, and resurrection is everywhere.
> As from the abyss full of the dead, Daniel ascended,
> as depicted in it the revival of the dead, even resurrection.
> It cast wonder upon that cohort forged of iniquity,
> for he had defeated death and without harm he climbed out of the pit.
>   (238–239)

> The truth dawned and showed itself clearly,
> and gave triumph to the faith of the house of God. (243)

IXa & X. Justice Requited;
The Dawn of Resurrection

This was the climax, but not yet the conclusion of Daniel 6's narrative, for which we might imagine that the congregation waits with baited breath. God's justice is about to be invoked.

> The iniquitous company saw the miracle and hid its face,
> and those of faith's side lifted up their heads. (245)

> In the evening they had pranced around because of that holy one who was
>   already dead,
> but morning came and shamed them through his resurrection. (247)

> The shadows triumphed against darkness during the night only,
> and like the day, Daniel dawned and made them flee. (250)

If there is a distinction between Daniel's time in the lions' den and Jesus' tenure in the tomb until Easter, it is that for Daniel it was only one night, while Jesus rose on the third day. Jonah was in the belly of the fish for three days and three nights, but the three young men walked through the fiery furnace in unmeasured time, a matter of minutes? What is parallel in symbolic imagination is that Daniel was cast into the den in the evening, if not night itself, and came up out of the den at dawn as the sun rose again, just as and when Christ rose on Easter morning.

IXb. Bitter Conclusion

The perpetrators of Daniel's conviction and attempted execution were quickly rounded up, along with their families—no squeamishness allowed here—and were thrown down into the very pit they had designed. The lions received them and renounced their previous discipline of fasting with Daniel. Jacob spends no more than five couplets to detail the gory conclusion without being gory. Then he offers a series of analogies and conclusions which epitomize the Gospel.

XI. Persian Furnace and Den:
The Purpose of Exegesis

Jacob limits his conclusions to the two incidents in the Book of Daniel, the Fiery Furnace and the Lions' Den, and demonstrates how these developed and were resolved, resulting in parallel and supporting truths.

> In the fire of Babylon and in the lions of Medea He taught
> that great is his power and all creatures obey Him.
> In the furnace and in the pit, He was triumphant,
> in order to make known His power to the Babylonians and to the Medes.
> The flame was the teacher to the sons of Babylon,
> and the lions as teachers to the Medes. (261–63)

> In the furnace He commanded the fire not to burn,
> and in the pit [He commanded] the lions and they did not destroy.
> He commanded and that blaze devoured the accusers,
> and the lions, moreover, destroyed the workers of iniquity. (269–70)

> Prudently, He guarded his own from injuries,
> so that the world might run to his refuge to be sheltered. (271)

The New Gospel in an Old Story

Jacob of Serugh has lavishly retold a familiar and beloved biblical saga, whose conclusion the listeners already knew. Simply knowing how the scriptural event ended is not the end of exegesis, especially for the congregants. How Daniel arrives at the end proves the dynamism of the Gospel for Jacob. The congregants watching and listening to the liturgy must have felt the weight of the darkness, and while enshrouded in this gloom, the congregants could have heard other possibilities—the meticulous and devoted worship and prayer practiced by Daniel, which they too could practice and mould the devotion of their lives and souls. King Darius is Daniel's unlikely supporter, and although fooled by his officials' deception, he is deeply affected by Daniel's execution. Yet, Darius holds onto hope that Daniel's God will intervene and prays to God, although he is a pagan. If Darius could pray to our God and be heard, then why should we hold back from praying to our God?

Daniel, besides being virtuous in conduct and faithful in the fear of God, is also an ascetical athlete whose discipline gives him the strength to transform others, even teaching fasting to lions. In Jacob's interpretation of what happened in the den, Daniel's spiritual fatherhood to these irrational beings brought about the miracle during the night. At dawn, Daniel ascended unscathed out of the pit and out of Sheol to prefigure Jesus' Easter sunrise resurrection. The Resurrection is not a one-time event, for see here—Jacob winks at the congregation—it happened once before, and indeed among the congregation it will happen once again.

Bibliography

Primary Sources

Akhrass, Roger and Imad Syryany, eds., *160 Unpublished Homilies of Jacob of Serugh*, 2 vols. (Damascus: Bab Touma Press, 2017).

J. Parisot, ed. *Aphraatis Sapientis Persae Demonstrationes*, (PS, vol. 1 & 2; Paris, 1894/1907); English translation by Adam Lehto, *The Demonstrations of Aphrahat, the Persian Sage* (Piscataway, NJ: Gorgias Press, 2010).

Gulten, Abgar Garis, *The Life Story of Mor Augin*. Syriac text and English translation (Glane, The Netherlands: Bar Hebraeus Verlag, 2012).

Bedjan, Paul, ed. *Homiliae S. Isaac Syri Antiocheni*, (Paris/Leipzig: Harrassowitz, 1903).

Bedjan, Paul, ed. *Homiliae selectae Mar-Jacobi Serugensis*, 5 vols. (Paris: Harrassowitz, 1905–10).

Bedjan, Paul, and Sebastian P. Brock, eds. *Homilies of Mar Jacob of Sarug*, 6 vols. (Piscataway, NJ: Gorgias Press, 2006).

Charlesworth, James H., edit. and translation *The Odes of Solomon* (Oxford: Clarendon Press, 1973).

Drijvers, Han J. W., *The Book of the Laws of the Countries: Dialogue on Fate of Bardaisan of Edessa* (Assen: Van Gorcum, 1965).

Golitzin, Alexander, ed. and trans. *Jacob of Serug's Homily on the Chariot that Prophet Ezekiel Saw*, TCLA 3, *The Metrical Homilies of Mar Jacob of Sarug* 14 (Piscataway, NJ: Gorgias Press, 2016).

Howard, George, *The Teaching of Addai*, SBL Texts and Translations 16 (Chico, CA: Scholars Press, 1981).

Klijn, A. F. J., *The Acts of Thomas: Introduction, Text, and Commentary*, 2nd revised edition (Leiden: Brill, 2003).

Krüger, Paul, ed. "Prose *mēmrā*, anonymous," *Oriens Christianus* 56 (1972): 80–111.

Lattke, Michael, *Odes of Solomon: A Commentary*. *Hermeneia* 86. Trans. by Marianne Ehrhardt (Minneapolis: Fortress Press, 2009).

Liber Graduum, ed. M. Kmosko (PS, vol. 3; Paris, 1926); English translation by R. A. Kitchen & M. F. G. Parmentier, *The Book of Steps: The Syriac Liber Graduum* (Kalamazoo, MI: Cistercian Publications, 2004).

Mathews, Jr., Edward G., and Joseph Amar, *St. Ephrem the Syrian. Selected Prose Works: Commentary on Genesis, Commentary on Exodus, Homily on Our Lord, Letter to Publius* (Washington, D.C.: The Catholic University of America Press, 1994).

McCarthy, Carmel, *Saint Ephrem's Commentary on Tatian's Diatessaron: An English Translation of Chester Beatty Syriac MS 709 with Introduction and Notes* (Oxford: Oxford University Press, 1993).

Mingana, Alphonse, ed. *Narsai doctoris syri homiliae et carmina*, 2 vol. (Mosul, 1905).

Romanos the Melodist, *Kontakia: On the Life of Christ*, trans. Archimandrite Ephrem Lash (New Haven & London: Yale University Press, 2014).

Wickes, Jeffrey T., *St. Ephrem the Syrian. The Hymns on Faith* (The Fathers of the Church; Washington, D.C.: The Catholic University of America Press, 2015).

Mēmrā by Ḥabib of Edessa, "On Jacob of Serugh"—CFMM 00130: 211vb7–216vb39, CFMM 00144: 225r7–243r4. (CFMM = Church of the Forty Martyrs Mardin, Turkey; Hill Museum & Manuscript Library, vhmml.org)

Mēmrā on Jacob of Serugh, CFMM 00256: 001va–005rb (vhmml.org).

Secondary Sources

Alfeyev, Hilarion, *Christ the Conqueror of Hell: The Descent unto Hades from an Orthodox Perspective* (Crestwood, NY: St. Vladimir's Seminary Press, 2009).

Alibertis, Demetrios, "East Meets East in the Chaldean Furnace: A Comparative Analysis of Romanos's Hymns and Jacob of Serugh's Homily on the Three Children," *JCSSS* 18 (2018): 24–41.

Brock, Sebastian P., *The Luminous Eye: The Spiritual World Vision of Saint Ephrem the Syrian* (CSS 124; Kalamazoo, MI: Cistercian Publications, 1985).

———. "Two Verse Homilies on the Binding of Isaac," *Le Muséon* 99 (1986): 61–129.

———. "Dramatic Dialogue Poems" in *IV Symposium Syriacum 1984*, eds. H. J. W. Drijvers, R. Lavenant, C. Molenberg, G. J. Reinink, OrChrAn 229 (Rome: Pontificium Institutum Orientalium Studiorum, 1987), 135–47.

———. "The Dispute Poem: From Sumer to Syriac," *JCSSS* 1 (2001): 3–10.

———. "The Dispute between the Cherub and the Thief," *Hugoye: Journal of Syriac Studies* 5:2 (2002): 169–93.

———. "The Syriac Orient: A Third "Lung" for the Church?," *OCP* 71:1 (2005): 5–20.

———. "Poetry and Hymnography (3): Syriac" in *The Oxford Handbook of Early Christian Studies*, eds. Susan Ashbrook Harvey & David G. Hunter (Oxford: Oxford University Press, 2008), 657–71.

———. trans. *Mary, Joseph, and Other Dialogue Poems on Mary* (TCLA 8; Piscataway, NJ: Gorgias Press, 2011) 9–30.

Bruns, Peter, "Arius hellienizans—Ephräm der Syrer und die neoarianischen Kontroversies seiner Zeit," *ZK* 101 (1990): 21–57.

Butts, Aaron M., "The Christian Arabic Transmission of Jacob of Serugh (d. 521): The Sammlungen," *JCSSS* 16 (2016): 39–59.

Butts, Aaron M., Kristian S. Heal, Robert A. Kitchen, *Narsai: Rethinking His Work and His World*, (Tübigen: Mohr-Siebeck, 2020).

Charlesworth, James H., ed. *The Odes of Solomon* (Oxford: Clarendon Press, 1973).

Coakley, James F., "Syriac Exegesis" in *The New Cambridge History of the Bible. Volume 1: From the Beginnings to 600*, eds. James Carleton Paget & Joachim Schaper (Cambridge: Cambridge University Press, 2013), 697–713.

Drijvers, Hans J. W., *Bardaisan of Edessa* (Assen: Van Gorcum, 1966).

Forness, Philip M., *Preaching Christology in the Roman Near East: A Study of Jacob of Serugh* (Oxford: Oxford University Press, 2018).

Griffin, Carl W., *Cyrillona: A Critical Study and Commentary* (GECS 46; Piscataway, NJ: Gorgias Press, 2016).

———. *The Works of Cyrillona* (TCLA 48. Piscataway, NJ: Gorgias Press, 2016).

Gusev, Andrey V., "The Sermon of the Greek Ephrem" on the Feast of Encaenia: Translation and Preliminary Observations," *Bulletin of the Ekaterinburg Theological Seminary* 2 [6] (2013):179–209.

Hilkens, Andy, "The Armenian Reception of the Homilies of Jacob of Serugh: New Findings," in *Caught in Translation: Studies on Versions of Late Antique Christian Literature*, eds. Madalina Toca & Dan Batovici (Texts and Studies in Eastern Christianity 17; Leiden: Brill, 2020), 64–84.

Kitchen, Robert A., "I, Mēmrā: This Is the Story Talking. Personification of Literary Genre in Jacob of Sarug" in Emidio Vergani & Sabino Chiala, eds, *Atti Symposium Syriacum XII, Roma August 2016* (OrChrAn 311 (2022) 319–27.

———. "The Pearl of Virginity: Death as the Reward of Asceticism in *Mēmrā* 191 of Jacob of Serug," *Hugoye: Journal of Syriac Studies* 7:2 (2004): 147–56.

———. "Jonah's Oar: Christian Typology in Jacob of Seug's *Mēmrā* 122 on Jonah," *Hugoye: Journal of Syriac Studies* 11:1 (2008): 29–62.

———. "On the Road to Nineveh: Dramatic Narrative in Jacob of Serug's *Mēmrā* on Jonah," in *Malphono w-Rabo d-Malphone: Studies in Honor of Sebastian P. Brock*, ed. George A. Kiraz (GECS 3; Piscataway, NJ: Gorgias Press, 2008), 365–81.

Loopstra, *Jonathan,* "Syriac Bible" in *The Syriac World*, ed. Daniel King (London: Routledge, 2019), 293–308.

Mathews, Edward G., "A Bibliographical Clavis to the Corpus of Works Attributed to Isaac of Antioch," *Hugoye: Journal of Syriac Studies* 5:1 (2002): 3–14.

———. "The Works Attributed to Isaac of Antioch: A[nother] Preliminary Checklist," *Hugoye: Journal of Syriac Studies* 6:1 (2003): 51–76.

Murray, Robert, "Aramaic and Syriac Dispute-Poems and Their Connections," in *Studia Aramaica: New Sources and New Approaches*, eds. Mark J. Geller, Jonas C. Greenfield & Michael P. Weitzman (Journal of Semitic Studies Supplement 4; Oxford / New York: Oxford University Press, 1995), 157–87.

Petersen, William L., *Tatian's Diatessaron: Its Creation, Dissemination, Significance, and History in Scholarship* (VCS 25; Leiden: E.J. Brill, 1994).

———. *The Diatessaron and Ephrem Syrus as Sources of Romanos the Melodist* (CSCO 475, Subs. 74; Louvain: Peeters 1985).

Papoutsakis, Manolis, "The Making of a Syriac Fable: From Ephrem to Romanos," *Le Muséon* 120:1–2 (2007): 29–75.

Pataridze, Tamara, "La version géorgienne d'une homélie de Jaques de Saroug Sur la Nativité. Étude et traduction," *Le Muséon* 121:3–4 (2008): 373–402.

Salvesen, Alison, *The Exodus Commentary of St. Ephrem* (Mōrān 'Eth'ō 8; Kottayam: St. Ephrem Ecumenical Research Institute, 1995).

Suciu, Alin, "The Sahidic Version of Jacob of Serugh's Mēmrā on the Ascension of Christ," *Le Muséon* 128:1–2 (2015): 49–83.

Taylor, David G. K., "St. Ephraim's Influence on the Greeks," *Hugoye: Journal of Syriac Studies* 1:2 (1998): 185–96.

Weitzman, Michael P., "The Interpretative Character of the Syriac Old Testament," in *Hebrew Bible / Old Testament: The History of Interpretation. Vol. I: From the Beginnings to the Middle Ages (Until 1300). Part 1: Antiquity*, ed. Magne Sæbø, (Göttingen: Vandenhoeck & Ruprecht, 1996), 587–611.

———. *The Syriac Version of the Old Testament: An Introduction* (University of Cambridge Oriental Publications 56; Cambridge / New York: Cambridge University Press, 1999).

Witakowski, Witold, "Jacob of Serug," in *Encyclopaedia Aethiopica*, ed. Siegbert Uhlig, (Wiesbaden: Harrassowitz Verlag, 2007), 262–63.
Zimbardi, Emanuele, "Translation from Syriac into Greek: The Case of Ephrem the Syrian and the Sermon on Jonah and the Repentance of the Ninivites," *ARAM* 30:1–2 (2018): 295–306.

Sarah Stewart-Kroeker

6. READING AUGUSTINE'S PSALM COMMENTARIES IN THE ANTHROPOCENE

Augustine practices and articulates a methodology of spiritual/allegorical reading in his biblical commentaries, the theoretical framework for which he lays out early in his career in *De doctrina christiana*.[1] It is worth noting that Augustine's writings on the Psalms are mostly homilies, however, and both the singing of the Psalms and his preaching on them reflect the central importance he assigns these texts in the spiritual and affective formation of his congregants.[2] He sees the Psalms as full of figurative meanings for the believer, that often—especially when they concern the nonhuman world (animals and natural phenomena)—require a movement beyond the literal reading of the texts. As a result, he consistently and overwhelmingly interprets verses in the Psalms that are about animals, natural phenomena, and the non-human world as speaking about human beings, the challenges of living in the world, and the difficulties of faith. He also interprets them as signifying truths about Christ and/or God. There is an evident and pervasive anthropomorphic and anthropocentric framework in play. This method may raise worries for a

---

1. *Teaching Christianity.* In *The Works of Saint Augustine* (I/11) (hereafter WSA), ed. John E. Rotelle; trans. Edmund Hill (New York: New City Press, 1996).

2. Michael Fiedrowicz, "General Introduction," *Expositions of the Psalms*, WSA, III/15, ed. John E. Rotelle. (New York: New City Press, 2000). See 37–43 in particular on the affective significance of the Psalms.

contemporary reader about whether, in Augustine's exegesis, natural phenomena become mere signs, signifying instruments, for human meaning. Like the
unfortunate party guest who seizes on every comment, no matter how small,
as an occasion to talk about himself, Augustine's exegesis can read like a kind
of human narcissism *par excellence*. It reinforces the human as the center of
creation and, indeed, of the universe. If one might have thought the Bible had
something to say about sparrows, harts, cedars, and flowing waters, Augustine's commentaries seem to indicate that it is really all about human creatures.
For a theologian who identifies pride as the first sin, this exegetical habit may
seem viciously hypocritical. In this essay, however, I argue that Augustine's allegorical and imagistic approach to the Psalms makes them a morally and aesthetically formative site of encounter with the more-than-human world.[3]

Allegory, Anthropomorphism, and Ecomorphism

In Augustine's commentaries, ecology becomes anthropology—this much
is clear. But conversely, does anthropology become ecology? In the shift from
natural phenomena to anthropological allegory, is there not necessarily a re-
imagining of the human on the model of the earth? At times, Augustine indeed
turns his hearers back to more-than-human phenomena as exemplary. We can
see this in his hortatory rhetoric—for example, he exhorts his hearers at some
length to imitate the ant.[4] He calls on his hearers to "chew" and "ruminate on
what you have received, and do not let it slip away into the bowels of oblivi-
on."[5] He urges them to "bring forth grass" to their hard-working pastor-oxen,
as the well-watered earth does for cattle.[6] These are just a few of many examples
of such moves.[7]

---

3. There has been relatively little discussion of the ecological dimensions of Augustine's thought
and its potential for constructive theological development. See for example Scott A. Dunham, *The Trinity and Creation in Augustine: An Ecological Analysis* (Albany: State University of New York Press, 2008);
Augustine and the Environment, eds. John Doody, Kim Paffenroth, Mark Smillie (Lanham, MD: Lexington Books, 2016).

4. *en. Ps.* 66.3; trans. Maria Boulding (4 WSA III/17, 311–13).

5. *en. Ps.* 103.4.19 (WSA III/19, 118).

6. *en. Ps.* 103.3.9 (WSA III/19, 148–49).

7. A few other examples from a series of sermons on Psalm 103 include Augustine exhorting his
hearers to obey God's commandments in order to have good, strong wings like a dove (*en. Ps.* 103.1.12,
WSA III/19, 123–24); to thirst like a parched land (*en. Ps.* 103.1.17, *WSA* III/19, 127); to be like valleys

On the other hand, sometimes his spiritual exhortations, which evidently respond to the human spiritual concerns he's detailing, are addressed directly to animals:

Wherever we are, we need to take refuge on the rock, whether it be the lofty crag in the mountains, or the reef at sea that is battered by waves but not broken, or the land rock that gives stability. To the rock flee the harts, the water-fowl, the coneys and the hedgehogs. Let the coneys beat their breasts and the hedgehogs confess their sins.[8]

Here, it would seem that human beings (the initial "we" who "need to take refuge") are personified as animals ("To the rock flee the harts ..."). Augustine shifts from the implicitly human "we" to the fleeing animals, to whom he addresses his words: let the coneys beat their breasts and the hedgehogs confess their sins! This is a striking image—the surprise one might have in reading it shows the extent to which we are habituated to seeing the allegorical exhortations move in one direction, from the nonhuman to the human, rather than the human to the nonhuman (it is also unsettling, in that Augustine envisions animals performing distinctly human gestures of penitence).

Augustine also sees mythical natural phenomena as representative of spiritual realities. For example, he describes a myth about the eagle, who upon reaching middle age dashes its beak against the rock to grow a new one, allowing it to live another several decades, in what Augustine takes as a metaphor of resurrection.[9] Not only animals but other creatures enter into his allegorizing: rocks, grass, trees, waters, skies (I will elaborate on some of these images below).

What should we make of these anthropomorphic personifications of the more-than-human world? Do they necessarily reinforce a noxious anthropocentrism? If not necessarily, what conditions or criteria might help distinguish between different personification practices?

In this vein, let me turn briefly to comments about anthropomorphic metaphor by Baptiste Morizot, the author of a book called *Les Diplomates* (*The Diplomats*) about cohabiting with wolves, in which he elaborates a set of ethological and spiritual practices that facilitate understanding and cohabitation.[10]

---

that let streams flow in them, bringing water to many places (*en. Ps.* 103.2.11, *WSA* III/19, 138); to drink like woodland beasts (*en. Ps.* 103.3.3, *WSA* III/19, 142).

8. *en. Ps.* 103.3.18 (WSA III/19, 160).

9. *en. Ps.* 66.10 (WSA III/17, 322), 102.9 (WSA III/19, 88–89).

10. Baptiste Morizot, *Les Diplomates. Cohabiter avec les loups sur une autre carte du vivant* (Marseille: Wildproject, 2016).

Appealing to the Yellowstone accounts of the wolf packs that draw on dynastic analogies, he articulates the need for a *narrative epistemology*.[11] Morizot contrasts this narrative and analogical way of accounting for animal behavior with the standard ethological presupposition that the natural world simply follows a set of fixed laws, which as long as human rationality discerns, render natural phenomena intelligible and basically predictable (as long as their habitats remain relatively stable). Morizot notes, however, that when it comes to observing wolves, narrative is critical to understanding, precisely because wolves do not follow fixed patterns. Packs develop distinctive dynamics that may shift over time as different leaders reconfigure relationships. Ethologists have started to develop a kind of "underground literature" that uses the narrative style their scientific disciplines exclude.

Narration operates a kind of *semantic wilding* (*ensauvagement sémantique*).[12] Narration (and presumably other forms of aesthetic or artistic representation) captures observed realities about wolves that mere data analysis does not, and a finer, more varied, more nuanced portrait of wolves emerges.[13] But this wilding of the semantic field, where feudal and dynastic metaphors intervene in an area typically dominated by biological terms, is tied to personification on human terms! Are these narrative accounts that borrow from feudal and dynastic analogies truly insightful into these specific wolf packs (or wolves as a species) or are they mere anthropomorphic projections that obscure rather than illuminate wolves *as wolves*?

Morizot distinguishes two kinds of anthropomorphism, for he claims, anthropomorphism is an analogical method like any other and subject to the same epistemological norms: it is always strictly hypothetical and subject to further comparison and contestation.[14] The first anthropomorphism falsely interprets the animal—passing too quickly from superficial observation to human analogy. This anthropomorphism occludes the wolf. But the second is a diplomatic anthropomorphism based on long and detailed observation—an

---

11. Morizot, *Les Diplomates*, 146–59.

12. Morizot, *Les Diplomates*,149.

13. I note that Morizot does not necessarily restrict this to narration alone. In a different section of the book where he develops an enlarged sense of the "mutualisms" possible between human and nonhuman creatures, he argues that attending to mutualisms should not be restricted to the scientific-ecological domain, but should encompass all mutually enriching interactions: ecological, ethological, evolutionary, symbolic, economic, aesthetic (278).

14. Morizot, *Les Diplomates*,158.

analogical reasoning that generates understanding through an *ascesis* of silent attention that precedes interpretation.[15] This second type is a form of respect: it interprets the wolves using methods and concepts as elaborate as those we have developed for ourselves.[16] The challenge is to do justice to an intimate alterity: the relationship with a creature one may recognize as at once like and unlike. Morizot thus sketches a kind of spiritual discipline of observation that can orient anthropomorphic analogy to foster understanding across life-forms.[17]

Morizot's account of "anthropomorphic metaphorology" provides a significant counterpoint to standard criticisms of anthropomorphism. For Morizot, anthropomorphic metaphorology can interpret the more-than-human world in rich ways that contribute to deeper understanding and relationship between human and nonhuman beings. Of course, Augustine's "anthropomorphic metaphorology" in his exegesis of the Psalms is by no means the same kind of enterprise as ethological accounts of animal behavior. Augustine is not seeking to generate deeper understanding of animals *as such*, but to understand and interpret Psalmic imagery of animals as a source of insight into the God who created both human and nonhuman animals and who "speaks" to human beings through these texts. Nevertheless, Morizot's account of anthropomorphism as an analogical mode that need not be strictly problematic demonstrates that appreciation for what such modes may offer is possible. I will suggest that Augustine's anthropormorphic metaphorology—albeit in a different context and with a different aim—may be read more constructively than we might assume.[18]

One aspect of Augustine's "metaphorology" that resonates with Morizot's emphasis on observing animals is that Augustine's knowledge about natural phenomena informs his allegorical reading. Take for example his puzzlement over the Psalm text that claims the sparrows will nest in the cedars, *but their leader is the home of the coots.*[19] How can this be, Augustine wonders?

***

15. Morizot, *Les Diplomates,*158–65.

16. Morizot, *Les Diplomates,*159.

17. Morizot, *Les Diplomates,*165.

18. I also discuss Morizot's anthropomorphic metaphorology in the context of an essay on reading Barth's commentary on the Epistle to the Romans (specifically Rom 8:18–25) eco-theologically, forthcoming in the volume *Karl Barth's Epistle to the Romans: Retrospect and Prospect,* ed. Christophe Chalamet, Andreas Dettwiler, and Sarah Stewart-Kroeker (Berlin: De Gruyter, forthcoming). For a full discussion of the book, see Sarah Stewart-Kroeker, "Exploring New and Renewed Eco-Spiritualities: French Contributions to Environmental Ethics," *Journal of Religious Ethics* 47/4 (2019): 790–817.

19. *en. Ps.* 103.1.18 (WSA III/19, 128); 103.3.16–17 (WSA III/19, 157–59).

If we confine our attention to the creatures before our eyes, the statement is unintelligible, for we know that coots or waterfowl are sea-birds or pond-dwellers. The *home* of the coot, or waterfowl, could mean its nest, but how could the home of the waterfowl be leader of the sparrows?[20]

Augustine comes back to this line of the Psalm after having glossed the cedars of Lebanon (where the sparrows nest) as the "nobles of this world, people illustrious by their birth, their wealth, their rank"—who will be satisfied but only if they are generous in hosting the sparrows, the spiritual ones not tied to any home of their own. So the sparrows will nest in the cedars, but the cedars are not their leader. Augustine reads that this way:

As we all know, coots are water birds. They live either on ponds or near the sea. Rarely if ever do they nest on shore; they prefer a place surrounded by water, especially on a rock with sea all around. We can well understand why a rock provides a good habitat for coots, for there could be none stronger or steadier. What kind of rock? A rock out to sea. It may be battered by waves, but it breaks their force; it is not broken itself.... How great are the billows that have poured over our rock, the Lord Christ!... Thus the dwelling of the coots is both strong and humble. A waterfowl does not build a nest in lofty places. Nothing is stronger than its dwelling, and nothing humbler. Sparrows nest in cedars on account of present needs; but they look to that rock as their leader, the rock that is battered by waves but not broken.[21]

Augustine integrates what he knows about the coots' habitat to interpret an otherwise ecologically puzzling passage in spiritual terms.

The nonhuman world is thus animated anthropomorphically and allegorically—but does this nonhuman imagery animate the Anthropos reciprocally? Do the ecological images for human spiritual life animate the spiritual landscape in ways that might decenter the human? To see the terms of one's spiritual life rendered as analogous to the ant, or the earth, or the waters, or the coots and sparrows and cedars, or as hedgehogs confessing their sins—does this alter the way human beings imagine themselves as human, as human embedded in a nonhuman world? Does it make us strange to ourselves specifically by disrupting an assumption that human beings by their rationality are the only morally relevant beings? Augustine makes clear affirmations of human uniqueness—and human superiority to "the beasts."[22] This is never dislocated; it is a feature of his cosmology. But his rhetorical strategy also thoroughly melds human and

---

20. *en. Ps.* 103.1.18 (WSA III/19, 128).
21. *en. Ps.* 103.3.17 (WSA III/19, 158–59).
22. *en. Ps.* 103.4.2 (WSA III/19, 168).

nonhuman imagery; he passes fluidly between the Psalmic images of the non-human world to images of the human spiritual and moral life.

Word, Speech, and Praise

This imagistic interplay rests on a semiotic interplay between the natural world, the Scriptures, and their signifying power. In interpreting the verse, *Arrayed in light as in a garment, he stretched out the sky like a skin*, Augustine begins with what he takes to be the literal sense: the passage shows the remarkable ease with which God creates the world. Turning to the figurative sense, he takes the reference *like a skin* to indicate a complex series of associations between the sky, skins as signs of mortality that he associates with words, as well as the Word whose wisdom stretches from end to end, and a scroll. Augustine thus begins this analogical series by taking the "skin" to signify the fact that God's authority and word passes through mortal human beings, drawing on the symbolism that he ties to the fact that Adam and Eve, in fleeing from the garden, put on skin tunics—skins, therefore, are a symbol of mortality, both the mortality of the animals whose skins become clothing and of the human beings whose error makes them both mortal and self-conscious in one go.[23] Skins signify mortality; the Scriptures are mortal human words but *also* God's eternal Word. How can this be? The Word of God is everywhere, stretched from end to end, for the world was created in God's wisdom—Christ ("God's wisdom" is a Christological formula for Augustine).[24] Indeed, "the earth is filled with Christ's creation,"[25] for everything that exists was created through Christ. But though God's wisdom is everywhere, we have not understood—and so God employed a mortal tongue and uttered mortal sounds, he employed the ministry of mortal men and made use of mortal instruments, and by this means a sky was made for you, so that in this mortal artifact you might come to know the immortal Word, and by participating in this Word you too might become immortal.[26] Through the words of the dead prophets therefore the sky was spread out like a skin, and so, "We read now under this

---

23. *en. Ps.* 103.1.8 (WSA III/19, 115).

24. *en. Ps.* 103.1.8 (WSA III/19, 115).

25. *en. Ps.* 103.3.26 (WSA III/19, 165). See Ron Haflidson's excellent treatment of the Christological association with creation in his essay on *Confessions* 12 in this volume, "The Differences the Son Makes: The Vocation of the Theologian-Exegete in Augustine's Confessions Book 12."

26. *en. Ps.* 103.1.8 (WSA III/19, 115–16).

sky, under this skin of the divine Scriptures spread out for us. Moreover, we are told that *the sky will be rolled up like a scroll* (Is 34:4; Rv 6:14)."[27]

The imagistic links between the sky like a skin and like a scroll make clear that Augustine assigns a semiotic quality to natural phenomena, which seems to be connected to his theory of allegorical reading itself (though I note that he does not make this connection explicitly). For Augustine, because all things were created in God's wisdom, they "speak" God's words. Human beings nevertheless need Scriptures—the incarnate words of the prophets, poets, and Christ—to help them to see and hear such words in all of their expressive range. Further, both the Biblical words, and human understanding of them, depend on *love*.

Augustine elaborates how words and understanding depends on love in commenting on the verse *He covers the sky's higher regions with waters*. Waters, here, signify love—the charity of the Holy Spirit poured out.[28] The sky is covered by the higher regions with waters but not weighted down by it:

(God) covers the sky with waters in such a way that the sky is uplifted by the divine Spirit. Now what uplifts something else is above that other thing; what is uplifted is below. The one suspends, the other is suspended. Well now, if one suspends the other, and the lower hangs from the higher, we might expect that the sky, by which I mean the scriptures, would hang from and depend on charity. And this is indeed the case, for there are two commands of love which are the most notable of all, and *on these two commandments depend all the law and the prophets* (Mt 22:40).[29]

The sky stretched out like a skin/scroll thus has multiple significations: it is itself a "sign" of God, a symbol of God's creation through the eternal Word, and a figure of mortal, incarnate speech accommodated to human capacities. This multi-layered signification (skies/skins/scrolls) is illuminated through the interplay of literal and figurative signs. But this illumination also depends on the outpouring of charity by the Holy Spirit and the response to that outpouring in creatures (the two commands of love).[30]

---

27. *en. Ps.* 103.1.8 (WSA III/19, 116).

28. Augustine's readings of water imagery are varied: flooding seawaters (representing persecution) make the earth sterile and barren and stormy seas signify trials and tribulations, whereas in other images thirsting for God or God's word makes water the object of holy desire (*en. Ps.* 103.2.11, 103.3.2–4) or central to images of abundance (all woodland beasts drinking, *en. Ps.* 103.3.2–4).

29. *en. Ps.* 103.1.10 (WSA III/19, 119).

30. This resonates with Haflidson's remarks on how Augustine appeals to the dual love command in relation to scriptural interpretations in his contribution to this volume.

For Augustine, a central *expression* of love is praise: praise that finds poetic expression in the Psalms, which in turn may inspire affective responses of love and praise—and which, further, become the fundamental liturgical speech of the early Church and the key texts for orienting the affective life, especially for Augustine.[31] Augustine's commentaries themselves, furthermore, double on this poetic and affective force in their literary and hortatory qualities.[32] I am tempted to say that insofar as poetic and rhetorical arts particularly aim at affective responses, including the love that issues in praise (for which the Psalms are remarkable), that there is a particularly strong connection between the aesthetic qualities of certain forms of "speech" and the affective formation in "charity" on which the Scriptures (imaged as skies in the passage above) "hang," as it were. The literary qualities of the Psalms—and of Augustine's commentaries on them—are not mere ornaments, but rather form the sinews that join the sky-skins (Scriptures) to the waters (love commands). They hold together words and loves, and precisely in this way, art forms exert formative pressure on worldviews. The expressions of praise in the Psalms, repeated in the liturgical recitation of the Psalms and further still in Augustine's commentaries on the Psalms, link words and desire—skies and waters, skin and love.

The linking of creature to Creator via praise hinges then on both Christological and pneumatological points. I will say a bit more on the Christological point before returning to the question of praise, which is tied to the pneumatological outpouring of love. The idea that all things are created in Christ, in the Word, in God's wisdom, is a critical hinge for a number of points I want to make here. First, it is the hinge for the ecological-anthropological analogy: not just human beings but *all flesh* is created in Christ. The Christological hinge that links humanity with creation allows for the ecological-anthropological interplay that may undo the human-nonhuman binary. Second, both the doctrine

31. See Fiedrowicz, "General Introduction," 13–37; Carol Harrison, "Getting Carried Away: Why Did Augustine Sing?," *AugStud* 46 no. 1 (2015): 1–22. I note that this also coheres with the sense in which, as Dan Opperwall points out in relation to Cassian's works in his essay in this volume, scriptural texts are understood to be transformative "technologies of the self" (a Foucauldian term Opperwall takes from Niki Clements' recent book, Niki Kasumi Clements, *Sites of the Ascetic Self: John Cassian and Christian Ethical Formation* (Notre Dame: Notre Dame, 2020)). Scriptural interpretation is thus importantly involved in one's spiritual, affective, and ethical (trans)formation.

32. This feature of Augustine's commentary coheres with Andrew Faulkner's discussion of poetic paraphrase as form of "creative" interpretation of Scripture with overlapping aesthetic and interpretive aims. See Andrew Faulkner's contribution to this collection, "Late Antique Poet as Scriptural Interpreter: The Case of the *Metaphrasis Psalmorum*."

of creation in Christ and the ecological-anthropological interplay it allows are the warrant for Augustine's method of allegorical reading. Recall that it is not just Scriptures that are stretched out like the sky but wisdom itself that is stretched out "from end to end"[33] and also hidden in common sights.[34] Precisely because everything was created through Christ—through the Word as John 1 maintains—everything may be saved through Christ.[35]

Further, because all things were created through the Word, they not only may be signs of their creator—signs that contribute to the beauty of the universe—they may praise God. In their beauty, they *reflect*—and in their praise they *respond to*—the charity from which all words are suspended. But note that Augustine does not think all creatures praise God in the same way.

… heavenly creatures have never fallen silent in their praise of their creator, any more than earthly creatures have ever ceased to praise God. Among them are some whose will to praise him springs from their delight in God, for an intelligent being praises only what is recognized as lovable. Other creatures there are which lack spiritual life and intelligence wherewith to praise God, but they too are good, and, being assigned their places within an ordered whole, they contribute to the beauty of the universe that God has created. These creatures do not praise him with their own voices and hearts, but, when they are contemplated by intelligent observers, God is praised through them. And, if God is praised through them, it can be said that in a way they too praise God.[36]

For Augustine, there is a hierarchy of being in place: animals who lack spiritual life and intelligence, human creatures who have spiritual life and intelligence, and heavenly creatures who contemplate and love God "without weakness or weariness."[37] This is a simplistic hierarchy, and it might and should be contested in various ways, at a minimum in terms of the presupposed definitions of spiritual life and intelligence. Augustine actually qualifies this somewhat in the following paragraph, when he affirms that nonhuman animals may not have a rational intelligence but they have a spirit and they manifest a life of their own that prompts them to distinguish between material things, so that,

---

33. *en. Ps.* 103.1.8 (WSA III/19, 115).

34. *en. Ps.* 103.3.2 (WSA III/19, 139).

35. *en. Ps.* 148.7 (WSA III/20, 481). Thus, the notion of the "cosmic Christ" on which much eco-theology rests can be discerned in Augustine.

36. *en. Ps.* 148.3 (WSA III/20, 478).

37. *en. Ps.* 148.3 (WSA III/20, 478).

like human animals, they are drawn toward what gives them pleasure and shun what hurts.[38]

To get back to the question of praise, however, we can observe that Augustine seems to affirm a kind of praise implicit in the beauty of creation: creatures already offer certain kinds of praise. Further, even for creatures who do not praise the creator "with their own voices and hearts," God is praised through them when they are contemplated as beautiful "by intelligent observers."[39] The idea that God is praised through the appreciative contemplation of nonhuman creatures by "intelligent observers" provides a *further* analogical meaning to the praise such creatures offer.

Human beings lend their voices to creatures who praise God implicitly by their beauty. This semiotic "lending" is perhaps not unlike how human beings may lend metaphors to animals and other creatures, as Morizot suggests, which fosters a sense of intimate alterity with them. Lending their voices and their metaphors is not just a way of fostering understanding, however, but of inspiring or even exhorting praise in others. The aesthetic appreciation of the beholder yields a confession of beauty—and Augustine has much to say about how confessing beauty is morally and aesthetically formative for the one who confesses *as well as* others who may hear that confession.[40]

Confessing beauty is a kind of praise of both the beauty itself and its source. Confessing the beauty of creation may form an ecologically-attuned imagination of the more-than-human world as a site of praise in two senses: 1) insofar as nonhuman creatures also engage in the activity of praise, and 2) insofar as the more-than-human world inspires praise in the form of confessing its beauty. These terms (confession, beauty, and praise) are central to Augustine's ethics, which are rooted in his understanding of ordering love.[41] When we see how these terms take their place in his Psalms commentaries relative to all creatures, they expand the scope of what we might otherwise take to be a narrow range of moral concern or of morally-relevant beings.

Without getting into the details of his aesthetic theory, Augustine accords

---

38. *en. Ps.* 148.3 (WSA III/20, 478–79).

39. *en. Ps.* 148.3 (WSA III/20, 478).

40. I discuss this at further length in *Pilgrimage as Moral and Aesthetic Formation in Augustine's Thought* (Oxford: Oxford University Press, 2017).

41. For elaboration, see *Pilgrimage as Moral and Aesthetic Formation*.

a high moral value to beauty, which we can see at work here—but interestingly, to use an anachronism on Augustine but one that I think is apt, Augustine also seems to have an implicit notion of what later works in aesthetics name the sublime.[42] The verse, *Praise the Lord from the earth, you dragons and all the depths* yields a remarkable interpretation by Augustine. He says that the Psalmist wanted us to praise God through our study of these dragons, "for, when they move us to praise God, they themselves are praising him."[43] So what do we know about dragons? Listening to Augustine here gives us a fascinating window onto one of the more fantastical (to the contemporary Western reader) elements of his cosmology, his earthly imagination:

You dragons and all the depths. The depths he means are the deep places of the ocean. Associated with them are all the seas and cloudy atmospheric conditions. Whatever kinds of weather God wishes to prevail on the earth—clouds, winds, storms, rain, lightning, thunder, hail, snow—all of them are generated by this damp, foggy air.... Now dragons favor watery habitats. They emerge from caves and take to the air. They create major atmospheric disturbance, for dragons are very large creatures, the largest of all on earth. This is probably why the psalm began its consideration of earthly creatures with them. There are caves in which hidden waters rise, and from them spring the fountains that issue in rivers. Some of these flow above ground, but others make their way below the surface, hidden from our gaze. All of them, together with the entire watery world, the sea, and our damp atmosphere here below, are called *the depths* in our psalm, they and the great deeps in which dragons live and praise God. What? Are we to imagine dragons forming a choir to praise God? Of course not, but when you think about dragons you are reminded of the dragons' designer, the dragons' creator. When they fill you with amazement you reflect, "How great must be the God who made them!" In this way dragons praise God through your voices, and so the psalm invites them, *Praise the Lord, you dragons and all the depths.*[44]

This is a wild and incredible evocation—a choir of dragons praising God! Or rather, as Augustine specifies, dragons praising God "through your voices"

---

42. The sublime features prominently in Immanuel Kant's highly influential treatise on aesthetics, *Critique of the Power of Judgment* (trans. Paul Guyer, Cambridge: Cambridge University Press, 2000), in which he distinguishes between the beautiful and the sublime—a distinction that dominantly marks the subsequent development of the field of philosophical aesthetics in the 18th and 19th centuries. For Kant, and his inheritors, while the term beauty applies to that which is pleasant, harmonious, and lovely, the sublime is imposing, awe-inspiring, and powerful. While the beautiful elicits delight, the sublime may inspire fear as much as amazement.

43. *en. Ps.* 148.9 (WSA III/20, 484).

44. *en. Ps.* 148.9 (WSA III/20, 483–84).

(which is only slightly less amazing an image).[45] Note the further implication: Augustine thinks dragons influence both water flows and weather systems, especially storms (a feature of Kant's account of the sublime, I note in passing[46]). Through the idea of the dragons' praise, water flows and weather systems praise too. This is significant in light of Augustine's often more negative images of turbulent seas and storms as the tribulations of earthly life—though it raises more questions than it answers about how to conjoin his aesthetic sense of how dragons and storms praise God and how these same storms signify obstacles or difficulties in the earthly moral life.

Conclusion

Human creatures lend their voices, their language, their images and metaphors, their poetical and rhetorical arts, to creatures of all sorts. Just as through Augustine's allegorical readings of the Psalms, animals of all sorts, trees, skies, waters and mists lend their behaviors, their patterns, their ecological texture and complexity to Augustine as images and metaphors of the human spiritual life. But they can only do so because creatures are *already engaged in praise simply by being what they are*—and their beauty and sublimity inspires praise and awe in the human beholder. In fact, this may be one way of further decentering an anthropocentric view of moral authority: for Augustine, the most apt expression of praise is nonverbal.[47]

---

45. *en. Ps.* 148.9 (WSA III/20, 484).

46. Immanuel Kant, *Critique of the Power of Judgment* (trans. Paul Guyer, Cambridge: Cambridge University Press, 2000), 139, 144, 146. For Kant, the sublimity lies not in the natural phenomena themselves but in the "mind of the one who judges" (139), but he repeatedly cites certain phenomena—such as stormy seas—as occasions propitious to such judgments.

47. "Do not worry, for he provides you with a technique for singing. Do not go seeking lyrics, as though you could spell out in words anything that will give God pleasure. Sing to him *in jubilation.* This is what acceptable singing to God means: to sing jubilantly. But what is that? It is to grasp the fact that what is sung in the heart cannot be articulated in words. Think of people who sing at harvest time, or in the vineyard, or at any work that goes with a swing. They begin by caroling their joy in words, but after a while they seem to be so full of gladness that they find words no longer adequate to express it, so they abandon distinct syllables and words, and resort to a single cry of jubilant happiness. Jubilation is a shout of joy; it indicates that the heart is bringing forth what defies speech. To whom, then, is this jubilation more fittingly offered than to God who surpasses all utterance? You cannot speak of him because he transcends our speech; and if you cannot speak of him, yet may not remain silent, what else can you do but cry out in jubilation, so that your heart may tell its joy without words, and the unbounded rush of gladness not be cramped by syllables?" (*en. Ps.* 32.2.8, WSA, III/15, 401).

In this regard, even as he portrays a kind of human "lending" of voice/ words to the more-than-human world, might we see this as primarily a confession destined to "converting" human beings to confessions of beauty and praise in/of the more-than-human world, and see the nonverbal praise of the more-than-human world as in fact already *closer to* true praise? Who is the audience of the poetical, rhetorical arts of the Psalms, of the Psalm commentaries, and of anthropomorphic/ecomorphic personification and metaphorology, if not fellow human beings—whose understanding of and relationship to the more-than-human world the psalmist (or the preacher of the Psalms, or the contemporary reader harboring ecological concerns) seeks to shape or reorient in particular ways? In ways that perhaps foster recognition of the very *poverty* of human temporal speech and praise in certain regards?

The poetical and rhetorical arts create an intimate interplay between the human and more-than-human world, between natural and spiritual landscapes which are in fact interwoven precisely in this allegorical reading in ways that— we might say—get lost in the modern rebuffing of allegorical exegesis that reinforces a division between the "natural" as literal and material, the "spiritual" as disincarnate and abstract. Anthropomorphic allegorical reading may also open onto ecomorphic imagery. This performs a kind of undoing of an antagonistic human/nonhuman distinction—to some extent. Perhaps it may also undo certain modern assumptions about the epistemological and hermeneutical value of allegory, personification, and metaphor. As Elaine James suggests, biblical poetry is an art: a technology that provides a mode of encounter *with* a mode of knowledge *about* the natural world.[48] In Augustine's commentaries on such biblical poetry, we might discern an art that integrates this mode of encounter and mode of knowledge about the natural world with a mode of encounter and understanding about the spiritual and ethical life as well.

---

48. See Elaine James, *Landscapes of the Song of Songs: Poetry and Place* (Oxford: Oxford University Press, 2017). This paper was originally conceived and presented in collaboration with James as a two-part set of complementary papers; hers on the Psalms themselves and mine on Augustine's commentaries on the Psalms. I am grateful to her particularly for this way of framing biblical poetry and the modes in which it engages the reader.

Bibliography

Augustine and the Environment. Edited by John Doody, Kim Paffenroth, Mark Smillie. Lanham, MD: Lexington Books, 2016.

Augustine. *Expositions of the Psalms.* In *The Works of Saint Augustine* (III/17), edited by John E. Rotelle, translated by Maria Boulding. New York: New City Press, 2001.

Augustine. *Expositions of the Psalms.* In *The Works of Saint Augustine* (III/19), edited by John E. Rotelle, translated by Maria Boulding. New York: New City Press, 2004.

Augustine. *Teaching Christianity.* In *The Works of Saint Augustine* (I/11), edited by John E. Rotelle, translated by Edmund Hill. New York: New City Press, 1996.

Clements, Niki Kasumi. *Sites of the Ascetic Self: John Cassian and Christian Ethical Formation.* Notre Dame, IN: University of Notre Dame Press, 2020.

Dunham, Scott A. *The Trinity and Creation in Augustine: An Ecological Analysis.* Albany: State University of New York Press, 2008.

Faulkner, Andrew. "The Late Antique Poet as Scriptural Interpreter: The Case of the *Metaphrasis Psalmorum.*" In *Exploring the Literary Contexts of Patristic Biblical Exegesis,* edited by Miriam De Cock and Elizabeth Klein, 114–29. Washington, DC: The Catholic University of America Press, 2023.

Fiedrowicz, Michael. "General Introduction." In *Expositions of the Psalms. The Works of Saint Augustine* (III/15), edited by John E. Rotelle, 13–66. New York: New City Press, 2000.

Haflidson, Ron. "The Differences the Son Makes: The Vocation of the Theologian-Exegete in Augustine's Confessions Book 12." In *Exploring the Literary Contexts of Patristic Biblical Exegesis,* edited by Miriam De Cock and Elizabeth Klein, 178–95. Washington, DC: The Catholic University of America Press, 2023.

Harrison, Carol. "Getting Carried Away: Why Did Augustine Sing?" *AugStud* 46 no. 1 (2015): 1–22.

James, Elaine. *Landscapes of the Song of Songs: Poetry and Place.* Oxford: Oxford University Press, 2017.

Kant, Immanuel. *Critique of the Power of Judgment.* Trans. Paul Guyer. Cambridge: Cambridge University Press, 2000.

Morizot, Baptiste. *Les Diplomates. Cohabiter avec les loups sur une autre carte du vivant.* Marseille: Wildproject, 2016.

Opperwall, Daniel. "Apocalyptic Imagery and the Transformation of Self: Matthew 24 and the Book of Revelation in John Cassian." In *Exploring the Literary Contexts of Patristic Biblical Exegesis,* edited by Miriam De Cock and Elizabeth Klein, 222–36. Washington, DC: Catholic University of America Press, 2023.

Stewart-Kroeker, Sarah. *Pilgrimage as Moral and Aesthetic Formation in Augustine's Thought.* Oxford: Oxford University Press, 2017.

Andrew Faulkner

7. LATE ANTIQUE POET AS SCRIPTURAL INTERPRETER

The Case of the *Metaphrasis Psalmorum*

Early Christian poets of the fourth and fifth centuries, writing in both Greek and Latin, engaged with Scripture through biblical poetic paraphrase, an innovative and bourgeoning Christian genre in which biblical texts were rendered in the language of classical poetry, especially that of Homer and Virgil.[1] As early as the first half of the fourth century, Juvencus composed an extensive and refined paraphrase of the Gospels in Latin,[2] while in the fifth century Victorius retold Genesis in his *Alethia* and an unknown poet penned a Latin paraphrase of the *Heptateuch*. On a smaller scale, Paulinus (c. 354–431) paraphrased in ornate verse a selection of Psalms (*Carm.* 6–9).[3] In the Greek East, highly sophisticated and extensive poetic paraphrase of Scripture seems to have emerged a bit later than in the Latin West, but not long after Juvencus in the fourth century some shorter poems of the Bodmer papyri, with close links to the typical exercises of the late antique school curriculum, creatively

---

1. For an overview of late antique biblical epic, which arose in the wake of the reforms of Constantine, see the foundational survey of Roberts 1985, 61–106; more recently Agosti 2012, 371–72, who calls such verse paraphrase the "most characteristic Christian genre," and McGill 2012, 344–45.

2. The poem is not later than the early 330s; see Green 2006, *passim* (on dating, see 3–7).

3. There is an extensive bibliography on these Latin works, but see e.g. Roberts 1985, 92–96, Trout 1999, 85–86, Green 2006, Cutino 2009, Jakobi 2010.

paraphrased Genesis and the Psalms.[4] The fifth century saw large-scale biblical paraphrases in Greek. Aelia Eudocia rendered the Octateuch, Zechariah, and Daniel in hexameter verse, although these works have not survived,[5] and Nonnus of Panopolis, author also of a 48-book hexameter poem on the exploits of the pagan god Dionysus, paraphrased St John's Gospel in florid verse.[6]

These poetic paraphrases render Scripture with varying levels of word-for-word fidelity to the biblical exemplar, yet all engage in some way with the creative interpretation of Scripture. On a very basic level, paraphrase and translation are interpretative acts.[7] Looking beyond poetry for a moment, late antique Christian prose paraphrases had interpretative aims:[8] Gregory of Nyssa, for example, indicates that he paraphrases Ps 57 (58): 2–3 "for the sake of clarity" (σαφηνείας χάριν), language used elsewhere of the exposition of Scripture.[9] Early Christian poets also engage actively in the tradition of Christian scriptural exegesis in their paraphrases,[10] adapting and expanding upon the scriptural source with both (and sometimes overlapping) aesthetic and interpretative aims. Juvencus, who explains in the epilogue to his *Evangeliorum Libri Quattuor* that through his poetic inspiration the "glory of the divine law willingly adopts the terrestrial ornaments of language" (*divinae gloria legis | ornamenta libens caperet terrestria linguae*, 4.804–5), is intensely concerned with the aesthetic and emotional power of his poetic narrative, but he is also concerned with teaching and scriptural interpretation.[11] Similarly Nonnus, al-

---

4. Hurst-Rudhardt 1999, 37–56, 119–26, 150–80. On these poems as paraphrase and their links to school exercises, especially *ethopoiea*, see Agosti 2001, 203–5, 2002, 90, 2005, 43–45; cf. Miguélez-Cavero 2008, 313.

5. As reported by Photius, *Bibliotheca* Codex 183–4. Eudocia's biblical centos also retell Scripture in hexameter verse, on which see Whitby 2007 with further bibliography.

6. On Nonnus' poem and his paraphrastic technique, see with further bibliography the excellent edition of *Paraphrasis* 11 by Spanoudakis 2014, part of the project to produce comprehensive editions and commentaries for the whole poem led by Enrico Livrea: see Livrea 1989 and 2000, Agosti 2003 etc.

7. More discussion of paraphrastic technique and the theory of translation can be found in Faulkner 2014.

8. See further Faulkner 2019, 212–13. Aramaic Targumim of the Hebrew Bible also had interpretative aims, on which see McNamara (2010).

9. See Lampe s.v. σαφήνεια.

10. Green 2006, 91–3 draws a distinction between instances where the poet makes an "active and conscious contribution" (where he makes a choice) and those where he follows a familiar tradition. This builds upon Röttger 1996, 17 who differentiates between "implicit" and "explicit" exegesis in Juvencus.

11. See Green 2006, 84–103 ("Teaching is as important to Juvencus as narrative. He presents Christ's *dicta*, or *doctrina*, as well as his *facta*."), with a survey of Juvencus' possible explanation or exegesis of Scripture; earlier Fichtner 1994, 201–4 and Colombi 1997. The didactic intention and exegetical

though more liberal with respect to amplification of his source text than Juvencus, expands creatively upon the scriptural model in his fifth-century Greek paraphrase of Saint John's Gospel, paying careful attention to both the narrative progression of his paraphrase and contemporary or well-known issues concerning the interpretation of the Gospel of John. He evidently consulted commentaries on the Gospel, especially that of Cyril of Alexandria, on which certain of his interventions seem to depend, as well as other patristic sources.[12]

The paraphrase of the Septuagint Psalms in Greek hexameters, the so-called *Metaphrasis Psalmorum*, is another prominent example of early Christian biblical poetry occupied with scriptural exegesis. The traditional attribution of the poem to the fourth-century bishop Apollinaris of Laodicea, who was condemned at the Council of Constantinople in 381,[13] was rejected in the last century by Joseph Golega in favour of a mid-fifth-century date, which has become the *communis opinio*.[14] He argued that the theology expressed in the poem is incompatible with the heretical views of Apollinaris and that the addressee of the prologue, a certain Markianos, is to be identified with the presbyter of that name who was an administrator under Patriarch Gennadius (458–71). I have written recently in support of a fourth-century date and Apollinaris' authorship of the poem, on the grounds that the Christology and Pneumatology of the paraphrase are in fact compatible with our fragmentary knowledge of Apollinaris' views, which may have changed and developed over time, and that comments of Gregory of Nazianzus' in his letter to Cledonius (*ep.* 101.73) probably refer to the poem.[15] One cannot be certain, but if the poem does belong to the fourth century, it is the earliest large-scale biblical poetic paraphrase in Greek.

---

interventions of later Latin biblical paraphrasts, such as Sedulius and Arator, becomes more explicit. See McGill 2012, 344–45.

12. The classic treatment of correspondence between Nonnus' paraphrase and Cyril of Alexandria's commentary is Golega 1930, 127–30. The influence of exegetical sources is discussed *passim* in the commentaries upon the poem, e.g., Livrea 1989, Agosti 2003. See recently Spanoudakis 2014, 18–23, who explores possible influence from the commentaries of Origen, John Chrysostom, and Theodore of Mopsuestia, as well as homilies on the Lazarus episode. However, Nonnus' sources were not limited to commentaries and strictly exegetical works. As Simelidis 2016, 289 argues, "Nonnus is not only aware of contemporary debates, but he treats patristic exegesis with a critical mind … he must have drawn on a variety of patristic works, other than commentaries."

13. *NPNF* 2, 14. See Young 2010, 253.

14. Golega 1939 and 1960, with bibliography of earlier views. More recently, see e.g., the helpful and nuanced review of the chronology by De Stefani 2008.

15. Faulkner 2020a, 1–31.

Whether it is a product of the fourth or the fifth century, the *Metaphrasis Psalmorum* also reflects influence from and conscious engagement with the Christian exegetical tradition. In contrast to Nonnus' paraphrase of Saint John's Gospel, which frequently amplifies the scriptural source with much rhetorical flourish, the *Metaphrasis Psalmorum* follows quite closely the structure and wording of the Septuagint text, with one hexameter verse most commonly corresponding to one stichus of the Septuagint. This difference, which is probably due to multiple factors (including individual authorial style and the influence of the stichometric structure of the Psalms), results in a difference of scale in interpretative and rhetorical intervention,[16] but the underlying paraphrastic principles appear similar in the two poems.[17] The expression of Christian truth is reclothed in the beauty of classical poetic language, whose nature simultaneously creates challenges for the precise rendering of Scripture and opportunities for rhetorical enhancement and exegetical intervention.[18] As noted above, some cases in the *Metaphrasis Psalmorum* show that the poet is in active dialogue with exegetical sources:[19] The paraphrase of LXX Ps 41:6/41: 12/42:5 ἵνα τί περίλυπος εἶ, ψυχή, καὶ ἵνα τί συνταράσσεις με; ("Why are you deeply grieved, soul, and why do you upset me?") by θυμέ, τί δηθύνεις; τί δε μοι νόον ἔνδον ὀρίνεις; ("Soul, why do you tarry? Why do you trouble my mind within me?" *Met.* 41.11/41.27 / 42.12), which in isolation appears to depart from the meaning of the model text,[20] is explained by the exegesis of the verse represented in Gregory of Nyssa's *On the Inscriptions of the Psalms*—he says that the verse is exclaimed both in the middle and at the end of the psalm because the soul is "eager to attain that for which it longs and considers the brief delay in the participation in good things a misfortune" (σπεύδουσα τοῦ ποθουμένου τυχεῖν καὶ τὴν ἐν ὀλίγῳ τῆς τῶν ἀγαθῶν μετουσίας ἀναβολὴν ἐν

---

16. As Spanoudakis 2014, 18 comments of Nonnus, "Paraphrasing a sacred text primarily by means of amplification involves much interpretation."

17. For a fuller comparison of the rhetorical style and paraphrastic technique of Nonnus and the *Metaphrasis Psalmorum*, see Faulkner 2014.

18. The poet of the *Metaphrasis Psalmorum* indicates in the prologue of the poem (lines 15–23) that he intends to restore the grace of the metre (χάρις μέτρων), which was lost in the Septuagint translation of the Hebrew.

19. For more on the examples of exegesis in the *Metaphrasis Psalmorum* discussed briefly here, see Faulkner 2019, 216–18, 2020, 51–56.

20. The opening of the line θυμέ, τί δηθύνεις; echoes the opening line of one of Gregory of Nazianzus' so-called *Poemata Arcana* (*carm.* I.1 3.1); see Moreschini-Sykes 1997, 115–16, who with Golega 1960, 84–85 assume that the poet of the *Metaphrasis* is imitating Gregory.

συμφορᾷ ποιουμένη).²¹ Elsewhere, in his paraphrase of LXX Ps 15: 3–4 the poet advances an interpretation of the verses which follows closely the exegetical exposition of Origen's first homily on the Psalm, both of whom invoke Is 29:13 (~Mt 15:8, Mk 7:6) in their positive interpretation of οὐδὲ μὴ μνησθῶ τῶν ὀνομάτων αὐτῶν διὰ χειλέων μου ("I will not recall their names with my lips.") as applying to the holy ones of God.²²

To what extent does the paraphrast identify with and broadcast this role as scriptural interpreter? As discussed above, the instructive intentions of Christian classicizing poetry are well known. Gregory of Nazianzus famously includes amongst his reasons for writing poetry that it might serve as a pleasant drug of persuasion (τερπνὸν ... φάρμακον πειθοῦς), which seems to relate to schools.²³ The recasting of Scripture into verse by Apollinaris of Laodicea (and by tradition his father) is also linked to the school curriculum by the fifth-century historians Socrates and Sozomen, who report that they undertook their project in response to the emperor Julian's edict of 362 banning Christians from teaching pagan texts.²⁴ Latin biblical epic also from its outset in the first half of the fourth century had didactic aims, most pronounced in later poets of the fifth and sixth centuries who openly express their objective to educate and interpret Scripture:²⁵ Victorius (5th c.), whose *Alethia* retells the beginning of Genesis, declares his purpose to lead the young to the true path of virtue.²⁶ In his *Carmen Paschale*, a poetic account of the Gospels, Sedulius (5th c.) interprets through quotation of other passages of Scripture in a manner characteristic of biblical commentary or homily.²⁷ Even in the

---

21. *Ps. titt.* 58 Reynard; translation Heine 1995.

22. Is 29:13: ἐγγίζει μοι ὁ λαὸς οὗτος ἐν τῷ στόματι αὐτοῦ καὶ ἐν τοῖς χείλεσιν αὐτῶν τιμῶσί με, ἡ δὲ καρδία αὐτῶν πόρρω ἀπέχει ἀπ' ἐμοῦ ("These people draw near me; they honour me with their lips, while their heart is far from me."). The paraphrast renders the Septuagint verse as *Met.* 9 οὔνομά τ' ἐκ πραπίδων οὐ χείλεσι, μνήσομαι αὐτῶν. See Origen, *Hom. I in Psalmum XV*, 7 ed. Perrone 2015, 84–86.

23. Greg. Naz. II.1.39 (ed. De Blasi 2017 = PG 37,1312–13). See Simelidis 2009, 24–30.

24. Aspects of this story about Apollinaris and his father may be fictional, and Julian's law cannot practically have had an enduring effect; see Agosti 2001, Speck 2003, 166–9. Nevertheless, Julian's law was widely condemned, even long after his death and its repeal, which attests to its rhetorical appeal for Christians citing pagan persecution: cf. Greg. Naz., *or.* 4; Ambrose, *ep.* 17. 4–5; Rufinus, *hist. eccl.* 10. 33; and Theodoret, *hist. eccl.* 3. 8.

25. See e.g. Trout 2009 and above n. 11.

26. *Precatio* 104–05 *dum teneros formare animos et corda paramus | ad verum virtutis iter puerilibus annis*, with McGill 2012, 345, Nodes 1993, 10–12. Cf. Hadjittofi 2020, 251 n. 8.

27. Green 2006, 230 points out, "A very conspicuous feature of Sedulius' exegesis is the principle that scripture has more than one sense. In this he conforms closely to the expository practice of the fourth and early fifth centuries, founded upon the work of Origen in the third."

case of Nonnus' paraphrase of Saint John's Gospel, whose defined narrative structure and lack of clear didactic markers aligns it more with narrative epic, has marked affinities with the didactic genre, broadly understood.[28] Instruction is also an element of late antique Christian paraphrastic poetry on extrabiblical themes. In the opening lines of her poetic paraphrase of the martyrdom of Saints Cyprian and Justina, the empress Eudocia portrays the deacon Praulius, whose preaching converts Justina to Christianity, as a poet singing Scripture, which enacts an identification of Praulius with Eudocia herself, a Christian poet whose versification of Christian narratives instructs and draws people to true faith.[29]

Indeed, an intention to teach, although not exclusive of other generic affiliations, seems to be a defining characteristic of early Christian biblical epic and poetic paraphrase. I have argued recently that the prologue to the *Metaphrasis Psalmorum* itself evokes the didactic tradition, both classical and Christian, in its form and language.[30] The prologue begins:

> ἔλπομαι ἀθανάτοιο θεοῦ κεκορυθμένος οἴμῃ
> σοὶ χάριν ἀντὶ πόνων φορέειν καὶ κέρδος ἐπ' ἔργῳ
> καὶ τυφλὸς γεγαὼς δοκέειν φάος ἄλλο κομίζειν,
> Μαρκιανὲ κλυτόμητι· τί γάρ νύ τοι ἔπρεπεν ἄλλο
> ἢ τό μοι εὑρέμεναι σέθεν ἄξιον; οὐ γὰρ ἐφετμῆς
> σεῖο, πάτερ, λαθόμην· ἐθέλω δέ τοι ἤπιος εἶναι
> εἰς ἀγαθὸν σπεύδοντι. τί δ' ἥδιον ἠὲ μερίμναις
> σῇσιν ἐπ' ἀτρύτοισι νόον φιλόμολπον ἐγείρειν,
> μεμνῆσθαι δ' ἐπέων, ὧν φθέγξαο τοῖα πιφαύσκων.

> I hope, armed with the song of immortal God,
> to bring to you joy in return for pains and reward for work,
> and, although being blind, to be able to convey another light,
> Markianos, famous for skill. For what else is indeed now more fitting,
> than for me to find something worthy of you? For your command
> I have not forgotten, father, and I want to be pleasing to you,
> who strive after good. But what is sweeter than to
> rouse the song-loving mind upon your limitless thoughts,
> and to recall the words, which you uttered speaking thus.

28. See the compelling discussion of Hadjittofi 2020. As she points out, the voice of Jesus in Nonnus' poem recalls both archaic and Hellenistic didactic poets.

29. For the text, see Bevegni 1982 and 2006. On Eudocia's portrayal of Praulius as poet, see Faulkner 2021.

30. Faulkner 2020b.

On the level of structure, the reader is immediately struck by the direct addressee, a prominent feature of Greek and Latin didactic poetry.[31] The precise
identity of Markianos has long been debated and has implications for the dating of the poem, but more important for the poetics of the paraphrase than
his real-world credentials is the literary construction of the addressee's identity.[32] The reported speech of Markianos which follows these opening lines,
recalled by the poet as a tribute to his mentor, advise undertaking the poetic
paraphrase of the Psalms "in order that others as well should know that every tongue will shout Christ the king and all nations of the earth will with all
speed supplicate him" (32-4 ἵνα γνώωσι καὶ ἄλλοι | γλῶσσ' ὅτι παντοίη Χριστὸν
βασιλῆα βοήσει | καί μιν πανσυδίη γουνάσσεται ἔθνεα γαίης); in other words,
with apostolic and broadly instructive aims, to spread true faith in Christ.
As a prototypical instructor, Markianos also provides hospitality to the poet
upon his arrival in Constantinople and teaches him the customs of the people
(πὰρ γὰρ ἐμοὶ πρώτῳ προμολὼν χθόνα Κωνσταντίνου | ἤθεα καὶ λαόν τ' ἐδάης καὶ
ἐπάσσαο σίτου, 42–3; "For through me above all, having come to Constantinople, you became familiar with its customs and people and partook of food.").

Importantly, this description of Marcianus' hospitality in the *Metaphrasis
Psalmorum* can be read figuratively as conversion or catechesis:[33] πὰρ γὰρ ἐμοὶ
πρώτῳ προμολὼν recalls the language of converts (οἱ πρώτως προσιόντες, *Const.
app.* 15), while ἐπάσσαο σίτου can be read as describing eucharistic communion.
Combined with the evocation of the Eucharist, the ἤθεα taught by Markianos may refer to the sacraments of the Church,[34] but by recalling the use of the
word a few lines earlier in the poem of the moral teachings of glorious David's
Psalter (Δαυίδου μὲν ἀγακλέος ἤθεα, 15), it may also refer to the ethical precepts
learned from Scripture, in which sense Origen also uses the term.[35] Given this
potential for an allegorical reading of his words, which constitute the most
detailed information we have about his relationship to the poet, it seems

<hr>

31. See Schiesaro-Mitsis-Strauss Clay 1994, *passim*.

32. As discussed above, Golega identified the addressee as the *oeconomus* Markianos active under
the emperor Gennadius (458–71 AD). Others have associated him with the fourth-century desert ascetic, or even the fifth-century emperor. See further Faulkner 2020, 25–30. The poet's description of Markianos includes certain details that evoke a real-world setting (e.g., his activity in Constantinople), but there
is no explicit link to a particular individual.

33. Argued persuasively by Agosti 2001, 90.

34. Agosti 2001, 90; for ἔθος in this sense cf. Gr. Nyss., *Eun.* 3.9.58.

35. Or. *princ.* 3.1.11–12 (cf. Lampe ad loc.).

legitimate to consider whether Markianos is a purely literary construct. In this vein, it is of note that the name Markianos had an existing history as addressee in Christian didactic prose reaching back to the second century. In his *Demonstration of the Apostolic Preaching*, a treatise aimed at Christian converts, Irenaeus' addresses a certain Markianos, of whose precise identity we are once again uncertain.[36] This treatise was circulating in the fourth century: Eusebius names not only Irenaeus' work but also his addressee Markianos (*h.e.* 5.26, καὶ ἄλλος [λόγος], ὃν ἀνατέθεικεν ἀδελφῷ Μαρκιανῷ τοὔνομα εἰς ἐπίδειξιν τοῦ ἀποστολικοῦ κηρύγματος.). The phraseology of the second line σοὶ χάριν ἀντὶ πόνων φορέειν καὶ κέρδος ἐπ' ἔργῳ simultaneously calls to mind Hesiod, as the poet subtly weaves together Christian and pagan didactic voices.[37] These elements of the prologue serve to create a generalized didactic atmosphere, rather than a precise reflection on the methodologies of Christian scriptural interpretation.

In what follows, I will nonetheless suggest that aspects of the poet's programmatic stance in the prologue and the imagery he employs associate the versifier of Scripture quite closely with the late antique Christian interpreter of Scripture. Peter Martens has recently sketched "some of the leading contours in early Christian portraits of ideal scriptural interpreters," which will serve as a helpful framework for the present investigation.[38] He organizes the ideal qualities of scriptural interpreters into three main categories, essential elements of which I summarize here:

1) Interpreter's Aim: "Early Christians invariably presented the aim of their scriptural exegesis as the discovery of a message capable of transforming its readers and hearers;" "The overarching expectation of scriptural interpreters was … to discover and communicate the divine message of salvation … [they] perceived themselves as agents of religious transformation.… they fundamentally saw themselves as brokers of salvation, linking audiences to the Christian way of life that was often recalcitrantly communicated in the Scriptures."

36. The *Demonstration* survives only in an Armenian translation: see Rousseau 1995, Behr 1997, Graham 2001.

37. The second half of the line combines *Works and Days* 381–82 σοὶ δ' εἰ πλούτου θυμὸς ἐέλδεται ἐν φρεσὶν ᾗσιν, | ὧδ' ἔρδειν, καὶ ἔργον ἐπ' ἔργῳ ἐργάζεσθαι ("If you desire wealth in your heart, act thus and undertake work upon work") and 644 μείζων μὲν φόρτος, μεῖζον δ' ἐπὶ κέρδει κέρδος ("The greater the cargo, the greater the profit piled upon profit."). For the broader structure of the line, cf. Th. 5.86 οὐκ ἂν ἀντὶ πόνων χάρις καθίσταιτο.

38. Martens 2019, especially 152–62; cf. his detailed exposition of Origen's exegetical approach 2012.

2) Interpreter's Education: "The prolific commentators on Scripture were highly learned scholars who had enjoyed an extended period of training under grammarians.... this education was intensely literary and oriented to the 'interpretation of the poets' (Quintilian, *inst.* 1.4.2);" "By extracting what was true and useful from this schooling and putting it to its proper use ... such interpreters were engaging in an act of worship. Both Origen and Augustine advanced this point, arguing that in repurposing 'pagan' learning for scriptural study, interpreters were symbolically re-enacting the plundering of the Egyptians ... (Origen, *ep.* 2 [*ad Gregorium*]; Augustine, *doct. chr.* 2. 40. 60–1)."

3) Interpreter's Manner:[39] a) *Moral and Doctrinal Qualities*—"Those who came to the text with what were considered to be disfigured moral and doctrinal sensibilities were poorly disposed to uncover Scripture's salutary message;" b) *Exegetical Precedent*—"Another feature of the successful interpreter was adherence to earlier exegetical authorities.... Paul in particular became the authority par excellence for a symbolic approach to Scripture;" c) *Exegetical Virtues*—"Early Christians employed a large moral lexicon to describe the virtues ideal interpreters ought to espouse while studying Scripture ... perhaps most frequently, the need to examine texts carefully and attentively;" d) *Inspiration*—"we frequently find interpreters turning their gaze heavenward in prayer, requesting divine help for deciphering Scripture's riddles.... Interpretation, then, often became an inspired affair, a conversation between human interpreter and divine author."

It will be immediately obvious from the preceding discussion that several of these qualities of the ideal scriptural interpreter were inherently shared by late antique poets of the fourth to sixth centuries, who were formed in the same educational milieu as exegetes such as Origen. Classical poetry was, as Martens observes, at the core of the school curriculum, which underlay the development of Christian classicizing poetry in both Greek and Latin.[40] Patristic authors, such as Basil in his *Letter to Young Men on Greek Literature*, recognized value in studying Hellenic "pagan" literature, and many early Christian poets, such as Gregory of Nazianzus or Apollinaris of Laodicea, were also prolific authors of prose engaged with elucidating Scripture and Christian

39. In his discussion of the ideal interpreter's manner, Martens draws attention to parallels with the portrait of the ideal philosopher.

40. See Cameron (2016), 163–84. On Christian poetry and schools, above *passim*.

morality. At the heart of the early Christian poetic agenda is the repurposing of classical learning to express Christian truth,[41] a point made unequivocally in the prologue of the *Metaphrasis Psalmorum*. In lines 15–34, the narrator states that he will restore the metrical grace of the original, which was lost in the Greek prose translation of the Septuagint, and on account of which the Greeks (i.e. non-Christians) have thought their songs better than Christian literature (21–3, ἔνθεν Ἀχαιοί | μείζονα μὲν φρονέεσκον ἐπὶ σφετέρῃσιν ἀοιδαῖς, | ἡμετέρας δ᾽ οὐ πάμπαν ἐθάμβεον, "The Greeks therefore always thought better of their own songs and did not at all marvel at ours."). Closely related is the transformational aim of the poet, as Martens says of ideal interpreters, to link 'audiences to the Christian way of life that was often recalcitrantly communicated in the Scriptures.' The beauty of classical "pagan" poetry is appropriated by the poet for the apostolic mission to transform the religious life of his audience and bring the message of Christ to the whole world (32-4, ἵνα γνώωσι καὶ ἄλλοι | γλῶσσ᾽ ὅτι παντοίη Χριστὸν βασιλῆα βοήσει | καί μιν πανσυδίῃ γουνάσσεται ἔθνεα γαίης ~ Phil 2:11, "in order that others as well should know that every tongue will shout Christ the king and all nations of the earth will with all speed supplicate him").[42] Building upon this and the other didactic markers in the prologue, the poet goes on to discuss at length the teaching of all nations by the Apostles through the inspiration of the Holy Spirit (44–104), echoing Acts 2:2–11 and openly linking his hexameter composition to the apostolic mission (105–110).

Beyond this overlap in the aims and education of early Christian poets and scriptural interpreters, there is considerable commonality in their manners. Perhaps most striking is the appeal that both make to divine inspiration. In the first line of the *Metaphrasis Psalmorum* quoted above, the poet claims to be inspired, literally "armed" by the song of God (1, ἔλπομαι ἀθανάτοιο θεοῦ κεκορυθμένος οἴμῃ). At the very end of the poem, he similarly claims Christ as a

---

41. The image of the Israelites taking the spoils of the Egyptians, used by Origen and Augustine of their use of classical learning, is also employed by early Christian poets. See Paulinus, *ep.* 16. 11, with Gnilka 2012, 132–40. On Gregory of Nazianzus' rhetorical prose, grounded in classical learning, and exegesis, see in this volume Robin Darling Young's chapter.

42. The Psalms were in their Septuagint version already highly valued by Patristic authors for their beauty and as a vehicle for education. E.g. Basil, *hom. in Ps.* 1. 1–2 τὸ ἐκ τῆς μελῳδίας τερπνὸν τοῖς δόγμασιν ἐγκατέμιξεν … κατὰ τοὺς σοφοὺς τῶν ἰατρῶν, οἳ τῶν φαρμάκων τὰ αὐστηρότερα πίνειν διδόντες τοῖς κακοσίτοις, μέλιτι πολλάκις τὴν κύλικα περιχρίουσι; Jer., *ep.* 107. 4 (of the education of the soul) *adhuc tenera lingua psalmis dulcibus inbuatur*, Gr. Nyss., *pss. titt.* 8. ὁ μέγας Δαυὶδ τῇ περὶ τῶν ἀρετῶν φιλοσοφίᾳ τὴν μελῳδίαν κατέμιξεν, οἷόν τινα μέλιτος ἡδονὴν τῶν ὑψηλῶν καταχέας δογμάτων.

support for his singing (110, Χριστὸν ἀεὶ ζώοντα … ἐπαρωγὸν ἀοιδῆς). It is common in Christian classicizing poetry for the poet to signal that he is divinely inspired by Christ or the Holy Spirit, which both takes the place of the traditional appeal to the Muses in classical texts and in the case of scriptural paraphrase justifies the poetic adaptations of the source text.[43]

The imagery of light in the opening lines of the *Metaphrasis Psalmorum* is also of note. The poet, inspired by God, conveys a "new light" despite himself being blind (3, καὶ τυφλὸς γεγαὼς δοκέειν φάος ἄλλο κομίζειν), which is again reminiscent of the imagery employed by exegetes.[44] Origen, in a fragment of his *Homilies on Luke*, explains that with careful study of Scripture, the Word illuminates the knowledge of his glory in our hearts, citing 2 Cor 4:6 (ἐκ σκότους φῶς λάμψει, ὃς ἔλαμψεν ἐν ταῖς καρδίαις ἡμῶν πρὸς φωτισμὸν τῆς γνώσεως τῆς δόξης τοῦ θεοῦ).[45] This passage of Corinthians reflects upon the revelation of gospel truth to the righteous, whereas God has blinded the minds of unbelievers so that they should not see the glorious light of the gospel (2 Cor 4:4, ὁ θεὸς τοῦ ἀιῶνος τούτου ἐτύφλωσεν τὰ νοήματα τῶν ἀπίστων εἰς τὸ μὴ αὐγάσαι τὸν φωτισμὸν τοῦ εὐαγγελίου τῆς δόξης τοῦ Χριστοῦ).[46]

The figure of the blind poet, which clearly evokes and announces the new Christian departure from Homer, the pagan bard *par excellence*, is also an expression of the poet's humility,[47] one of the exegetical virtues commended by

---

43. See Shorrock 2011, 22–33, Faulkner 2014, 200–05. For divine inspiration in Latin poets, cf. Juv. 1.25–27, Sedul. 1.85, Arat. 2.577–78, with Green 2006, 21–22, 300–02. Paulinus (*carm.* 10.19–32) explicitly rejects as a source of inspiration the Muses and deaf Apollo, who are replaced by a greater God (*nunc alia mentem vis agit, maior Deus*). In Greek poets, Greg. Naz., *Arc.* 1.22. On the appeal to divine aid in Origen, see further Martens 2012, 181–86.

44. For the poet's "new" or "different" light (φάος ἄλλο), one might compare Origen's discussion of true divine light as different from other forms of light: *hom. Ps.* I in Ps. 67. 10 (ed. Perrone 2015, 198) φῶς ἀληθινὸν ἕτερον παρὰ τὸ μὴ ἀληθινόν and *Io.* I. 9 καὶ ἕτερον ἀγαθὸν φῶς τοῦ κόσμου, φῶς τυγχάνον ἀληθινὸν καὶ φῶς τῶν ἀνθρώπων. In his famous programmatic response to Ausonius, defending his new Christian focus, Paulinus (*carm.* 10.1–32) repeatedly uses *alius* to underscore the novel and transformative otherness of his Christian poetry (cf. also *carm.* 22.6 *noua lux*); see Hardie 2019, 23, 161.

45. Origen, *fr. in Lc.* 151/GCS 9, 287.10–14, with Martens 2012, 183.

46. Cf. later Theodoret, *Ezech.* Pref., who calls upon readers to follow Ps 118:18 LXX ἀποκάλυψον τοὺς ὀφθαλμούς μου in asking God, who gives wisdom to the blind, to uncover their eyes. See Martens 2019, with further examples of requests for divine aid. The figure of spiritual sight and blindness is widespread (cf. Acts 9:17–19 of Paul's conversion). For τυφλός used metaphorically of a lack of understanding in early Christian literature, see also Bauer s.v.

47. On the poet's blindness as metaphorical rather than literal, cf. Gitschel 1936, Golega 1960, 26, Agosti 2001, 88. On the figure of Homer and the poet's engagement with the classical literary tradition in the opening lines, see Faulkner 2014, 202–03.

Origen.[48] The poet presents himself and his spiritual father Markianos as paradigms of faithfulness, who constantly read Scripture as a source of holiness and virtue. Markianos is one who "strives after good" (7, εἰς ἀγαθὸν σπεύδοντι), while his first words introducing his recommendation that the poet undertake the paraphrase of the Psalter state plainly that "one concerned with prudence ought not to do anything else than to nourish his human soul with virtues" (10–11, οὔ τις ἐχεφροσύνῃ μεμελημένος ἄλλό τι ῥέξειν | ὤφελεν ἢ ψυχὴν ἀρεταῖς μεροπηίδα φέρβειν). He is later described as having chosen the Psalter, clear-toned song, as his constant companion in old age, as he marvels in his soul at the miracles of God (50-3, λιγυρὴν ἠσπάσσατο μολπὴν | γήραος εὐφήμοιο συνέμπορον αἰὲν ἐλέσθαι. καὶ γὰρ ἐποπτεύων βασιλήια θαύματα θυμῷ). The poet himself works according to the model of Markianos, accomplishing his desire that God be hymned also in the Ionian language of Homer (109, Μαρκιανὸς ποθέεσκεν, ἐγὼ δὲ οἱ ἤνυσα βουλήν). The prologue to the *Metaphrasis Psalmorum* therefore builds a picture of the ideal versifier of Scripture as a humble servant of God, who devotes himself to constant study of Scripture involving the mystical contemplation of God's wonders.[49]

The poet also makes clear attempts in the prologue to establish his doctrinal credentials, as do exegetes. In lines 85–87 he describes the Apostles' preaching as telling of "the Word in a woman's womb, the son of God, and God appearing in true human form, and a mortal having an immortal Father" (καὶ λόγον ἐν λαγόνεσσι γυναίαις, υἷα θεοῖο, | καὶ θεὸν ἀνδρομέῃ προφανέντ' ἀψευδέϊ μορφῇ, | καὶ βροτὸν ἀθανάτοιο βίην γενετήρος ἔχοντα). Broadly Nicene in their formulation, these lines are much discussed as they relate to the thorny question of the poem's authorship and dating.[50] More important for the present discussion than the precise doctrine they express is that these lines fundamentally shape the portrait of the poet as doctrinally upright in the tradition of the Apostles. In justifying his paraphrastic project, the poet also appeals directly to the authority of the humble Apostle Paul: having in lines 33–34 paraphrased Phil 2:11, that every tongue will confess that Jesus Christ is Lord, the poet says that "the cobbler Paul did not lie saying this" (οὐδ' ὁ σκυτοτόμος τὸ λέγων ἐψεύσατο Παῦλος).[51]

48. *Comm. in Rom.* 7.17.4, with Martens 2019, 160–61.

49. On Origen's exegetical activity as "religious" or "mystical," see Martens 2012, 184 with earlier bibliography.

50. See above pages 3–4.

51. For the Apostles as poor and humble leatherworkers (σκυτοτόμοι), see Basil, *hom.* 23, *PG* 31, 593

In conclusion, the prologue to the *Metaphrasis Psalmorum* does not communicate a precise manifesto of exegetical methodology, with direct reflection upon allegorical and literal interpretations of Scripture, such as we find elsewhere in early Christian poetry.[52] It nevertheless conveys unmistakeably the poet's didactic intentions and paints a portrait of the poet which overlaps considerably with the fundamental qualities of the ideal early Christian interpreter of Scripture. Poets of course have broader aesthetic aims that diverge from those of the scriptural interpreter writing in prose. But it should come as no surprise to the reader of the prologue that the *Metaphrasis Psalmorum*, which like every translation or paraphrase is inherently an act of interpretation,[53] goes on to engage directly with the Christian exegetical tradition.

Bibliography

Agosti, Gianfranco. "Considerazioni preliminari sui generi letterari dei poemi del Codice Bodmer." *Aegyptus* 81 (2001): 185–217.

Agosti, Gianfranco. "I poemetti del *Codice Bodmer* e il loro ruolo nella storica della poesia tardoantica." In *Le Codex des Visions*, edited by André Hurst and J. Rudhardt (Geneva: Librarie Droz, 2002), 73–114.

Agosti, Gianfranco. *Nonno di Panopolis. Parafrasi del Vangelo di San Giovanni: Canto Quinto*. Firenze: Università degli studi di Firenze, 2003.

Agosti, Gianfranco. "L'etopea nella poesia greca tardoantica." in *ΗΘΟΠΟΙΙΑ. La représentation de caractères entre fiction scolaire et réalité vivante à l'époque impérial et tardive*, edited by Eugenio Amato and Jacques Schamp (Salerno : Helios, 2005), 34–60.

Gianfranco, Agosti. "Greek Poetry." In *The Oxford Handbook of Late Antiquity*, edited by Scott Johnson (Oxford: Oxford University Press, 2012), 361–404.

Behr, John. *St Irenaeus of Lyons: On the Apostolic Preaching*. New York: St Vladimirs Seminary, 1997.

Bevegni, Claudio. "Eudociae Augustae Martyrium S. Cypriani I, 1–99." *Prometheus* 8 (1982), 249–62.

ποιμὴν καὶ πένης, ταῦτα τῷ Χριστιανῷ τὰ σεμνολογήματα … ἐὰν τοὺς μαθητὰς [ζητήσῃς], σκυτοτόμοι πένητες. οὐδεὶς πλούσιος, οὐδαμοῦ περιφάνεια. In his *Commentary on Romans* (10.18.2), according to Rufinus' Latin translation, Origen interprets the controversial term σκηνοποιός used of Paul's profession at Acts 18:3 as "cobbler" (*sutor*). John Chrysostom and Theodoret also later identify Paul as σκυτοτόμος. On the anti-pagan irony of Paul's lowly yet authoritative position, cf. Golega (1939), 21.

52. See, for example, the iambic *praefatio* to Prudentius' overtly allegorical *Psychomachia*, which as Hardie 2019, 205 puts it "sketches a framework of interpretation reaching from Genesis to the New Testament and applicable to Prudentius's individual reader, and puts on the table a range of the kinds of allegory deployed in the poem." Glau 2000 ties the allegory in the *Psychomachia* closely to Origen's hermeneutic.

53. On translation/paraphrase as interpretation see further Faulkner 2014, 2019 with bibliography.

Bevegni, Claudio. *Eudocia Augusta: Storia di San Cipriano*. Milan: Adelphi, 2006.

Cameron, Allen. *Wandering Poets and Other Essays on Late Greek Literature and Philosophy*. Oxford: Oxford University Press, 2016.

Colombi, Emanuela. "*Paene ad verbus:* gli *Evangeliorum libri* di Giovenco tra parafrasi e commento." *Cassiodorus* 3 (1997): 9–36.

Cutino, Michele. *L'Alethia di Claudio Mario Vittorio: la parafrasi biblica come forma di espressione teológica*. Rome: Institutum Patristicum Augustianum, 2009).

De Blasi, Alessandro. *Gregorio di Nazianzo εἰς τὰ ἔμμετρα (carme II 1, 39)*. Master's Thesis, Università degli studi di Padova, 2017.

Faulkner Andrew. "Faith and Fidelity in Biblical Epic: The *Metaphrasis Psalmorum*, Nonnus, and the Theory of Translation." In *Nonnus of Panopolis in Context*, edited by Konstantinos Spanoudakis (Berlin: De Gruyter, 2014), 195–210.

Faulkner, Andrew. "Paraphrase and Metaphrase." In *The Oxford Handbook of Early Christian Biblical Interpretation*, edited by Paul M. Blowers and Peter W. Martens (Oxford: Oxford University Press, 2019), 210–20.

Faulkner, Andrew. *Apollinaris of Laodicea:* Metaphrasis Psalmorum. Oxford: Oxford University Press, 2020a.

Faulkner, Andrew. "Davidic Didactic Hexameters: the Generic Stance of the *Metaphrasis Psalmorum*." In *The Genres of Late Antique Christian Poetry: Between Modulations and Transpositions*, edited by Anna Lefteratou and Fotini Hadjittofi (Berlin: De Gruyter, 2020b), 265–74.

Faulkner, Andrew. "Eudocia's Singing Deacon: Another Programmatic Passage in Late Antique Christian Verse." *JHS* 141 (2021): 1–8.

Fichtner, Rudolf. *Taufe und Versuchung Jesu in den Evangeliorum Libri quattor des Bibeldichters Juvencus*. (Stuttgart: Teubner, 1994).

Gitschel, J. "War der Verfasser der dem Apolinarius zugeschriebenen Psalmenmetaphrase wirklich körperlich blind?" In *Munera philologica L. Ćwikliński oblata* (Posnan: 1936), 104–10.

Glau, Katherina. "Allegorie als Reflex der Origenischen Hermeneutik in der *Psychomachia* des Prudentius." In *Hortus litterarum antiquarum: Festschrift für Hans Armin Gärtner zum 70. Geburtstag*, edited by Andreas Haltenhoff and Fritz-Heiner Mutschler, (Heidelberg: C. Winter, 2000), 161–75.

Gnilka, Christian. *Der Begriff des rechten Gebrauchs*. 2nd ed. (Basel: Schwabe Verlag, 2012).

Golega, Joseph. *Studien über die Evangeliendichtung des Nonnos von Panopolis: Ein Beitrag zur Geschichte der Bibeldichtung im Altertum* (Breslau: Verlag Müller & Seiffert, 1930).

Golega, Joseph. "Verfasser und Zeit der Psalterparaphrase des Apolinarios." *Byzantinische Zeitschrift* 39 (1939): 1–22.

Golega, Joseph. *Der Homerische Psalter. Studien über die dem Apolinarios von Laodikeia zugeschriebenen Psalmenparaphrase* (Ettal: Buch-Kunstverlag Ettal, 1960).

Graham, Susan. "Structure and Purpose of Irenaeus' *Epideixis*." StPatr 36 (2001): 210–21.

Green, Roger. *Latin Epics of the New Testament* (Oxford: Oxford University Press, 2006).

Hadjittofi, Fotini. "Nonnus *Paraphrase* as Didactic Epic." In *The Genres of Late Antique Christian Poetry: Between Modulations and Transpositions*, edited by Anna Lefteratou and Fotini Hadjittofi (Berlin: De Gruyter, 2020), 250–64.

Hardie, Philip. *Classicism and Christianity in Late Antique Latin Poetry*. Berkeley: University of California Press, 2019.

Heine, Ronald. *Gregory of Nyssa's Treatise on the Inscriptions of the Psalms*. Oxford: Oxford University Press, 1995.

Hurst, André and Rudhardt, Jean. *Papyrus Bodmer XXX–XXXVII. « Codex des Visions » : Poèmes divers*. Munich : K. G. Saur, 1999.

Jakobi, Rainer. "Zur Datierung der Heptateuchdichtung." *Hermes* 138 (2010): 124–29.

Livrea, Enrico. *Nonno di Panopoli. Parafrasi del Vangelo di S. Giovanni: Canto XVIII*. Napoli: M. D'Auria Editore, 1989.

Livrea, Enrico. *Nonno di Panopoli. Parafrasi del Vangelo di S. Giovanni: Canto B*. Bologna: Biblioteca patristica, 2000.

Martens, Peter. *Origen and Scripture: the Contours of the Exegetical Life*. Oxford: Oxford University Press, 2012.

Martens, Peter. "Ideal Interpreters." In *The Oxford Handbook of Early Christian Biblical Interpretation*, edited by Paul M. Blowers and Peter W. Martens (Oxford: Oxford University Press, 2019), 149–65.

McGill, Scott. "Latin Poetry." In *The Oxford Handbook of Late Antiquity*, edited by Scott Johnson (Oxford: Oxford University Press, 2012), 335–60.

McNamara, Martin. *Targum and Testament Revisited: Aramaic Paraphrases of the Hebrew Bible*. 2nd ed. Grand Rapids, MI: Eerdmans, 2010).

Miguélez-Cavero, Laura. *Poems in Context: Greek Poetry in the Egyptian Thebaid 200–600 AD*. Berlin: De Gruyter, 2008.

Moreschini, Claudio and Sykes, David. *St Gregory of Nazianzus: Poemata Arcana*. Oxford: Oxford University Press, 1997.

Nodes, Daniel Joseph. *Doctrine and Exegesis in Biblical Latin Poetry*. Leeds: Cairns, 1993.

Perrone, Lorenzo. *Origenes XIII: Die neuen Psalmenhomilien*. Berlin: De Gruyter, 2015.

Roberts Michael. *Biblical Epic and Rhetorical Paraphrase in Late Antiquity*. Liverpool: Cairns, 1985.

Röttger, Wilfried. *Studien zur Lichtmotivik bei Iuvencus*. Münster: Lehmanns 1996.

Rousseau, Adelin. *Irénée de Lyon: Démonstration de la prédication apostolique*. Paris: Le Cerf, 1995.

Schiesaro, Alessandro, Mitsis, Phillip, and Strauss Clay, Jenny (eds.). *Mega nepios. Il destinatario nell'epos didascalico. The addressee in Didactic Epic*. Pisa : Materiali e discussion per l'analisi dei testi classici 31, 1994.

Shorrock, Robert. *The Myth of Paganism: Nonnus, Dionysus and the World of Late Antiquity*. London: Bristol Classical Press, 2011).

Simelidis, Christos. "Nonnus and Christian Literature." In *Brill's Companion to Nonnus of Panopolis*, edited by Domenico Accorinti (Leiden: Brill), 289–307.

Spanoudakis, Konstantinos. *Nonnus of Panopolis: Paraphrasis of the Gospel of John XI*. Oxford: Oxford University Press, 2014.

Speck, Paul. "A More Charitable Verdict: Review of N. G. Wilson, *Scholars of Byzantium*"
    In *Understanding Byzantium: Studies in Byzantine Historical Sources*, edited by Paul
    Speck and Saroltà Takács (Aldershot: Ashgate, 2003), 163–78.
Trout, Dennis. *Paulinus of Nola*. Berkeley: University of California Press, 1999.
Trout, Dennis. "Latin Christian epics of Late Antiquity." In *A Companion to Ancient Epic*,
    edited by John Miles Foley (Malden, MA and Oxford: Blackwell, 2009), 550–61.
Young, Frances. *From Nicaea to Chalcedon*. 2nd ed. London: Baker, 2010.

Robin Darling Young

8. EXEGETICAL BIOGRAPHY

Gregory of Nazianzus' Oration
on his Sister, Gorgonia

At the end of the fourth century two early Christian authors, elaborating on the works of Origen and Clement of Alexandria, described their sisters as philosophers and holy women. Where Origen had both consulted with Christian women thinkers and envisioned a biblical woman as an apostle, his fourth-century heirs—Gregory of Nazianzus, Gregory of Nyssa—went much further, praising their kinswomen. They wrote detailed accounts of their sisters as ascetic philosophers, far outstripping Clement's and Origen's in length and detail, and adapted scriptural exegesis to apply it to the lives of women in their own region of Asia Minor in the second half of the fourth century.[1] Both authors may have inspired Evagrius of Pontus to interpret Melania the Elder similarly.[2]

1. Among other scholarly treatments of Gregory's exegesis, see Frances Young, *Biblical Exegesis and the Formation of Christian Culture,* (Cambridge and New York: Cambridge University Press, 1997), 49–118; see also her "Paideia and the Myth of Static Dogma," in Sarah Coakley and David Palin, *The Making and Remaking of Christian Doctrine: Essays in Honour of Maurice Wiles* (Oxford: Clarendon Press, 1993), 265–83; Frederick Norris, "Gregory Nazianzen: Constructing and Constructed by Scripture," in *The Bible in Greek Christian Antiquity*, edited by Paul Blowers (Notre Dame, IN: University of Notre Dame Press, 1997) Paul Gallay, "La Bible dans l'oeuvre de Grégoire de Nazianze le Théologien," in *Le monde grec ancien et la Bible*, ed. Claude Mondésert (Paris: Beauchesne, 1984; and Brian Daley, "Walking through the Word of God: Gregory of Nazianzus as a Biblical Interpreter," in *The Word Leaps the Gap: Essays in Honor of Richard B. Hays,* ed. J. Ross Wagner (Grand Rapids, MI: Eerdmans, 2008).

2. See Robin Darling Young, "The Lady Advances: Prophets and Pilgrims in Early Christianity," forthcoming in *JECS* (Winter, 2023).

This essay is a close reading of one of those exemplary lives, told as a funeral oration. Gregory of Nazianzus used the classical form of the *epitaphios logos* now infused with biblical interpretation, to present his sister as an exegete and holy woman—not only to celebrate his own family, but to propose how Christian lives should be lived, particularly by his own social class. He inscribed those lives into the biblical story as he understood it. As a rhetor of consummate skill, Gregory was able to weave scriptural language and stories into literary forms—both poetry and prose—with deep roots in ancient, pagan Hellenic.[3] True to the practices of fourth-century exegesis, Gorgonia becomes a hero like Job or Solomon, the living fulfillment of a scriptural type. His *Epitaphios Logos* exemplifies a local discussion about Christian women's devotion to discipline, interpretation, and ascetic philosophy.

Studying Gorgonia

At the turn of the twenty-first century, Gorgonia of Iconium[4] had briefly enjoyed attention among historians of early Christianity.[5] Some scholars examined her brother's oratorical portrait of her life in connection with a more general interest in the portrayal of the activity of women among early Christians. Others were interested primarily in the work of its author, but touched on the subject of the *Epitaphios Logos*[6] itself and the poetic composi-

3. An excellent description of Gregory's method in the context of poetry may be found in Brian Dunkle, *Poems on Scripture: Saint Gregory Nazianzus* (Crestwood, NY: St. Vladimir's Seminary Press, 2013).

4. Iconium is not named in the logos; Marie Madeleine Hauser-Meury records that Elias of Crete identified it as her city. See *Prosopography zu den Schriften Gregors von Nazianz* (Bonn: P. Hanstein, 1960), and Jacobus Billius, ed. Eliae Cretensis Commentarius in Gregorii Nazianzeni, Gregorii Theologi, v. 2 (Cologne: Coloniae, 1690); Jean Bernardi, *La prédication des pères cappadociens. Le prédicateur et son auditoire* (Paris: P.U.F., 1968) accepted the location of the grave and logos as Iconium.

5. For instance, in three articles in 2006: Tomas Hägg, "Playing with expectations: Gregory's funeral orations on his brother, sister and father," in *Gregory of Nazianzus Images and Reflections*, ed. Jostein Bortnes and Tomas Hägg (University of Copenhagen: Museum Tusculanum Press, 2006), 133–52; Virginia Burrus, "Life after Death: The Martyrdom of Gorgonia and the Birth of Female Hagiography," 153–70, and Susanna Elm, "Gregory's Women: Creating a Philosopher's Family," 171–93.

6. The critical edition of the text with French translation is Marie-Ange Calvet-Sebasti, *Grégoire de Nazianze, Discours 6–12* (Paris: Cerf, 1995), 246–99. The most recent English translation is in Brian E. Daley, SJ, *Gregory of Nazianzus* (London and New York: Routledge, 2006), 63–74. An earlier English translation is by Leo P. McCauley et al, *Funeral Orations by Saint Gregory Nazianzen and Saint Ambrose* (New York: Fathers of the Church, 1953). Older studies of interest are Robert C. Gregg, *Consolation Philosophy* (Philadelphia: Patristic Foundation, 1975); see also, for the long history of the logos celebrating the Attic military dead, communicating a notion of personal nobility and the character of the

tions[7] that he composed in her honor, after her death.[8] This single and philosophical ascetic became the *paterfamilias* after the death of his father and brother; long after Gorgonia's death, Gregory sent a letter to one of her children about the prospects of her grandchild, his great nephew, when he was studying rhetoric.[9] Gregory had a compelling interest in his sister and her family, both as elite members of the social world of fourth-century Asia Minor, and as emblems of Christian public life.

Certainly Gorgonia was such an elite actor. In her brother's oration, she became an example of a scriptural exegete and teacher, a philosophical woman and an ascetic wife, and a wealthy and charitable authority among the Christians of Iconium.[10] Although like almost all women in late antiquity, she did not write for or about herself, she may well have agreed with the aims of her brother's eulogy. As a wealthy Christian and a leader in the Christian community of her city, she was also a fulfillment of scriptural models; like Job, a model of patience in suffering, and like the good wife of Proverbs, a generous benefactor to the poor—or so Gregory claimed. Unlike another sister of bishops—Macrina, in her younger brother Gregory of Nyssa's portrait of a female ascetic adroit in philosophical[11] dialogue—the older Gorgonia was an example of a

---

politeia, Nicole Loraux, *The Invention of Athens: The Funeral Oration in the Classical City*, tr. Alan Sheridan (Cambridge, MA: Harvard University Press, 19860, 123–24 and for Gregory on married women, Elena Giannarelli, *La tipologia femminile nella biografia e nell'autobiografia cristiana del IVo secolo* (Rome: Sede del Istituto, 1980), 67–86.

7. PG 38, columns 21–22

8. See among others, Justin Mossay, *La mort et l'au-delà dans saint Grégoire de Nazianze* (Louvain: Université de Louvain, 1966) and "Notes sur l'herméneutique des sources littéraires de l'histoire byzantine," (*Recherches de philologie et de linguistique, III Series, Section de philologie classique* 3), 39–51; John McGuckin, *St. Gregory of Nazianzus: An Intellectual Biography* (Crestwood, NY: St. Vladimir's, 2001), 8–18; and Raymond Van Dam, *Families and Friends in Late Roman Cappadocia* (Philadelphia: University of Pennsylvania Press, 2003), 85, 93–96.

9. Ibid., *Families and Friends,* 212.

10. "In his later funeral eulogies for his brother, sister, and father, Gregory explicitly wrote himself a sacred philosophical family, closely affiliated (through *oikeiōsis*) with the divine.... His sister, Gorgonia, epitomized *sōphrosynē* as the philosopher as matriarch and mother of future philosophers.... Since Gregory issued from a sacred, philosophical, family, his closest kin were also more oikeios to God than most." Susanna Elm, *Sons of Hellenism, Fathers of the Church: Emperor Julian, Gregory of Nazianzus, and the Vision of Rome* (Berkeley: University of California Press, 2012), 219.

11. Gregory's employment of philosophy, and his understanding of himself and others as philosophers, deserves a thorough study. The last comprehensive treatment of the subject was Henri Pinault, *Le Platonisme de Saint Grégoire de Nazianze. Essai sur les relations du Christianisme et de l'Hellénisme dans son oeuvre théologique* (La Roche sur Yon: Romain, 1925). But now see Bradley Storin, "Father of Philosophers," 121–45 in *Self-Portrait in Three Colors: Gregory of Nazianzus's Epistolary Autobiography* (Berkeley: University of California Press, 2019).

married, family philosopher who had grown up in a philosophical household and also modelled silence (1 Cor 4:34) until the very end of her life.[12]

Gorgonia bore a powerful, pagan apotropaic name, invoking Athena to ward off the beheaded monster with serpentine tresses; it was customary in Cappadocia.[13] Like the names of her brothers, Gregory and Caesarius, it was not Christian or Jewish in origin, but a family name likely honoring an ancestor. The area remained strongly pagan into the sixth century, and names did not have to be Christian.[14] Thus far from signifying "the monstrosity of the female subject,"[15] the name Gorgonia's parents gave her was protective, invoking the *gorgonia*, the ancient term for red coral, "Gorgon's stone."[16] According to Pliny the Elder, Metrodoros of Skepsis[17] had reported that the coral hardened after softening in the sea, and, often affixed to a ship's mast, was reported to have repelled lightning and storms.[18] It also appears in an Egyptian *defixio*, a curse-tablet of late antiquity, as the name of a woman subject to enchantment by another woman, for erotic purposes.[19] Gorgonia may have been named after an ancestress, possibly a grandmother; but in the fourth century, Christian names had not been substituted for traditional names, and Gorgonia's was likely to have been thought unremarkable.[20]

Other features, however, do make this discourse remarkable, and worth further study. For instance, when Gregory delivered his *epitaphios logos,* possibly before the tomb, he was the first Christian to deliver a public discourse in memory of a woman.[21] He used the skills of a rhetor to persuade an audience

12. See the discussion of Susanna Elm, *Sons of Hellenism, Fathers of the Church,* 219.

13. *Iliad* 5.7.41, 8.348, 11.036.

14. See Frank R. Trombley, *Hellenic Religion and Christianization,* 2 ed (Leiden and New York: Brill, 1995), vol. 2, 74–134.

15. Op cit., 170.

16. On gorgonian corals: see Francesca Balzan and Alan Deidun, "Notes for a history of coral fishing and coral artefacts in Malta—The Significance of Coral: Apotropaic, Medical, Symbolic, Precious" in *60th anniversary of the Malta Historical Society: a commemoration,* Joseph F. Grima, ed. (Zabbar, Malta: Veritas Press 2010), 435–54.

17. See most recently Seth Long, *Excavating the Memory Palace* (Chicago: University of Chicago Press, 2020), 55, 85.

18. See Pliny the Elder, *Natural History* 37.164.

19. By another woman; see Bernadette J. Brooten, *Love Between Women: Early Christian Responses to Female Homoeroticism.* (Chicago: The University of Chicago Press, 1996), 103–10.

20. Sylvain Destephen, "Christianisation and Local Names in Asia Minor: Fall and Rise in Late Antiquity," in Robert Parker, *Changing Names: Tradition and Innovation in Greek Onomastics* (Oxford: University Press/Proceedings of the British Academy, 2019), 258–76.

21. The emperor Julian's *Thanksgiving Speech in Honor of the Empress Eusebia* may have been

of notables whom he had no power to compel; he tried to strengthen his own kinship group in the city of Iconium; he gave a practical model for the wealthy to practice the charity incumbent upon wealthy Christians.[22] He had already made a number of careful choices among the ideal qualities with which to invest her. As a wife, Gorgonia had been fruitful, hospitable, modest; as a daughter, she had emulated the example given her by her parents, the "Abraham and Sarah" of Nazianzus; as a Christian, she had been devoted to good works and prayer. Her practice of silence was notable, and for most of her life, Gregory states, it constrained her.

According to her brother, Gorgonia's silence, along with her other virtues, made her an apt model for the ostentatious Christian women of her city, Iconium.[23] They stubbornly had refused to abandon ornamentation, even for the memorial of the death of this local holy woman,[24] and at her death they had probably engaged in the traditional wailing condemned by other Christian orators of the period.[25] Yet Gregory's chief object here was not to harry the overdressed, but to create a portrait worthy of imitation mingling both the customary themes of the good wife, securely placed in a family of the curial class,[26] with attributes of the Christian ascetic, now understood as foreshadowed in the scriptural narrative—an interpretation already accomplished in the works of Athanasius.[27] Gregory is thus responsible for one of the earliest depictions of a married female ascetic, composed when Christian authors were debating the relative merits of marriage and virginity.

---

delivered after her death, but Julian was no longer a Christian when he delivered it. See Shaun Tougher, "The Advocacy of an Empress: Julian and Eusebia," *The Classical Quarterly* 48, no. 2 (1998): 595–99.

22. The latter a well-known approach since Clement of Alexandria's treatise, *Who Is the Rich Man Who is Going to Be Saved?*

23. Bernardi accepts in *Predication* 110–11, the traditional site of Iconium for Gorgonia's tomb, and that the epitaphios was pronounced before it.

24. A cult of Gorgonia developed not long after her death. See François Halkin, *Bibliotheca Hagiographica Graeca 3ed* (Brussels: Société des Bollandistes, 1951) v. 1, 227; her feast day of February 23 appears in the Martyrology of Rabban Sliba, attesting to the spread of her cult to Syria; see R. Janin, "Gorgonia," in *Bibliotheca Sanctorum* (Rome: Nuova Editrice, 1966), 121–22.

25. See Eric Rebillard, "Christian Funerals and Funerals of Christians: The Church and the Death Ritual in Late Antiquity" in *The Care of the Dead in Late Antiquity* (Ithaca, NY: Cornell University Press, 2010), 123–39.

26. Thomas A. Kopecek, "The Social Class of the Cappadocian Fathers," *CH* 42, no. 4 (December, 1973): 453–66. Kopecek demonstrated from Gregory's Letter 429 that his father had belonged to the curial class before becoming a bishop, as did Gregory himself and his cousin Amphilochius of Iconium.

27. See the prologue to the *Life of Anthony*, and in the same tradition, (Pseudo) Athanasius, *Discourse on Salvation, to a Virgin*.

Another notable feature of this work occurs in its very first line, where Gregory speaks in the register of local rhetors and philosophers. "Praising a sister, I am amazed at my own (τὰ ὀικεῖα)—but I will not speak falsely because they are my own; it is because they are true that they merit praise." Gregory opens the work by recalling, for his educated listeners, an ancient philosophical conundrum: is "one's own," primarily family fortune and obligations, opposed to civic concord? His refined listeners knew that, in the *Republic*, Plato thought family obligations obstructed political concord, though Aristotle took the opposite point of view. Plato's aim is admirable, Aristotle thought, but impractical.[28] Gregory also recalls Plato for his audience by citing, favorably, a quotation from Gorgias' *Praise of Helen*.[29] But like earlier rhetors, he adds that a discourse is a necessity to fulfill a debt of piety, to lead others to desire the same virtue, and to conduct others to perfection or completion (*katartizein*). No listener could have doubted his learning before Gregory returns to praising his own family in his parents, having already praised it in his oration at the death of his brother. But he shows his audience that he will accomplish this praise by inscribing not just a Christian ascetic, but his own family into the scriptural narrative of the righteous—for which he had to enlist the most prominent family of the Septuagint, that of Abraham.[30] Gregory's skillful combination of philosophy and Scripture in the very first line of his oration—all to the benefit of his own family—could not have been lost on his audience, just as the name of his sister would also have been familiar to his listeners.

It is not possible to arrive at a full comprehension of Gorgonia's ascetic life in its context; Gregory's tribute, along with his memorial poems, still reflects his own purposes, and she herself might have chosen a different list of qualities to emphasize. Yet Gregory may accurately have reported what he also wished to stress when he spoke in front of a gathering of those who knew her—her children, possibly, and the notables of her city: that his sister developed a practice harmonizing both the ascetic and the domestic realms; and more remarkably, she did so unobtrusively. Gorgonia's discipline both anticipated and defused the threat of domestic disruption. Before the more famous Macrina had

28. *Republic* 5459d–61e and *Politics* II.5 ff.

29. For a discussion, see Robert Wardy, *The Birth of Rhetoric: Gorgias, Plato and their Successors* (London: Routledge, 1996).

30. It is worth noting that he had already given an oration on the family of the Maccabees. See Daniel Joslyn-Siemiatkoski, *Christian Memories of the Maccabean Martyrs* (London: Palgrave-Macmillan, 2009).

converted her family's wealthy household into an ascetic gathering, Gorgonia in effect encompassed her marriage with a life of strict *askesis* and prayer, perhaps modifying an established custom of her region, a place where women who had rejected marriage could remain at home in their father's household, in living as solitaries.[31] Her practices contrast with the norms of Christian marriage Gregory also ascribes to her. She was a responsible wife of a wealthy man, with all her domestic skills deployed, including, very likely, the deployment of slaves, common at the time among the wealthy.[32]

On the other hand, Gorgonia's ascetic practice—rigorous fasting, constant prayer, vigils, meditation on Scripture, even her careful teachings—are similar to those of other Christian ascetic women in fourth-century Asia Minor, of various groups. She probably knew of and shared some of the practices of the local Encratite and Montanist women. Gorgonia's collaborator, her bishop Faustinus,[33] may have been judged too tolerant of these groups, since his successor, Amphilochius, was urged to bring them under control.

Several parts of the text may indicate a local debate, grounded in scriptural exegesis and philosophy, about authentic forms of Christian existence, particularly for women. Why, for instance, did Gregory emphasize Gorgonia's silence and her practice of staying at home while at the same time including episodes of her teaching, travelling, and her incubation in a shrine? Perhaps to distinguish her from women like the Montanists, who were known to travel, were not bound by silence and allowed audibly to prophesy in a meeting.[34] Furthermore, Iconium was associated with that celebrated ascetic and rebel against her own marriage, the self-baptized apostle Thecla;[35] and two generations before Gorgonia's residence had produced the famous Chariton, later considered the protomonk of Palestine.[36] The city gained after Gorgonia's

31. Basil of Ancyra, On Virginity, in PG 30, cols 669–809. Frazee, Charles A. "Anatolian Asceticism in the Fourth Century: Eustathios of Sebastea and Basil of Caesarea." *CHR* 66, no. 1 (1980): 16–33.

32. See Kyle Harper, *Slavery in the Late Roman World, AD 275–425* (Cambridge: Cambridge University Press, 2011), 546.

33. See Basil, *Letter* 138, on the death of Faustus and his possible replacement.

34. See Nicola Denzey, "What did the Montanists Read?" *HTR* 94:4 (October, 2001): 427–48 and Christine Trevette, *Montanism: Gender, Authority and the New Prophecy* (Cambridge: Cambridge University Press, 1996)

35. See Scott Fitzgerald Johnson, *The Life and Miracles of Thecla* (Cambridge, MA: Harvard Center for Hellenic Studies, 2006), 17–18.

36. Leah Di Segni: *The Life of Chariton*, in *Ascetic Behavior in Greco-Roman Antiquity: A Sourcebook*

death a bishop charged specifically with reforming the Church and freeing it from, among other difficulties, Encratite groups. Basil, as we know from his correspondence with Amphilochius of Iconium, had wanted the removal of rigorist groups from the Church there, among whom were "Marcionites," presumably Christian ascetics who rejected the validity of marriage altogether.[37] Could this extreme asceticism, a different form of which is often associated with Eustathius of Sebaste,[38] be one reason why Gregory emphasized his sister's loyalty to her spouse and her childbearing?. It is entirely plausible that Gregory emphasized certain features of Gorgonia's life in order to instruct an audience composed not only of the members of the Church aligned with imperial councils, but of the dissenting communities as well.[39]

Gregory asserts that Gorgonia established her own religious life—modelling her life on her parents'—during a period when, in Asia Minor and elsewhere, numerous women, singly and in groups, adopted the ascetical way. A variety of documents attest to patterns of life similar to Gorgonia's. The *Epitaphios* and its subject offer more than a pious encomium in order to place Gorgonia in the company of the women who were the forerunners of monasticism in Asia Minor.

The Structure of the Epitaphios on Gorgonia

The oration on Gorgonia followed her death by about a year. She had died not long after the death of their younger brother, Caesarius, in the winter of 368/369; hence Gregory delivered it in 370.[40] These two deaths saddened Gregory;[41] the younger brother had been inclined toward some form of monasticism following an ambitious career in Constantinople after narrowly

(Studies in Antiquity and Christianity), Vincent L. Wimbush (Minneapolis: Continuum International Publishers, 1990), 393–421

37. For Amphilochius, see Cornelius Datema, ed. *Contra Haereticos* (CCSG 3), 181–214. See also Basil, *Letter* 199.47

38. Frazee, Charles A. "Anatolian Asceticism in the Fourth Century: Eustathios of Sebastea and Basil of Caesarea." *CHR* 66, no. 1 (1980): 16–33. Philip Rousseau, "Eustathius and Friends," *Basil of Caesarea* (Berkeley: University of California Press, 1995).

39. Among other studies, see Stephen Mitchell, "The Life of Saint Theodotus of Ancyra," *Anatolian Studies* 32 (1982): 93–113.

40. Jean Bernardi, *La prédication des pères cappadociens: Le prédicateur et son auditoire* (Paris: Beauchesne, 1968), 108–13.

41. See his *Carmina* 2.1.1 (PG 37). Lines 177–78.

escaping with his life in the earthquake of Nicaea/Nicomedia in 368.[42] Baptized during Easter 369, he died shortly thereafter. He had lived in Constantinople and had not seen Gregory for years. Likewise, Gorgonia lived far from her brother if she really lived in Iconium and he seems not to have attended her funeral; at least, he does not mention his own presence at these occasions.

This distance and the time that separated brother and sister accounts in part for the lack of any of the consolatory language customary in a funeral oration. Similarly, Gregory includes no lament in the *Epitaphios*, as he had in the oration for Basil; the two rhetorical apostrophes stand in place of a lament. Instead, as Gregory himself states in the prologue of *Oration* 8 (sections 1–3), he departed from the "laws of panegyric" in order to instruct his entire audience to imitate the virtue of Gorgonia. Lest it be thought that Gregory unduly praised his own family, he remarked that even one's own family shouldn't be deprived of the praise due it; and at any rate, since the heroine was dead, it was too late for effective flattery. The primary object of the oration, however, was Gorgonia's *akroatēs* (in contemporary Greek, either a disciple or a lecturer) and the bishop of Iconium, Faustinus. He had been present at Gorgonia's deathbed, and may have been the source, along with her children, of Gregory's information about his sister's life. At the time of the oration, her husband, Alypius, was already dead.

The *Epitaphios* has four sections: the prologue, discussed above; the virtues of Gorgonia; her actions and ascetic discipline; her illnesses and her death. These larger sections may be subdivided as follows: paragraphs one through three, the Prologue, justifies the discourse, and exhorts the listener to a eulogy, albeit one (Gregory says, with a show of modesty) rhetorically unadorned, since his sister had not decked herself out in glamorous clothing. The object of the oration was only to pay his debt to Gorgonia and also to "instruct many to zeal and imitation of her virtue" since we strive "in every word and work to perfect (*katartizein*) those entrusted to us." This remark in itself raises an interesting question: was Gregory, not a member of the local clergy, speaking for himself as a Christian rhetor, or as one of the clergy, or on behalf of Faustinus?

The next paragraphs move to the biography of Gorgonia. Here the oration turns to Gorgonia's parents as examples of virtue. Gregory the Elder and

42. See *Oration* 7, 773B.

Nonna he compares to Sarah and Abraham,[43] the first because of his departure from paganism[44] and spiritual fatherhood of the local population. Nonna actually even surpassed her type, Sarah, since she labored successfully to achieve Gregory the Elder's conversion. In Gregory's description, his mother seems to be both inferior, equal and even superior to her husband; following his conversion she regards him as lord, yet in the next paragraph Gregory asserts the parity of each member of the couple in the realm of virtue: they share a mind and a soul, as well as a yoke for the purpose of familiarity with God. They are each a pattern for the men and women of their Church and city.

The following section (six through twelve) lists Gorgonia's virtues; these Gregory has asserted, she had gained by observing her parents and modelling herself after them, but they also come from the imitation of Christ (6), as will be discussed below. She achieves "true nobility" ; she has virtue, desire and knowledge (7); modesty (8); is the good wife of Prov 31:10 (9) and even exceeds her; she avoids ornamentation in clothing and jewelry (10); knew the Scriptures, respected priests and donated money to "temples" (*naoi*), i.e. the churches of Iconium (11); and engaged in hospitality, while maintaining a tranquil mind (12)31/. Section 13, with 11 and 12, forms a section describing Gorgonia's praxis. In particular, 13 outlines her ascetic discipline, and concludes that she possessed the totality of virtues.

Another transitional passage is section 14, an exclamatory section which leads to the account of Gorgonia's last illness and death. This portion of the *epitaphios* strengthens the comparison between Gorgonia and the monk, as it describes her longing for heaven, her hope for death and resurrection, and her last, barely audible words: a recitation of Ps 4:9, "In peace I will lie down and sleep"—i.e., to awake in Paradise. Gregory has already exhorted his listeners to imitate Gorgonia; is he now recommending that they imitate Gorgonia's final abandonment of marital or sexual coupling, which he thinks permitted Gorgonia to regain her chastity and to adopt the angelic life near her death? To what was Gregory trying to persuade his audience? The advice to imitate Gorgonia's virtue, generally considered, is the obvious answer. Yet the specific nature of her practices are as much objects of imitation as they were of

43. See *Epitaphion* 27 for Nonna as a fulfillment of the biblical type of a mother, like Elijah's, who consecrates a child to God.

44. See Pieter W. van der Horst, "Judaism in Asia Minor," in SAJEC (Leiden: Brill, 2014), 143–60.

veneration, according to Gregory. These were what enabled her "image" to ascend to her archetype, Christ, and presumably would allow his listeners to accomplish the same if they followed in her steps.

Gorgonia as Virtuous Wife

Gorgonia learned her domestic virtues from her mother, described briefly in this oration and at length elsewhere.[45] Nonna had married a non-Christian; during her youth when she was less pious than in her middle age, and perhaps this accounted for her early willingness to mix with the "polluted,"[46] an attitude she later abandoned. Like her daughter in Iconium, Nonna directed her attention toward the Christians of Nazianzus, upon whom she spent her time and wealth. Gorgonia too gave a substantial amount of money both to the poor and to the monks, and to the churches of Iconium. Not married to a priest, as her mother was, she nevertheless worked closely with Faustinus, who was her spiritual "father" and at her deathbed was the only one close enough to hear her last words, even though her husband was still alive at the time. Thus she occupied a position in the Church at Iconium for which her parents' example had partly prepared her.

The characterization of Nonna and Gregory the Elder is instructive here, for Gregory and other patristic authors assert Abraham's spiritual parentage, following Paul, against the Jewish claim to descendants by the flesh. If Gregory/Abraham and Nonna/Sarah were the spiritual progenitors of the Christians at Nazianzus, they were pre-eminently the spiritual parents of Gorgonia, rather than the fleshly ones:

From them Gorgonia received both her being and her good repute. They were the source of the seeds (Gal 3:16, citing Gn 12:7) of her piety, of her noble life, and of her joyful departure with better hopes.[47]

---

45. See *Orations* 8 and 18 on Gorgonia and his father, respectively, in the *Epitaphioi*, and in his autobiographical poems.

46. *Oration* 18.11, *On the Death of His Father*, claims that Nonna increased her piety with age; she refused to share salt with those of the family who were unbaptized, and crossed herself in the presence of pagans. Peter Brown, in *The Body and Society: Men Women and Sexual Renunciation in Early Christianity* (New York: Columbia University Press, 1918), 285, regarded Nonna, like Gregory of Nyssa's parents, as one from "families of Old Believers" who held to a "stern, ceremonious Christianity, firmly rooted in the continued life of great households." Bernardi, *Prédication*, 127, regards Gorgonia's life as similar to her mother's.

47. *para toutōn Gorgonia kai to einai, kai to eudokimon. Enteuthen autē ta tēs eusebias spermata....*

Her parents had given a noble birth and reputation, but this was their least important patrimony; more important was her exit, prepared by them, to the fatherland which was "the Jerusalem above."[48]

Here Gregory provides an interpretative passage that shapes the descriptions of Gorgonia's actual life. It agrees with his own view of the goal of the Christian life as he expresses that goal consistently throughout his works. This remark, he stated, was included because it was necessary to "pass on to a more philosophical and elevated [level]" from accounts of her parentage. Gorgonia's life had been dictated by her heavenly citizenship, apparent only to the inner eye: Iconium was not her city, but Jerusalem, "the city, then, not observable [to the eye] but perceived, where we live as citizens and toward which we rush." Gregory describes that city, following Heb 12:22–23 as an eternal feast, the contemplation of the city's founder.

Gorgonia had recognized the pre-eminence of her heavenly citizenship, which accounts for the correct ordering of her life in the *polis kato*. The core of her *eugenia*, however much it owed to the spiritual filiation of her parents, was the practice of Christian *mnemosynē*, which Gregory presents in other writings as human perfection, the assimilation to God.

This process of assimilation toward the archetype constitutes, according to Gregory, the goal of the redeemed human being—the anticipation during this life of the heavenly chorus to which this passage also alludes.[49] Elsewhere, Gregory makes this process of assimilation to Christ the archetype an absolute prerequisite for ordination to the priesthood, and it is the lack of this quality in himself which, he writes in *On [His] Flight,* led to his terrified escape after his own ordination.[50] The "assimilation to the archetype, "Christ, Gorgonia achieved by her practice of the virtues, guided by reason. Gregory employs a

48. Gregory perhaps exaggerated his father's "humble birth," to stress his resemblance to Abraham and his spiritual nobility. But he seems also to emphasize Gorgonia's *mega eugenia,* presumably acquired through her mother.

49. Cf. *Theological Orations* 2 (*Or.* 28.17) in which the human inability to know God persists until "that which resembles God and is divine, I mean to indicate our spirit and reason, will be mixed with that to which it is similar (tō oikeiō), when the image will return upward (anelthe) to its archetype, toward which it now tends. This seems to me to be philosophy generally speaking…;" *Or.* 28.17 in Gregoire de Nazianze, *Discours theologiques*, ed. P. Gallay (Paris: Cerf, 1978), 134.

50. *De Fuga* 91 (*Oration* 2): "Before one has, as far as possible, risen above the passions, has sufficiently purified his mind, and has passed others in nearness to God, I do not see how one could expect to undertake the rule over souls or the role of mediator between man and God for this, I believe, is what a priest is."

kind of ladder of virtues that had been used widely by past Christian authors and was coming to be one of the characteristics of descriptions of monastic *praktikē*. In Gregory's hands, this collection of virtues also served the purpose of criticizing the Iconian women who lacked them, although like the other Cappadocians, he had also inherited the Neoplatonic philosophical doctrine that women and men are equally bound to good behavior.[51]

Here Gregory rhetorically invited his listeners to "contribute some particular [virtue] (of Gorgonia's) and aid me in my discourse." First listed was *sophrosynē,* a traditional virtue not only for males but for the married woman. Next (9) came a comparison of Gorgonia to the good wife of Proverbs. Here it is noticeable that Gregory begins with Gorgonia's more domesticated self, although when the portrait is complete it seems that Gorgonia had little interest in housekeeping and vinelike fruitfulness. She is an instructive example for Iconian women, but even more than that, she achieves the Aristotelian mean of behavior; she achieved a balance between "gravity and gaiety;" she exercised "control of the eyes," avoided laughter,[52] and listened and spoke sparingly.[53]

Next Gorgonia is praised for prudence and piety, sagacity, generosity to the Church, hospitality, kindness to the poor, and for providing, like her mother, an example of virtue to her children.[54] She exercised magnanimity, practiced the religious life assiduously, and owned the entire corpus of virtues.

If Gregory had been satisfied to end his list of his sister's accomplishments in the domestic realm, he would have left a portrait of her as an example of the chaste married woman. But she had in effect departed from her marriage: Gorgonia's particular exercise of those virtues had modified the domestic order in such a way that she had been able to regain the status of virginity.

Early in the oration Gregory indicated that Gorgonia had modified the

51. See Kathleen O'Brien Wicker, *Mulerium Virtutes (Moralia* 242E–263E), in Hans Dieter Betz, ed. *Plutarch's Ethical Writings and Early Christian Literature,*: (Leiden: Brill, 1978)

52. Clement of Alexandria is the first to discuss the problem of laughter for Christians, *Paidagogos* 2.5.

53. See Ambrose G. Wathen, *Silence: The Meaning of Silence in the Rule of St. Benedict* (Collegeville, MN: Cisetercian Publications, 1973).

54. Gorgonia's benefactions are a continuation of the practice of other women in Hellenistic cities, not specifically Christian, and particularly those of late-ancient Asia Minor; see Riet van Bremen, "Women and Wealth," in Amelie Kuhrt and Averil Cameron, eds., *Images of Women in Antiquity* (Detroit: Wayne State University Press, 1983), 232–42.

domestic life in two ways: first, by her allegiance to Christ she had rendered her husband a friend instead of a commander[55] and after baptism she had abandoned the marriage bed to live a fully a celibate life within the confines of her house.[56] Gregory also implies that this kind of life was responsible for two miraculous cures experienced by her in later life, and it was certainly responsible for her own spiritual parentage, by example of her children and grandchildren. Among her children there were two priests and one nun. Thus the example of her parents was duplicated for successive generations, both in the married and the monastic spheres.

Gorgonia as Ascetic

Ironically, Gregory begins his description of Gorgonia's discipline by praising the virtue of temperance, although her portrait actually suggests extreme zeal. This virtue guided her marriage and her prayer through her *nous*, which rules both the married and unmarried lives and with the *technitēs Logos* ("craftsman Word [of God]) makes it possible that 'both … are ordered and fashioned to virtue").

Though yet joined in the flesh, she was not because of it distanced from the spirit; although she had her husband as a head, she was not ignorant of her first head. But when she had performed her service (λειτουργήσασα) to the world and to nature a little bit, to the extent that the law according to the flesh willed, or better, that the lawgiver to the flesh (willed), she consecrated herself in every way to God (καθιέρωσεν).[57]

As evidence of Gorgonia's modesty, Gregory lists her lack of pride in balancing duties of the married life with those of the unmarried life. Sections eight and nine were devoted to her performance as a good and dutiful wife, with the presence of children and grandchildren as proof, but the remaining portion of the oration shows that Gorgonia later withdrew from these duties, especially sexual duties. Perhaps her parents had practiced chastity, as the oration hints. In chapter twenty, Gregory tells his audience that after Gorgonia's baptism, she and her husband embraced a life of chastity. The passage reads as follows:

55. Husband and wife can be friends based on a mutual love of philosophy: Plutarch, Coniugalia praecepta 19 in Plutarch's *Moralia*, v. 2, ed. Frank Babbit (Cambridge: Harvard University Press, 1956), 311.
56. *Epitaphios* 8.17
57. *Epitaphios* 8.22.

"She wished to be consecrated to God in her whole body, and not depart this life only half-perfected, nor leave behind any part of herself imperfect. She did not fail to obtain an answer even from him who does the will of them that fear him (Ps 114:19) and brings their petitions to fulfillment."

Even more interesting than this cessation of the sexual activities was the way in which Gorgonia, according to Gregory, seems to have overturned the customary arrangements of marriage. Chapter eight goes on to say, "What is most excellent and most honorable, that she made her husband toward herself, not a strange tyrant, but gained a good fellow-slave [of God]" (*ou despotēn atopon, all' homodoulon agathon presektēsato*). In that achievement, and in making her household, "the fruit of her body," into "the fruit of her spirit," she "made marriage praiseworthy by her well-pleasing conduct in marriage." She showed herself an example of every good to her family because of this; and moreover, this remained after her death as a legacy to her household.

In chapter eleven, Gregory qualifies the wifely qualities of prudence and piety, attested by her silence. Gorgonia, once again deriving her goodness and illumination from the example of her parents, possessed a capacity beyond her "prudent silence" and "Wise words." She offered to her family and others (these are not specified, but may be the Christians of Iconium) "precepts and exhortations." Likewise, beyond her regular silence, she was able to "know divine things, some from the divine Scriptures, and some from her own intelligence (*tes oikeias syneseos*)."

Yet Gregory reemphasizes her silence: "Who spoke less, remaining within the bounds of female piety?" Gorgonia, a wealthy woman, could make donations to local churches; Gregory speaks of her as adorning not only "this temple but other temples as well," and of her respect for priests in general and Faustinus in particular. Their cooperation seems to have gone well beyond that of lay married woman and local priest; Faustinus was her fellow-fighter and teacher and most interestingly, depicted as a second husband: he was, with her, the possessor of "good seedsand the yoke of sons consecrated to God." This phrase in particular suggests that Gorgonia and Faustinus were like Nonna and Gregory the Elder in their spiritual parentage. Again, Alypios is not mentioned.

Gorgonia's wealth also gave her an opportunity to exercise hospitality, and Gregory makes her conform to the Old Testament model of the magnanimous

Job. Although hospitality was a traditional domestic virtue, in Gregory's treatment, Gorgonia's hospitality suggests a manifestation of the monastic *koinos bios*. She distributes her largess, furthermore, in silence: "in secret she husbanded piety for the one who sees secrets."[58] Again, Gorgonia was able to do this because of her trained mind: she possessed a "mind undisturbed in suffering and a soul sympathetic to the distressed." Gorgonia's *philanthropia* resembles an important characteristic of Christ himself. Here again, Gorgonia is assimilated to her archetype as she practices rather traditional and scriptural, domestic virtues—however, the archetype is not the wife of Proverbs 31 but the Christ of the ascetic imagination of Gregory.

Like Nonna, Gorgonia is said to have exhausted her savings by providing for the Church and its poor. Like Nonna, she transformed her marriage into an occasion for θεωρία. Unlike Nonna, and unlike Gregory himself, it seems, Gorgonia practiced a severe self-discipline which, when catalogued, rivals that of the Basilian reorganization and goes well beyond the recorded practices of Macrina and other domestic, ascetic women. She engaged in rigorous fasting; at night she lay upon the ground instead of sleeping in bed; she deprived herself of sleep; she sometimes slept standing up, a "struggle especially marked among philosophical men," i.e. ascetics; she made numerous genuflections during prayer; she wept copiously due to her "contrite heart and humility of spirit." In addition to her ascetic praxis, she was also able to engage in prayer which led to spiritual ascent because she had a mind "steady and raised on high;" this, for Gregory, is another way of portraying the ideal ascetic theologian; her "reading, explanation and timely recall" of the Scriptures, and her devotion to the psalmody—doubtless the daily office of the Church—would have given her little time for many domestic activities beyond those of having before the end of her life abandoned sexual "yoking" and delegated the housework, Gorgonia essentially lived the life of a monk. Her mother had not gone so far.

To his list of her practices, Gregory adds a revealing exclamation: "Oh feminine nature, which conquered that of man in the common struggle for

---

58. See Pierre de Labriolle, "'Mulieres in ecclesia taceant.' Un aspect de la lutte antimontaniste I," *Bulletin d'ancienne littérature et d'archéologie chrètiennes* 1, no. 1 (1911) : 3–24. But Gregory may also be referring to the silence of the philosopher. Cf. Evagrius of Pontus *Gnostikos* 41, "The inexpressible is to be adored in silence," (cf. *The Gnostic Trilogy* ed and trans. Robin Darling Young et al (forthcoming) and Jean Souilhe, "Le silence mystique," in *Révue d'ascetique et de mystique* 4 (1923), 128–40.

salvation, and proved male and female a distinction, not of soul but of body! Oh chastity (*hagneia*) after baptism, and soul the bride of Christ in the pure bridal chamber of the body!"[59]

Thus Gorgonia has reclaimed the virgin's betrothal to Christ—and even attained the restoration of the original human condition:

Oh bitter taste, and Eve the mother of our race and sin, and erring snake and death, conquered by her *enkrateia*! Oh emptying of Christ, and form of a servant, and sufferings, rendered honorable by her mortification![60]

Gorgonia's chastity consecrated her physical ailments, which Gregory details in chapters fifteen and seventeen. In each case, Gorgonia was healed not by physicians, whom she was too modest to consult, but by her faith, a result Gregory considered miraculous.

Gregory comments later in the oration that Gorgonia, even before her tardy baptism, looked forward to her death: she "desired to be purely joined with her fair one and embrace her beloved completely and, I will add further, her Lover." Gregory likely knew Origen's *Commentary on the Song of Songs*, as well as his set of homilies on the book; here the reference to Christ as her lover depends upon that text.[61] Apparently this desire, characterized by prognosis, or foreknowledge, and many vigils was rewarded by a vision of Christ. Yet Gorgonia did not publicize this; even her deathbed scene was characterized by silence. Her mother was present, as was Bishop Faustinus, and the assembly successfully stifled its natural reaction to her "dissolution." Gorgonia, however, had a final, virtuous act to display. When it was thought that she had died, after her discourse on the following section (six through twelve) lists Gorgonia's virtues; this portion of the *epitaphios* strengthens the comparison between Gorgonia and the monk, as it describes her longing for heaven, her hope for death and resurrection, and her last, barely audible words. Gregory has already exhorted his audience to imitate Gorgonia, is he now recommending that they imitate Gorgonia's final abandonment of marital duties or sexual

---

59. *Epitaphios* 14.

60. Gregory has not mentioned Mary as the antitype of Eve here, but see the discussion in Nicholas [now Maximos] P. Constas, "Weaving the Body of God: Proclus of Constantinople, the Theotooks, and the Loom of the Flesh," in *JECS* 3, no. 2 (Summer, 1995): 169–94.

61. See Nathalie Henry, "The Song of Songs and the Liturgy of the *Velatio* in the Fourth Century: From Literary Metaphor to Liturgical Reality," *Studies in Church History*, vol 35, Continuity and Change in Christian Worship (Cambridge: Ecclesiastical History Society, 1999): 18–23.

coupling, which he seems to think permitted Gorgonia to regain her chastity and to adopt the angelic life near her death.

Gorgonia and Scripture

One previously-unexplored aspect of the logos on Gorgonia is Gregory's abundant use of Scripture in the interpretation of his sister's life. Gregory views his sister as a philosopher[62] and therefore a competent exponent of Scripture, when he says that she, like "males dedicated to philosophy" undertook the practice of strict asceticism. She was "a person of courage—more courageous not only than women but surpassing even men of noble heart." And in one passage Gregory gives his listeners or readers a clue that Gorgonia was not as dedicated to the practice of silence as his discourse would strive to present her:

In her intelligent *tonos* of psalmody, in her reading of divine scriptures, of their explanation or her ready recollection of them, in the bending of her hardened knees, which almost seemed glued to the ground, in the her purifying tears "with a contrite heart and a humble spirit," (Ps 50:3, Dan 3:19) or a prayer lifted up on high, or a mind unwavering and raised on high—in all these things, who would be able to boast of themselves to have surpassed her, man or woman?[63]

Gregory knew that Gorgonia not only sang the Psalms, presumably in Church as well as in private devotion, but knew how to interpret them, along with the rest of Scripture. Gregory presents her as having adopted philosophy, but he is not simply applying a synonym for "ascetic" here; it is her "mind unwavering and raised on high" that qualifies her to understand and explicate Scripture, because she has adopted a practice that enables her to gain θεωρία, the observation and contemplation of the immaterial realities fundamental to the late-ancient Platonism adopted by Gregory and many of his contemporaries.[64]

Gregory had implicitly begun to connect Gorgonia with Scripture early in the discourse, where he discusses Gorgonia's parents and his own, Gregory the Elder and his wife Nonna. But an earlier passage had already placed Gorgonia in the company of philosophers. Gregory tells his hearers that Gorgonia

62. Without using the noun "philosopher;" nonetheless, she has the qualifications for the designation (*Or.* 8.8, 11. 13, 15–16).

63. *Epitaphios* 18.

64. *Epitaphios* 13.

had learned from her parents "to live well and to depart happily, with the best of hopes:"

But if it is necessary to converse further about her more highly and philosophical-ly, the fatherland was for Gorgonia "the Jerusalem above," the not seen, but under-stood intellectually in which we might gather as a polis and toward which we hurry, in which Christ (or a Christ?) is a compatriot, and fellow-citizens the assembly "and a church of the first born written in the heavens," and around the great city-founder cel-ebrating with the observation/contemplation[65] of glory, and circling an indestructi-ble choir. Nobility (*eugeneia*) is the conservation of the image and the likening to the archetype, which the logos and virtue and pure longing accomplishes, always shaping according to God the genuine mystic initiates of the above, and knowing whence and who we are, and where we are going.[66]

In these two passages—and again at the close of the discourse—Gregory has portrayed Gorgonia not only as an ascetic, but as a philosopher. She had been educated to the level where she could understand the inner meaning of Scrip-ture, which had anticipated the philosophy with which Gregory and his audi-ence—and his family—were also familiar. Gregory subordinates family and city—the "republic" that his Platonic references recall—not only to the Chris-tian community, but that he makes Christian community equivalent to a soci-ety of philosophers.

As he closes his *epitaphios*, Gregory addresses Gorgonia directly, for the benefit of her community, certainly, but also to indicate the high philosophi-cal achievement of this particular woman:

I know well that the good things in which you now rejoice surpass by far everything that we are able to see, and are more precious: the echo of festivals, the choir of an-gels, the celestial rank, the observation of glory, and above all, another, higher and more pure and more perfect illumination of the Triad that no longer flees from a mind enchained and dispersed by the senses, but is contemplated as a whole by the whole mind, and illuminating with its radiance our souls with the whole light of the godhead.[67]

Gorgonia's practice of asceticism and observation or contemplation has, Greg-ory asserts, led her above this world, to return from Iconium and her family, to the city of God. And Gregory's interweaving of scriptural vocabulary and

65. The Greek word *theôria* can be translated in either way; here both meanings may be intended.
66. *Epitaphios* 6
67. *Epitaphios* 23.

themes, and philosophical terminology, allows Gorgonia to be portrayed as a genuine philosopher.

Another critical aspect of Gregory's portrayal, however, is his portrait of Gorgonia as a scriptural hero. Early in the discourse he identifies Gorgonia with the virtuous wife of Proverbs, primarily by connecting her with chapter 31:10–31. This would seem to portray Gorgonia as having stayed largely inside the home; but Gorgonia not only circulates through the city—she spends the night in a Church, seeking a cure for her illness.

Beginning in chapter 7 of the work, Gregory had already compared his sister's life to that of Job. "The soul of this [woman]," he wrote, "was more well-born 'than all those [sons] of the East." He returns to the theme in chapter 12, where he describes Gorgonia's charity.

I do not hesitate to compare her, for my part, with the words of Job: "Her door was open to everyone who came, and no stranger ever had to camp outside [it];" "She was an eye for the blind, a foot for the lame;" a mother of orphans (cf., Job 31:32; 29:15; 29:16).

In the fourth century, the figure of Job was becoming a model for ascetics; Didymus the Blind commented on the work, Evagrius of Pontus composed scholia on Job, possibly taking their cue from Origen, who had discussed him in *On Prayer* 29.11. This interest in Job was rooted in the Letter of James (5:11), where Job is "happy": "We call those happy who persevered: you have heard of the perseverance of Job, and you have seen the purpose of the Lord, how the Lord is compassionate and merciful."

If Gorgonia was one fulfillment of these biblical types, she could also be explained by a running set of allusions to biblical texts. In addition to the figures of Job and the ideal wife of Proverbs, Gregory has laced every section of the work with biblical quotations, usually by citing or alluding to Old Testament texts and New Testament verses to which they relate; for example, in his portrait of her parents interweaving single words of texts from Genesis 12, 15 and 17 (the story of Abraham) with texts from Romans, Galatians and Hebrews; or in the description of Gorgonia's philosophical orientation toward the "Jerusalem above," with texts from Galatians, Hebrews, Revelation, Ephesians, and the Gospel of John.[68]

68. *Epitaphios* 4 and 6, respectively. Calvet-Sebasti does not discuss this running chain of biblical allusions, but does provide a general outline of scriptural precedents for the virtuous woman, op cit., 53–84.

Re-evaluating Gorgonia's Life

To summarize: Gorgonia was the eldest of the three children of Gregory the Elder, bishop Nazianzen in 325–374, and his wife Nonna; she bore the name of her maternal grandmother. Born around 326, Gorgonia died in 369 or 370. If she had married between the ages of twelve and sixteen, as was customary for girls of the period, she would have spent the next ten to fifteen years bearing the five children of her marriage between 338 and 342, and since she renounced sexual intercourse after the birth of her children, the period of her celibacy would have lasted from 352 or 357, approximately, to her death, or from thirteen to eighteen years. At the time of her death two of her sons had become priests, and she was already a grandmother.[69]

Gregory communicated no details of Gorgonia's childhood in Nazianzus or the nearby family villa at Arianzus. He noted her intelligence, but mentioned only his mother's instruction in virtue, which he knew well. Gorgonia's *askēsis* is not merely an imitation of Nonna's, but seems to have developed from hers. The extent of Gorgonia's formal education is unknown—or, possibly, Gregory did not know it; but her ability to read and sing the Psalms, noted above, attest to her literacy and interpretive abilities. By contrast, Gregory and his brother, Caesarius, both successful rhetors, had been tutored at home by the future monk Carterius.[70] A skillful exegete, Gorgonia perhaps received some education from him as well; her contemporary Macrina was educated at home, as was her brother, Gregory of Nyssa. The wealth of Gorgonia's family, although not as substantial as Macrina's, could easily have provided her with tutors.[71]

Once married, certainly to a man of the same class, Gorgonia seems to have controlled her own funds, because she, like her mother, exhausted for the benefit of the poor that portion of the family money she controlled. She also endowed churches in Iconium, including the one near which she was buried. Unlike Macrina, Gorgonia seems not to have gathered any other women around her, but

---

69. See Marie-Madelein Hauser-Meury, *Prosopographie zu den Schriften Gregors von Nazianz* (Bonn: Peter Hanstein, 1960) and Raymond Van Dam, *Families and Friends*, 93–96.

70. See *Epitaphia*, numbers 142–146 (PG 38) 11–32. *Carmina* 2.2.1.139–42, *Epitaphia* III, 115–18= Anthologia Graeca 8.148, 142, 143, 144–46 and see P. Gallay, La vie de saint Grégoire de Nazianze (E. Vitte: Lyon and Paris, 1943), 31, 46.

71. In addition to the studies of McGuckin and Van Dam, see Thomas Kopecek, "The Social Class of the Cappadocian Fathers, *CH* 42 (1973): 453–66; the family was already well-connected in Constantinople through their cousin Amphilochius' sister Theodosia.

to have developed a strict ascetic regimen within her own house. If she actually followed the regimen Gregory describes, including severe fasting and night-long vigils, she would have needed to retain servants for the maintenance of her household while she adopted a life of discipline and prayer.[72]

Gorgonia's husband agreed to their eventual renunciation of the marriage bed, but is not mentioned as a fellow-ascetic, and his late-in-life baptism was credited to Gorgonia's prayers. Gorgonia endured one serious injury, the result of an accidental wreck of her carriage, and suffered one mysterious illness, the latter possibly brought on by her self-discipline. In one case she received a miraculous cure. She died at forty-four, survived by her parents and brother as well as children and grandchildren. Perhaps because of her local reputation for holiness, assisted by her brother's praise, Gorgonia became the object of a popular devotion attested as early as the fifth century.

During Gorgonia's life, many Christian women in Asia Minor experimented with different forms of the "philosophical life."[73] A map of the area would show female asceticism thickly planted in Cappadocia, Pontus, and Lycaonia. In Gorgonia's immediate neighborhood of Iconium there was an order of virgins, and a variety of ascetic enthusiasts which had flourished, or at least had not been opposed, during the episcopacy of her mentor Faustinos.[74] Thecla was locally revered, and a shrine at Seleucia, to the southwest, honored her relics and contained a community of monks and nuns, with whom Gregory lived from 374 to 379.[75] In Ancyra to the northeast, bishop Basil in the 350s described female asceticism in terms very similar to descriptions of Gorgonia's own life[76] and in Annesi to the east, Macrina's ascetic life grew to include a community which drew in her mother and two brothers, and almost certainly provided a model for Basil's emulation, despite his silence about her.

72. The most comprehensive study remains Susanna Elm, *Virgins of God: The Making of Asceticism in Late Antiquity* (Berkeley: University of California Press, 1996).

73. For the growth of Christianity of all stripes in Anatolia, see Stephen Mitchell, *Anatolia: Land, Men and Gods in Asia Minor*, vol. 2: *The Rise of the Church* (Oxford: Clarendon Press, 1993) and idem and Philipp Pilhofer, *Early Christianity in Asia Minor and Cyprus: From the Margins to the Mainstream* (Leiden: Brill, 2019).

74. See Basil of Caesarea, *ep.* 188 to Amphilochius of Iconium three years after Gorgonia's death, complaining about fallen virgins.

75. Now see Scott Fitzgerald Johnson, *The Life and Miracles of Thekla: A Literary Study* (Washington, DC: Center for Hellenic Studies, 2006) and Stephen J. Davis, *The Cult of Saint Thecla: A Tradition of Women's Piety in Late Antiquity* (Oxford: Oxford University Press, 2001).

76. See Theresa M. Shaw, "Creation, Virginity and Diet in Fourth-Century Christianity: Basil of Ancyra's On the True Purity of Virginity," *Gender and History* 9:3 (November, 1997): 579–96.

In the late 350s, Eustathius had just been ordained bishop of Sebaste, an attestation of his popularity despite his prior synodal condemnation (at the Synod of Gangra, in about 340), and from 358 to 360 Basil was visiting well-established groups of male and female ascetics.[77] Furthermore, the composition in 361–363 of Montanist hagiography right in the vicinity of Iconium demonstrates the continuing existence of a group in which women not only prophesied publicly but possibly reclaimed the title of virgin even though they had once been married.[78] In fact, the practice of female asceticism is attested far earlier, in 235, with the solitary domestic ascetic Juliana of Caesarea, with whom Origen stayed as a guest, and in the prophetess described in a letter of Firmilian, bishop of Caesarea in the 250s.[79] In addition, syneisaktism, condemned at two synods—Ancyra in 314 and Neocaesarea between 314 and 325, provided another way of practicing Christian askesis; perhaps (without the enforcing power of the state yet deployed) it did not disappear despite its condemnation. It is hard to say precisely how widespread was the practice, but its continuity is highly likely.[80] Gorgonia and Macrina seem to have been developing, in different ways, customs perhaps known to them already in the churches of Asia Minor—Gorgonia as a wealthy married woman who developed a domestic asceticism while tending to a family, and Macrina as a wealthy dedicated virgin who refused marriage to convert the family's villa into the site of a somewhat egalitarian community of ascetic women.[81] Even though Gregory depicts Gorgonia as a dutiful daughter and pious housewife, the very incidents he relates point to a more complicated state of life for his sister, that of a woman who joined the common experimentation of her age in drastically shrinking her marriage.[82]

<hr>

77. See Jean Gribomont, "Un aristocrate révolutionnaire, évêque et moine: s. Basile, *Augustinianum* 7 (1977): 179–91 and more generally, Philip Rousseau, *Basil of Caesarea* (Berkeley: University of California Press, 1994), 190–269.

78. Stephen Mitchell, The Life of Theodotus of Ancyra, *Anatolian Studies* 32 (December, 1982), 93–113.

79. Cf., *Letter of Firmilian* (Cyprian Letter 75); for discussion, see Gaetano Spampinato, "Autorita profetica e amministrazione dei sacramenti: Il caso della profetessa nella lettera di Firmiliani di Cesarea a Cipriano, *Cristianesimo nella storia* 2 (May–August 2002): 547–62.

80. Miller, Patricia Cox, ed. *Women in Early Christianity: Translations from Greek Texts* (Washington, DC: Catholic University of America Press, 2012), 117 and Clark, Elizabeth A. "John Chrysostom and the 'Subintroductae'" *CH* 46, no. 2 (1977), 183; Elm, 139–140, notes that in Macrina's community, *parthenos* was a title, not a physical description.

81. Cf. Evagrius, *To A Virgin* "Do not say "yours" and "mine" cf. Robert Sinkiewicz, ed. and trans., *Evagrius of Pontus: The Greek Ascetic Corpus* (Oxford: Oxford University Press, 2003), p. 132.

82. Cf. Gregory on a more positive view of marriage: Letters 232, 231 and *Or.* 40, 18 on Holy Baptism

Like Basil and Gregory of Nyssa he may hve thought that the differences between men and women were external, operating within the pronoia of God, but temporary.[83]

Conclusion

In his oration on Gorgonia, Gregory created an elaborate record of a virtuous, and even an ideal woman—one who could be praised as the fulfillment of scriptural models of female virtue, but one who also ascended to philosophy. It was that ascent that enabled Gregory, he thought, to say that her true *polis* was the "Jerusalem above." Gregory claimed that his sister was both a fulfillment of biblical types of virtue, and that her virtues allowed her to understand the deeper meaning of Scripture:

In my opinion, it seems no small matter, nothing suited for the narrow of spirit, 'to give to each his measure of grain' from Scripture 'in due season,' and to distribute the truth of our teachings with discernment, whether we are speculating about the world or worlds, about matter, about the soul, about the intellect and intellectual natures, good and evil, about the providence that holds all things together and guides their course—whatever seems true according to the whole of reason, and whatever lies beyond this human reason here below.[84]

In his *Epitaphios Logos* Gregory uses a typological and moral interpretive strategy to teach his audience how Gorgonia lived by fulfilling virtuous types found in the Scriptures, or adhering to virtues and directives contained in them. In the penultimate section of the work, though, Gregory hints at her deeper level of understanding. Only her "shepherd" could lean close to her deathbed, to hear her "murmuring" Ps 4:9, "In peace, all at once, I shall lie down and fall asleep." Already surrounded by a chorus "of family and 'strangers,'" singing, perhaps, Psalms, Gorgonia now is "blessed"[85] and a prophet: "the psalm-verse," Gregory says, "both described what happened, and was the *epitaphios* of her departure."

As an adherent of the practice of *synkatabasis* Origen had recommended,

---

83. On the equality of men and women at the intellectual level, in Cappadocian thought: Verna E. F. Harrison, "Male and Female in Cappadocian Theology," *JTS* N.S. 41 (1990): 441–71.

84. *Or.* 2.35; trans.Brian Daley, op. cit., 53.

85. The word *makarios* points to Mt 5:3–11, and suggests that Gorgonia is not only holy, but one of Christ's disciples.

Gregory could only sketch, on this very public occasion, at his sister's practice of philosophy. He supported his account of her life with details of the numerous scriptural exempla she followed, and merely pointed to her deeper understanding of the text that arose from her practice. In this early work, however, he may well have practiced the approach to the *mysterion* that he would later delineate in the *Theological Orations*. Few were able, like Moses, to ascend the mountain, but he hints that his sister was one.

Bibliography

Babbit, Frank. Ed. *Plutarch. Moralia.* Cambridge: Harvard University Press, 1956.

Balzan, Francesca and Alan Deidun. "Notes for a history of coral fishing and coral artefacts in Malta—The Significance of Coral: Apotropaic, Medical, Symbolic, Precious," 435–54 as in *60th anniversary of the Malta Historical Society: a commemoration*, ed. Joseph F. Grima. Zabbar, Malta: Veritas Press 2010.

Bernardi, Jean. *La prédication des pères cappadociens. Le prédicateur et son auditoire.* Paris: Beauchesne, 1968.

Billius, Jacobus. *Eliae Cretensis Commentarius in Gregorii Nazianzeni.* Gregorii Theologi. v. 2 Cologne: Coloniae, 1690.

Brakke, David. "Reading the New Testament and Transforming the Self in Evagrius of Pontus." Pages 284–99 in *Asceticism and Exegesis in Early Christianity: The Reception of New Testament Texts in Ancient Ascetic Discourses.* Edited by Hans-Ulrich Wiedeann. Göttingen: Vandenhoeck & Ruprecht, 2013.

Brooten, Bernadette J. *Love Between Women: Early Christian Responses to Female Homoeroticism.* Chicago: The University of Chicago Press, 1996.

Brown, Peter. *The Body and Society: Men Women and Sexual Renunciation in Early Christianity.* New York: Columbia University Press, 1988.

Burrus, Virginia. "Life after Death: The Martyrdom of Gorgonia and the Birth of Female Hagiography." Pages 153–70 in *Gregory of Nazianzus: Images and Reflections.* Edited by Jostein Bortnes and Tomas Hägg. University of Copenhagen: Museum Tusculanum Press, 2006.

Calvet-Sebasti, Marie-Ange. *Grégoire de Nazianze, Discours 6–12.* SC 405. Paris: Cerf, 1995.

Chin, C. M. "'Who is the Ascetic Exegete?:' Angels, Enchantments and Transformative Food in Origen's Homilies on Joshua." Pages 203–18 in *Asceticism and Exegesis in Early Christianity: The Reception of New Testament Texts in Ancient Ascetic Discourses.* Edited by Hans-Ulrich Wiedeann. Göttingen: Vandenhoeck & Ruprecht, 2013.

Clark, Elizabeth A. "John Chrysostom and the 'Subintroductae'" *Church History* 46, no. 2 (1977): 171–85.

Constas, Nicholas P. "Weaving the Body of God: Proclus of Constantinople, the Theotooks, and the Loom of the Flesh." *JECS* 3, no. 2 (Summer, 1995): 169–94.

Cox Miller, Patricia. ed. *Women in Early Christianity : Translations from Greek Texts*. Washington, D.C.: Catholic University of America Press, 2012.

Daley, Brian E. *Gregory of Nazianzus*. London and New York: Routledge, 2006.

———. "Walking through the Word of God: Gregory of Nazianzus as a Biblical Interpreter." Pages 514–31 in *The Word Leaps the Gap: Essays in Honor of Richard B. Hays*. Edited by J. Ross Wagner, C. Kavin Rowe, and A. Katherine Grieb. Grand Rapids, MI: Eerdmans, 2008.

Datema, Cornelius. Ed. *Contra Haereticos*. CCSG 3. Turnhout: Brepols, 1978.

Davis, Stephen J. *The Cult of Saint Thecla: A Tradition of Women's Piety in Late Antiquity*. Oxford: Oxford University Press, 2001.

de Labriolle, Pierre. "'Mulieres in ecclesia taceant.' Un aspect de la lutte antimontaniste I," *Bulletin d'ancienne littérature et d'archéologie chrètiennes* 1, no. 1 (1911): 3–24.

Denzey, Nicola. "What did the Montanists Read?" *HTR* 94:4 (October, 2001): 427–48.

Destephen, Sylvain. "Christianisation and Local Names in Asia Minor: Fall and Rise in Late Antiquity." Pages 258–76 in *Changing Names: Tradition and Innovation in Greek Onomastics*. Edited by Robert Parker. Oxford: Oxford University Press/Proceedings of the British Academy, 2019.

Dilley, P. *Monasteries and the Care of Souls in Late Antiquity*. Cambridge: Cambridge University Press, 2017.

Di Segni, Leah. "The Life of Chariton." Pages 393–421 in *Ascetic Behavior in Greco-Roman Antiquity: A Sourcebook*. Studies in Antiquity and Christianity. Edited by Vincent L. Wimbush. Minneapolis: Continuum International Publishing, 1990.

Dunkle, Brian. *Poems on Scripture: Saint Gregory Nazianzus*. Crestwood, NY: St. Vladimir's Seminary Press, 2013.

Elm, Susanna. "Gregory's Women: Creating a Philosopher's Family." Pages 171–93 in *Gregory of Nazianzus: Images and Reflections*. Edited by Jostein Bortnes and Tomas Hägg. University of Copenhagen: Museum Tusculanum Press, 2006.

———. *Sons of Hellenism, Fathers of the Church: Emperor Julian, Gregory of Nazianzus, and the Vision of Rome*. Berkeley: University of California Press, 2012.

———. *Virgins of God: The Making of Asceticism in Late Antiquity*. Berkeley: University of California Press, 1996.

Fitzgerald Johnson, Scott. *The Life and Miracles of Thecla: A Literary Study*. HSS 13; Harvard: HUP; Center for Hellenic Studies, 2006.

Frazee, Charles A. "Anatolian Asceticism in the Fourth Century: Eustathios of Sebastea and Basil of Caesarea." *The Catholic Historical Review* 66, no. 1 (1980): 16–33.

Gallay, P. *Grégoire de Nazianze, Discours 27–31 (Discours théologiques)*. SC 250. Paris : Cerf, 1978.

———. "La Bible dans l'oeuvre de Grégoire de Nazianze le Théologien." Pages 313–34 in *Le monde grec ancien et la Bible*. Edited by Claude Mondésert. Paris: Beauchesne, 1984.

Giannarelli, Elena. *La tipologia femminile nella biografia e nell'autobiografia cristiana del IVo secolo*. Rome: Sede del Istituto, 1980.

Gregg, Robert C. *Consolation Philosophy: Greek and Christian Paideia in Basil and the Two Gregories*. Philadelphia: Patristic Foundation, 1975.

Gribomont, Jean. "Un aristocrate révolutionnaire, évêque et moine: s. Basile. *Augustinianum* 7 (1977): 179–91.

Halkin, François. *Bibliotheca Hagiographica Graeca 3ed*. Brussels: Société des Bollandistes, 1957.

Harl, Marguerite. Ed. *Origène, Philocalie 1–20 sur les écritures*. Nicholas de Lange. Ed. *La lettre à Africanus sur l'histoire de Suzanne*. SC 302. Paris: Cerf, 1983.

Harper, Kyle. *Slavery in the Late Roman World, AD 275–425*. Cambridge: Cambridge University Press, 2011.

Harrison, Verna E. F. "Male and Female in Cappadocian Theology," *JTS* N.S. 41 (1990): 441–71.

Hauser-Meury, Marie Madeleine. *Prosopography zu den Schriften Gregors von Nazianz*. Bonn: P. Hanstein, 1960.

Henry, Nathalie. "The Song of Songs and the Liturgy of the Velatio in the Fourth Century: From Literary Metaphor to Liturgical Reality." Pages 18–23 in *Studies in Church History*, vol 35, *Continuity and Change in Christian Worship*. Cambridge: Ecclesiastical History Society, 1999.

Hägg, Tomas. "Playing with expectations: Gregory's funeral orations on his brother, sister and father." Pages 133–52 in *Gregory of Nazianzus: Images and Reflections*. Edited by Jostein Bortnes and Tomas Hägg. University of Copenhagen: Museum Tusculanum Press, 2006.

Janin, R. "Gorgonia." Pages 121–22 in *Bibliotheca Sanctorum*. Rome: Nuova Editrice, 1966.

Joslyn-Siemiatkoski, Daniel. *Christian Memories of the Maccabean Martyrs*. London: Palgrave-Macmillan, 2009.

Kopecek, Thomas A. "The Social Class of the Cappadocian Fathers," *Church History* 42, no. 4 (December, 1973): 453–66.

Krueger, Derek. *Liturgical Subjects: Christian Ritual, Biblical Narrative, and the Formation of the Self in Byzantium*. Divinations: Rereading Late Ancient Religion; Philadelphia: University of Pennsylvania Press, 2014.

Long, Seth. *Excavating the Memory Palace*. Chicago: University of Chicago Press, 2020.

Loraux, Nicole *The Invention of Athens: The Funeral Oration in the Classical City*. Translated by Alan Sheridan. Cambridge, MA: Harvard University Press, 2006.

McCauley Leo P. et al. *Funeral Orations by Saint Gregory Nazianzen and Saint Ambrose*. New York: Fathers of the Church, 1953.

McGuckin, John. *St. Gregory of Nazianzus: An Intellectual Biography*. Crestwood, NY: St. Vladimir's Press, 2001.

J. P. Migne. Ed. *Basil of Ancyra, De Virginitate*. PG 30, 669–809. Paris: Migne, 1857–66.

———. *Gregory of Nazianzus. Carmina*. PG 37, 397ff. Paris: Migne, 1857–66.

———. *Gregory of Nazianzus. Epitaphia*. PG 38, 21–22. Paris: Migne, 1857–66.

Mitchell, Stephen. *Anatolia: Land, Men and Gods in Asia Minor*, vol. 2: *The Rise of the Church*. Oxford: Clarendon Press, 1993.

———. "The Life of Saint Theodotus of Ancyra." *Anatolian Studies* 32 (1982): 93–113.

Mitchell, Stephen and Philipp Pilhofer. *Early Christianity in Asia Minor and Cyprus: From the Margins to the Mainstream.* Leiden: Brill, 2019.

Mossay, Justin. *La mort et l'au-delà dans saint Grégoire de Nazianze.* Louvain: Université de Louvain, 1966.

———. "Notes sur l'herméneutique des sources littéraires de l'histoire byzantine." *Recherches de philologie et de linguistique, III Series, Section de philologie classique* 3. Louvain, 1972, 39–51

Norris, Frederick. "Gregory Nazianzen: Constructing and Constructed by Scripture." Pages 149–62 in *The Bible in Greek Christian Antiquity.* Edited by Paul Blowers. Notre Dame, IN: University of Notre Dame Press, 1997.

O'Brien Wicker, Kathleen. *Muleriumm Virtutes* (Moralia 242E–263E). Pages 106–34 in *Plutarch's Ethical Writings and Early Christian Literature.* Edited by Hans Dieter Betz. Leiden: Brill, 1978.

Pinault, Henri. *Le Platonisme de Saint Grégoire de Nazianze. Essai sur les relations du Christianisme et de l'Hellénisme dans son oeuvre théologique.* La Roche sur Yon: Romain, 1925.

Rebillard, Eric. "Christian Funerals and Funerals of Christians: The Church and the Death Ritual in Late Antiquity." Pages 123–39 in *The Care of the Dead in Late Antiquity.* Ithaca, NY: Cornell University Press, 2010.

Rousseau, Philip. *Basil of Caesarea.* Berkeley: University of California Press, 1995.

Shaw, Theresa M. "Creation, Virginity and Diet in Fourth-Century Christianity: Basil of Ancyra's On the True Purity of Virginity." *Gender and History* 9:3 (November, 1997): 579–96

Souilhe, Jean. "Le silence mystique." *Révue d'ascetique et de mystique* 4 (1923): 128–140.

Storin, Bradley. "Father of Philosophers." Pages 121–45 in *Self-Portrait in Three Colors: Gregory of Nazianzus's Epistolary Autobiography.* Berkeley: University of California Press, 2019.

Strutwolf, Holger. *Gnosis als System: Zur Rezeption der valentinianischen Gnosis bei Origenes.* Göttingen: Vandenhoeck & Ruprecht, 1993.

Tougher, Shaun. "The Advocacy of an Empress: Julian and Eusebia." *The Classical Quarterly* 48, no. 2 (1998): 595–599.

Trevette, Christine. *Montanism: Gender, Authority and the New Prophecy.* Cambridge: Cambridge University Press, 1996.

Trombley, Frank R. *Hellenic Religion and Christianization,* 2 ed. Vol. 2. Leiden and New York: Brill, 1995.

van Bremen, Riet. "Women and Wealth." Pages 232–42 in *Images of Women in Antiquity.* Edited by Amelie Kuhrt and Averil Cameron. Detroit: Wayne State Press, 1983.

Van Dam, Raymond. *Families and Friends in Late Roman Cappadocia.* Philadelphia: University of Pennsylvania Press, 2003.

van der Horst, Pieter W. "Judaism in Asia Minor." Pages 143–60 in *Studies in Ancient Judaism and Early Christiaity.* Leiden: Brill, 2014.

Wardy, Robert. *The Birth of Rhetoric: Gorgias, Plato and their Successors*. London: Routledge, 1996.
Wathen, Ambrose G. *Silence: The Meaning of Silence in the Rule of St. Benedict*. Collegeville, MN: Cistercian Publications, 1973.
Young, Frances. *Biblical Exegesis and the Formation of Christian Culture*. Cambridge and New York: Cambridge University Press, 1997.
———. "Paideia and the Myth of Static Dogma." Pages 265–83 in *The Making and Remaking of Christian Doctrine: Essays in Honour of Maurice Wiles*. Edited by Sarah Coakley and David Palin. Oxford: Clarendon Press, 1993.

Brian E. Daley, SJ

9. "THE BEGINNING OF HIS WAYS"

Christ as God's Personified Wisdom
in the Early Greek Fathers

Near the beginning of his First Letter to the Corinthians, Paul contrasts the criteria of credibility presupposed by religious Jews and philosophically literate Greeks in his own day with what he presents as the shocking simplicity of the early apostolic preaching: "Jews demand signs," he insists, "and Greeks desire wisdom, but we proclaim Christ crucified, a stumbling-block to Jews and foolishness to Gentiles, but to those who are called—both Jews and Greeks—Christ, the power of God and the wisdom of God" (1 Cor 1:23–24).[1] Like the search for signs of divine power in the world, which animated the long tradition of Jewish faith, the *quest for wisdom* in ancient Mediterranean society, Paul knew, was not limited to Greek philosophical speculation; it was, in its broadest terms, the human search for knowledge of the world and oneself that could be put to use in making life better, more predictable, more controllable. It was not necessarily abstract argument, either. Early in the *Phaedo*, for instance, Plato has Socrates tell of a frequent dream he had earlier in life, urging him to cultivate "the arts" (*mousikē*); but "since the loving pursuit of wisdom (*philosophia*) is the greatest of the arts," Socrates says, he

1. An earlier version of this article was given as the Everett Ferguson Lecture, at the Christian Scholars' Conference, Lubbock Christian University, June 6, 2019.

159

was convinced he was already doing what the voice in his dream commanded.[2] To ask hard questions honestly—to draw on the fruit of long experience, in producing the outlines of an art of living and acting well—was for Plato and his forebears the most beautiful of enterprises.

Ancient Jewish literature, too, as we know, had its own approach not just to "seeking signs" of God's power and presence, but to finding and growing in wisdom. Mainstream Western biblical scholarship since the 19th century, dominated by a narrative that sees the Hebrew Bible as thematically centered on the history of the covenant people, once tended to assume that what we know as the "Wisdom-literature" of the Bible—less historically focused than the narrative of election, engaged with wider human aspirations than simply the historic fate of Israel—is generally late and literarily dependent on other religious traditions of the ancient Near East. Nevertheless, more recent biblical interpreters, beginning with Gerhard von Rad in the 1950s, have argued that the Hebrew tradition of wisdom literature may, in fact, be equally ancient with the Covenant narrative, expressing in terse, aphoristic form traditional advice for living productively and peacefully in a land whose religious center was the God of the exodus and the Jerusalem Temple.[3] Although this non-narrative stream in biblical literature is notoriously difficult to date, von Rad suggests that some classic passages, including parts of the Book of Proverbs, may be quite ancient, representing reflections of pre-exilic authors on how members of the early Jewish Kingdom might learn to cope well with life's challenges. Wisdom of this kind, most biblical passages agree, is in every age the rarest and most precious of resources.[4]

Some passages in the Hebrew Bible, as von Rad pointed out, quite clearly understand this gift of "wisdom" to be a kind of intelligible coherence, a deeper level of meaning, known to God himself and inscribed in the history and structure of the world, yet also at least partially accessible to the human mind that searches for it diligently, and a personal force involved in shaping the world.[5] The best-known instance of this is surely Wisdom's lyrical declara-

---

2. Plato, *Phaedo*, 61a.

3. See Gerhard von Rad, *Wisdom in Israel* (Neukirchen: Neukirchener Verlag,1970; Eng. trans. Nashville: Abingdon, 1972). For an overview of earlier scholarship on the Wisdom tradition, see R. B. Y. Scott, "The Study of the Wisdom Literature," *Interpretation* 24 (1970): 20 ff.

4. See, for example, Job 28:12–19; Prv 8:10–11; 16.16; Wis 6:21; 7.13–14; Sir 24:1–22.

5. So, Job 28:12–19; Ps 104 (103):24.

tion in Proverbs 8, later celebrated by Christian writers through being applied to Christ:

The Lord created me at the beginning of his work,[6] the first of his acts of long ago. Ages ago I was set up, at the first, before the beginning of the earth… When he marked out the foundations of the earth, then I was beside him, like a master-worker, and I was daily his delight, rejoicing before him always, rejoicing in his inhabited world, and delighting in the human race. And now, my children listen to me: happy are those who keep my ways… Happy is the one who listens to me, watching daily at my gates… He who finds me finds life, and obtains favor from the Lord.[7]

A few features of this passage stand out for their influence on the way the figure of Wisdom is later understood by both Jews and Christians: she is the first of God's productions; she is present in the world with God from the start of his activity outside himself, as a kind of willing assistant in the complex, ongoing work of creation; God delights in her presence and help, and she in turn delights in the works of his creation, especially in the human race; so to learn from her, to "keep her ways," brings humans life and blessing. God creates, in other words, *through* the action of the Wisdom that has originally come from him; this Wisdom—"at God's side"—plays a key role in God's ordering of non-divine reality as the world, the *kosmos*, we know; we find our own well-being by seeking out, in the world around us, this same friendly, ordering, life-giving Wisdom for ourselves.

It should not be surprising, then, that some of the earliest Christian witnesses to faith in Jesus refer to him in unmistakably similar terms. Jesus taught and worked in Galilee, some recent New Testament scholars argue, less as a prophet or even a Messianic figure than as a *sage*, a wise man and teacher.[8] Although he sometimes spoke in terms of prophetic warnings or hinted at apocalyptic expectations, most of what we have of his teaching in the Gospels would fall better into the formal categories of biblical wisdom-teachings: aphorisms, parables, challenging or puzzling sayings that draw on his hearers' experience of daily life to stimulate further reflection about God's demands and promises. If this was central to how Jesus was remembered, it is understandable, too,

6. The Septuagint translates, "at the beginning of his ways, for his works"—a version that will figure significantly in fourth-century theological debates about the application of the passage to Christ.

7. Prv 8:22–36.

8. See especially Ben Witherington III, *Jesus the Sage: The Pilgrimage of Wisdom* (Minneapolis: Fortress, 1989).

that some New Testament passages actually refer to him in terms reminiscent of the Wisdom tradition of Israel: not only as speaking in a sapiential style, but as being himself that benevolent figure who realizes and reveals God's ordering work.

This understanding of Jesus' person appears not only in the passage in Paul's First Letter to the Corinthians we quoted at the start, in which "Christ" is referred to explicitly as "the power of God and the Wisdom of God,"[9] but also in such passages as Col 1:15–20 or Eph 1:3–12, where the Christ that Paul and his companions are preaching is described as "the first-born of all creation" and the unifying center of all created after him[10]—the active, personal key to understanding God's provident plan to unify and vivify all he has made.[11] Strikingly, too, Jesus' words to his disciples in Matthew 11, on their return from their first solo adventure, preaching and working signs in his name, might themselves be spoken by God's creative, nurturing Wisdom in Proverbs 8:

I thank you, Father, Lord of heaven and earth, because you have hidden these things from the wise and intelligent and have revealed them to infants… Come to me, all you who are weary and are carrying heavy burdens, and I will give you rest. Take my yoke upon you, and learn from me; for I am gentle and humble of heart, and you will find rest for your souls. For my yoke is easy, and my burden is light.[12]

Jesus here, like Wisdom, presents himself as a "kindly spirit,"[13] inviting those followers humble enough to listen to be consoled by his revelation of God's light and goodness,[14] and so to become themselves "friends of God and prophets."[15] The disciple of Jesus, thinking of the teaching of Jesus as he presents himself at the end of Matthew 11 and dwelling in the "house" of the Church, could well echo the words of the author of the Wisdom of Solomon, "When I enter my house, I shall find rest with her [Wisdom], for companionship with her has no bitterness, and life with her has no pain, but gladness and joy."[16]

9. 1 Cor 1:24.
10. Col 1:15.
11. So especially Eph 1:4–5, 7–10.
12. Mt 11:25, 28–30.
13. See Wis 1:6.
14. Wis 7:25–26.
15. Wis 7:27–28.
16. Wis 8:16.

Second-Century Writers

This subtle but pervasive feature of the portrait of Jesus in the New Testament can give us a clearer sense of why he is so widely referred to, in the writings of influential early Christian theologians, not only as the incarnate form of the divine *Logos*—God's communicative reason or Word—but as himself the *Wisdom* of God. The figure of God's Logos or articulate intelligence, actively present in creation and the moving force in God's self-revelation to Israel, had been emphasized strongly by Philo, the Jewish philosopher and exegete, around the time of Jesus; this conception of the Logos, too, is famously echoed, identified with the person of Jesus, in the prologue to the Gospel of John—a passage that itself decisively shaped the theological understanding of Jesus in early Christianity. But understanding Jesus also as God's personified Wisdom, as we shall see, was a related line of interpretation, subtly different from identifying him as God's Logos: more biblical, less philosophical in its origins, and also an image with a different literary resonance. Still, the difference in theological implications between Christ as divine Logos and Christ as divine Wisdom seems not to have been immediately apparent to early Christian theologians.

Justin, for instance (often styled in early Christian texts as "philosopher and martyr") in his *First Apology*, datable to the early 150s, uses the Johannine characterization of Jesus, as the divine Logos made flesh, to argue that the object of the Christians' faith and worship is really the same universal reason that shaped the speculations of the classical philosophers. He writes:

We have been taught that Christ is the First-begotten of God (*prototokon tou Theou*), and have already testified that he is the reason (*Logos*) of which every race of humanity partakes. Those who lived in accordance with reason are Christians, even though they were called godless, such as—among the Greeks—Socrates and Heraclitus and others like them; among the barbarians, Abraham, Ananiah, Azariah and Mishael, and Elijah, and many others...[17]

In his "Second Apology," which may originally have been simply an explanatory appendix to the "First," Justin repeats this assertion, affirming that "Christ was and is the Reason (*logos*) that is in everyone, who both foretold the things

---

17. Justin, *Apology I*, 46 trans. Edward R. Hardy; in Cyril C. Richardson ed. *Early Christian Fathers* (New York: Macmillan, 1970), 272.

that were to happen through the prophets, and then in his own person, when he became able to experience suffering as we do, and taught these things."[18] Jesus is, in other words, for Justin's version of this early Logos-Christology, the human realization of the same divine universal mind that is the guiding force in creation and active in all reasonable people.

In his other major work, the *Dialogue with Trypho*, which probably also comes from the 150s, Justin also argues—now ostensibly with a group of critical Jewish rabbis—that Jesus is, in the core of his divine identity, a unique "rational power" who proceeds from God the creator.

God begot as a beginning, before all creatures, a kind of rational power (*dynamin logikēn*) from himself, which is called by the Holy Spirit "the glory of the Lord," and sometimes "Son," sometimes "Wisdom," sometimes "Angel," sometimes "God," sometimes "Lord" and "Logos;" at another time, he calls himself "leader of the Army," when he appears in human form to Joshua, the son of Nun… The Word of Wisdom, who is himself God, begotten from the Father of all things, existing as Word and Wisdom and Power and Glory of the one who begot him, bears witness to this through Solomon when he says: "If I declare to you all the things that happen every day, I shall [also] remind you how to number the things that are from eternity. The Lord created me as the beginning of his ways, for his works…"[19]

Here Justin seems to lay special emphasis on the same passage from Proverbs 8 that would play a central role in later attempts to identify the person of Christ as divine. But he makes no attempt to distinguish the divine Wisdom, as described here, from the other terms in the Hebrew Bible that seem to refer to the self-communication or revelatory appearances in creation of the God of Israel. A word, it seems, is a word of wisdom, especially when it comes from God.

Perhaps even more than the figure of Wisdom in the Book of Proverbs and other parts of the Hebrew Bible, however, the concept of God's Logos suffered from a built-in ambiguity, due to the wide range of meanings it conveyed. In Greek, the term could mean, among other possibilities, simply a *word* or unit of language; a *story* or narrative; a *unit* in a larger piece of prose

---

18. Justin, *Apology II*, 10, trans. A, Roberts and J. Donaldson, *ANF* 1 (Grand Rapids: Eerdmans, repr. 1979), 191.

19. Justin, *Dialogue with Trypho* 61 (*ibid..* 227–228). At the end of this passage, Justin quotes Prv 8:22–36, but in the Septuagint version, which includes at the beginning (as verse 22a) a verse not found in the Hebrew: "If I declare to you … the things that are from eternity."

(what in English is usually called a "book"); even the whole of *Scripture*. In a less literary context, it could also signify the *proportion* between two measured entities; the *intelligible structure* or meaning of an argument or a thing; or the human faculty of *reason* itself, in which speech and analysis abide. Philo's works often refer to a *divine* Logos or rationality as a power, by which God has formed the world, revealed himself to the descendants of Abraham, and continues to be present to, and communicate with, rational creatures. Philo seems to think of this Logos—which he sometimes also simply identifies with the biblical figure of God's Wisdom—as linked to the divine reality at the heart of things, yet which also is an *agent* that is, in some sense, independently operative. When God communicates with human beings, Philo understands that it normally happens through God's Logos; so the human experience of God is fundamentally an intellectual "vision" or reception of the divine Logos, as God's image, understood through the ordered universe of sensible, intelligible things that lie "under the feet" of the Word that produced them.[20] This same understanding may well lie behind language about God's Logos in the Prologue to John's Gospel, and also in the works of Justin. Yet despite this ability of Logos-language to link the biblical view of God, who creates and calls a people by intelligible speech, with the dominant late antique cosmological assumptions of Middle Platonism, it is unclear in most of these passages whether Logos-language primarily suggested an *activity* of a radically single God or a distinct divine *agent*. And this, in turn, raised questions for some early Christian writers about the ability of Logos-language alone to do full justice to the implications of the Bible in referring to the identity of Jesus Christ.

Irenaeus, alone among early Christian theologians, avoids the problems of identifying *Logos* and *Sophia* by identifying the Son with the Word of God, but the Wisdom mentioned in Proverbs 8 and similar biblical passages with the Holy Spirit, whom he conceives of as the Father's other "hand" in the work of creation and salvation.[21] Clement of Alexandria, also writing in the last two decades of the second century, emphasizes the distinctive role of the Son in realizing and activating the benevolent power of the Father in creation; so, in

20. So, for example, Philo, *On the Confusion of Tongues* 97; *On Flight and Finding* 92. On the much-discussed subject of Philo's understanding of the divine Logos, see David Winston, *Logos and Mystical Theology in Philo of Alexandria* (Cincinnati: Hebrew Union College Press, 1985); David Runia, "Philo of Alexandria and the *Timaeus* of Plato," *Philosophia Antiqua* 44 (1986): 446–51.

21. See, for example, *Adversus Haereses* IV, 20.3

chapter 2 of Book VII of his *Stromateis* (an extended treatment of God's involvement in all the activities of human intelligence) Clement argues that God providentially "gave philosophy to the Greeks," as well as revealing himself and his will in historical events to Israel.[22] Clement tends, however, to look still farther back, beyond the creation of the universe, and to identify the "Wisdom in which God delighted"—the Wisdom celebrated in Proverbs 8 and elsewhere—simply with the power of God and his "most ancient Word, before the production of all things."[23] God's eternal intelligence, holding within itself all the ideas and forms of things, always stands ready to reach out and communicate with creatures when they happen to appear.

Origen

It is in Origen's work that one first begins to notice the sense of a significant, if subtle, difference between God's Word or *Logos* and God's *Wisdom*. In the first book of his monumental, unfinished *Commentary on John*, Origen first reflects on what a Gospel is, and why the Fourth Gospel should be regarded as the "first-fruits" of Scripture's proclamation of Jesus. As the work of the disciple "whom Jesus loved," who reclined on Jesus' breast at the Last Supper and had learned the secrets of his heart, this Gospel, among the four, most authentically identifies the Savior.[24] For most of Book I, Origen sees the exegete's main work of proclaiming Jesus as carried out by explaining concepts or images (*epinoiai*), which—scattered throughout the Gospels and especially throughout John—reveal to the thoughtful reader central, defining ways of imagining Jesus' unique role in created history. So, the main work Origen undertakes in Book I of his *Commentary* is to reflect on and order the thirty-five or so titles that are given to Jesus in the Fourth Gospel, confident that these names or images are the fundamental key to our understanding who he is, as the Evangelist proclaims him.

The first exegetical task, then, that Origen sees confronting him here, in explaining Christ's identity, is to interpret the Gospel's opening phrase, "In the beginning was the Word." With his characteristic mix of close verbal attention

22. Clement of Alexandria, *Stromateis* VII, 2
23. Clement of Alexandria, *Stromateis* VII, 2
24. Origen, *ComJn* I, 6.

to the biblical text and imaginative freedom, Origen asks what that *archē*, the beginning of all created history, must be *in which* the creative Word (*Logos*) of God first existed. His carefully crafted answer, in chapter 22 of the first book of his *Commentary*, is to point to Christ's primal identity as Wisdom. So Origen writes:

It is in virtue of his being Wisdom that he is called *archē*. For Wisdom says in Solomon (i.e., the *Book of Proverbs*), "God created me the beginning (*archē*) of his ways, for his works," so that the Word might be in an *archē*, namely in *wisdom*. Considered in relation to the structure (*systasis*) of contemplation and thoughts (*noēmatōn*) about the whole of things, it is regarded as Wisdom; but in relation to the communication of the objects of thought with reasonable beings (*ta logika*), it is rewarded as the Word.[25]

Origen's point seems to be that while both the categories of Wisdom and Word, representing fundamental aspects of God's eternal being, suggest the divine, creative, intellectually fertile origin of all things, as the source of creation's identity, "Wisdom" carries with it more the notion of a timeless repository of the divine ideas, the forms of things in themselves, while "Word" suggests the divine act of *communicating* these forms "outwards." The parallel to the Middle Platonic understanding of creation seems clear: it is the work of a divine agent or "second God," who both contains within himself, as divine mind, the intelligible principles of all things, and actively employs them in the formation of an ordered world (*kosmos*);[26] but here in Origen, this conception is used as a tool to interpret *Scripture*. He continues:

For I consider that as a house or a ship is built or fashioned in accordance with the sketches of the builder or designer, while the house and the ship have their beginning (*archē*) in the sketches (*typous*) and calculations (*logous*) inside the builder himself, so all things came into being in accordance with the structures (*logous*) of things that were to exist, as previously defined by God in his Wisdom; "for in wisdom he made all things."[27]

25. Origen, *ComJn* I, 22 (trans. Allan Menzies; *ANF* 9.307 [alt.]).

26. This admittedly Platonic way of thinking about the Son as agent in creation, recalling Plato's own narration of the origin of the world we know, in *Timaeus* 36b-c, had already been employed by Justin in *Apology I*, 60 and *Dialogue* 56. In this sense, Origen is here echoing earlier Greek Patristic tradition. For a broad treatment of later Platonism, including its understanding of the divine mind or *nous* and its use of its own store of ideas in the creation of the universe, see John Dillon, *The Middle Platonists* (London: Duckworth, 1977).

27. Origen, *ComJn* I, 22. (trans. Menzies 307–308 [alt.]) Origen's conclusion of this passage is a brief quotation from Ps 103 (104):24.

The Word, by which God creates all things, thus becomes a kind of executor for the plans or ideas of God that already exist, with a view to creation, in the eternal treasury of God's Wisdom.

Origen takes pains to emphasize, a few chapters further on in Book I of the *Commentary*, that in God, this all-containing Wisdom is not simply a mental function or activity of a monadic divinity, but has a concrete, if wholly spiritual, existence in itself alongside the Father, as the Bible suggests. He writes:

For the Wisdom of the God and Father of all things does not have his concrete existence (*hypostasin*) in mere imagination, like the mental images analogous to our human thoughts. But if someone is able to think of a bodiless individual existence, living and, as it were, vivified by the various ideas that express the intelligible structures of all things, he will know the Wisdom of God that is above all creation, and that beautifully says of itself, "God created me as the beginning of his ways, for his works."[28]

God's Wisdom, for Origen, is a *hypostasis*, then—a concrete individual—which God has produced specifically to be the living mind that holds in itself all knowable ideas, and that then expresses itself actively in the process of time as God's creative, revealing Word. Later, in Book XIX of the *Commentary*, Origen suggests that this hypostasis, who is the Son and Christ and who, as Wisdom, contains the principles of intelligibility for all creation, can himself be thought of as a *kosmos*, an "ordered world;" he writes:

You may wonder whether in some way, according to our discussion, the "first-born of all creation" (Col 1:15) could be called a "world," especially in that he is Wisdom in all its diversity. For because of the fact that the principles (*logoi*) of everything whatsoever, according to which everything created in Wisdom by God has come into being in him (for as the Prophet says, "You have made all things in Wisdom" [Ps. 103 [104]:24), he himself would be Wisdom: so much more varied than the perceptible world, differing from it so much, just as the rational structure (*logos*) of the whole world, free of all matter, differs from the material world—since it is ordered not by matter, but by participating in the rational principle (*logos*) and wisdom that give matter its order.[29]

In his work *On First Principles*, apparently written to outline the basic assumptions of Christian biblical interpretation[30] around 230–231, after he had

28. Origen, *ComJn* I, 39 (my trans.).
29. Origen, *ComJn* XIX, 5 (my trans.).
30. For further reflection on the purpose and content of this influential and controversial work, see my article, "Origen's *De Principiis*: A Guide to the ʻPrinciples' of Christian Scriptural Interpretation" in

begun the *Commentary on John* but before he had finished it, Origen also stresses that the Wisdom of God, referred to in the Bible, is not just a *quality* of God, but a distinct hypostasis, although one without bodily characteristics.[31] Yet if God is eternal, and eternally wise, his hypostatized Wisdom must always have been *with* him, carrying out God's work of forming an ordered world.

Wisdom, therefore, must be believed to have been begotten beyond the limits of any beginning that we can speak of or understand. And because in this very subsistence of Wisdom there was implicit every capacity and form of the creation that was to be, the form both of those things that exist in a primary sense and of those which happen in consequence of them—the whole being fashioned and arranged beforehand by the power of foreknowledge—Wisdom, speaking through Solomon in regard to these very created things that had been, as it were, outlined and prefigured in herself, says that she was created as a 'beginning of the ways' of God, which means that she contains within herself both the beginnings and causes and species of the whole creation.[32]

Later on, in Book IV of the same work, Origen will emphasize that the Wisdom of God always remains inexhaustible to the inquiring human mind: "for however far one may advance in the search and make progress through an increasingly earnest study, even when aided and enlightened in mind by God's grace, he will never be able to reach the final goal of his inquiries."[33] Even though God's Wisdom is oriented towards the created world, it remains itself divine, not a part of creation.

Some years later, in the mid-240s, Origen wrote his great apologetic work against the Middle Platonist philosopher Celsus, who had sharply criticized the Christians as religiously ignorant and unsophisticated. Here, in the course of defending the Jewish and Christian focus on worshipping the transcendent Creator alone, Origen remarks:

For we ought not to imagine that because they are feminine nouns, wisdom and righteousness are feminine in their being. In our view, the Son of God *is* these things, as his genuine disciple showed when he said of him: 'who was made unto us wisdom from God, and righteousness, and sanctification, and redemption.' (1 Cor 1:30). Therefore,

---

John Petruccione, ed. *Nova et Vetera: Patristic Studies in Honor of Thomas Patrick Halton* (Catholic University of America Press, 1998), 3–21.

31. Origen, *Princ* I, 2.2.

32. Origen, *Princ* I, 2.2 (trans. G. W. Butterworth [New York: Harper Torchbook, 1966] 16).

33. Origen, *Princ* IV, 3.14 (trans. Butterworth, 311).

though we may call him a 'second God,' it should be understood by this that we do not mean anything but the virtue (*aretē*) which includes all virtues, and the Logos which includes every logos whatever, of the beings which have been made according to nature... We say that this Logos dwelt in the soul of Jesus and was united with it in a closer union than that of any other soul, because he [i.e., Jesus] alone has been able perfectly to receive the highest participation in him who is the Logos itself, and Wisdom itself, and Righteousness itself.[34]

In these and numerous other passages, Origen draws on the biblical figure of God's creative Wisdom as a way of reflecting more deeply on the uniquely divine identity of Jesus. The Son *is*, as John's prologue affirms, the eternal, creative Word of God, who in God's plan "came to his own" by being "made flesh" and dwelling "among us."[35] Yet that Word of creation and revelation is also God's eternal Wisdom, present at God's side (as Proverbs 8 picturesquely asserts) throughout God's work, residing as revealer in the midst of God's people, delighting to be among them and clarifying for them the virtues and practices that draw an ordered world closer to God. Some modern scholars have suggested that Origen, a contemporary of the (mainly Western) "monarchian" controversy of the early third century, presents divine Wisdom as being even more primordial than the divine Word, because the term suggests a more stable, enduring, "hypostatic" presence, both with God and in the world; thus it avoids the possibly "modalist" implications of Word-language, which might imply the Logos is simply a divine faculty, God's passing activity, by pointing to the figure of the divine Wisdom who is always *there*, at God's side.[36] Whether or not Monarchian theology was a real concern for Origen, he clearly sees in the late Hebrew conception of Wisdom an explanation for how the intelligible structures of the world are contained and rooted in God, ready to be used by God in the formation of a cosmos "outside" himself: not just as forms to be mirrored in concrete things, but as the dynamic possessions of a creative mind, which is involved in the process from the start.[37]

---

34. Origen, *CCels* V, 39 (trans. Henry Chadwick [Cambridge: Cambridge University Press, 1965] 296 [alt.]

35. See Jn 1:3, 11, 14.

36. See Wolfgang Ullmann, "Die Sophialehre des Origenes im 1. Buch seines Johanneskommentars," StPatr 16 (= Texte und Untersuchungen 129; Berlin: Akademieverlag, 12985): 271–76; Stephen E. Waers, "Wisdom Christology and Monarchianism in Origen's *Commentary on John*," GOTR 60 (2015): 93–113. For a hint of Origen's own resistance to heretical Monarchianism, see his *Dialogue with Heracleides* 4.1–9 (ed. J. Scherer: SC 67, 60–62).

37. So Cécile Blanc, commenting on *ComJn* 19.5 (147) (SC 290, 136–37), observes that divine

The Arian Controversy

In the early fourth century, the tradition of drawing on the figure of personified wisdom in the Hebrew Bible took on a new importance in the controversy over Arius's Christology. The outspoken Alexandrian presbyter had insisted, as we know, that Christ is above all a mediator between an essentially unknowable God and the world of finite creatures: himself *created from nothing* in time by the Father ("but not as one of the creatures!"[38]) to be God's agent in both the rest of the act of creating and in the redemption of fallen creatures. Arius's interpretation seems to reflect a wider habit of early fourth-century thinking, possibly inspired by Origen's Wisdom Christology, that stressed the hypostatic, active independence of the Word and that also saw the origin of the Word's being and activity in God's creative act.

Eusebius of Caesaraea, for example—the devoted leader of the Origenist school of exegesis and theological speculation, fifty years after Origen's death—struggles to explain the relationship of God the Son, as divine Wisdom, to God the Father, concluding that it is one of the most "unexplained and inconceivable" aspects of Scripture's mysteries.[39] In reflecting on Proverbs 8, as one of the key biblical sources dealing with the origin of the Son, Eusebius insists in his work, *The Proof of the Gospel*, that the coming-to-be of hypostatic Wisdom cannot be compared with the physical generation of offspring as we know it, or with the separation and launching of what was originally simply an aspect of God's unique and unified being:

For the Son was certainly *not unbegotten* for ages infinite and without beginning within the Father, as one thing within another that differs from itself, being a part of him which afterwards was changed and cast out from him, for such a being would be

---

Wisdom, in Origen's understanding of creation, is not just a "world of ideas" on which the creator, like a skilled artisan, models the realities of the world he creates; it is an actual agent, drawing on the intelligible realities it eternally has within itself to bring the Father's will to full realization. It is a living partner, not a book of plans.

38. See *Confession of Faith of Arius and his Associates to Alexander of Alexandria* (ed. H.-G. Opitz, *Athanasius Werke* III/1 [Leipzig: De Gruyter, 1934], Urkunde 6.2; p. 12, ll. 9–10). Cf. *Letter of Arius to Eusebius of Nicomedia* (Opitz III/1. Urkunde 1.4; p. 3, ll. 1–4). For a summary view of Arius's often obscure theological intentions, see Rowan William, *Arius. Heresy and Tradition* (London: Darton, Longman and Todd, 1987), 230–32.

39. Eusebius of Caesaraea, *The Proof of the Gospel* V, 1 (trans. W.J. Ferrar [London: SPCK, 1920; repr. Grand Rapids: Baker Books, 1981] 233). This work was probably written in the early 320s, and thus would be contemporaneous with Arius's preaching and just prior to the Council of Nicaea.

subject to change… [But] it is equally perilous to take the opposite road, and say thus without qualification that the Son was *begotten of things that were not*, similarly to the other begotten beings; for the generation of the Son differs from Creation *through* the Son.[40]

Eusebius does not understand the Son as simply a "part of God," then, but also refuses to follow Arius's path, and say that the Son was created in time from nothing, to do the Father's will. He also resists the "modalist" solution of comparing the Son's relationship to the Father to the relation of fragrance to an aromatic ointment, or of a ray of light to its source: "the Word of God has its own essence and existence in itself."[41] Eusebius opts for understanding the Son as "a living image" of the Father—in some radical sense subsequent and dependent on the Father in his being, but not formed by him in a material way:

For neither was he brought into being from the Unbegotten Being by way of any event, or by division, nor was he eternally existent with the Father—since the one is unbegotten and the other begotten, and the one is Father and the other is Son, and all would agree that a father must exist before and precede his son. Thus the image of God would be a kind of *living image of the living God*, in a mode that is beyond our words and reasoning, and existing in itself immaterially and unembodied and unmixed with anything opposite to itself—but not such an image as *we* connote by the term, which *differs* in its essential substance and its species, but one which itself *contains the whole* of its species, and is *like in its own essence* to the Father…[42]

Eusebius is laboring hard here to describe the Son, in the context of strict monotheism, as genuinely both divine and derived: not a "second God," co-eternal with the Father, but also not "made out of nothing," as worldly creatures are.

Arius's challenge forced Christian preachers and leaders to move a step farther and to take a stand, in the name of the Church's faith, on the divinity of the Son of God. The classic expression of this, of course—one that remained controversial for some fifty years, driving theological debate through most of the fourth century—was the creed formulated by the Council of Nicaea in 325, affirming that the "only Son of God," encountered historically in Jesus, was "generated from the Father—that is, from the essence (*ousia*) of the Father—God from God, light from light, true God from true God; begotten,

40. Eusebius of Caesaraea, *The Proof of the Gospel* V, 1 (trans. Ferrar, 232–33).

41. *Kath' heauton ousiōtai kai hyphestēke*: Eusebius of Caesaraea, *The Proof of the Gospel* V, 1 (trans Ferrar, 234).

42. Eusebius of Caesaraea, *The Proof of the Gospel* V, 1 (trans. Ferrar, 234 [alt.]).

not made; of the same substance (*homoousion*) as the Father; through whom all things came to be…"[43] This undisguised affirmation that the Son—the divine Wisdom, the Word that became flesh—is *God* in the same sense, belongs to the same eternal substance, as the one God confessed by the Bible, was the council's real challenge to Arius, and even to the more nuanced position of Eusebius, who could not move beyond saying that the Son and the Father, whose image he is, are "*like in essence.*"

The strongest defense of the Nicene position, as things turned out, came from Athanasius, bishop of Alexandria from 328, through five periods of exile, until his death in 373. In his longest anti-Arian polemic, the three *Orations against the Arians*,[44] probably composed during his Roman exile in the 340s, Athanasius deals at length with some fifteen major biblical texts that had been used in argument by all sides in the current debate about Christ. His most extended discussion, towards the end of the *Second Oration*, deals with the now-famous meditation on divine Wisdom in Proverbs 8; especially with Wisdom's affirmation in her own voice, in Prv 8:22 (LXX): "The Lord created me as a beginning of his ways, for his works." Here, in the midst of the controversy over Arius's Christology, the central point at issue has now become Wisdom's claim, in this text, that she is "created" to do the Lord's work. If divine Wisdom here is identified—as the Christian tradition since Paul had identified it—with Christ the Son, in his pre-incarnate existence, then Prv 8:22 seemed to support Arius's claim that the Son himself is essentially the first of creatures, formed by God from nothing in order to be the "first of his ways," the instrument of God's further creating and of his saving work—but clearly not a transcendent or strictly eternal being, as his Father is. Athanasius begins his response by insisting that creation, in its full sense of the formation of something from nothing, is clearly a work that can be done by God alone; so if God's Wisdom is himself a creature from nothing, however exalted his assigned work in history, he himself will simply be engaged in re-shaping what is already created by God, and will need another mediator to have created him.[45] There have been many mediators between God and humanity

---

43. Text from Socrates, *Church History* I,8; in E. J. Jonkers (ed.), *Acta et Symbola Conciliorum quae Saeculo Quarto Habita Sunt* (Leiden: Brill, 1974), 38–39 (my trans.).

44. The so-called *Fourth Oration* is generally agreed today not to be a work of Athanasius, although its author remains unknown. It shows theological resemblances to the thought of the fourth-century modalist writer and correspondent of Athanasius, Marcellus of Ancyra.

45. *Second Oration against the Arians* 16.22.

in history, Athanasius argues—the angels and the Apostles, for example, or
Moses and Aaron:

If then, he were a creature, and one of things that have come to be, there must have
been many such sons, so that God might have many such ministers… But if this is not
possible to see [as correct], but if, while there are many creatures, the Word is one, anyone will conclude from this that the Son differs from them all, and is not on a level
with creatures, but is proper (*idios*) to the Father.[46]

In fact, Athanasius goes on, God creates not through a created Mediator, but
simply by his will, speaking out the Word that is always within him, proper to
him.[47]

The crux of this difficult verse in Proverbs 8, Athanasius realizes, is the
meaning of the phrase, "God *created* me … for his *works*." His subtle interpretation begins from the assumption that "creation," in this text, refers not to the
identity of divine Wisdom itself, but to Wisdom's role in the Economy—the
realm of God's "works"—in the created human person of Jesus. In this passage
(he writes),

it is not as signifying the essence of the Godhead, nor his own everlasting and genuine
generation from the Father, that the Word has spoken through Solomon, but rather
his human economy, directed towards us. And as I said before, he has not said, "I am a
creature," or "I became a creature," but only: "He created…." This mere term, "He created," does not necessarily signify the essence or the generation [of the Son], but indicates something else as coming to pass in him of whom it speaks, not simply that he
who is said to be created is at once, in his nature and essence, a creature.[48]

The passage in Proverbs, then, is for Athanasius really an affirmation that the
created aspect of God's Wisdom, as the "beginning of his ways, for his works,"
is what Wisdom will take upon herself for the sake of fallen creatures: a *created*
humanity that now belongs to God's own Word and Wisdom, assumed in order to transform the human creature from within.

For the Lord, knowing his own essence to be that of the only-begotten Wisdom and
Offspring of the Father, and other than things that have come to be—natural creatures—says in love to humanity, "The Lord created me as a beginning of his ways,"
as if to say: "My Father has prepared for me a body, and has created me, for human

---

46. *Second Oration against the Arians* 17. 27 (trans. John Henry Newman; NPNF II, 4 [repr. Peabody, MA: Hendrickson, 1994] 363).

47. *Second Oration against the Arians* 18.31.

48. *Second Oration against the Arians* 19.45 (trans. Newman, 372 [alt.]).

beings, on behalf of their salvation…" So we must not conceive that the whole Word is in nature a creature, but that he put on a created body and that God "created" him for our sakes: "preparing for him the created body," as it is written, for us, that in him we might be capable of being renewed and deified.[49]

He who is eternally begotten as Son and Word and Wisdom, Athanasius argues, receives a human, created nature—becomes himself a creature—so that the human creature might come to be a child of God in the "new creation."[50] Our renewal in Christ is founded in God's eternal Wisdom, which thus reveals itself in the Incarnation as truly "the beginning of his ways."[51]

Conclusion

Speculation on the figure of divine Wisdom in the Hebrew Bible by early Greek theologians, as a way of identifying the person and work of Christ was—as even these brief reflections suggest—an increasingly important Scriptural means of reflecting on the Son's role of bringing God's saving work in history, God's unfathomable "ways," to their climax and fulfilment. Is it possible, one might ask, to see some coherent direction in how early Christian writers drew on the biblical picture of divine Wisdom to understand Jesus?

1) Jewish reflection on God's work in the world, creating it from nothing, revealing himself in the midst of space and time, calling a people and entering into a covenant with them, seems increasingly to have evoked a sense that God's radical, mysterious unity could be expressed in terms of a plurality of agents that together engage with creatures in a single plan for their good. The personal self-presentation of divine Wisdom in Proverbs 8 and 9, in the Wisdom of Solomon 6–8, and in Sirach 24, among other passages, probably laid the foundation for Philo's reflection on the divine Logos as God's regular agent in creation. The portrait of Jesus in the Synoptic Gospels and the Logos-theology of

---

49. *Second Oration against the Arians* 19.47 (trans. Newman, 374 [alt.]). Athanasius alludes in the final sentence here to Ps 40 [39]:6, as it is quoted in Heb 10:5b: "a body you have prepared for me." The original text of the Psalm, in Hebrew and in the Greek of the LXX, is: "an ear you have given to me…."

50. *Second Oration against the Arians* 21.60–61. So Athanasius writes in 20.61: "For as human beings, receiving the Spirit of the Son, become children through him, so the Word of God, when he himself puts on the flesh of humans, then is said both to be created and to have been made. If then we are by nature sons and daughters, then he is by nature creature and work; but if we become sons and daughters by adoption and grace, then the Word also, when in grace towards us he became human, said, 'The Lord created me.'" (trans. Newman, 381 [alt.]).

51. See *Second Oration against the Arians* 22.77–81.

John, along with phrases in the Pauline corpus, show traces of an early Christian conviction that Jesus could preach and act as he did because he was himself the realization in human history of God's healing, enlightening Wisdom.

2) In Christian theological literature of the second and third centuries, the increasing use of this interpretive theme was not long in coming. Justin recognizes the titles of divine Logos and divine Wisdom as two of the principal biblical titles applicable to Jesus, enabling Christian believers to identify him as the fulfilment of God's historical plan of salvation. Clement of Alexandria sees the communication of wisdom to the human race as one of God's most constant blessings, brought to its fullness in Christ. Origen, a generation later, argues at some length that divine Wisdom is the most basic title or concept (*epinoia*) given in Scripture to identify Jesus and his work. Like Justin and Clement, Origen draws on the Middle Platonic conception of a divine mind containing the whole realm of intelligible, communicable ideas, all of which play a key role in forming an ordered, regular world (*kosmos*), a world where rational (*logikos*) speech and thought are key to well-being. Somewhat differently from the Platonic "world of ideas," these are ordered to the development and perfection of things in history, because they constitute the mind of God's ever-present agent in creation and salvation: divine Wisdom, the Son, the Word who became flesh—Jesus.

3) In the fourth-century controversy over the identity and precise role of Christ, much of the debate was centered on this tradition of identifying him as the divine Wisdom. For Arius and, to a lesser extent, for Eusebius of Caesaraea, identifying Jesus as divine Wisdom implied that he was less than God in the full, transcendent sense—an agent or mediator deliberately formed by God in his image. For Athanasius, on the contrary, Jesus could only do God's work if he were himself fully and eternally divine. Prv 8:22, he argued, must be interpreted as referring not primarily to the identity of divine Wisdom, but to his role in the economy of salvation, as Wisdom enfleshed. Apollinarius of Laodicaea, who claimed to be a disciple of Athanasius, even insists in one fragment that Christ must *be* the divine mind or Wisdom itself, hypostatically distinctive but now "enfleshed," if he is not just to be identified with "the wisdom that enlightens the human mind" in general. For Apollinarius, to be a key to Jesus' identity, divine Wisdom must take the place of a created mind in Jesus.[52]

52. Apollinarius, *Frag.* 70 (in Hans Lietzmann, *Apollinarius von Laodicaea und seine Schule* [repr. Hildesheim: Georg Olms, 1970] 220).

4) In these early reflections on Jesus as the divine Wisdom, one sees an important line of thought that would lead, in the context of growing controversy, in the late fourth century and especially in the work of the three Cappadocian Fathers, to the formal articulation of the distinctively Christian understanding of God as a Trinity of related persons or hypostases, all of whom act as one to create and to save, and who share a radically single, ultimately unknowable divine nature or substance. This Trinitarian understanding of God was offered not as the explanation of a Mystery, but as a way of drawing together into a single conceptual model the convictions about who and what the saving, revealing God of the Bible is. It is also a major step towards the debates and reflections on who Jesus the Savior is in himself, debates that preoccupied the fifth, sixth and seventh centuries, and indeed has led to the continuing development of the whole breadth of our Christian reflection that we call "theology." In Christ, after all, as Paul reminds the Colossians, "all the fullness of God was pleased to dwell"—a fullness that still beckons us to delight in God's own Wisdom, and to "walk in her ways."

Bibliography

Daley, Brian. "Origen's *De Principiis*: A Guide to the `Principles' of Christian Scriptural Interpretation" in John Petruccione,ed. *Nova et Vetera: Patristic Studies in Honor of Thomas Patrick Halton.* Washington, DC: The Catholic University of America Press, 1998, 3–21.

Dillon, John. *The Middle Platonists.* London: Duckworth, 1977.

Runia, David. "Philo of Alexandria and the *Timaeus* of Plato," *Philosophia Antiqua* 44 (1986): 446–51.

Scott, R. B. Y., "The Study of the Wisdom Literature," *Interpretation* 24 (1970): 20–45.

von Rad, Gerhard. *Wisdom in Israel.* Neukirchen: Neukirchener Verlag,1970; Eng. trans. Nashville: Abingdon, 1972.

Ullmann, Wolfgang "Die Sophialehre des Origenes im 1. Buch seines Johanneskommentars," StPatr 16 (= Texte und Untersuchungen 129; Berlin: Akademieverlag, 12985): 271–76.

Waers, Stephen E. "Wisdom Christology and Monarchianism in Origen's *Commentary on John*," GOTR 60 (2015): 93–113.

Williams, Rowan. *Arius. Heresy and Tradition.* London: Darton, Longman and Todd, 1987, 230–32.

Winston, David. *Logos and Mystical Theology in Philo of Alexandria.* Cincinnati: Hebrew Union College Press, 1985.

Witherington, Ben III. *Jesus the Sage: The Pilgrimage of Wisdom.* Minneapolis: Fortress, 1989.

10. THE DIFFERENCES THE SON MAKES

The Vocation of the Theologian-Exegete in Augustine's *Confessions* Book 12

In *Biblical Exegesis and the Formation of Christian Culture*, Frances Young devotes the final chapter to Augustine, whom she describes as a "fitting climax" to her study.[1] Augustine's writings serve as a perfect demonstration of Young's claim that the early Church believed in the "inseparability of theology, exegesis … and spirituality, an integration by no means apparent in the modern world."[2] By brief and penetrating analyses of a range of Augustine's works— from his homilies on the Psalms to his doctrinal masterpiece *On the Trinity*—Young shows how Augustine's works are always and everywhere exegetical. As she pithily puts the point, for Augustine "[t]he theologian is exegete; the exegete is theologian."[3] In and through the remarkable variety of his works, there is this remarkable consistency.

In this volume devoted to the genres of early Christian interpretation, I

---

1. The reading of *Confessions* 12 developed here was born during my master's thesis at McMaster University, under the unfailingly insightful and generous supervision of Professor Peter Widdicombe. I continue to aspire to the careful, rigorous and above-all illuminating reading of texts that so mark Professor Widdicombe's work as a scholar, teacher and preacher.

2. Frances Young, *Biblical Exegesis and the Formation of Christian Culture* (Cambridge: Cambridge University Press, 1997), 265.

3. Young, *Biblical Exegesis and the Formation of Christian Culture*, 282.

want to build on Young's analysis by dwelling on that variety. Consider that in the same short period around the end of the 4th century, Augustine was at work on *Confessions, On Christian Instruction, Questions on the Gospels, Harmony of the Gospels, The Work of Monks, Against Faustus the Manichean, Against Felix, The Nature of the Good,* and *Catechizing the Uninstructed.*[4] These works reflect a diverse range of genres from an exegetical instruction manual to a polemical treatise, from a scriptural commentary to a rule of life for monks; and this description sidesteps the challenging question of how to characterize *Confessions* in terms of genre. I assume that this diversity was not unintentional, but reflects Augustine's sense of his vocation as a theologian. While his responsibilities as a priest and bishop explain some of this diversity, I think there is more to it than that. So, then, what motivated Augustine to write in such a range of genres, and arguably also to be an innovator and inventor in some of them?

I will explore this question through a reading of *Confessions* Book 12. I approach that text as an extended reflection on the theologian's role as exegete in and for the Church. Augustine's reflection seems thrust on him by diverse interpretations of "heaven and earth" (Gn 1:1) that he feels the need to address. I will argue that, by the conclusion of Book 12, Augustine has not only reconciled himself to that diversity, but has decided to play a role in generating even more interpretations of that verse. By considering why Augustine does so, we can see his theological justification for the wide-ranging and often experimental use of genre that characterizes his works. Such justification derives from a distinguishing feature of Augustine's Trinitarian theology, the work of the Son in creation.[5] I build on the work of other scholars who see Books 11, 12 and 13 focusing on the activity of Father, Son and Spirit

---

4. I owe this chronologically-based observation to Thomas F. Martin, "Book Twelve: Exegesis and *Confessio,*" in *A Reader's Companion to Augustine's Confessions,* ed. Kim Paffenroth and Robert P. Kennedy (Louisville, KY: Westminster John Knox Press, 2003), 196.

5. We do not have space or need to consider the debated question of the coherence of *Confessions,* and in particular the relation of the final three so-called "exegetical" books (11 to 13) to the earlier ten so-called "autobiographical" books (1 to 10). My own approach has been influenced most by Robert Crouse and Robert McMahon: Robert Crouse, "'*Recurrens in te unum:*' The Pattern of St. Augustine's *Confessions,*" StPatr 14, no. 3 (1976): 389–418; Robert McMahon, *Augustine's Prayerful Ascent: An Essay on the Literary Form of the* Confessions, (Athens: The University of Georgia Press, 1989). For an up-to-date and comprehensive survey of different approaches to the unity of *Confessions,* see Annemare Kotzé, "Structure and Genre of the *Confessions,*" in *The Cambridge Companion to Augustine's* Confessions (Cambridge: Cambridge University Press, 2020), 28–45.

respectively.[6] Book 12 turns, in my reading, on how the Son's particular work in creation and the Church is centered on difference: the different natures given to "heaven and earth" and the different interpretations of Scripture among believers. In creation and the Church, the Son's particular work is to form and re-form different natures so that they fulfill their purposes in creation. As Augustine encounters the work of the Son over the course of Book 12, he discerns a responsibility to offer different scriptural interpretations that will meet the needs of different believers. This sense of responsibility offers one source of motivation for the variety of genres he writes in and experiments with. I also intend to show how this focus on the Son's work in *Confessions* 12 will uncover the deep coherence of this book. As I detail further below,[7] the question of its coherence has either been side-stepped, or led to divergent conclusions. I demonstrate that the work of the Son draws together the seemingly different subjects discussed over the course of Book 12.

The Son and Difference within Creation

The first work of the Son in *Confessions* 12 relates to the first two creatures God makes. And according to Augustine's exegesis of "heaven and earth," the first two creatures God makes could not be more different. It may even be accurate to say that the pair of creatures God makes in the beginning are opposites. For Augustine the "heaven" of Gn 1:1 is not the sky we see overhead, but the heaven's heaven of Psalm 115, known by God alone, home to the saints and angels. This heaven, from its first existence, has contemplated God, and so participates in God's nature, making it "independent of the spinning changes of time."[8] The "earth," on the other hand, is the lowest of God's creations, the formless matter out of which God created the world we know. Formless matter hovers right next to nothingness; out of this God gave form to all things.[9] We can see how different they are: heaven's heaven enjoys immediate perfection and is united with God eternally, whereas formless matter teeters right next to

---

6. James O'Donnell, *Augustine's Confessions: Text and Commentary* (Oxford: Oxford University Press, 1992), online edition, introductory comment to Book 11, http://www.stoa.org/hippo/framesii.html. See also Crouse, "Pattern" and McMahon, *Augustine's Prayerful Ascent.*

7. See note 19 below.

8. *Confessions,* 12.9.9. Throughout I use Maria Boulding's translation (New York: New City Press, 1997).

9. *Confessions,* 12.4.4.

non-being and will need to be given further form to achieve God's purposes for it. What is most relevant for our inquiry is that these starkly different creatures, in Augustine's reading of Gn 1:1, are both intended by God as his first creations. Especially surprising is that formless matter is a good creature made by God. Colin Starnes contrasts Augustine's approach to formless matter with a Neoplatonic approach where what exists comes by "the result of a lengthy cascade of descending emanations from the One."[10] The result of Augustine's view is that difference, even as staggering a difference as that between heaven's heaven and formless matter, defines creation from the very first two creatures God makes. That is, difference is intended and directly created by God.

Heaven's heaven and formless matter are made different by the Son, the person of the Trinity who gives all created things their distinct natures. As O'Donnell notes, Augustine's discussion of these two creatures involves repeated reference to their respective natures (*species*).[11] *Species* is the second term of a triad that repeats throughout *Confessions* of *modus/species/ordo*.[12] In Augustine's doctrine of creation, Father, Son and Holy Spirit are all inseparably involved in the creation of all things, and yet they also play identifiably distinct roles that reflect their personhood within the Trinity: the Father gives existence to each creature (*modus*), the Son defines its particular nature (*species*), and the Spirit ensures it abides in its nature and flourishes (*ordo*). By discerning the defining features of heaven and earth, then, Augustine is focusing on the work of the Son in giving each its particular nature. As the person who gives distinct natures to each creature, the Son is the origin of difference within creation.[13]

The Son's role as the origin of difference within creation reflects the Son's

10. Colin Starnes, "Prolegomena to the Last Three Books," paper presented at "Celebrating Augustine's *Confessions*: Reading the *Confessions* for the New Millennium," (Pruitt Memorial Symposium, Baylor University, Waco, TX, October 4, 2001), 16.

11. O'Donnell, *Commentary*, introductory comment to Book 12, http://www.stoa.org/hippo/comm12.html.

12. For O'Donnell's brief but helpful introduction to this triad, see his *Commentary*, comment on 1.7.12, http://www.stoa.org/hippo/comm1.html. For the early development of this triad, see Chad Gerber, *The Spirit of Augustine's Early Theology: Contextualizing Augustine's Pneumatology* (Surrey: Ashgate, 2012), 159–62. This triad is related to another favorite triad of measure, number and weight; for this triad's presence in *Confessions*, see Jared Ortiz, '*You Made Us For Yourself*:' *Creation in Augustine's* Confessions (Minneapolis: Augsburg Fortress Press, 2016), chapter one.

13. For further reflection on the significance of Augustine's Christology for our understanding of creation, see Sarah Stewart-Kroeker's searching chapter in this volume.

personhood within the Trinity. After Augustine's initial explication of "heaven and earth," he sums up what he has learned from his exegesis to that point, and begins by affirming that God "created something out of nothing, and created it in that Beginning who is from your very self, in your Wisdom, born of your own substance."[14] Augustine expands on both titles for the Son with descriptions that affirm the Son's unity with and distinction from the Father: as Beginning, the Son is "from" the Father, and so distinct from the Father as his origin, and yet the Son is also "from your very self," and so of the same substance with the Father. As "Wisdom," the Son is "born" from the Father, and so distinct from the Father as the one who begets, and yet the Son is born "of your own substance."[15] Robert Crouse helpfully says that for Augustine the Son is the "principle of intelligible distinction" within the Trinity.[16]

When Augustine then pivots to the creatures that God made, his description returns again and again to distinctions: "heaven and earth, a great thing and a small thing … a mighty heaven and a tiny earth … heaven and earth, two realities: one near to yourself, the other bordering on nothingness; one, to which you alone would be superior, the other, than which nothing would be lower."[17] By moving from the distinction between Father and Son to the distinctions that define creation, Augustine subtly connects the Son's personhood within the Triune life to the Son's role in creation. As the Son has his own distinct personhood through his relation to the Father, so the Son gives creatures their distinct natures within creation. To state this more simply, what the Son does in creation reflects who the Son is in the Trinity.

Our emphasis on difference allows us to interpret a remarkable fact about *Confessions*: in the whole of the work, Augustine does not address God as Trinity until Book 12.[18] In this same passage in which Augustine describes the Son's nature and the distinctions within creation, Augustine addresses God as Trinity

14. *Confessions,* 12.7.7.

15. Brian Daley's essay in this volume offers a rich synthesis of scriptural and early Greek patristic reflections on divine Wisdom. Augustine's approach to the Son as Wisdom discussed here has some powerful resonances with the Eastern figures Daley considers.

16. R. D. Crouse, "Augustinian Platonism in Early Medieval Theology," in *Augustine: From Rhetor to Theologian,* ed. Joanne McWilliam (Waterloo, Ontario: Wilfrid Laurier University Press, 1992), 112.

17. *Confessions,* 12.7.7.

18. O'Donnell also notes this; see *Commentary,* comment on 12.7.7, http://www.stoa.org/hippo/comm12.html. He provides an overview of addresses to the Trinity in Augustine's prior works, but does not address the looming interpretive question of why Augustine saves addressing the Trinity in *Confessions* until this very late stage.

for the first time: "O God, undivided Trinity and threefold Unity."[19] Of course, the Trinity is present implicitly, and the persons of the Trinity are individually addressed explicitly, throughout *Confessions*.[20] And reflections of the Trinity dominate the text in the numerous triads, including the pattern mentioned above of *modus/species/ordo*. Yet God is never addressed specifically as Trinity prior to this occurrence in Book 12. Why has Augustine delayed this long? I suggest that Augustine's exegesis of "heaven and earth" has given him newfound insight into the personhood and role of the Son in creation, and this makes possible his first address to God as Trinity. While in Book 11 Augustine interpreted the "beginning" of "In the beginning" as referring to the Son, his focus on only those first words of the verse meant that the Son was not yet active in creating. When he turns in *Confessions* 12 to "heaven and earth," Augustine's exegesis leads to a description of how the Son is involved in giving particular natures to the first two creatures and so distinguishing them from each other. As I argued above, this particular role of the Son in granting definition and so distinction to creatures reflects the Son's own definition and distinction in relation to the Father. While the full role of the Holy Spirit does not come until *Confessions* 13, with this clarity about the personhood and role of Father and Son, Augustine can address God as Trinity for the first time in *Confessions* 12. If this argument is right, it provides further evidence for the inextricable connection Augustine sees between difference within creation and the Son; as we have seen, interpreting the differences between heaven's heaven and formless matter leads Augustine to his fullest exposition of the work of the Son in creation and the Son's personhood within the Trinity. The distinctiveness of those first creatures yields further insight into the distinctiveness of the Son.

The Son and Difference within the Church

Following his elaborate discussion of heaven's heaven and formless matter, Augustine then turns to consider different interpretations of Gn 1:1. He does so by staging an imaginary dialogue with interlocutors who object to his interpretation and have another to offer. It might seem that Augustine shifts his

---

19. *Confessions*, 12.7.7.

20. The nearest I can find to a Trinitarian address occurs following his Platonic ascent when Augustine calls God, "Eternal truth and true love and beloved eternity" (*Conf.* 7.10.16).

focus from his own interpretation of "heaven and earth" to other interpretations of it because he was aware of an array of alternate readings of Gn 1:1 and the potential conflict this could cause in the Church. No doubt that is part of what is at work. By focusing on the role the Son, I believe that we can discern an even deeper coherence between Augustine's discussion of the creation of "heaven and earth" and that of different scriptural interpretations.[21] As Oliver O'Donovan notes in an essay on the coherence of *Confessions* 10, "Augustine was a self-conscious architect, a designer of literary structures large and small… Augustine liked to think through an intellectual problem organizationally."[22] Following O'Donovan's approach, if Augustine does "think through an intellectual problem organizationally," then the two subjects of *Confessions* 12 are not only contingently related.

Two of Augustine's most able interpreters have sought for the coherence to Book 12, and have come to divergent conclusions. O'Donnell pictures *Confessions* 12 in terms of a contrast, writing that Augustine "sets the unity and clarity of the Word side by side with the plurality and ambiguity of the words through which we approach the Word."[23] The Son's coherent work, then, highlights the unruly diversity of human interpretations of Scripture. McMahon, instead, sees Book 12 following the ever-present logic of ascent, as Augustine gradually returns to God, the Origin of all things. Specifically in Book 12, McMahon argues that Augustine first comes to the "timeless matter of Creation" with formless matter and then pushes further to "the original principles of Scripture,"

---

21. I think a search for such a coherence has been largely neglected in scholarly work on *Confessions* 12. Generally, scholars focus either on the metaphysical claims present in Augustine's interpretation of "heaven and earth" or on how Augustine addresses the fraught issue of diverse interpretations of Scripture. For examples of the former, see Robert J. O'Connell, *St. Augustine's Confessions: The Odyssey of the Soul* (Cambridge, MA: Harvard University Press, 1969), chapter 15, and Roland Teske, *To Know God and the Soul: Essays on the Thought of Saint Augustine* (Washington, DC: The Catholic University of America Press, 2008), chapter 14. For examples of the latter, see Martin, "Book Twelve" and Thomas Williams, "Hermeneutics and reading Scripture" in *The Cambridge Companion to Saint Augustine*, second edition, ed. David Meconi and Elenore Stump (Cambridge: Cambridge University Press, 2014). Of course, I cannot fault scholars for focusing their attention on what is most relevant to their inquiry in Book 12. Even so, I hope to demonstrate that Augustine is relating the challenge of diverse scriptural interpretations within the Church to what Gn 1:1 reveals about the first acts of creation. In other words, the doctrine of creation is decisively informing this exegetical and ecclesial issue.

22. Oliver O'Donovan, "'Repellent Text:' The Transition from Wisdom to Ethics in Augustine's *Confessions* 10," in *Love and Christian Ethics: Tradition, Theory, and Society*, ed. Frederick V. Simmons (Washington, DC: Georgetown University Press, 2016), 51.

23. O'Donnell, *Commentary*, introductory comment to Book 12, http://www.stoa.org/hippo/comm 12.html.

and, by so doing, "he progresses even closer to eternity, as it were."[24] I hope to offer an interpretation of *Confessions* 12 that integrates both of these approaches and shows that they are, ultimately complementary. I argue that by focusing on the work of the Son we can see how the "plurality and ambiguity" of human interpretations do reflect "the original principles of Scripture." I will show that Augustine's affirmation of differing scriptural interpretations follows God's affirmation of difference in creation. As Colin Starnes suggests, in an intriguing but underdeveloped claim, the "divinely ordered multiplicity" revealed by Augustine's interpretation of "heaven and earth" is then further reflected in his conclusion "that there can be multiple and different true interpretations."[25] I think Starnes' insight needs to be developed in terms of the consistent work of the Son. The Son as Word and Wisdom gives heaven's heaven and formless matter different natures appropriate to their purposes within creation, and so the Son as Truth illumines believers' minds with different Scriptural interpretations appropriate for them.

To begin, the only source of contention Augustine has with his imagined interlocutors—though it takes a while to establish that this is the case—is over what Moses really meant by "heaven and earth." Augustine only admits into his imagined discussion those whom he regards as orthodox Christians, who believe that the Scriptures are inspired by the Holy Spirit and submit themselves to the authority of the Church.[26] His approach to their disagreement over "heaven and earth" is to argue that discerning the true meaning of the author is not the primary purpose of exegesis; instead, he suggests, the primary purpose of Christians should be to learn the truth from Scripture. If so, when Christians cannot agree about the author's meaning behind a particular verse, but they agree about the truth that each has gleaned from that verse, they should recognize that they are united in their dependence on "the light of all truthful minds (*lux omnium veridicarum mentium*)," the Son.[27] If we disagree, for example, about whether or not Moses intended the heaven of Gn 1:1 to refer to the literal sky overhead, but we agree that God made all things good, then the difference over Moses' intention lacks any substantial consequence. There is also the practical reality that direct access to the author's mind is

24. McMahon, *Prayer Ascent*, 133.
25. Starnes, "Prolegomena," 17.
26. *Confessions,* 12.17.24; 12.16.23.
27. *Confessions,* 12.18.27.

unavailable, but we all have a relation to God's Truth, the Son, through our "inner eye."[28] Even if the author's intention is a goal in interpretation, as it should be, reference to it will not resolve disagreement. All interpretations that yield truth, no matter how differently they may understand the author's intention, can be traced back to the illumination of Truth within the believer's mind.

To recall the earlier section, the Son's work in giving distinct natures to heaven and earth mirrors the Son's work in illuminating distinct interpretations for individual believers. Just as the Son is involved in making different creatures, each good in their own way, so the Son offers different believers different interpretations, each true according to their needs. The differences between creatures, like the differences between interpretations, are affirmed because they reflect the Son's creative activity. Thus Augustine proceeds to argue that Genesis itself was inspired by God to communicate truth to a variety of believers. Genesis, he says, is like a small fount which is confined to a small space and yet "by means of its branching streams it is a source of richer fertility, and waters wider tracts of countryside, than can any one of the derivative streams alone, far though this may flow from its parent fount."[29] By dividing up into differing streams, the fount is able to cover the greatest area. In their interpretation of Scripture, all believers draw from the same fount, but may discover different truths: "Everyone draws for himself whatever truth he can from it … each a different point, and then hauls his discovery through the meandering channels of his discourse."[30] Later in Book 12, Augustine refers to God as the "fount of truth;"[31] and again in Book 13 he will praise the Son, the Word, as "fount of eternal life" and "fount of life."[32] The gushing fount, then, as an image of the scriptural text, is connected to the image of the Son as the fount of eternal life. The differing scriptural interpretations are intended to make truth accessible to all, regardless of spiritual and intellectual capacity. Just as the Son gives form to the extremes of creation, heaven's heaven and formless matter, so the Son informs all Christians with true scriptural interpretations, from the spiritually adept to the spiritually naïve.[33]

---

28. *Confessions,* 12.20.29.

29. *Confessions,* 12.27.37.

30. *Confessions,* 12.27.37.

31. *Confessions,* 12.30.41.

32. *Confessions,* 13.21.31.

33. Miriam DeCock's essay in this volume provides insight into how another Patristic theologian, Origen, understood different levels of spiritual maturity in the Church.

Especially relevant for our focus is Augustine's decision, following this image of the fount, to offer a brutally materialist interpretation of Gn 1:1. He acknowledges that some will read that verse and imagine God has a body and that heaven and earth refer to two huge bodies. For those "carnal Christians," who are unable to acknowledge the existence of anything immaterial, such an interpretation is the best they can do. Augustine affirms this interpretation—an interpretation, I want to stress, that contains the *falsity* that God has a body—on the grounds that it still communicates the truths that God made all things and made them good. He says that this is the same truth that those who recognize the existence of immaterial things will learn, though these "spiritual Christians" are not so constrained in their interpretations of what "God" and "heaven and earth" refer to.[34] With both interpretations, Augustine emphasizes that believers will learn that created things, in their difference, are good. So, for the more materialist interpreters, he says Gn 1:1 will communicate that: "God made all those natural things which their senses observe all around them in amazing variety;" and, so too, for the more spiritually mature interpreters, they will learn that God made all things "exceedingly good, whether they remain closely grouped around you or, arrayed in ever-widening circles through time and space, they bring about changes or themselves beautifully evolve."[35] The truths that these believers come to, in their different ways, underline the affirmation of difference in creation and the Church that suffuses Book 12.[36]

And, most importantly, by offering his brutally materialist interpretation of Gn 1:1, Augustine is himself affirming the goodness of difference within creation. By giving an interpretation of Gn 1:1 that is accessible to "carnal Christians," he has travelled a long way from his own interpretation of "heaven and earth" as heaven's heaven and formless matter. I believe we are to see an analogy between the extremes of creation, heaven's heaven and formless matter, and the "extremes" within the Church, "spiritual Christians" and "carnal Christians."[37] While Augustine began *Confessions* 12 giving an interpretation only

34. *Confessions,* 12.27.37.

35. *Confessions,* 12.28.38.

36. I suspect Augustine's approach to exegesis here could be helpfully explored further in the light of Geoffrey Dunn's essay in this volume on Augustine's use of the parable of the dragnet in Matthew 13 to counter the Donatists' understanding of the Church. I believe, in other words, that there are connections between Augustine's approach to exegesis discussed here and his approach to the Church discussed by Dunn, in particular that the ultimate discrimination between true Christians and false belongs to God at the final judgment.

37. The distinction between these two kinds of Christians, and the stages of development of a

available to the former, towards the end of the book he is concerned with the latter too. He gradually offers a variety of interpretations that are available for those who can conceive of immaterial existence and those who cannot. Just as the Son gave formless matter, that lowest of creatures, its own particular nature, so Augustine—eventually—comes to support even the most spiritually naïve in their reading of Scripture.

Christ's Authoritative Teaching on Love of Neighbor

Thus far the two roles of the Son in creation and the Church that we have considered are not explicitly related to the Son in his incarnate work. In this final section, we return again to Augustine's consideration of differing scriptural interpretations to discover a crucial role for the Word made flesh; in particular, Christ's command to love God and neighbor serves as an authoritative teaching which defines Augustine's approach. Thus as Jesus of Nazareth, too, the Son's work is focused on difference. Augustine returns to the command to love God and neighbor three times and each time it distinctly informs his approach to alternate scriptural interpretations; under the influence of these verses, we gradually see Augustine first restrain himself from arguing over the right interpretation of "heaven and earth" to then adding other interpretations that will be accessible to "carnal Christians." The authoritative teaching of Christ on love of God and neighbor serves to ensure that differing scriptural interpretations do not threaten the unity of the Church. Thus while the Son as Truth grants differing interpretations to different believers, that same Son as Jesus commands love of God and neighbor which serves to unite Christians in their difference. This final role of the Son is essential to developing Augustine's vocation as an exegete who writes so that all abilities within the Church can glean truth from Scripture. It seems that it is through obedience to Christ's dual-love command that he comes to most fully embrace—and even participate in—the Son's individual care for different believers within the Church.[38]

"carnal Christian" into a "spiritual Christian," is returned to in *Confessions* 13 with Augustine's interpretation of the seven days of creation.

38. Thus Book 12 reflects Augustine's continual wrestling with the dual-love command, a defining concern of his thought. For an illuminating overview of Augustine's approach to the relation of love of

Augustine explicitly refers to the dual-love command three times in the second half of *Confessions* 12. The first reference occurs at what is roughly the *middle* of Book 12.[39] Returning yet again to O'Donovan's description of Augustine as a "self-conscious architect" who thought things through "organizationally," this location identifies the dual-love command as the turning point in Augustine's thinking about diverse scriptural interpretations. In my reading, that first mention prevents Augustine from getting into a potentially nasty argument. Augustine and his rhetorical interlocutors all seem on edge about their disagreement. I believe we can discern some snark in Augustine's opening challenge to them: "Well, my opponents, what have you to say to that? Are these statements incorrect?... You surely are not going to accuse me of error."[40] Augustine's opponents, too, when he has them speak for themselves, do not mince words about their disagreement with Augustine's interpretation: "'What we say is what the author meant... We can explain what he enunciated in those words."[41] Augustine requests divine intervention early on because he is concerned things are about to get even more combative.[42] His turn to the dual-love command shortly thereafter can be seen as one way that God is responding to Augustine's desire for help.

What effect does the dual-love command have? In its first use, Augustine is deliberating about whether he should continue to argue with his interlocutors. He considers whether he bears some responsibility to correct others when they have a false interpretation of "heaven and earth" according to Moses' intention for that verse, yet that false interpretation yields truth. In the background is Augustine's understanding of the relation between Christ's commands to love God and neighbor. As he argues in *On Christian Teaching*, love of God defines the content of both self-love and neighbor-love. Apart from love of God, a human being does not fulfill her purpose, and so she does not enjoy the happiness for which she was made. And since Christ specifies that we are to love our neighbor "as ourselves," if love of self consists in love

---

God and love of neighbor, see John Rist, *Augustine: Ancient Thought Baptized* (Cambridge: Cambridge University Press, 1994), 159–68.

39. Book 12 has 43 chapters. The first reference to the dual-love command is in chapter 27, so there are 26 chapters before this chapter and 26 chapters afterwards. While Augustine himself was not responsible for the chapter divisions, they do provide an approximate means to identify the center of the book.

40. *Confessions*, 12.15.19.

41. *Confessions*, 12.17.24.

42. *Confessions,* 12.16.23.

of God, then it follows that love of neighbor also consists in supporting the other's love of God.[43] In *Confessions* 12, Augustine is wondering whether letting his neighbor persist in a false interpretation of "heaven and earth" would count as a failure of neighbor-love. Love of neighbor may demand, in other words, trying to correct another about what Moses really meant.

With this statement of Augustine's dilemma in mind, we turn to his first words after he refers to the dual-love command:

I confess this with burning love, O my God, O secret light of my eyes, what does it matter to me if what I think the author thought is different from what someone else thinks he thought? I repeat, what does it matter to me if what I think the author thought is different from what someone else thinks he thought?[44]

The repeated phrase "what does it matter to me" indicates that Augustine has decided that his responsibility to love his neighbor does not include correcting him about what "heaven and earth" really means. Why not? Augustine's repeated references to "truth" in the next lines are the most crucial: if my neighbor is learning truths from his reading of Scripture, truths that can only come from illumination by the Son—"the light of all truthful minds"— then my neighbor is loving God, and so I do not need to step in. Though Augustine does not spell it out, the converse is also true: if my neighbor is learning falsities from his reading of Scripture, it very well may be my responsibility to do what I can to correct him (and I believe many of Augustine's own works demonstrate how he felt this responsibility acutely). The dual-love command comes in first, then, to assist Augustine to see that, although he and his interlocutors differ about what "heaven and earth" means, they are united in their devotion to truth, which is itself evidence of their love of God. To argue, then, would not be an act of neighbor-love. Christ's dual-love command ensures that different scriptural interpretations do not cause conflict within the Church as long as there is unity around truth. As O'Donnell puts it, "allowing the plurality of views to thrive [is] an embodiment of the command to love one's neighbor."[45]

Augustine's second and third references to the dual-love command come quickly one after the other and both center on what Christians should believe

---

43. *On Christian Teaching*, Book I.24.25–30.31.
44. *Confessions*, 12.18.27.
45. O'Donnell, *Commentary*, comment on 12.31.42, http://www.stoa.org/hippo/comm12.html.

about Moses, the author of Genesis. He brings up Moses in order to respond to a persistent imagined interlocutor who is not satisfied with Augustine's refusal to argue about what Moses really meant; despite conceding that he and Augustine do agree on the truths of the faith, and disagree only about how to interpret particular verses, this interlocutor does not want to give up. Augustine's response is both cunning and cutting. He distinguishes between what we might call Moses' primary authorial intention and secondary ones: "Unless we believe that Moses meant whatever he did mean in his books with an eye to those twin commandments of charity, we shall make the Lord out to be a liar, by attributing to our fellow-servant a purpose which is at odds with the Lord's teaching."[46] Augustine is making a strong argument from authority, including the authority of both Christ and Moses. Christ teaches that the primary purpose of the Hebrew Scriptures is to inculcate love of God and neighbor, and so that must be Moses' primary purpose too. To cause conflict over what could only be seen as Moses' secondary intentions in writing, then (for example, what he really meant by "heaven and earth"), demonstrates that one is not truly devoted to Moses.[47] As with the first reference to Christ's dual-love command, this second reference too prevents differing scriptural interpretations from causing conflict.

In the third and final reference, Augustine uses it to suggest a particular responsibility of all exegetes. With this instance, too, the command to love one's neighbor is applied to Moses. We might consider Augustine's thinking here to be rather peculiar:

I would have wished that such a gift of eloquence should be given me, and such skill in weaving words, that readers unable to understand how God created would not reject what I said as too difficult for them, while those who could already understand it, whatever might be the true idea they had arrived at by their own reasoning, should not find that their idea had been overlooked in your servant's few words. Finally, I would hope to have written in such a way that if anyone else had in the light of truth seen some other valid meaning, that too should not be excluded, but present itself as a possible way of understanding in what I had said.[48]

---

46. O'Donnell, *Commentary*, 12.25.35.

47. I also suspect there may be another—subtler—way in which the dual-love command is at work. Not to read as Christ has taught us to read is to fail to love God; and to assume that Moses's writings were not devoted to love of God and neighbor is to think poorly of him, and thus to fail to love your neighbor.

48. *Confessions*, 12.26.36.

The dual-love command has two applications here. First, if Augustine is to love Moses as himself—that is, if he is to recognize Moses' equality with himself—then he should attribute to Moses the same admirable goals Augustine has for his own writing. This application of love-of-neighbor justifies Augustine in assuming that Moses himself actually wanted his words to be interpreted differently by different people. The second use of the dual-love command, although it seems rather implicit, is that Augustine (and Moses) both desire for their words to be diversely interpreted as a means of serving their neighbors. This second use is what is most relevant for us. Augustine ultimately comes to offer a variety of interpretations of Gn 1:1 because he believes that this is what love of neighbor requires of him.

Thanks to Augustine's repeated return to the dual-love command, then, he has ended up imitating the Son's own work in creation and the Church as detailed in the previous two parts. As we saw in the first part of this essay, the Son is responsible for giving all creatures their distinctive natures; he does so right from the beginning, with the first two creatures who seem to represent opposite poles of creation, heaven's heaven and formless matter. Further, in the second part of this essay, we saw that within the Church the Son is inwardly present to each believer ensuring that Scripture provides truths that are appropriate to the individual. The same Son who gives believers their individual natures, then, ensures that they glean truths that are comprehensible to them. In this third and final part, we saw how, by submitting himself to the authority of Christ's dual-love command, Augustine eventually ended up by multiplying readings of "heaven and earth" to ensure that all Christians, especially the "carnal" ones, had an interpretation that communicated truth and was accessible to them. Because of this, Augustine's own work as an exegete in *Confessions* 12 ultimately reflects the work of the Son in creation and the Church. Further, I also suggest that by writing in a variety of genres, Augustine would continue to love his neighbors by making the truths of Scripture available to them.

Conclusion

In his recent book on *Confessions*, Jared Ortiz advises us to take Augustine's comments on Moses in Book 12 as a statement of Augustine's own goal as an author. The conclusion Ortiz draws is that Augustine wrote so that his works "had layers of meaning [which] allowed for a multiplicity of interpretations, so that it could reach as many people as possible in order to lead them back to the truth."[49] Ortiz then proceeds to explicate the significance of this approach for interpreters of *Confessions*. Augustine has designed his one book so that it will engage and communicate with a great variety of readers. That is one approach for Augustine to take to be like Moses. Another, complementary approach, is to write in a variety of genres to engage with a variety of readers. I think that approach is evident in the list of works that I referred to at the beginning, all composed around the same time that Augustine was at work on *Confessions*: *Confessions, On Christian Teaching, Questions on the Gospels, Harmony of the Gospels, The Work of Monks, Against Faustus the Manichean, Against Felix, The Nature of the Good*, and *Catechizing the Uninstructed*. As I argued above, *Confessions* 12 establishes an analogy between the stark differences between heaven's heaven and formless matter in creation and those between "spiritual Christians" and "carnal Christians." Augustine's works show his devotion to communicating truth to both kinds of Christians and all the variations in-between these two poles. Further, the work of Christ is the means of salvation for both kinds of Christians, and also the source of harmony between them.

In this essay, I have sketched a possible theological justification for the variety of genres Augustine wrote in and experimented with. The diverse interpretations of Gn 1:1 which Augustine considers in *Confessions* 12 provoke him to reflect on his vocation as an exegete within the Church. I argued that his interpretation of "heaven and earth" serves as the indispensable context for this reflection. The same Son who was at work in giving particular natures to heaven's heaven and formless matter continues to be at work as the One who illuminates different interpretations of Scripture for individual believers. Augustine eventually affirms diverse interpretations within the Church as long as they all reflect the illumination of Truth, the Son inwardly present to every mind, just as, despite their staggering differences, heaven's heaven and formless matter are both creatures made by God. Further, we saw a third way in which the Son was present, through the authoritative teaching of Jesus of Nazareth. The dual-love command first restrained Augustine from arguing over differing scriptural interpretations, and then empowered him to add more

---

49. Ortiz, *You Made Us For Yourself*, 193.

interpretations to meet the needs of his fellow believers. Thus Augustine's own vocation as a theologian as it gets refined over the course of *Confessions* 12 depended on exegesis of the authoritative words of Christ. By obeying Christ's command to love his neighbor in the context of different interpretations of Scripture, Augustine comes to participate in the Son's work by multiplying interpretations of the same verse to make truth accessible to all.

Bibliography

Augustine. *Confessions.* Translated by Maria Boulding. New York: New City Press, 1997.

Augustine. *On Christian Teaching.* Translated by R. P. H. Green. Oxford: Oxford University Press, 1997.

Crouse, R. D. "'*Recurrens in te unum:*' The Pattern of St. Augustine's *Confessions.*" StPatr 14, no. 3 (1976): 389–418.

——— "Augustinian Platonism in Early Medieval Theology." In *Augustine: From Rhetor to Theologian,* edited by Joanne McWilliam, 109–20. Waterloo: Wilfred Laurier University Press, 1992.

Gerber, Chad. *The Spirit of Augustine's Early Theology: Contextualizing Augustine's Pneumatology.* Surrey: Ashgate, 2012.

Kotzé, Annemare. "Structure and Genre of the *Confessions.*" In *The Cambridge Companion to Augustine's* Confessions, edited by Tarmo Toom, 28–45. Cambridge: Cambridge University Press, 2020.

Martin, Thomas F. "Book Twelve: Exegesis and *Confessio.*" In *A Reader's Companion to Augustine's Confessions*, edited by Kim Paffenroth and Robert P. Kennedy, 185–206. Louisville, KY: Westminster John Knox Press, 2003.

McMahon, Robert. *Augustine's Prayerful Ascent: An Essay on the Literary Form of the* Confessions. Athens: The University of Georgia Press, 1989.

O'Connell, Robert J. *St. Augustine's Confessions: The Odyssey of the Soul.* Cambridge, MA: Harvard University Press, 1969.

O'Donnell, James. *Augustine's Confessions: Text and Commentary.* Oxford: Oxford University Press, 1992. http://www.stoa.org/hippo/frames11.html

O'Donovan, Oliver. "'Repellent Text:' The Transition from Wisdom to Ethics in Augustine's *Confessions* 10." In *Love and Christian Ethics: Tradition, Theory, and Society*, edited by Frederick V. Simmons, 51–58. Washington, DC: Georgetown University Press, 2016.

Ortiz, Jared. '*You Made Us For Yourself:' Creation in Augustine's* Confessions. Minneapolis: Augsburg Fortress Press, 2016.

Starnes, Colin. "Prolegomena to the Last Three Books." Paper presented at "Celebrating Augustine's *Confessions*: Reading the Confessions for the New Millennium." Pruitt Memorial Symposium, Baylor University, Waco, TX, October 4, 2001.

Rist, John. *Augustine: Ancient Thought Baptized.* Cambridge: Cambridge University Press, 1994.

Teske, Roland. *To know God and the Soul: Essays on the Thought of Saint Augustine.* Washington, DC: The Catholic University of America Press, 2008.

Williams, Thomas. "Hermeneutics and reading Scripture." In *The Cambridge Companion to Saint Augustine*, second edition, edited by David Vincent Meconi and Elenore Stump, 311–30. Cambridge: Cambridge University Press, 2014.

Young, Frances. *Biblical Exegesis and the Formation of Christian Culture.* Cambridge: Cambridge University Press, 1997.

Geoffrey D. Dunn

11. AUGUSTINE, THE FISHERMEN'S DRAGNET, THE DONATISTS, AND EXCOMMUNICATION

What today we call Donatism was a movement within North African Christianity that emerged in the early years of the fourth century in response to Christian failings during Diocletian's persecution of Christians.[1] At its heart, stirred by bitter betrayal and righteous indignation, Donatism was concerned to preserve the holiness of the Church and the purity of its members by maintaining strict boundaries of inclusion and exclusion. Such a rigorist, elitist, and separatist perspective on Christianity was long a characteristic of North African Christianity, balanced (or not) in tension with the necessity for the unity

1. On Diocletian, see Stephen Williams, *Diocletian and the Roman Recovery* (New York and London: Routledge, 1997); and Roger Rees, *Diocletian and the Tetrarchy*, DDAH (Edinburgh: Edinburgh University Press, 2004). On the persecution see Lactantius, *De mort. per.* (SC 39); Eusebius, *Hist. eccl.* 9 (SC 55); W. H. C. Frend, *The Donatist Church: A Movement of Protest in Roman North Africa* (Oxford: Clarendon Press, 1985 [2nd ed]), 3–25; Timothy D. Barnes, *Constantine and Eusebius* (Cambridge, MA and London: Harvard University Press, 1981), 15–27; Bill Leadbetter, *Galerius and the Will of Diocletian*, RIB (New York and London: Routledge, 2009), 114–34; Brent D. Shaw, *Sacred Violence: African Christians and Sectarian Hatred in the Age of Augustine* (Cambridge: Cambridge University Press, 2011), 66–106; and Jonathan P. Conant, "Memories of Trauma and the Formation of a Christian Identity," in Bronwen Neil and Kosta Simic (eds), *Memories of Utopia: The Revision of Histories and Landscapes in Late Antiquity*, RMCS (London and New York: Routledge, 2020), 36–56.

of the Church.[2] This is a point we could exemplify in Klein's chapter on Perpetua's *passio* and the importance of martyrdom. We need not rehearse the history of the Donatist-Caecilianist sectarian controversy[3] in North Africa during the fourth and fifth centuries (to say nothing about its continued existence in those that followed).[4]

In arguing about the conditions of membership within the Church, both the Donatists and the Caecilianists relied on their readings of the Bible. As Maureen Tilley wrote, "In the Church of the Donatists, the Bible became the storehouse for texts that made sense of their own world, that approved or disapproved both the characters who inhabited that world and the conduct enacted there."[5] In a similar vein we find Richard Miles writing that "… the Donatist textual community put strong emphasis on the scriptures as the key to understanding the world and Church."[6] While the voice of the Donatists themselves has been heard increasingly in recent decades,[7] it still remains drowned out by

2. J. Patout Burns, *Cyprian the Bishop*, RECM (London and New York: Routledge, 2002), 100–165; J. Patout Burns and Robin Jensen, *Christianity in Roman Africa: The Development of its Practices and Beliefs* (Grand Rapids, MI: Eerdmans, 2014), 601–21; and David E. Wilhite, *Ancient African Christianity: An Introduction to a Unique Context and Tradition* (London and New York: Routledge, 2017), 195–239, especially 220–21. cf. Jane E. Merdinger, "In League with the Devil? Donatist and Catholic Perspectives on Pre-Baptismal Exsufflation," in Anthony Dupont, Matthew Alan Gaumer, and Mathijs Lamberigts (eds), *The Uniquely African Controversy: Studies on Donatist Christianity*, LAHR, vol. 9 (Leuven: Peeters, 2015), 172.

3. While both sides laid claim to the epithet 'Catholic' and the Donatists rejected being labelled 'Donatist,' since they found it a term of abuse, and while the choice by Shaw, *Sacred Violence*, 5–6, in calling Donatists 'dissenters' has the unfortunate result of still viewing them from a later perspective, naming both parties in this dispute after their founding or principal leaders is today perhaps the most neutral way of branding them, as leading scholars have started to do. See Maureen A. Tilley, "Redefining Donatism: Moving Forward," *AugStud* 42 (2011): 21–32; and Jesse A. Hoover, *The Donatist Church in an Apocalyptic Age*, OECS (Oxford: Oxford University Press, 2018), 18–24.

4. See Stanisław Adamiak, "When Did Donatist Christianity End?" in Dupont et al., *The Uniquely African Controversy*, 211–36; and Jonathan Conant, "Donatism in the Fifth and Sixth Centuries," in Richard Miles, (ed.), *The Donatist Schism: Controversy and Contexts*, Translated Texts for Historians, Contexts, vol. 2 (Liverpool: Liverpool University Press, 2016), 345–61.

5. Maureen A. Tilley, *The Bible in Christian North Africa: The Donatist World* (Minneapolis: Fortress Press, 1997), 7.

6. Richard Miles, "Textual Communities and the Donatist Controversy," in Miles, *The Donatist Schism*, 255.

7. See Maureen A. Tilley, *Donatist Martyr Stories: The Church in Conflict in Roman North Africa*, Translated Texts for Historians, vol. 24 (Liverpool: Liverpool University Press, 1996); Maureen A. Tilley, "Sustaining Donatist Self-Identity: From the Church of the Martyrs to the *Collecta* of the Desert," *JECS* 5 (1997): 21–35; François Leroy, "L'homilétique africaine masque sous le Chrysostomus latinus, Sévérien de Céramussa et la catéchèse donatiste de Vienne;" *Revhistecclés Ecclésiastique* 99 (2004):

the fate suffered by schismatic literature in general at the hands of victors in controversies and by the sheer size of the literary output from the victors, like the two Numidian bishops Optatus of Milevis (modern El Milia) and Augustine of Hippo Regius (modern Annaba), who were equally adept at offering biblical interpretations.[8]

Of fundamental importance in the disputation about who belonged and did not belong to the Church was the question of who had the right to judge the failings and sins of a Christian and expel them from the community, and when such a judgement should be made. The Donatists, according to Augustine, believed that the Church had the right and duty to remove sinful Christians from the flock as soon as their serious transgression became known, in order to align their interior reality as sinful with their exterior position as outside the Church, while Augustine championed the idea that such decisions were God's alone to be made at the final judgement. Augustine found the parables of Matthew 13 very helpful in this regard. Elsewhere, I have examined the parable of the wheat and the weeds (cf. Mt 13:24–30) as it was used in the African tradition and particularly in Augustine's assessment of the Donatists.[9] Here we shall consider the last of the parables in Matthew 13, that of the dragnet (σαγήνη; Mt 13:47–50).[10]

Our examination concerns how this parable was used by Augustine in his

---

425–34; Alan C. M. Dearn, "The Abitinian Martyrs and the Outbreak of the Donatist Schism," *JEH* 55 (2004): 1–18; Alan C. M. Dearn, "Persecution and Donatist Identity in the Liber Genealogus," in H. Amirav and R. B. ter Haar Romeny, (eds), *From Rome to Constantinople: Studies in Honour of Averil Cameron*, LAHR, vol. 1 (Leuven: Peeters, 2007), 127–35; Leslie Dossey, *Peasant and Empire in Christian North Africa*, The Transformation of the Classical Heritage, vol. 47 (Berkeley and Los Angeles: University of California Press, 2010), 162–67; Alden Bass, "An Example of Pelagian Exegesis in the Donatist Vienna Homilies (Ö.N.B. lat. 4147)," in Dupont et al., *The Uniquely African Controversy*, 197–209; Alden L. Bass, "*Justus sibi lex est*: The Donatist Interpretation of the Law in Romans 2:14," in David V. Meconi (ed.), *Sacred Scripture and Secular Struggles,* BAC 9 (Leiden and Boston: Brill, 2015), 162–78; Maureen Tilley, "Donatist Sermons," in Anthony Dupont et al. (eds), *Preaching in the Patristic Era: Sermons, Preachers, and Audiences in the Latin West*, A New History of the Sermon, vol. 6 (Leiden and Boston: Brill, 2018), 373–402; and Miles, "Textual Communities," 249–83.

8. On Optatus and the African tradition see Geoffrey D. Dunn, "Optatus and Parmenian on the Authority of Cyprian," in Dupont et al., *The Uniquely African Controversy*, 179–96. See André Mandouze, *Prosopographie Chrétienne du Bas-Empire*, vol. 1: *Afrique (303–533) = PCBE* 1 (Paris: Éditions du Centre national de la Recherche scientifique, 1982), 795–97 (Optatus 1).

9. Geoffrey D. Dunn, "Ecclesiology in Early North African Christianity: The Parable of the Wheat and the Weeds," *Augustinianum* 57 (2017): 371–401.

10. In this chapter I am not using any particular modern text of the Bible but using the verses as they were used in the sources, with either my own translation or of others, as acknowledged.

writing against the Donatists and how it played a part at the 411 confrontation between Caecilianists and Donatists in Carthage before the imperial commissioner (a rather under-utilised source until recently).[11] Luckily, not only do we have Augustine's summary of the proceedings of the confrontation of 411[12] and his later recapitulation of events during an encounter in 418 in Caesarea Mauretania (modern Cherchell) with Emeritus, one of his chief Donatist protagonists,[13] but we also have most of the stenographic record of the proceedings, as preserved in a somewhat later edition by Marcellus.[14] From it we see just how arguments about sacramentality, ecclesiology and the very legitimacy of one's version of Christianity depended upon advancing an interpretation of key scriptural passages deemed acceptable to the imperial commissioner. As we shall see, the scriptural arguments employed on both sides during that confrontation were not used for the first time in 411 but had been played and counter-played in the literary battles concerning this controversy in previous years. This is an example of Augustine using biblical texts not as the basis for commentary, but to provide ammunition in theological and legal polemic.

11. See James S. Alexander, "The Donatist Case at the Conference of Carthage of A.D. 411," (PhD diss., St Andrews, 1970); James S. Alexander, "A Note on the Interpretation of the Parable of the Threshing Floor at the Conference of Carthage of A.D. 411," *JTS*, n.s. 24 (1973): 512–19; James S. Alexander, "A Note on the Identity of the 'Man of God' of 1 Kgs: XIII in Gesta coll. Carthag. 3," *JTS* n.s. 28 (1977): 109–12; James S. Alexander, "Aspects of Donatist Scriptural Interpretation at the Conference of Carthage of 411," in Elizabeth A. Livingstone, (ed.), StPatr, vol. 15, papers presented at the Seventh International Conference on Patristic Studies, Oxford 1971, Texte und Untersuchungen zur Geschichte der altchristlichen Literatur, vol. 128 (Berlin: Akademie-Verlag, 1984): 125–30; Erika T. Hermanowicz, *Possidius of Calama: A Study of the North African Episcopate at the Time of Augustine*, OECS (Oxford; Oxford University Press, 2008), 188–220; Thomas Graumann, "Upstanding Donatists: Symbolic Communication at the Conference of Carthage (411)," *Zeitschrift für Antikes Christentum* 15 (2011): 329–55; Neil McLynn, "The Conference of Carthage Reconsidered," in Miles, *The Donatist Schism*, 220–48; and Richard Miles, "Textual Communities," 274–80.

12. I prefer to translation *collocatio* as 'confrontation' rather than the more usual 'conference' because, as Maureen A. Tilley, "Dilatory Donatists or Procrastinating Catholics: The Trial at the Conference of Carthage," *CH* 60 (1991), 14, notes the gathering was not simply a meeting or even a theological disputation but a civil legal proceeding. On Augustine's summary, see Augustine, *Brev.* (CSEL 53.39–92).

13. Augustine, *Gesta cum Emerito* (CSEL 53.181–96). See Geoffrey D. Dunn, "*Romani principes adversum nos provocantur*: Augustine of Hippo's *Epistula* 87 to Emeritus of Caesarea," *Scrinium* 14 (2018): 1–18; and Geoffrey D. Dunn, "Augustine's Memory of the 411 Confrontation with Emeritus of Cherchell," in Neil and Simic, *Memories of Utopia*, 57–72.

14. *Gesta conl. Carth.* (SC 194, 195, 224, 383; CCL 149A; and CSEL 104). See Clemens Weidmann, "Recording and Reporting the *Gesta collationis Carthaginiensis*: Problems and Solutions," in Dupont et al., *The Uniquely African Controversy*, 85–100.

Unlike Haflidson's chapter, examining the variety of genres in which Augustine employed biblical exegesis, centred on *Confessiones*, or Stewart-Kroeker's look at Augustine and the psalms, the presentation here is restricted to Augustine's use of scriptural passages to support his notions of Christian identity and belonging.

It will be argued that the parable of the dragnet usually functions for Augustine as an additional example to support the meaning found in the parable of the wheat and the weeds, that until the final judgement the Church will consist of good and bad people alike (*ecclesia permixta*), and that efforts to remove them are contrary to the divine will. On one or two occasions, the parable of the dragnet functions to demonstrate how numerous the members of the Church are (given how full the dragnet is when it is hauled ashore) and that, even if there are numerous sinners among them, this is no reason for good Christians to panic. The Donatists interpreted the parable, at least according to Augustine, not eschatologically but for the events of the present moment. The fact that the parable barely features in African Christian writers before its extensive use in this controversy is indicative of a long-established concern for purity over tolerance. Tertullian and Cyprian would have had a great deal of sympathy for the Donatist position, with the caveat that Cyprian also accepted that those removed from the Church because of sin were able later to be reconciled.

The results of this investigation of Augustine's use of the parable of the dragnet in his anti-Donatist works reveal what could appear to be an incongruity in Augustine's writings. On the one hand, his use of the parable would suggest that only God could remove someone from the Church. On the other hand, we know that Augustine supported the excommunication of other dissident Christians, such as the Pelagians. This contribution will argue that Augustine, perhaps idiosyncratically and semantically, did not understand excommunication as a separation or removal from the Church as much as it was a means of bringing sinners to penance while suspending their participation in the sacramental life of the Church.

The Parable of the Dragnet in the
Earlier Christian Tradition

Whatever way modern scholars calculate the structure of Matthew's Gospel, all agree that the parables of chapter 13 including that of the dragnet, directed to the disciples and not the crowd, concern the eschatological judgement of the Church that has been collecting members in the present age.[15] The fullness (ἐπληρώθη) of the dragnet refers to the fullness of time and the variety of fish in the catch (ἐκ παντὸς γένους) refers to God's universal outreach for salvation. Apart from the parable of the sower (cf. Mt 13:1–24), the mustard seed (cf. Mt 13:31–32), and the yeast (cf. Mt 13:33), the parables of chapter 13 are unique to Matthew.[16] It is instructive to see the eschatological framework in which to interpret scriptural verses as examined by Opperwall in his chapter on John Cassian.

Within the African tradition prior to Augustine, this parable does not feature much at all in extant writings. We do not find it in Tertullian. It is hard to sustain an argument from silence, but it would be reasonable to say that he did not find the story helpful in confronting any of the opponents against whom he wrote. Why he did not find it useful is imponderable. One could speculate that, as a hardliner, Tertullian supported removing from the Church those who failed to live up to the high demands of Christian initiation. The Church must remain pure.[17] His changing views on how reconcil-

15. Daniel Patte, *The Gospel According to Matthew: A Structural Commentary on Matthew's Faith* (Philadelphia: Fortress Press, 1987), 138, and 198–99; Jack Dean Kingsbury, *Matthew: Structure, Christology, Kingdom* (Minneapolis: Fortress Press, 1989 [rev. ed.]), 144–45; Craig L. Blomberg, *Jesus and the Gospels: An Introduction and Survey* (Nashville: B & H Publishing Group, 2009 [2nd ed.]), 143–46; Charles H. Talbert, *Matthew*, Paideia Commentaries on the New Testament (Grand Rapids, MI: Baker Academic, 2010), 162–73.

16. *Gospel of Thomas* 8 (James M. Robinson, [ed.], *The Nag Hammadi Library* [Leiden: E. J. Brill, 1988 (2nd ed.)], 127), which has a saying about a fisherman and a net and the two stories differ in some respects, there being only one fisherman in the non-canonical version who catches lots of small fish, which are discarded, and he saves the one large fish. This differs from the fishermen in Matthew who separate the pristine (καλὰ) from the rotten (σαπρὰ). There is enough overlap for the conclusion to be reached that they are versions of the same story. See W. G. Morrice, "The Parable of the Dragnet and the Gospel of Thomas," *ExpTim* 95 (1984): 269–73.

17. On Tertullian and repentance see Timothy David Barnes, *Tertullian: A Historical and Literary Study* (Oxford: Clarendon Press, 1985 [rev. ed.]), 119–20 and 141; David Rankin, *Tertullian and the Church* (Cambridge: Cambridge University Press, 1995), 168; Christine Trevett, *Montanism: Gender, Authority and the New Prophecy* (Cambridge: Cambridge University Press, 1996), 114–16; Eric Osborn, *Tertullian: First Theologian of the West* (Cambridge: Cambridge University Press, 1997), 171–76;

iation of those who committed serious offences, from being limited to once after initiation in *De paenitentia* to not being possible at all in *De pudicitia*, reveal an increasingly uncompromising zealot, and would suggest that he did not believe in leaving such matters only for God. Indeed, Tertullian wrote in the latter pamphlet that once discovered, the guilty person is to be excommunicated immediately.[18] As noted in his references to the parable of the wheat and the weeds, Tertullian never referred to the eschatological dimension in these parables of leaving the final judgement to God, but found a way of interpreting it as referring to a separation of good from bad in the here-and-now.[19]

Although Cyprian had made use of the parable of the wheat and the weeds in his developing reflection on Novatian and other rigorists who denied the possibility of reconciliation for penitent *lapsi* who had denied their faith as a result of Decius' policy of religious revival,[20] the parable of the dragnet never features in his surviving letters or pamphlets. This is somewhat surprising given that the parable would have been just as helpful in his argument against rigorists and laxists as the parable of the wheat and the weeds was.[21] Yet, even though Cyprian ultimately did take a moderate position between the two extremes, it remains true that all parties in this controversy did accept that those who apostatised during this time were removed from the Church's communion; where they differed was in the possibility and difficulty of reconciliation. Thus, even Cyprian seems out of step with the thrust of the parable, which seems to indicate that no one is to be excommunicated in the present age.

We do not find use of the parable of the dragnet in *Aduersus nationes* of Arnobius of Sicca (modern El Kef) or in Tyconius. Given that Arnobius was writing to non-Christians and focused on topics like the immortality of the soul this is not surprising. As I have argued elsewhere, given that Tyconius' second rule in *Liber regularum* is about the bipartite nature of the Church, it is surprising that the parables of chapter 13, including that of the dragnet, are

---

Geoffrey D. Dunn, *Tertullian,* The Early Church Fathers (London and New York: Routledge, 2004), 10; Burns and Jensen, *Christianity in Roman Africa,* 296–313; and Geoffrey D. Dunn, "Tertullian," in Philip F. Esler, (ed.), *The Early Christian World* (London and New York: Routledge, 2017 [2nd ed.]), 973.

18. Tertullian, *De pud.* 7, no. 22 (CCL 2.1294): "Simul apparuit, statim homo de ecclesia expellitur ..."

19. Dunn, "Ecclesiology in Early North African Christianity," 374–80.

20. Dunn, "Ecclesiology in Early North African Christianity," 380–89.

21. On Cyprian see Geoffrey D. Dunn, *Cyprian and the Bishops of Rome: Questions of Papal Primacy in the Early Church,* ECS, vol. 11 (Strathfield: St Paul's Publications, 2007).

not used as illustrations.[22] Optatus gives some hint of a reference to the parable in book 4 of his *De schismate Donatistarum.* In interpreting Jer 2:13, he speaks about the people forsaking the living water and digging broken cisterns for themselves, and there criticises Parmenian, claiming that the Donatist bishop has used a dragnet to make every reference to water a reference to the Caecilianists abandoning the true Church (i.e. the of Donatists), whereas, Optatus argued, God was angry with the Jews for having abandoned God and not with Caecilianists, for it was the Donatists who had separated and not the Caecilianists.[23] If there is any hint of a reference to Matthew 13 here, it is vague and of no relevance for our purposes.

The Parable of the Dragnet
at the 411 Confrontation

On 3 June 411, as Caecilianist and Donatist bishops assembled in Carthage in response to the summons by Marcellinus, tribune and notary,[24] to determine whether or not the Donatists had any right to call themselves Catholic, the Donatists complained about the procedural rules Marcellinus had laid down.[25] Even prior to that, the Caecilianists had agreed to a number of Donatist demands about procedures in a letter they sent to Marcellinus and which was read into the *gesta* of the confrontation.[26] Aurelius of Carthage and Silvanus of Summa, the two leading Caecilianist primates, no doubt using Augustine as their ghost-writer, could not resist the opportunity to argue for the legitimacy of Caecilian, the figure whose episcopal ordination a century previously had provoked this schism. Even if Caecilian and Felix of Aptungi, the suspect bishop involved in Caecilian's ordination, had been wrong, Aurelian and Silvanus argued, they would not have been a problem to the Church, since

22. Dunn, "Ecclesiology in Early North African Christianity," 390. On Augustine's non-dependence on Tyconius for the idea of *ecclesia permixta* see Mrcela Andoková, *"Fusca sum et decora*: The Influence of Tyconius on Augustine's Teaching of the *Ecclesia permixta," Acta Universitatis Carolinae. Philosophica et historica* 2 (2015), 61–76.

23. Optatus, *De schis.* 4, no. 9 (SC 412.104–08), especially 4.9.5.

24. On Marcellinus see J. R. Martindale, *Prosopography of the Later Roman Empire* [= *PLRE*], vol. 2: *AD 395–527* (Cambridge: Cambridge University Press, 1980), 711–12 (Marcellinus 10).

25. For the procedural rules see *Gesta conl. Carth.* 1.10 and 14 (SC 195.576–86 and 588–90). For the complaint see *Gesta* 1.14 (SC 195.590). For discussion see Tilley, "Dilatory Donatists," 9–14.

26. Augustine, *Ep.* 129 (CSEL 44.34–39) = *Gesta conl. Carth.* 1.18 (SC 195.602–16).

the Church was going to have mixed fish in it until the time it was brought to the shore, which the two leading African bishop presumed was not then but at the end of time.[27] The parable is not the only evidence; there is reference to the wheat and weeds of Mt 13:24–30 (and 36–43) and to the grain and chaff of Mt 3:12.

After the procedural matters had been adjudicated by Marcellinus, the Caecilianists read out their *mandatum*, their brief of evidence as it were, summarising their position. The Church was a mixed reality (*ecclesia permixta*), consisting of wheat and weeds, grain and chaff, sheep and goats, and good and bad fish. These fish are all in the same net and are only separated when that net comes to shore, which will be at the end of the world.[28]

The Donatists had not prepared a *mandatum* but several days later issued a letter in reply to the Caecilianist position. In part, they reinterpreted the Caecilianist reading of the Matthean parables by rejecting their idea of a morally mixed Church. While they took the field in which the wheat and the weeds grow as the world rather than the Church,[29] they did take the dragnet in which the two types of fish are caught as the Church.[30] The Donatists accurately described the Caecilianist position: the good and the bad are together until the net is dragged ashore at the end of the world.[31] This does not mean that they conceded the Caecilianist interpretation. For them, the shore is not the end time but the time when sinners are discovered within the Church's membership. Sinners can only be part of the Church while they are undetected, while the dragnet is still submerged in the sea; once discovered they must be cast out. This discovery comes through divine judgement (*in divino iudicio*). The Donatists then produced a string of scriptural passages to affirm their position on divine judgement, such as the second part of the parable of the wedding banquet concerning the uninvited guest without the wedding garment (cf. Mt 22:11–13) and God purifying Israel like separating dross from

27. Augustine, *Ep.* 129.5 (CSEL 44.37) = *Gesta conl. Carth.* 1.18 (SC 195.610): "… et piscibus malis futurama esse promissam usque ad tempus … litoris …"

28. *Gesta conl. Carth.* 1.55 (SC 195.656): "… vel mali pisces a bonis, qui nunc intra eadem retia simul trahuntur ad litus, in eodema litore, hoc est in fine saeculi …"

29. *Gesta conl. Carth.* 3.258 (SC 224.1198–200). This is what is found in Mt 13:38, which the Caecilianists had to reinterpret.

30. *Gesta conl. Carth.* 3.258 (SC 224.1202).

31. *Gesta conl. Carth.* 3.258 (SC 224.1202): "Pisces etiam bonos et malos uno retiaculo usque ad litus, id est iustos et iniustos usque in finem saeculi simul contineri et protrahi confirmant …"

silver in a furnace (cf. Ez 22:18–22).[32] No doubt, the Caecilianists would agree with all this, except for the question of timing. The Donatists had removed this from its eschatological timeframe, which is explicit in Matthew, and located the divine and ecclesial separation as happening in the here-and-now.[33] In his own summary of the 411 proceedings, Augustine removed much of the Donatist argument concerning the dragnet and did not deal with their time shift but simply noted that they had conceded that the evil or the unjust can currently exist (even though undetected) within the Church,[34] which is a kind of twisting of the Donatist position.

For the Donatists, the issue of tolerance was inescapably linked to the question of contamination. The Church's purity would be destroyed as the rot caused by one sinner left unremoved would spread. Caecilian's guilt had infected his followers.[35] The Caecilianist response to the Donatist interpretation of Matthew 13 and the other key scriptural passages followed. Augustine was able to make the point that his side accepted that a mixed Church only existed in the present and that a pure Church (as the Donatists wanted) would exist only in the future, at the end of time.[36] However, before the response turned to the parable of the dragnet, the text of *Gesta conlationis Carthaginiensis* breaks off and we have to rely upon Augustine who informs us again that the parable refers only to a separation at the end of time.[37] As Alexander notes:

32. *Gesta conl. Carth.* 3.258 (SC 224.1202–204).

33. This point is not made by Alexander, "The Donatist Case," 19–20; and Alexander, "Aspects of Donatist Scriptural Interpretation," 126–28. He does suggest that this present dimension in the scriptural application might have been traditional in Africa. Tilley, *The Bible in Christian North Africa*, 165, noted the fact that the Donatists had eliminated the eschatological dimension of the Matthean parable.

34. Augustine, *Brev.* 3.8.10 (CSEL 53.59–61). See Alexander, "The Donatist Case," 27–29.

35. Augustine, *Brev.* 3.8.14 (CSEL 53.63–64).

36. *Gesta conl. Carth.* 3.161 (SC 224.1220–22) = Augustine, *Brev.* 3.9.16 (CSEL 53.65–66). See William C. Weinrich, "Cyprian, Donatism, Augustine, and Augustana VIII: Remarks on the Church and the Validity of Sacraments," *CTQ* 55 (1991): 281: "It [the church] has not yet arrived at its end and, therefore, possesses within it both the saints, those destined to arrive at the end, and the sinners, those destined not to arrive at the end."

37. Augustine, *Brev.* 3.9.16 (CSEL 53.66): "… de tali ecclesia dictum esse quod per illam non erit transiturus incircumcisus et immundus; ad immundos enim pertinere schismaticas separations, quae tunc non erunt, quia retia non sunt dirupta; hoc etiam significasse quod corvus avis immunda exierit de arca et non redierit; quae tamen arca, exeunte corvo, non utique omnibus immundis animalibus caruit, sed in ea fuerunt et munda et immunda usque ad diluvium, sicut in ecclesia boni et mali usque ad saeculti finem. Sed finem non de immundis, sed de mundis animalibus Noe obtulit sacrificium, ita non hi qui mali sunt in ecclesia, sed hi qui boni sunt perveniunt ad Deum." The scriptural allusions are to Is 52:1 and Gn 7:8; 8:6 (the unclean raven in Noah's ark) and 20 (the sacrifice of clean animals after the flood). See Alexander, "The Donatist Case," 57.

So far as can be judged from Augustine's account in the Breviculus, the Catholic Extended Reply did not provide a very comprehensive answer to the arguments developed by the Donatists in their Letter. Nevertheless, his distinction between two periods of the Church was a crucial element in the Catholic argument for a morally mixed Church and on this distinction the remainder of the doctrinal debate between the two sides at the Conference was concentrated.[38]

The Parable of the Dragnet Elsewhere in the Donatist Controversy

The use of the parables of Matthew 13, including that of the dragnet, did not appear in this controversy for the first time at the 411 confrontation. It had appeared in the literary exchange between the Donatists and Augustine for over nearly two decades.[39] Yet, as an investigation of the use of Mt 13:47–50 in Augustine reveals, this parable does not feature heavily. Here we can outline the argument presented and suggest why it did not feature more prominently.

In Augustine's first anti-Donatist work, *Psalmus contra partem Donati*, written in 393 while he was still a presbyter, in the first stanza of the abecedarian psalm, we find *abundantia* as the term for the letter A to demonstrate the Caeciliant theological position. The word is explained by reference to the parable of the dragnet.[40] For Augustine the interpretation is clear: the net, which is full and full of an abundance of fish varieties, is the Church, the sea is the world, the shore is the end of the world. With that time reference Augustine can say, "… then is the time for sorting."[41] In trying to get the bad fish out of the net before it comes to shore the Donatists are accused of tearing holes in it, i.e., destroying the unity of the Church. This parable rather than any of the others in Matthew 13 seems to have been chosen because it offered an

38. Alexander, "The Donatist Case," 59.

39. For a summary of Augustine's prior literary dealings with the Donatists see Maureen A. Tilley, "Anti-Donatist Works," in Allan D. Fitzgerald (ed.), *Augustine through the Ages: An Encyclopedia* (Grand Rapids, MI: William B. Eerdmans, 1999), 34–39; and Éric Rebillard, "Augustine in Controversy with the Donatists before 411," in Miles, *The Donatist Schism*, 297–316.

40. See Daniel J. Nodes, "The Organization of Augustine's *Psalmus contra Partem Donati*," *VC* 63 (2009): 390–408; and Geert Van Reyn, "Hippo's Got Talent: Augustine's *Psalmus contra partem Donati* as a Pop(ular) Song," in Dupont et al., *The Uniquely African Controversy*, 251–68.

41. Augustine, *Ps. c. Don.* 11 (CSEL 51.3): "… tunc est tempus separare;" English translation in Maureen Tilley and Boniface Ramsey, *The Donatist Controversy I*, The Works of Saint Augustine: A Translation for the 21st Century, part I – Books, vol. 21: The Donatist Controversy (Hyde Park, NY: New City Press, 2019).

insight into the Church in the present age: it was full of fish (*multos pisces*)[42] and therefore illustrated *abundantia* perfectly, since the parable itself says that the net was filled with all kinds of things (cf. Mt 13:47).[43]

Augustine's *Contra epistulam Parmeniani* was completed *c.* 400 against Parmenian's (the Donatist bishop of Carthage from *c.* 350–392) critique of his fellow Donatist, Tyconius.[44] Augustine rehabilitated Tyconius and found his arguments helpful and effective in use against the latter's fellow Donatists (a reminder, if one were needed, that neither side in this controversy had a single strand to it). In responding to Parmenian's interpretation of Jer 23:28b, Augustine noted that the separation of the grain and the chaff of Matthew 13 is not in the field or even on the threshing floor but in the barn, which must be the end time. The grain and the chaff are like the sheep and the goats of Matthew 25 and the good and bad fish of our parable. Those who think that they are good fish and have gotten rid of the bad fish while still in the net are themselves bad fish: "... and those who do not think that they are grouped together with bad fish are not only bad fish but have even broken the nets of unity."[45] In turning to Cyprian to stress the importance of unity over purity, Augustine noted that the righteous will only no longer mingle with the sinner when in heaven (cf. Phil 3:20; Col 3:1–3; Eph 2:6; Rom 8:24–25; Prv 1:33; 1 Jn 3:2). Heaven is identified with the harvest time, with the last winnowing, with the shore upon which the good and bad fish, who had been held together in the same net, are separated, with the end when the sheep and goats are divided.[46]

It is worth noting that in Augustine's largest anti-Donatist work, *De baptismo contra Donatistas* from 400–401, written after *Contra epistulam Parmeniani*, there is no mention of this parable of the dragnet nor of any other of the parables in Matthew 13, apart from a brief mention of the devil being the enemy who sowed weeds among wheat.[47] This is not to say that the idea is not

---

42. Augustine, *Ps. c. Don.* 17 (CSEL 51.3).

43. It also recalls the post-resurrection story in Jn 21:6 and 11 of the net full to bursting with fish.

44. On Parmenian, see *PCBE* 1.816–821. See Jennifer Ebbeler, "Charitable Correction and Ecclesiastical Unity in Augustine's *Contra epistulam Parmeniani*," in Miles, *The Donatist Schism*, 284–96, who wants to date the work to *c.* 405.

45. Augustine, *C. Parm.* 3.3.19 (CSEL 51.124): "... et qui cum malis piscibus se congregatos esse non putant, non solum mali pisces sunt, sed etiam unitatis retia dirruperunt." English translation in Tilley and Ramsey, *Donatist Controversy I*.

46. Augustine, *C. Parm.* 3..5.27 (CSEL 51.136).

47. Augustine, *De bapt.* 4.9.13 (CSEL 51.237).

canvassed. Augustine noted that the chaff will be blown out of the Church for the Church is indeed "without stain or wrinkle" (Eph 5:27), even though the sinner seems to belong.[48] The Church, as the house of God, could both turn a cold shoulder to anyone who rejected the Church's reproaches and correction (cf. Mt 18:17) and at the same time contain within it those who did not really belong (in other words, their belonging was only illusory), just as a house could contain both precious and common vessels (cf. 2 Tim 2:20). Those outside the Church in heresy or schism had placed themselves there rather than having been placed there.[49] What is not stressed in this treatise is the timing of such a revelation of who really does and does not belong to the Church. A point of interest to the argument of this essay is Augustine's comments in these passages that no one is to be abandoned as a prospect for salvation whether they are sinners within the Church or have been expelled or withdrawn from it.[50] Augustine seems to acknowledge that excommunication occurs, with the hint that it was something the Church rarely did, and that ultimately excommunication was a test rather than a punishment, since God will make the final and correct decision.

Another instance where the parable of the dragnet appears is in book 3 of *Contra litteras Petiliani Donatistae Cortensis*, written about 401, after Augustine had seen the full version of a letter written against Augustine by Petilian, bishop of Cirta (ancient Ciuitas Constantina Cirtensium in the province of Numidia) from *c.* 394 to 419 or 422.[51] Augustine wanted to stress that even if the Church contained bad people that was no reason for anyone to abandon it, as he accused the Donatists of having done. A Christian was called to trust in God and not in people (cf. 1 Cor 3:21–23; Jer 17:5). On that basis, one would never desert the threshing floor (cf. Matthew 13), the house with

48. Augustine, *De bapt.* 1.17.26 (CSEL 51.169–70); 3.18.23 (CSEL 51.214–15); 4.3.4 (CSEL 51.225); and 7.10.19 (CSEL 51.350). Later, in *Retract.* 2.18.45 (CSEL 36.153), Augustine would express regret that his comments about Eph 5:27 were not more clearly expressed. His point was that even though a sinner is left within the church in reality they do not belong (they were false Christians, even though they had true baptism). The stainless nature of the Church will only be revealed fully at the end of time.

49. Augustine, *De bapt.* 7.51.99 (CSEL 51.370–71). Interestingly, Augustine said that those outside the Church in heresy or schism were there "after the nets had burst" (*dirruptis retibus*). There is nothing in the parable or even in Jn 21:11 about nets bursting.

50. Of course, the point he was making in this treatise is about the non-repeatability of valid baptism.

51. On Petilian, see *PCBE* 1.855–868.

common drinking vessels (cf. 2 Timothy 2), break the net to escape from the bad fish, which will be separated out on the shore (our parable), leave the pasture that has goats among the sheep (cf. Matthew 25), nor the field that has weeds mixed in with the wheat (cf. Matthew 13). Augustine wanted to stress that judgement is not in the present age and will be done by God.[52] We are to put up with the bad. In this age there is not a physical or corporeal separation of good and bad but only a spiritual one:

For it is permitted to be separated and to part now from the wicked in life, behaviour, heart and will, which is a separation that must always be maintained. But let corporeal separation be looked forward to at the end of the world with confidence, patience and courage.[53]

In *Epistula ad Catholicos de secta Donatistarum* from 401 Augustine dwelt at length on issues raised by the Donatists, one of which was the mixture of good and bad in the Church. He sought to mention scriptural texts that supported his interpretation (cf. Sg 2:2; Ez 9:4; Mt 13:30, 38–39). The parable of the dragnet is cited in full and called a "very clear parable" about the commingling of good and bad in the Church and as a text that indicates that the good need have no apprehension about being in the company of the bad. Once again, Augustine makes it clear that the shore is the end of the world and that the task of separating good from bad is a divine not a human one.[54] Later, in pointing out Donatist inconsistency, Augustine argues that even if it were true that, at the time of Diocletian's persecution, there were those who sinned in handing over sacred books to be burned, the cleansing of the Church will take place at the last judgement. Those who are righteous put up with (*tolerat*) rather than purge the sinner, with the clear message that Donatists, who purge rather than endure, are not among the righteous. The good fish put up with (*tolerant*) the bad fish, no matter what the bad fish have done.[55] Augustine then has to confront the serious question of why, if a good Christian is

52. Augustine, *C. Pet.* 3.2.3 (CSEL 52.164).

53. Augustine, *C. Pet.* 3.3.4 (CSEL 52.165): "Licet enim a malis interim vita, moribus, corde ac voluntate separari atque discedere: quae separatio semper oportet custodiatur. Corporalis autem separatio ad saeculi finem fidenter, patienter, fortiter exspectetur ..."

54. Augustine, *Ep. ad Cath.* 14.35 (CSEL 52.278): "... similitude apertissima ... malis piscibus se congregatos esse non putant, non solum mali pisces sunt, sed etiam unitatis retia dirruperunt." English translation in Tilley and Ramsey, *Donatist Controversy I.*

55. Augustine, *Ep. ad Cath.* 18.48 (CSEL 52.294).

a tolerant one, Caecilianists were persecuting (*persequendo*) Donatists.[56] For him this was not punishment but correction.[57] If they were being persecuted they ought to rejoice (cf. Mt 5:12), but if they were schismatics, then they were being recalled to righteousness through corrective discipline. If some have gone too far in correcting the Donatists then they too will be separated out at the end, but not now in order that the net not be torn.[58]

In addition, we may observe that following the 411 confrontation, reference to the parable diminishes markedly. In fact, leaving aside *Breviculus*, we only find it in *Contra Donatistas post collationem* of 412, an extended examination of the issues and a response to Donatist post-confrontation statements, and *Contra Gaudentium* from *c.* 420, which responded to a Donatist bishop of Thamugadi (modern Timgad) who was protesting the enforcement of imperial anti-Donatist legislation by threatening to immolate himself and his congregation in their Church.[59]

In the earlier of these two works Augustine again stressed that the shore represented the end of the world and not the present age, that the good and the bad had to live together in the Church until then, and that the good would not be contaminated by the bad.[60] In the second book against Gaudentius, in which Augustine replied to a letter sent directly to him by the Donatist bishop (whereas in the first book he replied to Gaudentius' argument contained in a letter sent to imperial officials), Augustine simply made the point that the good are to have patience at the presence of the bad within the Church and are not to try to break out of the net simply because there are bad fish in it.[61]

---

56. Augustine, *Ep. ad Cath.* 19.52 (CSEL 52.300–01).

57. See Leslie Dossey, "Judicial Violence and the Ecclesiastical Courts in Late Antique North Africa," in Ralph W. Mathisen, (ed.), *Law, Society, and Authority in Late Antiquity* (Oxford: Oxford University Press, 2001), 98–114; Jennifer Ebbeler, *Disciplining Christians: Correction and Community in Augustine's Letters*, OSLA (Oxford: Oxford University Press, 2012); Paul van Geest, "*Timor est servus caritatis* (*s.* 156.13–14): Augustine's Vision on Coercion in the Process of Returning Heretics to the Catholic Church and his Underlying Principles," in Dupont et al., *The Uniquely African Controversy*, 289–309; and Geoffrey D. Dunn, "Discipline, Coercion, and Correction: Augustine against the Violence of the Donatists in Epistula 185," *Scrinium* 13 (2017): 114–30.

58. Augustine, *Ep. ad Cath.* 20.55 (CSEL 52.303–05).

59. See Brent D. Shaw, "State Intervention and Holy Violence: Timgad/Paleostrovsk/Waco," *JAAR* 77 (2009): 853–94.

60. Augustine, *C. Don.* 4.6; 8.11; and 21.36 (CSEL 53.103–04, 108–09, and 137–38).

61. Augustine, *C. Gaud.* 2.3.3 (CSEL 53.257–58).

Augustine and Excommunication

If this were all one read of Augustine, one could be forgiven for thinking that he was a very tolerant bishop and represented a branch of Christianity that took seriously Mt 7:1 about not judging lest one be judged.[62] Yet, this was not the case. Excommunication, as a form of judging serious sinners[63] and removing them from active membership of the Church, existed in the African churches, as elsewhere. This is to be distinguished from the use of coercion and violence, as discussed most notably in *Epistula* 185, which has been the subject of recent study.[64] Here we can only give an overview of Augustine's complex thinking on this. Of course, both coercion and excommunication were intended as corrective, but one was state inflicted and the other Church imposed. Serious sin cut a person off from communion within the Church and it needed a process of penance and reconciliation to restore membership.[65] Augustine made this clear in *Epistula* 153 to Macedonius, vicar of Africa in 413–414,[66] when he stated:

For we remove from the fellowship of the altar certain persons whose grave sins are public, although they were released from your severity, in order that by doing penance and by punishing themselves they may appease him whom they held in contempt by sinning.[67]

The most famous example comes in *Epistula* 250, written in response to a protest from Classicianus, an imperial official, against having been excommunicated by Auxilius, bishop of Nurco in Mauretania Caesariensis. Augustine was most concerned that Auxilius had excommunicated the entire household,[68] but

---

62. This is a verse that does not appear in Augustine's anti-Donatist writings, although it would have suited his argument.

63. For a sense of which sins were more serious than others see Augustine, *En. Ps.* 129.5 (CSEL 95.251).

64. See n. 57 above.

65. See Allan D. Fitzgerald, "Penance," in Fitzgerald, *Augustine through the Ages*, 640–46.

66. See *PLRE* 2.697 (Macedonius 3).

67. Augustine, *Ep.* 153.3.6 (CSEL 44.401): "Nam quosdam, quorum crimina manifesta sunt, a vestra severitate liberatos a societate tamen removemus altaris, ut paenitendo placare possint, quem peccando contempserant, seque ipsos puniendo." English translation in Roland A. Teske, *Letters 100–155,* The Works of Saint Augustine: A Translation for the 21st Century, part II – Letters, vol. 2 (Hyde Park, NY: New City Press, 2003).

68. Augustine, *Ep.* 250.2 (CSEL 57.595–96).

he was also concerned that, even though excommunication was a valid punishment, Classicianus was the victim of Auxilius' rage.[69]

A few further examples will help illustrate the point. In *Sermo* 232, one of Augustine's Easter homilies, we find Augustine complaining that many penitents, whether they had chosen the status for themselves or had been so designated by Augustine through excommunication, and who seemingly took up the challenge to conversion, were not actually using the time to repent but to continue sinning.[70] The purpose of excommunication (and of loving one's enemies) was to induce penance,[71] and to correct rather than punish.[72] As he said in *Enarrationes in Psalmos* 54: "Let us love our enemies, and correct them, punish them, excommunicate them, even cast them out from our society, provided we do so in love."[73] The Christian is still to love the excommunicated person in the hope of winning their reconciliation. Finally, we could mention the excommunication of Pelagius and Caelestius by the Africans, supported by Innocent I, bishop of Rome.[74]

Conclusion: Augustine Reconciling his Thoughts

Was Augustine inconsistent, rhetorically selective in what he said to the Donatists, or able to reconcile these two seemingly contradictory points of view? Could excommunication be held at the same time as accepting an *ecclesia permixta*? Augustine was not unaware of the apparent contradictions here, but obviously, in his anti-Donatist works, he would not have wanted to draw

69. Augustine, *Ep.* 250.3 (CSEL 57.596–97).

70. Augustine, *Sermo* 232.8 (SC 116.276): "Et qui sibi petierunt hoc volunt facere quod faciebat et qui a nobis excommunicati in paenitentium locum redacti sunt nolunt inde surgere, quasi electus sit locus paenitentium." See A.-M. La Bonnardière, "Pénitence et reconciliation des Pénitents d'après Saint Augustin," *Revue des Études Augustiniennes* 13 (1967) : 31–53 and 249–83 and 14 (1968): 181–204.

71. Augustine, *F. et op.* 2.3 (CSEL 41.37); and Augustine, *Ep.* 265.7 (CSEL 57.645).

72. Augustine, *En. Ps.* 78.14 (CCL 39.1106–107).

73. Augustine, *En. Ps.* 54.9 (CSEL 94/1.149): "… diligamus inimicos, corripiamus castigemus excommunicemus, cum dilectione a nobis etiam separemus."

74. Augustine, *Epp.* 175 (CSEL 44.652–62); 176 (CSEL 44.663–68); and 177 (CSEL 44.669–88); and Innocent I, *Epp.* 29 (*In requirendis*) (PL 20.582–88);30 (*Inter caeteras*) (PL 20.588–93); and 31 (*Fraternitatis vestrae*) (PL 20.594–97) = [Augustine], *Epp.* 181 (CSEL 44.701–15); 182 (CSEL 44.715–23); and 183 (CSEL 44.724–30). Innocent's three letters are numbered as 708, 709, and 710 in Philippe Jaffé, *Regesta Pontificum Romanorum ab condita ecclesia ad annum post Christum natum MCXCVIII*, rev. Marcus Schütz (Göttingen: Vandenhoeck and Ruprecht, 206 [3rd edn]). See Otto Wermelinger, *Rom und Pelagius*, Päpste und Papsttum, Bd 7 (Stuttgart: Hiersemann, 1975), 94–101 and 116–30; and Ebbeler, *Discipling Christians*, 221–23.

attention to what could have been exploited as a flaw in his argument (and it is to the Donatists' detriment that they did not, to our knowledge, attempt to exploit it). At the same time, Augustine did make some mention in his anti-Donatist writings of how the reality of excommunication was not contrary to the belief in an *ecclesia permixta*.

Augustine turned to a passage like 1 Cor 5:11–13, noting that Parmenian only cited "Remove the evil from yourselves" and not the rest of the section where Paul said that good Christians should not so much as eat a meal with notorious sinners.[75] Taking Cyprian as his example, Augustine argued that, for the sake of unity, Cyprian physically tolerated sinful Christians but spiritually separated from them, and at one point stated his position:

Is it that, because they could not be bodily separated from them, lest they also uproot the wheat at the same time, it was enough for them to be separated from such persons in their hearts and to be set apart by their life and their conduct, in exchange for the preservation of peace and unity, for the sake of the salvation of the grains that were nurslings and frail, as it were, so that they would not tear to pieces the members of Christ's body by sacrilegious schisms?[76]

While accusing Parmenian of being loose with the truth, Augustine conveniently failed to mention that Cyprian had done more than separate from sinners in his heart. All the lapsed were excommunicated, and several laxist clergy, including Felicissimus, were excommunicated, which led to the establishment of a laxist schismatic Church in Carthage (and in Rome).[77] The purpose might have been corrective, but such an action certainly ruptured ecclesial unity. Augustine's tactic was to chastise Donatists for not tolerating sinners within their own community, perhaps in an effort to divert scrutiny away from the weakness in his argument.

However, Augustine had opened book three of *Contra epistulam Paremniani* by saying that although sinners were not to be removed from the assembly, good Christians, by not consenting or encouraging the evil committed by

75. Augustine, *C. Parm.* 3.2.7 (CSEL 51.108).

76. Augustine, *C. Parm.* 3.2.9 (CSEL 51.111): "An quia non poterant ab eis corporaliter separari, ne simul eradicarent et triticum, sufficiebat eis a talibus corde seiungi, vita moribusque distingui, propter compensationem custodiendae pacis et unitatis, propter salute informorum et tamquam lactentum frumentorum, ne membra corporis Christi per sacrilege schismata laniarent?" Augustine's reclaiming of Cyprian from the Donatists has only just begun to be studied. See Matthew Alan Gaumer, *Augustine's Cyprian: Authority in Roman Africa*, Brill's Series in Church History and Religious Culture, vol. 73 (Leiden and Boston: Brill, 2016).

77. Cyprian, *Ep.* 42 (CCL 3B.199).

sinners, keep the evil away from themselves. Augustine went further: the failure of good Christians to chastise sinners, even by removing them from the sacraments, was a product of evil.[78] In other words, for Augustine excommunication was a mere cessation of sacramental participation and not a separation of wheat from weeds or good fish from bad fish. This he made clear later in book three, where he stated that someone in serious sin may be subject to anathema provided there is no risk of schism (i.e., no risk of others wanting to follow such a person's obvious evil): "In other words, he is not to be uprooted but corrected." If such persons choose not to take the correction, then they have separated themselves from the Church.[79] Rather than talk of the removal of evil from good, Augustine urged his community to remove good from evil. Through the corrective of separation (*per correptionem separationis*) the sinner remained within the Church but shunned, although in a healing and not destructive manner.[80] In this way the Lord's commands both not to separate wheat from weeds and to have nothing to do with the one who does not follow the correction by the Church (cf. Mt 18:17) can be kept.[81] Further, in *De baptismo* Augustine wanted to connect the idea of sinners within the Church with that of the validity of sacraments presided over by sinful clerics.[82]

The holding of two contradictory scriptural injunctions as though they are not is something we find mentioned briefly in the 411 confrontation itself, but only in Augustine's *Breviculus*. Thus, there is a need for a moral rather than physical separation between sinners and good Christians within the Church of the present age. Even though Church discipline requires rebuking and even excommunication and degradation from office, this is not the same as the separation of the wheat from the weeds.[83] The Caecilianists, however, focused their comments on the timing of the separation rather than on the

78. Augustine, *C. Parm.* 3.1.2 (CSEL 51.100): "Quapropter quisquis etiam contempserit ecclesiae disciplinam, ut malos cum quibus non peccat et quibus non favet desistat monere corripere arguer, etsi talem personam gerit et pax ecclesiae patitur etiam a sacramentorum participatione separare, non alieno malo peccat sed suo ..."

79. Augustine, *C. Parm.* 3.2.13 (CSEL 51.114–15): "Non enim ad eracidandum fit, sed ad corrigendum."

80. Augustine, *C. Parm.* 3.2.15 (CSEL 51.118). Thus, Ebbeler, "Charitable Correction and Ecclesiastical Unity," 289, is not attuned to the subtle qualifications Augustine was employing in his use of the term 'excommunication' when she writes: "... the responsibility of Christians to correct sin within the community rather than excommunicate sinners from the community."

81. Augustine, *C. Parm.* 3.2.16 (CSEL 51.120).

82. Augustine, *De bapt.* 7.52.100 (CSEL 51.371–72). See also *Ad Cresc.* 2.28 35 (CSEL 52.395–96).

83. Augustine, *Brev.* 3.9.16–18 (CSEL 53.65–68).

significance of excommunication. As Alexander noted, "... the distinction between a moral and a physical separation between good and bad in the Church of the present ... do[es] not appear to have played any further part in the debate ..."[84] Since Augustine was not seeking to have Donatists excommunicated, it probably did not help him to make too much of the role of excommunication as a corrective action, lest the matter get too waylaid. In *Contra Donatistas post collationem* we find this point mentioned again, that the excommunicated person was still a member of the Church.[85]

The opening parable of Matthew 13, the lengthy one of the wheat and the weeds, was the one most frequently employed by Augustine in his argument about the mixed nature of the Church. His argument was more impressive when he could pile up the examples: the grain and the chaff, the sheep and the goats, the precious and common drinking vessels, and, of course, the good and bad fish. The unique contribution of the dragnet parable was the Matthean comment about the fullness of the dragnet as it was being taken to the shore. From this Augustine could argue that there could be many sinners within the Church, but no matter how numerous they were it was a divine and not a human prerogative to separate the good from the bad, not in the here-and-now but only at the last judgement. Even though he argued passionately with the Donatists in favour of an *ecclesia permixta*, Augustine also accepted excommunication as a tool at the Church's disposal. For him, however, excommunication was not a way of separating good fish from bad or wheat from weeds or chaff, but instead was a way to induce serious sinners correctively onto the path of penance and reconciliation, limiting but not ending their membership of the Church. Augustine could have been accused of hair splitting or semantics in his understanding of the term 'excommunication' since someone cut off from the sacramental life of the Church was to all intents and purposes separated from the Church, but it seems this was not the way the Donatists sought to counter his arguments.

84. Alexander, "The Donatist Case," 59.
85. Augustine, *C. Don.* 20.28 (CSEL 53.127). See also *En. Ps.* 101.1.2 (95/1.28).

Bibliography

Primary Sources

Augustine, *Ad Crescnium grammaticum partis Donati*, CSEL 52, ed. M. Petschenig, Vienna: F. Tempsy, 1909.

Augustine, *Breviculus collationis cum Donatistas*, CSEL 53, ed. M. Petschenig, Vienna: F. Tempsky, 1910.

Augustine, *Contra Donatistas post collationem*, CSEL 53, ed. M. Petschenig, Vienna: F. Tempsky, 1910.

Augustine, *Contra epistulam Parmeniani*, CSEL 51, ed. M. Petschenig, Vienna: F. Tempsky, 1908.

Augustine, *Contra Gaudentium*, CSEL 53, ed. M. Petschenig, Vienna: F. Tempsky, 1910.

Augustine, *Contra litteras Petiliani Donatistae Cortensis*, CSEL 52, ed. M. Petschenig, Vienna: F. Tempsky, 1909.

Augustine, *De baptismo contra Donatistas*, CSEL 51, ed. M. Petschenig, Vienna: F. Tempsky, 1908.

Augustine, *De fide et operibus*, CSEL 41, ed. J. Zycha, Vienna: F. Tempsky, 1900.

Augustine, *Enarrationes in Psalmos*, CSEL 93, 94, and 95, ed. C. Weidmann, H. Müller F. Gori, Vienna: Österreichische Akademie der Wissenschaften, 2001–11.

Augustine, *Epistulae*, CSEL 34, 44 and 57, ed. A. Goldbacher, Vienna: F. Tempsky, 1895–1911.

Augustine, *Epistula ad Catholicos de secta Donatistarum*, CSEL 52, ed. M. Petschenig, Vienna: F. Tempsky, 1909.

Augustine, *Gesta cum Emerito*, CSEL 53, ed. M. Petschenig, Vienna: F. Tempsky, 1910.

Augustine, *Psalmus contra partem Donati*, CSEL 51, ed. M. Petschenig, Vienna: F. Tempsky, 1908.

Augustine, *Retractationes*, CSEL 36, ed. P. Knöll, Vienna: F. Tempsky, 1902.

Cyprian, *Epistulae*, CCSL 3B and C, ed. G. F. Diercks, Turnhout, Brepols, 1994–96.

Eusebius, *Historia ecclesistica*, SC 31, 41, 55, and 73, ed. G. Bardy, Paris: Éditions du Cerf, 1952–2008.

Gesta conlationis Carthaginiensis, SC 194, 195, 224, and 383, ed. S. Lancel, Paris: Éditions du Cerf, 1972–1991 = CCSL 149A, ed. S. Lancel, Turnhout: Brepols, 1974 = CSEL 104, ed. C. Weidmann, Berlin: De Gruyter, 2018.

Gospel of Thomas ed. James M. Robinson, *The Nag Hammadi Library* [Leiden: E. J. Brill, 1988].

Lactantius, *De mortibus persecutorum*, SC 39, ed. J. Moreau, Paris: Éditions du Cerf, 1954.

Optatus, *De schismate Donatistarum*, SC 412 and 413, ed. M. Labrousse, Paris: Éditions du Cerf, 1995–1996.

Tertullian, *De pudicitia*, CCSL 2, ed. E. Dekkers, Turnhout: Brepols, 1954.

Secondary Sources

Adamiak, Stanisław, "When Did Donatist Christianity End?" in Dupont et al., *The Uniquely African Controversy*, 211–36.

Alexander, James S., "The Donatist Case at the Conference of Carthage of A.D. 411," (PhD diss., St Andrews, 1970).

Alexander, James S., "A Note on the Interpretation of the Parable of the Threshing Floor at the Conference of Carthage of A.D. 411," *JTS* n.s. 24 (1973): 512–19.

Alexander, James S., "A Note on the Identity of the 'Man of God' of 1 Kgs: XIII in Gesta coll. Carthag. 3," *JTS* n.s. 28 (1977): 109–12.

Alexander, James S., "Aspects of Donatist Scriptural Interpretation at the Conference of Carthage of 411," in Elizabeth A. Livingstone (ed.), *StPatr* vol. 15, papers presented at the Seventh International Conference on Patristic Studies, Oxford 1971, Texte und Untersuchungen zur Geschichte der altchistlichen Literatur, vol. 128. Berlin: Akademie-Verlag, 1984: 125–30.

Andoková, Mrcela, "*Fusca sum et decora*: The Influence of Tyconius on Augustine's Teaching of the *Ecclsia permixta*," *Acta Universitatis Carolinae. Philosophica et historica* 2 (2015), 61–76.

Barnes, Timothy D., *Constantine and Eusebius*. Cambridge, MA: Harvard University Press, 1981.

Barnes, Timthy D., *Tertullian: A Historical and literary Study*. Oxford: Clarendon Press, 1985 [rev. ed.].

Bass, Alden, "An Example of Pelagian Exegesis in the Donatist Vienna Homilies (ÖNB lat. 4147)," in Dupont et al., *The Uniquely African Controversy*, 197–209.

Bass, Alden, "*Justus sibi lex est*: The Donatist Interpretation of the Law in Romans 2:14," in David V. Meconi (ed.), *Sacred Scripture and Secular Struggles*, BAC 9. Leiden: Brill, 2015, 162–78.

Blomberg, Craig L., *Jesus and the Gospels: An Introduction and Survey*. Nashville: B & H Publishing Group, 2009 [2nd ed.].

Burns, J. Patout, *Cyprian the Bishop*, RECM. London and New York: Routledge, 2002.

Burns, J. Patout and Robin Jensen, *Christianity in Roman Africa: The Development of its Practices and Beliefs*. Grand Rapids, MI: Eerdmans, 2014.

Conant, Jonathan P., "Donatism in the Fifth and Sixth Centuries," in Miles, *The Donatist Schism*, 345–61.

Conant, Jonathan P., "Memories of Trauma and the Formation of Christian Identity," in Neil and Simic, *Memories of Utopia*, 100–165.

Dearn, Alan C. M., "The Abitinian Martyrs and the Outbreak of the Donatist Schism," *JEH* 55 (2004): 1–18.

Dearn, Alan C. M., "Persecution and Donatist Identity in the Liber Genealogus," in H. Amirav and R. B. ter Haar Romeny (eds), *From Rome to Constantinople:*

Studies in Honour of Averil Cameron, LAHR, vol. 1. Leuven: Peeters, 2007, 127–35.

Dossey, Leslie, "Judicial Violence and the Ecclesiastical Courts in Late Antique North Africa," in Ralph W. Mathisen, (ed.), *Law, Society, and Authority in Late Antiquity*. Oxford: Oxford University Press, 2001, 98–114.

Dossey, Leslie, *Peasant and Empire in Christian North Africa*, The Transformation of the Classical Heritage, vol. 47. Berkeley and Los Angeles: University of California Press, 2010.

Dunn, Geoffrey D., *Tertullian*, The Early Church Fathers. London and New York: Routledge, 2004.

Dunn, Geoffrey D., *Cyprian and the Bishops of Rome: Questions of Papal Primacy in the Early Church*, ECS, vol. 11. Strathfield: St Pauls Publications, 2007.

Dunn, Geoffrey D., "Optatus and Parmenian on the Authority of Cyprian," in Dupont et al., *The Uniquely African Controversy*, 179–96.

Dunn, Geoffrey D., "Discipline, Coercion, and Correctio: Augustine against the Violence of the Donatists in Epistua 185," *Scrinium* 13 (2017): 114–30.

Dunn, Geoffrey D., "Ecclesiology in Early North African Christianity: The Parable of the Wheat and the Weeds," *Augustinianum* 57 (2017): 371–401.

Dunn, Geoffrey D., "Tertullian," in Philip F. Esler, (ed.), *The Early Christian World*. London and New York: Routledge, 2017 [2nd ed.], 959–75.

Dunn, Geoffrey D., "*Romani principes adversum nos provocantur*: Augustine of Hippo's *Epistula* 87 to Emeritus of Caesarea," *Scrinium* 14 (2018): 1–18.

Dunn, Geoffrey D., "Augustine's Memory of the 411 Confrontation with Emeritus of Cherchell," in Neil ad Simic, *Memories of Utopia*, 57–72.

Dupont, Anthony, Matthew Alan Gaumer, and Marhijs Lamberigts (eds), *The Uniquely African Controversy: Studies on Donatist Christianity*, LAHR, vol. 9. Leuven: Peeters, 2015.

Ebbeler, Jennifer, *Disciplining Christians: Correction and Community in Augustine's Letters*, OSLA. Oxford: Oxford University Press, 2012.

Ebbeler, Jennifer, "Charitable Correction and Ecclesiastical Unity in Augustine's *Contra epistulam Parmeniani*," in Miles, *The Donatist Schism*, 284–96.

Fitzgerald, Allan D., "Penance," in Allan D. Fitzgerald (ed.), *Augustine through the Ages: An Encyclopedia*. Grand Rapids, MI: Eerdmans, 1999, 640–46.

Frend, W. H. C., *The Donatist Church: A Movement of Protest in Roman North Africa*. Oxford: Clarendon, 1985 [2nd ed.].

Gaumer, Matthew Alan, *Augustine's Cyprian: Authority in Roman Africa*, Brill's Series in Church History and Religious Culture, vol. 73. Leiden: Brill, 2016.

Graumann, Thomas, "Upstanding Donatists: Symbolic Communication at the Conference of Carthage 411," *Zeitschrift für Antikes Christentum* 15 (2011): 329–55.

Hermanowicz, Erika T., *Possidius of Calama: A Study of the North African Episcopat at the Time of Augustine*, OECS. Oxford: Oxford University Press, 2008.

Hoover, Jesse A., *The Donatist Church in an Apocalyptic Age*, OECS. Oxford: Oxford University Press, 2018.

Jaffé, Philippe, *Regesta Pontifium Romanorum ab condita ecclesia ad annum post Christum natum MCXCVIII*, rev. Marcus Schütz. Göttingen: Vandenhoeck and Ruprecht, 2016 [3rd ed.].

Kingsbury, Jack Dean, *Matthew: Structure, Christology, Kingdom* (Minneapolis: Fortress Press, 1989 [rev. ed.]).

La Bonnardière, A.-M., "Pénitence et reconciliation des Pénitents d'après Saint Augustin," *Revue des Études Augustiniennes* 13 (1967) : 31–53 and 249–83 and 14 (1968) : 181–204.

Leadbetter, Bill, *Galerius and the Will of Diocletian*, RIB. New York and London: Routledge, 2009.

Leroy François, "L'homilétique africaine masque sous le chrysostomus latinus, Sévérien de Céramussa et la catéchèse donatiste d Vienne," *Revue d'Histoire Ecclésiastique* 99 (2004) : 425–34.

McLynn, Neil, "The Conference of Carthage Reconsidered," in Richard Miles, *The Donatist Schism: Controversy and Contexts*, Translated Texts for Historians, Contexts, vol. 2. Liverpool: Liverpool University Press, 2016, 220–28.

Mandouze, André, *Prosopographie Chrétienne du Bas-Empire*, vol. 1: *Afrique (303–533)*. Paris: Éditions du Centre national de la Recherche scientifique, 1982.

Martindale, J. R., *Prosopography of the Later Roman Empire*, vol. 2: *AD 395–527*. Cambridge: Cambridge University Press, 1980.

Merdinger, Jane E., "In League with the Devil? Donatist and Catholic Perspectives on Pr-Baptismal Exsufflation," in Dupont et al., *The Uniquely African Controversy*, 153–77.

Miles, Richard (ed.), *The Donatist Schism: Controversy and Contexts*, Translated Texts for Historians, Contexts, vol. 2. Liverpool: Liverpool University Press, 2016.

Miles, Richard, "Textual Communities and the Donatist Controversy," in Miles, *The Donatist Schism: Controversy and Contexts*, Translated Texts for Historians, Contexts, vol. 2. Liverpool: Liverpool University Press, 2016, 249–83.

Morrice, W. G., "The Parable of the Dragnet and the Gospel of Thomas," *ExpTim* 95 (1984): 269–73.

Neil, Bronwen, and Kosta Simic (eds), *Memories of Utopia: The Revision of Histories and Landscapes in Late Antiquity*, RMCS. London and New York: Routledge, 2020.

Nodes, Daniel J., "The Organization of Augustine's *Psalmus contra Partem Donati*," *VC* 63 (2009), 390–408.

Osborn, Eric, *Tertullian: First Theologian of the West*. Cambridge: Cambridge University Press, 1997.

Patte, Daniel, *The Gospel According to Matthew: A Structural Commentary on Matthew's Faith*. Philadelphia: Fortress Press, 1987.

Rankin, David, *Tertullian and the Church*. Cambridge: Cambridge University Press, 1995.

Rebillard, Éric, "Augustine in Controversy with the Donatists before 411," in Miles, *The Donatist Schism*, 297–316.

Rees, Roger, *Diocletian and the Tetrarchy*, DDAH.
Edinburgh: Edinburgh University Press, 2004.

Shaw, Brent D., "State Intervention and Holy Violence: Timgad/Paleostrovsk/Waco," *JAAR* 77 (2009), 853–94.

Shaw, Brent D., *Sacred Violence: African Christians and Sectarian Hatred in the Augustine*. Cambridge: Cambridge University Press, 2011.

Talbot, Charles H., *Matthew*, Paideia Commentaries on the New Testament. Grand Rapids, MI: Baker Academic, 2010.

Teske, Roland A., *Letters 100–155*, The Works of Saint Augustine: A Translation for the 21st Century, part II – Letters, vol. 2. Hyde Park, NY: New City Press, 2003.

Tilley, Maureen A., "Dilatory Donatists or Procrastinating Catholics: The Trial at the Conference of Carthage," *Church History* 60 (1991): 7–19.

Tilley, Maureen, *Donatist Martyr Stories: The Church in Conflict in Roman North Africa* Translated Texts for Historians, vol. 24. Liverpool: Liverpool University Press, 1996.

Tilley, Maureen A., *The Bible in Christian North Africa: The Donatist World*. Minneapolis: Fortress Press, 1997.

Tilley, Maureen A., "Sustaining Donatist Self-Identity: From the Church of the Martyrs to the *Collecta* of the Desert," *JECS* 5 (1997):, 21–35.

Tilley, Maureen A., "Anti-Donatist Works," in Allan D. Fitzgerald (ed.), *Augustine through the Ages: An Encyclopedia*. Grand Rapids, MI: Eerdmans, 1999, 34–39.

Tilley, Maureen A., "Redefining Donatism: Moving Forward," *AugStud* 42 (2011)" 21–32.

Tilley, Maureen A., "Donatist Sermons," in Anthony Dupont et al. (eds), *Preaching in the Patristic Era: Sermons, Preachers, and Audiences in the Latin West*, A New History of the Sermon, vol. 6. Leiden and Boston: Brill, 2018, 373–402.

Tilley, Maureen A. and Boniface Ramsey, *The Donatist Controversy I*, The Works of Saint Augustine: A Translation for the 21st Century, part I – Books, vol. 21: The Donatist Controversy. Hyde Park, NY: New City Press, 2019.

Trevett, Christine, *Montanism: Gender, Authority and the New Prophecy*. Cambridge: Cambridge University Press, 1996.

Van Geest, Paul "*Timor est servus caritatis* (*s.* 156,13–14): Augustine's Vision on Coercion in the Process of Returning Heretics to the Catholic Church and his Underlying Principles," in Dupont et al., *The Uniquely African Controversy*, 289–309.

Van Reyn, Geert, "Hippo's Got Talent: Augustine's *Psalmus contra partem Donati* as a Pop(ular) Song," in Dupont et al., *The Uniquely African Controversy*, 251–68.

Weidmann, Clemens, "Recording and Reporting the *Gesta collationis Carthaginensis*: Problems and Solutions," in Dupont et al., *The Uniquely African Controversy*, 85–100.

Weinrich, William C., "Cyprian, Donatism, Augustine, and Augustana VIII: Remarks on the Church and the Validity of Sacraments," *CTQ* 55 (1991): 267–96.

Werelinger, Otto, *Rom und Pelagius*, Päpste und Papsttum, Bd 7. Stuttgart: Hiersemann, 1975.
Wilhite, David E., *Ancient African Christianity: An Introduction to a Unique Context and Tradition*. London and New York: Routledge, 2017.
Williams, Stephen, *Diocletian and the Roman Recovery*. New York and London: Routledge, 1997.

Daniel Opperwall

12. APOCALYPTIC IMAGERY AND THE TRANSFORMATION OF THE SELF

Matthew 24 and the Book of Revelation in John Cassian

I began work on this essay with a fairly straightforward question. How does John Cassian approach apocalyptic and eschatological imagery from the New Testament and what might that tell us about how he uses Scripture more broadly?[1] As it happens, the period of time during which I was reviewing apocalyptic texts in Cassian witnessed the release of Niki Kasumi Clements' 2020 masterful work, *Sites of the Ascetic Self: John Cassian and Christian Ethical Formation*.[2] Clements has argued with brilliant force that what lies at the heart of Cassian's writings overall is an approach to asceticism in which its

1. I am inspired here by the studies of scriptural reception and exegesis in the ancient world by Peter Widdicombe (to whom this volume is dedicated). For just a few examples see: Peter Widdicombe, "The Two Thieves of Luke 23:32–43 in Patristic Exegesis," *StPatr* 43 (2006): 273–80; "The Drunkenness of Noah and the Patristic Legacy," *StPatr* 44 (2010): 9–13; "A Trinity of Delights: Proverbs 8:30–31 and its Theological Interpretation in Patristic Thought," *Theoforum* 42 (2012): 119–33; "Noah and Foxes: Song of Songs 2:15 and the Patristic Legacy in Text and Art," *StPatr* 59 (2013): 39–52; and *Drunkenness, Nakedness, and the Redemption and Fall of an Image: Noah and Christ* (Grand Rapids, MI: Eerdmans, forthcoming).

2. Niki Kasumi Clements, *Sites of the Ascetic Self: John Cassian and Christian Ethical Formation* (Notre Dame, IN: University of Notre Dame Press, 2020).

practice is designed to be transformative of the human being with regard to both body and soul as they exist within the complex interplay of the individual and the many layers of communal and social life which create and define the self.[3] Asceticism, for Clements' Cassian, is employed not for the ultimate purpose of dour or moralistic self-denial, but is rather carried out in search of the kind of fundamental change that renders human beings complete and able properly to live and relate to God, which is to say to live ethically in the fullest possible sense. The ascetic, therefore, must be trained in the usage of a variety of psychological, affective, and physical tools and techniques by which to seek such transformation, and it is the training of the ascetic in this way that is Cassian's focus in the main body of his writings.

While scriptural exegesis is not a focus of her recent book, Clements' work helps to build a vocabulary for describing some key aspects of the ancient monastic usage of Scripture. In short, it seems to me that for early Christian ascetics Scripture was most often used and cited as, in effect, one of the many tools of transformation, or "technologies of the self," that Clements observes at play in Cassian's project overall.[4] A seminal articulation of a very similar idea is found in the work of Douglas Burton-Christie, who draws primarily from the *Sayings of the Desert Fathers*. For Burton-Christie, the culture of scriptural interpretation in the *Sayings* was one in which "monks sought to reshape their imaginations around the world of Scripture and allow it to penetrate to the core of their beings and their communities."[5] Something similar is afoot with Evagrius. Indeed, his writings may offer the most explicit examples of Scripture used as a spiritual tool, especially in the *Antirhetikos* in which passages of Scripture are deliberately used as weapons in the ascetic's battle with demons.[6] Reminiscent (and fascinating) trends in the Syriac as-

3. See Clements, *Sites of the Ascetic Self*, 1–26.

4. The phrase "technologies of the self" is taken from Foucault, who is a major influence on Clements' work. Clements, *Sites of the Ascetic Self*, 16.

5. Douglas Burton-Christie, *The Word in the Desert: Scripture and the Quest for Holiness in Early Christian Monasticism* (Oxford: Oxford University Press 1993), vii.

6. See David Brakke, "Reading the New Testament and Transforming the Self in Evagrius of Pontus," in *Asceticism and Exegesis in Early Christianity: The Reception of New Testament Texts in Ancient Ascetic Discourses*, ed. Hans-Ulrich Wiederman (Göttingen: Vandenhoeck & Ruprecht, 2013), 284–99; and Augustine Casiday, *Reconstructing the Theology of Evagrius Ponticus: Beyond Heresy* (Cambridge: Cambridge University Press, 2013), 100–132. The kind of direct "talking back" with demons advocated by Evagrius is not discussed explicitly by Cassian. Evagrius' "talking back" as a specific technique is rather more delimited than Cassian's use of Scripture insofar as Cassian seems to deploy Scripture as a means of

cetical use of biblical literature, especially by way of metrical homilies meant to shape the listener's mind by re-forming it around key biblical themes and motifs, have also been explored by Robert Kitchen in this volume.[7]

And indeed, similar patterns are at play in John Cassian. Cassian reads Scripture on a variety of levels and for many reasons, and certainly engages in (and reflects on) the traditional forms of exegesis and commentary of his time.[8] This includes, at times, reading Scripture in search of literal, allegorical, moral, and anagogical meaning by way of exegetical processes that are familiar to the scholar of ancient Christianity.[9] Yet sustained and explicit exegesis is fairly rare in Cassian overall. Instead, Christopher J Kelley, in the sole monograph in English that focuses entirely on Cassian's approach to Scripture, emphasizes the imitation of key biblical figures as being central to Cassian's usage of Scripture.[10] Similarly, Rebecca Harden Weaver emphasizes the interaction between Scripture and the purified heart as the driving force in Cassian's usage.[11] If these observations are correct (and I think they are), then an approach to Cassian begins to emerge in which Scripture serves as one of the many tools and techniques—both simple and complex—that lead the ascetic toward transformation in Clements' reading of his work overall. Like such tools as communal obedience and monastic institutional structure, or the myriad bodily practices that mark the ascetic's way of life, soaking the

---

helping to shape the mind of the monk holistically, with the aim of self-transformation, where Evagrius in the *Antirhetikos* frames it as a weapon of combat meant to help conquer specific demons in the heat of battle. On the issue of eschatology in Scripture (my topic here), Evagrius appears to engage more frequently in exegesis as such, and also seems to pay more explicit attention to temporal eschatology. I do not wish to imply, however, that these are differences in kind—the connection between Cassian's approach and that of his master is certainly clear.

7. Robert Kitchen, "Teaching Lions to Fast: Jacob of Serugh on Daniel 6," in this volume. While the metrical re-working of Scripture for such purposes is strongly associated with the Syriac literary tradition, the work of Andrew Faulkner, "Late Antique Poet as Scriptural Interpreter: The Case of the *Metaphrasis Psalmorum*," in this volume reminds us that the approach was common across the Christian world in early centuries.

8. *Conlat.* 14 is the most obvious example.

9. See Niki Kasumi Clements, "The Asceticism of Interpretation: John Cassian, Hermeneutical *Askesis*, and Religious Ethics," in *Scripture, Tradition, and Reason in Christian Ethics,* ed. Bharat Ranganathan and Derek Alan Woodard-Lehman (London: Palgrave MacMillan, 2019), 67–88.

10. Christopher J. Kelley, *Cassian's Conferences: Scriptural Interpretation and the Monastic Ideal* (London: Ashgate, 2012). Kelley's monograph focuses heavily on the use of biblical narrative in Cassian, leaving many questions to be explored regarding Cassian's use of non-narrative scriptural passages (such as those I am looking at here).

11. Rebecca Harden Weaver, "Access to scripture: experiencing the text." *Interpretation* 52, no. 4 (1998): 367–79.

mind in Scripture, and referring back to it again and again serve for Cassian as cognitive techniques that help to reshape the ascetic at every level.

Treated this way, Scripture, for Cassian, is a tool of a very particular sort—a kind of store-house of symbols, advice, and promises with which the ascetic can populate his or her mind in order to remain on the road to the goal of spiritual and physical transformation. Cassian's usage of Scripture as a tool of transformation is, therefore, highly varied, and changes shape depending on what topic he is considering at a given moment, and of course on the nature of the scriptural passages with which he is working.

So, then, what use does Cassian make of apocalyptic and eschatological imagery, in particular, in his writings? As it turns out, Cassian will use apocalyptic imagery in his writings most often (though not exclusively) to give ascetics access to a group of emotionally charged mental images and exhortations meant to help strengthen their spiritual resolve when they are struggling in light of some of the most essential and salient problems of his day—especially problems of monastic authority and different types of affective discouragement. To explore this, I will focus especially on New Testament apocalyptic texts by examining the handful of Cassian's references to Matthew 24,[12] along with his more numerous references to the book of Revelation.

Cassian brings up Matthew 24 and Revelation most often for three specific reasons. First, to address the problem of individual ascetics who are losing heart or are tempted to give up on the struggle of their chosen life. Second (and closely related), to assist those who are vexed with especially intractable difficulties and help them frame their struggles in a more productive way. Third, to warn ascetics against submitting to the wrong authorities, be they heretics or poor spiritual leaders, and to assert his own authority as a teacher and guide.[13] Of note, Cassian gives almost no attention at all to the temporal or historical dimensions of Matthew 24 or Revelation, or the question of how the world might ultimately end.[14]

12. The similar apocalyptic pericopes found in Luke 21 and Mark 13 do not appear to be cited directly by Cassian, who seems to prefer Matthew's account (in fact he strongly prefers Matthew's Gospel in general; see note 26 below).

13. The question of how Cassian frames religious and spiritual authority continues to fascinate scholars. See for instance Richard J. Goodrich, *Contextualizing Cassian: Aristocrats, Asceticism, and Reformation in Fifth Century Gaul* (Oxford: Oxford, 2007); George Demacopoulos, *Five Models of Spiritual Direction in the Early Church* (Notre Dame: Notre Dame, 2007); and Philip Rousseau, *Ascetics, Authority and the Church in the age of Jerome and Cassian* (Oxford: Oxford, 1978).

14. There is some degree of contrast here in respect to the observations of Burton-Christie, *The*

I must emphasize the word "almost" here, however, because Cassian does on one occasion address the potential historical dimensions of Matthew 24, and does so in a way that helps set the stage for the more dominant treatment of eschatological and apocalyptic texts in his works.[15] I turn first to this, Cassian's brief discussion of end-times imagery framed in temporal and historical terms, before returning to his much more typical usage of these texts as having meaning for ascetics in regards to specific issues here and now.

Matthew 24 as Temporal Eschatology

In *Conference* 8, John Cassian takes a rare moment to discuss eschatology with reference to the end of temporal history, though he does so in a way that makes quite clear that this is not his primary interest with regard to the passage. His comments in this respect come in the context of a broader discussion about the nature of demons and their origins. Cassian begins the dialogue with one of his few extended discussions of the challenges of scriptural exegesis, explaining that certain aspects of Scripture's meaning are buried so deeply that they can never be known with certainty, and that they thus become matters of opinion for individual readers. This, Cassian tells us, is not necessarily a problem if none of the possible interpretations of a given passage "is found to oppose the faith."[16] In short, there are some speculative questions for which Scripture does not have a definitive answer, and for which no such final answer is ultimately essential. As an example of such a speculative question, Cassian mentions the abomination of desolation from Matthew 24:

Word in the Desert, 181–92. In reference mainly to the *Sayings of the Desert Fathers,* Burton-Christie emphasizes that eschatological passages were often used to spur repentance by reminding ascetics of the threat of judgement and eternal punishment, especially in a context in which they saw themselves as living in the last times already. In this respect, eschatological themes in Scripture were certainly serving to help ascetics transform themselves as Burton-Christie argues explicitly. Interestingly, however, the threat of judgment seems not to be as great a focus for Cassian's approach to this transformation as we shall see, and there are few if any passages in Cassian's writings that would seem to imply a belief that he and his readers were living in the end times themselves. This is not to say, however, that Burton-Christie's conclusions do not hold true for the *Sayings* necessarily.

15. He will also refer once to Revelation in a similar way, which I will explore below.

16. *Conlat.* 8.4.2. Unless otherwise noted, all translations of Cassian's works from Boniface Ramsey, *John Cassian: The Conferences*, ACW 57 (New York: Newman, 1997); or *John Cassian: The Institutes*, ACW 58 (New York: Newman, 2000).

Such is the case … with the abomination of desolation (Mt 24:15) which stood in the holy place and which was that likeness of Jupiter which we read was placed in the Temple at Jerusalem, and that it is to stand again in the Church with the coming of the Antichrist, and all those other things that follow in the Gospel and that are understood to have been fulfilled before the captivity of Jerusalem and as going to be fulfilled before the end of this world.[17]

Cassian is here delineating two (or perhaps three) possible positions that a Christian could take with respect to the "abomination of desolation" from Matthew 24. Either the item referenced by Jesus in the passage has already (by Cassian's time) been placed in the temple as Jesus predicted, in the form of a pagan statue,[18] or it is to stand before the future coming of the antichrist in the Church in some way, or possibly both. Most crucially, however, Cassian's overall point here is that a given Christian is free to take a speculative position on a question like this one without problematic consequences. Ultimately, the question is, for him, a curiosity and not a matter of serious theological or spiritual importance.

Cassian seems to bear no antipathy for those who might dive into a speculative issue like the meaning of the abomination of desolation. Indeed, he himself will go on to present a long and interesting discourse on what he considers to be similar speculative questions about the nature of demons. Yet, it is telling that he uses a historical and temporal reading of the imagery in Matthew 24 as an example of something about which Christians cannot have and really do not need to have any final certainty. And with that, John Cassian has more or less fully dispensed with the question of how Christians should understand potential signs of the end times. Yet, this is not to say that Cassian has no interest in texts like Matthew 24 in themselves. Rather, he tends to have a different use for them.

Matthew 24 in the Present Tense

To see Cassian's typical approach to Matthew 24, we can examine two other substantive references to the passage. The first comes in *Conference* 15,

---

17. *Conlat.* 8.4.2.

18. This would seem to be the statue that would have been housed in the temple to Jupiter constructed on the temple mount by Hadrian sometime around 130. Hadrian's temple is mentioned by Cassius Dio, *Roman History,* 69.12, which may be the text that Cassian here mentions having read. Today, the specifics of Hadrian's construction project have become the subject of debate. For details, see Weksler-Bdolah, Shmolit, *Aelia Capitolina: Jerusalem in the Roman Period in Light of Archeological Research,* MNS 432 (Leiden: Brill, 2019), 51–60.

which explores spiritual gifts—in particular, healing miracles. Cassian begins the conference by delineating the various types of healing miracles, and some of the parameters within which they can be performed. One key source of healing miracles, he observes, is in fact demons who try to deceive the faithful by giving the gift of healing to those whose way of life is corrupt,

so that, when a person who is entangled in obvious sins is believed to be holy and a friend of God out of admiration for his miracles, the imitation of his vices might also appear desirable.[19]

Cassian then cites two examples of Scripture warning that such people will arise. The first is from Dt 13:1–3, which refers to false prophets leading God's people astray. The second is Mt 24:24, "for false messiahs and false prophets will appear and produce great signs and omens, to lead astray, if possible, even the elect."[20]

The problem of bad elders and other spiritual authorities is one that Cassian addresses frequently, especially within the *Conferences*. Indeed, it would have been arguably the most challenging and pressing political and social issue facing many of his implied readers. The political structure of the ascetic communities that Cassian writes for and about relied heavily on charismatic leadership as an organizing principle, and the rise of this form of spiritual authority was one of the hallmarks of the heyday of eremitic monasticism in which Cassian sets his *Conferences*.[21] Moreover, healing miracles in particular were arguably the most important public signifiers used to establish the authority of a specific ascetic in Egypt and Palestine (these types of miracles dominate the hagiographies of holy men from the age), and in the popular consciousness healing power may have been considered sufficient on its own to prove the holiness of a given figure.[22] As such, apparently real healing miracles performed by sinful charismatics could have at times created an outright existential threat to the monastic project as a whole and its (generally) esteemed status in Cassian's society, and certainly could have undermined Cassian's own authority substantially.

19. *Conlat.* 15.1.5.

20. Mt 24:24 (NRSV translation).

21. This is naturally the thesis of Peter Brown, "The Rise and Function of the Holy Man in Late Antiquity," *The Journal of Roman Studies* 61 (1971): 80–101. However, Brown's approach has been importantly critiqued of late by Ramsay MacMullen, "The Place of the Holy Man in the Later Roman Empire," *HTR* 112, no. 1 (2019): 1–32.

22. MacMullen, "The Place of the Holy Man," 10–16.

Cassian's ultimate response to the issue of healing miracles performed by sinful leaders is to encourage his readers to focus more on the virtue of those they follow rather than the flashy special effects of miraculous healing. The witness of Matthew 24 becomes a key justification of this approach and a source of useful imagery that Cassian can draw on to frame it. For Cassian, the false Christs described in Matthew are present here and now in the form of one of the great social and political threats to his own communities and way of life. Charismatic systems of authority have their dangers, and Cassian knows it well. Yet the ascetic armed with discernment, who focuses on virtue much more than miracles, can stay safe; the warnings and images of Matthew 24 and Deuteronomy serve here as intellectual sign-posts reminding the ascetic to do so, and are thus tools of mental formation that help ready an ascetic to meet a notable obstacle on the road to transformation.

Cassian cites Matthew 24 in a similar vein in *Institutes* 4. As with the rest of the *Institutes*, the context of his discussion is one of his monastic communities in Gaul. As Cassian finishes the opening section of the *Institutes*, which deals explicitly with the rules for his monasteries, he presents an extended exhortation to his readers that they persevere through the challenges and temptations of communal monastic life. He warns the reader not to turn back after having given up material possessions and family,

for it would be a miserable affair if, when you were supposed to advance from your first beginnings and to aim at perfection, you began to slide even from them to still lower things. For it is not he who has begun in these things but he who has persevered in them to the end who will be saved (Mt 24:13).[23]

Once again, Cassian here applies Jesus' words in Matthew 24 to a common problem facing the communities of his day, namely the problem of people joining one of Cassian's communities but finding life there too difficult and thus returning to the world. While Jesus is speaking of those who endure apocalyptic suffering, Cassian applies the same words of exhortation to those who endure the challenges of asceticism. This deployment of Matthew 24 adds tremendous rhetorical weight to Cassian's encouragements, helping to raise the emotional stakes of his warnings about backsliding in the spiritual life (as he will continue to do throughout the rest of *Institutes* 4). As such, this usage of Matthew's text invites Cassian's readers to place themselves here and now

23. *Inst.* 4.36.2.

within the intense struggles discussed by Jesus in Matthew's original. As Jesus'
own words serve as both comfort and warning with respect to the apocalyptic
trials he describes, so does Cassian comfort and warn his readers in their ascetical struggles.[24]

The Book of Revelation

The book of Revelation is cited with notable frequency by Cassian, especially in his *Conferences,* with a total of at least twelve clear citations appearing. For comparison one can count roughly the same number of citations for
the letter of James, and only about half as many for the gospel of Mark, indicating that Revelation held a place of similar significance for Cassian as compared with many other New Testament books.[25]

Cassian's use of apocalyptic imagery as a tool for framing the struggles
and problems of his own day is perhaps even more pronounced with respect
to his use of Revelation than it is when he is quoting Matthew 24. Once again,
there seems to be a single notable exception to Cassian's tendency to read Revelation with an eye to the present, and the exception comes again in *Conference* 8. As I have noted, Cassian is here discussing the origins of demons, and
in doing so he references the dragon of Rev 12:4 which sweeps down a third of
the stars with its tail. The stars, for Cassian, represent angels who have fallen
and have thus become demons.[26] Once again, however, *Conference* 8 stands as
the exception that proves the rule, for everywhere else that Cassian cites Revelation he does so with a focus on some of the most essential current challenges
facing the ascetics to whom he writes.

It would become tedious to dissect all of Cassian's references to Revelation in detail, so I will summarize several here briefly to begin. First, Cassian
brings up the mysterious Nicolaitans (mentioned in Rev 2:6–16) in the context of counselling ascetics against following heretics.[27] The threat of purport-

---

24. See also *Inst.* 7.30 where Cassian cites another New Testament apocalyptic text, 1 Thes 5:2, to
very similar effect.

25. Precise counts are of course difficult, but the Gospel of Matthew appears to be far and away
Cassian's favorite book of the New Testament with upwards of 200 references and allusions. For a detailed qualitative analysis of scriptural citations in Cassian see Ansgar Kristensen, "Cassian's use of Scripture," *ABR* 28, no. 3 (1977): 277–79.

26. *Conlat.* 8.8.3.

27. *Conlats.* 18.16.6; and 24.17.3.

edly heretical teachers tearing ascetics away from Cassian's communities and the way of life he deemed suitable was naturally a major potential threat to Cassian's authority and that of his Church. The Nicolaitans once again provide Cassian and his reader with mental imagery to help keep them alert in a world where not all spiritual authorities can be trusted.

Second, Cassian often encourages ascetics not to fall into the temptation of becoming lukewarm—neither hot nor cold (cf. Rev 3:16)—which is to say losing the drive to continue seeking the transformation that they have set out to enact in themselves.[28] Similarly, he reminds struggling readers that God chastises those he loves (cf. Rev 3:19),[29] and gives several other similar exhortations to persevere in the ascetical life, drawn from Revelation.[30] His references here come with the evident intention of offering comfort and reassurance to those for whom the ascetical life has begun to feel overly burdensome or painful, with Revelation serving as a means to give hope to those who are flagging in their struggle in much the same way as Mt 24:13 did. In his treatment of the Nicolaitans and Rev 3:16, then, we continue to see Cassian deploying apocalyptic scriptural passages to help warn against false authorities using weighty images, and to exhort ascetics to persevere. Three more of his citations, all of which follow a similar pattern in their own way, are worth exploring more fully.

The first comes in *Conference* 22, Cassian's somewhat infamous extended discussion of nocturnal emissions and their spiritual and sacramental consequences. It is clear from Cassian's own treatment of this problem that it remained one of the most vexing concerns facing male ascetics whether in isolation or in a monastery. The male body, Cassian himself admits, cannot be permanently and completely prevented from some level of sexual excitement leading to ejaculation; even the most hardened ascetic will experience this during sleep a few times a year at least.[31] Among the problems that this evidently caused for Cassian's readers was a serious question about whether communion can be received after experiencing such a night-time emission, the implication being that many in Cassian's time were teaching against receiving the Eucharist in such circumstances.

28. *Conlat.* 4.12–19.
29. *Conlat.* 6.11.2.
30. *Conlats.* 3.9.2; 1.14.4.
31. *Conlat.* 23.1–4.

Cassian's own approach is nuanced, and involves an extended effort to dissect various causes of such emissions to seek out the real state of a given man with respect to chastity. Nocturnal emissions, in effect, may or may not be the fault of the ascetic, depending on whether the ascetic's heart is truly pure. Those who have examined the situation and prove to have done nothing to invite such an emission (such as going lax in their fasting, or entertaining lustful thoughts without resistance) can and should receive communion lest they allow the devil to trap them through the device of unwanted emissions. Others, however, certainly should abstain if a nocturnal emission is a sign of a deeper lack of real chastity.[32]

For Cassian, as a result, nocturnal emissions become in effect a spur to an ever deeper self-exploration, such that the male ascetic who has just experienced one must ask himself whether he is truly pure at heart. The bad news is that he may well not be, but the good news is that if he is, then regardless of any nocturnal emission, he stands among the true virgins discussed in Revelation. These persons, because of their purity of heart and body, also enjoy the special and unique blessing of being able to sing constantly the canticle that none of the other holy ones can sing, but only those who follow the Lamb wherever he goes, "for they are virgins and have not soiled themselves with women" (Rev 14:4).[33] The alternative is to be a mere foolish virgin (cf. Mt 25:1–13), perhaps outwardly chaste, but corrupt and impure within.

It is tempting for modern readers to set aside Cassian's discussion of nocturnal emissions as at best rather quaint, and at worst bizarre. Yet, for Cassian's readers the issue was clearly a cause of substantial angst as every such emission was a potential sign of an unknown failure in the quest to transform the self. For Cassian, though, it is not outward chastity that really counts, nor does the evident unchastity of a nighttime emission necessarily sully the ascetic. He thus deploys the virgins of Revelation alongside the equally apocalyptic virgins of Matthew 25 to provide imagery that helps his reader frame the space of self-inquiry that is necessary to face his problem and learn something about his inner state from it, neither ignoring the risk that a nocturnal emission might represent nor allowing it a power that it does not deserve.

Cassian uses Revelation in a similar way in *Institutes* 5, in one of the most revealing passages in his corpus with respect to his eschatology as such. At this

32. *Conlat.* 23.6.
33. *Conlat.* 23.6.9.

juncture in the *Institutes*, Cassian has transitioned from a discussion of rules for his communities into his extended presentation of the eight principal vices that the ascetic must struggle to overcome. Amidst an assessment of gluttony (the first of these vices), Cassian offers yet more exhortations and reassurances to his reader, including a long meditation on Paul's metaphor in 1 Cor 9 and 2 Tim 4 of running a spiritual race. Cassian is explicit that the reader is meant to take comfort in the knowledge that there are rewards here and now for those who persevere.

> Thus [Paul] declares that we shall have a part in his crown on the day of judgment if we love the coming of Christ—not only when he will appear even to the unwilling but also as he daily visits holy souls.... Of this coming the Lord says ... "behold, I stand at the door and knock. If anyone hears my voice and opens the door, I shall go in to him and I shall eat with him and he with me" (Rev 3:20).[34]

Cassian here notes explicitly what we have seen implicitly at work in his way of reading eschatological and apocalyptic passages so far. Namely, he expects a final second coming of Christ in which He will be revealed to everyone (whether they like it or not), yet he also believes that the second coming is a present reality in some sense to those who live a life of faith. On the basis of Cassian's reading of Matthew 24 in *Conference* 8, it would seem that the final coming of Christ is indeed historical, taking place at the end of time. But this is again not a major concern for Cassian in *Institutes* 7. It is Christ's coming in judgement here and now that he takes as the context of the words of Revelation, and once again his purpose is to exhort and reassure those who are flagging in the hard work of self-transformation while also encouraging those who are making good headway.

Cassian's final reference to Revelation in his *Conferences* puts a fine point on this approach by way of a poetic flourish. He introduces his final conference this way.

> With this twenty-fourth conference of Abba Abraham, forged with the help of Christ, the teachings and precepts of all the elders come to an end. Once it is concluded, thanks to your prayers, and the number mystically corresponds to that of the twenty-four elders who in the holy Apocalypse are said to offer their crowns to the Lamb (Rev 4:4), we believe that we shall be relieved of the debts of all our promises.[35]

34. *Inst.* 5.17.3.
35. *Conlat.* 24.1.1.

In the context of his era, Cassian appears less interested in numerology than many authors, but here he employs it to remarkable effect in order to bring the intensely apocalyptic imagery of Revelation 4 to bear on his reader's immediate context—indeed, on the very act of reading the conferences themselves! Recall the context of the throne imagery from Rev 4 that Cassian cites here. Just before the description of the thrones, the author of Revelation has imputed to Christ these words. "To the one who conquers I will give a place with me on my throne, just as I myself conquered and sat down with my Father on his throne" (Rev 3:21). Christ's words here stand as the summation of the letters He has dictated to the seven churches, detailing their struggles and triumphs and where they stand in His books. Those who have conquered it all are here reassured that they too may sit on a throne, immediately after which the author of Revelation is shown the vision of the 24 elders on their 24 thrones. The elders, it would seem, are at least in part a representation of those who have conquered as Christ would have them.

Throughout his conferences, Cassian has striven to introduce the great sages of the desert in ways that are approachable, and deeply human, giving them an exceptional level of personality and authenticity. Now, as he closes his magnum opus, these elders become in some sense the elders of the thrones of Revelation, and thus the imagery of Revelation comes alive and blooms throughout the conferences themselves, giving new and deeper authority to Cassian's text, and most importantly inviting the reader to identify more closely with those who live eternally in the light of Christ—a group that she, the reader, may join if she continues in the work of transforming herself. To follow Cassian's elders as presented in his conferences, to persist in the ascetical life of transformation through their teachings—all this brings the reader to the very throne of Christ. That reward, and the elders who already enjoy it, can be viewed here and now, even on the very pages held in the reader's hands, a fact that the imagery from Revelation helps the reader to apprehend. Once again, persistence in the hard life of the ascetic, and the authority of Cassian's own writings, are the emphasis as he fills his readers' minds with imagery from Revelation a final time before closing his greatest work.

Conclusion

For Cassian, just as there are threats to the Christian in the apocalyptic and eschatological passages of the New Testament, there are threats to the ascetic's way of life in the present. Disillusionment, vexing problems that might threaten any sense of progress, and bad authorities are high on the list of such threats in his mind, as is born out throughout his writings. But in Matthew 24, Revelation, and other apocalyptic passages of Scripture Cassians finds a wellspring of images and exhortations that can help ascetics face (if not wholly resolve) these particular roadblocks. In the work of self-transformation, calling apocalyptic and eschatological imagery to mind is meant to serve, for Cassian's reader, as a protective and exhortative technique, and therefore an important tool for those who find themselves uncertain or in despair. To reflect on the end of all things in such a context is to recall the profound rewards of a life transformed, to frame the mind such that rigorous self-inquiry becomes possible, and to remember the risks of following those who might lead one astray. While this approach to Scripture is of interest to observe in itself, it also strikes me that there are likely to be similar patterns of deployment when studying specific types of scriptural literature or biblical passages as they are used by early ascetical authors like Cassian when these passages are treated as "technologies of the self" as I have done here. Further study of such trends may indeed reveal much about the details of how such authors and their readers utilized Scripture as they pursued their work of self-transformation in Christ.

Bibliography

Brakke, David. "Reading the New Testament and Transforming the Self in Evagrius of Pontus." Pages 284–99 in *Asceticism and Exegesis in Early Christianity: The Reception of New Testament Texts in Ancient Ascetic Discourses*. Edited by Hans-Ulrich Wiederman. Göttingen: Vandenhoeck & Ruprecht, 2013.

Brown, Peter. "The Rise and Function of the Holy Man in Late Antiquity," *The Journal of Roman Studies* 61 (1971): 80–101.

Burton-Christie, Douglas. *The Word in the Desert: Scripture and the Quest for Holiness in Early Christian Monasticism*. Oxford: Oxford University Press 1993.

Casiday, Augustine. *Reconstructing the Theology of Evagrius Ponticus: Beyond Heresy*. Cambridge: Cambridge University Press, 2013.

Clements, Niki Kasumi. *Sites of the Ascetic Self: John Cassian and Christian Ethical Formation*. Notre Dame, IN: University of Notre Dame Press, 2020.

———"The Asceticism of Interpretation: John Cassian, Hermeneutical *Askesis*, and Religious Ethics." Pages 67–88 in *Scripture, Tradition, and Reason in Christian Ethics*. Edited by Bharat Ranganathan and Derek Alan Woodard-Lehman. London: Palgrave MacMillan, 2019.

Demacopoulos, George. *Five Models of Spiritual Direction in the Early Church*. Notre Dame, IN: University of Notre Dame Press, 2007.

Faulkner, Andrew. "Late Antique Poet as Scriptural Interpreter: The Case of the *Metaphrasis Psalmorum*." In *Exploring the Literary Contexts of Patristic Biblical Exegesis*, edited by Miriam De Cock and Elizabeth Klein, 114–29. Washington, DC: The Catholic University of America Press, 2023.

Goodrich, Richard J., *Contextualizing Cassian: Aristocrats, Asceticism, and Reformation in Fifth Century Gaul*. Oxford: Oxford, 2007.

Harden Weaver, Rebecca. "Access to scripture: experiencing the text." Interpretation 52, no. 4 (1998): 367–79.

Kelley, Christopher J. *Cassian's Conferences: Scriptural Interpretation and the Monastic Ideal*. London: Ashgate, 2012.

Kitchen, Robert. "Teaching Lions to Fast: Jacob of Serugh on Daniel 6." In *Exploring the Genres of Early Christian Interpretation*, edited by Miriam De Cock and Elizabeth Klein, [###]. Washington, DC: The Catholic University of America Press, 2023.

Kristensen, Ansgar. "Cassian's use of Scripture," *ABR* 28, no. 3 (1977): 277–79.

MacMullen, Ramsay. "The Place of the Holy Man in the Later Roman Empire," *HTR 112*, no. 1 (2019): 1–32.

Ramsey, Boniface. *John Cassian: The Conferences*, ACW 57. New York: Newman, 1997.

———*John Cassian: The Institutes*, ACW 58. New York: Newman, 2000.

Rousseau, Philip. *Ascetics, Authority and the Church in the age of Jerome and Cassian*. Oxford: Oxford, 1978.

Weksler-Bdolah, Shmolit. *Aelia Capitolina: Jerusalem in the Roman Period in Light of Archeological Research*, MNS 432. Leiden: Brill, 2019.

Widdicombe, Peter, "The Two Thieves of Luke 23:32–43 in Patristic Exegesis," StPatr 43 (2006): 273–80.

———"The Drunkenness of Noah and the Patristic Legacy," StPatr 44 (2010): 9–13

———"A Trinity of Delights: Proverbs 8:30–31 and its Theological Interpretation in Patristic Thought," *Theoforum* 42 (2012): 119–33

———"Noah and Foxes: Song of Songs 2:15 and the Patristic Legacy in Text and Art," StPatr 59 (2013): 39–52.

———*Drunkenness, Nakedness, and the Redemption and Fall of an Image: Noah and Christ*. Grand Rapids, MI: Eerdmans, forthcoming.

13. ORIGEN ON JOHN 20:25 AND ON THE NAME OF THE APOSTLE THOMAS (*IN IOHANNEM*, FRAGMENT 106)

Origen's great *Commentary on the Gospel of John* probably numbered 32 books and ran from the beginning of the Fourth Gospel to Jn 13:33. There is no indication that Origen continued it beyond chapter 13 or even intended to do so,[1] although two fragments drawn from catenae—that is, collections or "chains" of excerpts from the Church Fathers gathered to offer a continuous commentary on the Scriptures—which are attributed to Origen, comment on chapters 14 and 20 of the Gospel. Ronald E. Heine has established that one could not, in general, place much confidence in these fragments of the *Commentary on John*.[2] He argues that almost all the fragments attributed to Origen by the catenae must be considered of doubtful attribution and concludes that "all of them must be used with extreme caution as witnesses to Origen's comments on the Gospel of John."[3] Nevertheless, it is one of these fragments

1. Cf. Cécile Blanc, *Origène. Commentaire sur saint Jean. Tome V (Livres XXVIII et XXXII)*, *SC* 385 (Paris: Cerf, 1992), 9.

2. Cf. Ronald Heine, "Can the Catena Fragments of Origen's Commentary on John Be Trusted?," *VC* 40 (1986).

3. Heine, "Can the Catena Fragments of Origen's Commentary on John Be Trusted?," 119.

which will interest us here, namely, fragment 106 of the editions of Alan England Brooke and Erwin Preuschen.[4]

This fragment deals with the episode of Thomas' doubt in Jn 20:25, which in fact only serves as a starting point for a development on the double name of the apostle, Θωμᾶς ὁ λεγόμενος Δίδυμος, "Thomas, called the twin" mentioned in Jn 20:24.[5] We know how important the nickname given to the apostle was in the birth of the rich apocryphal literature that was dedicated to him.[6] If the Johannine addition invites us to understand Thomas' name in the sense of "twin," the question we naturally ask ourselves—and which will give rise to several different answers—is: whose twin? The later Thomasian tradition answered this question quite clearly: Thomas is the twin or double of Jesus, whether in the literal, physical sense, or in the sense of a spiritual or mystical twinship. The idea of the twinship of Thomas and his master was thus the driving force of the Thomasian literature. This theme is expressed in a privileged way through three writings quite closely related to each other, the *Gospel according to Thomas*,[7] the *Book of Thomas*[8]—also known under the erroneous title of *The Book of Thomas the Contender*—and the *Acts of Thomas*.[9] A Coptic version of the first two writings was discovered at Nag Hammadi, in Upper Egypt, in December 1945, while the *Acts of Thomas*, which has been known for a long time, is extant in two versions, Greek and Syriac, and in numerous adaptations in various languages.[10]

4. Cf. Alan England Brooke, *The Commentary of Origen on S. John's Gospel*, Vol. II (Cambridge: Cambridge University Press, 1896) 309–10; Erwin Preuschen, *Origenes Werke*, vol. 4: *Der Johanneskommentar*. GCS 40 (Leipzig: J. C. Hinrichs, 1903), 561–62.

5. I quote *The English Standard Version Bible*, Oxford : Oxford University Press, 2008.

6. For an overview of the Thomasian corpus, see Risto Uro, Thomas: *Seeking the Historical Context of the Gospel of Thomas* (London and New York: T&T Clark, 2003), 8–30.

7. Bentley Layton and Thomas Lambdin. "The Gospel According to Thomas," vol 1, as in Layton, B. (ed.), *Nag Hammadi Codex* II, 2–7 together with XIII, 2*, Brit. Lib. Or. 4926(1), and P. Oxy. 1, 6J4, 655 1, NHS 20 (Leiden: Brill, 1989): 2–7.

8. Cf. Turner and Layton, "The Gospel According to Thomas," (1989).

9. Cf. Drijvers, *Acts of Thomas* (1992); Attridge, *Acts of Thomas* (210).

10. For an inventory of this literature, see Geerard, the Greek and Coptic *Gospel of Thomas*, Clavis Apocryphorum Novi Testamenti (1992), 9–10; the Greek and Coptic *Gospel of Thomas*, 34–39; the *Infancy Gospel of Thomas*, 147–52; *Acts of Thomas* and the *Apocalypse of Thomas*, 210ff.; for the late *Acts of Thomas*, see Holste and Spittler, "The Acts of Thomas and His Wonderworking Skin," New Testament Apocrypha. More Noncanonical Scriptures, vol. 2, ed. Tony Burke (Grand Rapid, MI: Eerdmans, 2020) 316–39.

As already mentioned, fragment 106 is part of a "catena." This catena[11] is known by several manuscripts and was first edited in 1530 by Balthasar Cordier who used a defective manuscript,[12] the 11th century *Codex Cusanus* 18 of Bernkastel-Kues (Germany).[13] The fragments attributed to Origen by the catena were reedited by A. E. Brooke from two 10th–11th century manuscripts, and Brooke's edition served as a basis for E. Preuschen's own edition.[14]

Since Origen's commentary did not go beyond chapter 13 of John's Gospel, it is doubtful that fragment 106 comes from it. In fact, some of the fragments attributed to Origen by the catena have been attributed to authors other than Origen.[15] However, this is not the case for fragment 106. As for this fragment, we can even suppose, with Stephen C. Carlson, that it could have been taken from books 26 or 27 of the commentary of Origen, which are lost and must have been devoted in whole or in part to chapter 11 of John, since book 28, which is preserved, begins with Jn 11:39.[16] The commentary would therefore have been on Jn 11:16, where the first occurrence of Thomas' surname appears, rather than on Jn 20:24–25 or 21:2. Furthermore, nothing in the style of the fragment contradicts an attribution to Origen, even if the catenist could have, as it is the case with the fragments examined by R. E. Heine, shortened or reworked his source.[17]

Whatever one makes of this question of Origenian authorship, fragment

11. Cf. "Catena Typus F, as in Geerard, Maurits and Jacques, Noret, Jacques, *CPG*, vol. IV (Turnhout: Brepols, 2018), 376–77 (no. C 145).

12. Cf. Balthasar Cordier, *Catena Patrum Graecorum in Sanctum Johannem* (Antwerp: Officina Plantiniana, Balthasar Moretus Pub., 1630); this edition is considered the "editio optimae notae" by Geerard and Noret, *CPG*, vol. IV (1980), 247.

13. The manuscript was identified by Robert Devreesse, "Notes sur les chaînes grecques de saint Jean," *Revue biblique* 36 (1927): 192–215; 193; cf. Heitlinger, "Der 'Codex Cusanus 18.' Die Vorlagehandschrift der 'Corderius-Katene' zum Johannesevangelium," *Biblica* 42 (1961): 443–54.

14. The Preuschen edition is considered the standard one of Origen's *Commentary of the Gospel of John*. However, Brooke's edition is still worth considering.

15. Cf. Geerard, *CPG*, vol. 1, *Patres Antenicaeni, Corpus Christianorum* (Turnhout: Brepols, 1983), 163 (no. 1453); Devreesse, "Notes sur les chaînes grecques de saint Jean," 203–07; Joseph Reuss, *Matthäus-, Markus- und Johannes-Katenen nach den handschriftlichen Quellen untersucht*, Neutestamentliche Abhandlungen 18, 4–5 (Münster: Aschendorff, 1941): 173, 193, 202–03.

16. Carlson, "Origen's Use of the Gospel of Thomas," 149.

17. We must however consider the severe judgment of Devreesse: "[N]on seulement nombre des fragments ne sont que de très larges résumés, mais la plupart de ces extraits édités par Brooke et Preuschen n'ont que peu de rapport avec la pensée d'Origène. L'explication mystique, l'allégorie si chères au docteur alexandrin ne tiennent plus aucune place: Origène s'y exprime souvent comme un antiochien," *Notes* (1927), 204.

106 is a precious testimony of the circulation of the Thomasian traditions and the speculations to which they could give place in the middle of the third century. This first complete translation of the fragment[18] is based on Brooke's edition.[19]

Ἔοικέ τι ἀκριβὲς καὶ ἐξητασμένον ἔχειν ὁ Θωμᾶς, ὅπερ παρίσταται καὶ ἐκ τῶν ὑπ' αὐτοῦ λεγομένον, ἄπερ οἶμαι αὐτὸν εἰρηκέναι μὴ ἀπιστοῦντα τοῖς λέγουσι τεθεωρηκέναι τὸν κύριον, ἀλλ' εὐλαβούμενον μήποτε φάντασμά ἐστι, καὶ μεμνημένον τοῦ· *Πολλοὶ ἐλεύσονται ἐπὶ τῷ ὀνόματί μου λέγοντες ὅτι Ἐγώ εἰμι.* τοῦτο δὲ οἶμαι πεπονθέναι καὶ τοὺς λοιποὺς ἀποστόλους, ἀλλὰ κατ' ἐξοχὴν τὸν Θωμᾶν. ὅτι δὲ καὶ οἱ λοιποὶ ἀπόστολοι τοιοῦτόν τι ἐνενόησαν ἰδόντες τὸν Ἰησοῦν δῆλον ἐκ τοῦ γεγράφθαι ὅτι *Ἐδόκουν ὅτι φάντασμά ἐστι·* καὶ ἀπεκρίθη καὶ εἶπεν αὐτοῖς *Ψηλαφήσατέ με καὶ ἴδετε, ὅτι πνεῦμα ὀστᾶ καὶ σάρκα οὐκ ἔχει, καθὼς ἐμὲ θεωρεῖτε ἔχοντα.* περὶ δὲ τοῦ πῶς λέγεται αὐτῷ *Μὴ γίνου ἄπιστος ἀλλὰ πιστός·* καὶ εἰς τὸ ὄνομα δὲ τοῦ Θωμᾶ

Thomas seems to have something meticulous and inquisitive about him, which is expressed in his own words (Jn 20:25), which I believe he said, not because he did not believe those who said they had seen the Lord, but because he was careful that it was not a ghost, and that he remembered these words: "Many will come in my name, who will say, 'It is me'" (Mk 13:6). I believe that the other apostles also felt that way, but especially Thomas. The other apostles had also thought something similar when they saw Jesus, as is clear from what is written: "They thought it was a ghost" (Mk 6:49), and he answered them and said: "Touch me and see that a spirit has neither bone nor flesh, as you see that I have" (Lk 24:39). Concerning the way it is said to

18. There are four partial translations of fragment 106: Cordier, *Catenae Patrum* (1630), 460–61 (from Ἔοικέ τι ἀκριβὲς to θεωρεῖτε ἔχοντα); Rolf Gögler, *Origenes. Das Evangelium nach Johannes, Menschen der Kirche* (Zurich: Benziger, 1959), 405–06 (a paraphrase of the whole fragment); Stephen Carlson, "Origen's Use of the Gospel of Thomas," Paper presented at the Annual Meeting of the Society of Biblical Literature. New Orleans (November 24, 2009), 17; Stephen Carlson, "Origen's Use of the Gospel of Thomas," in Sacra Scriptura. *How "Non-Canonical" Texts Functioned in Early Judaism and Early Christianity,* JCTCRS 20, ed. James H. Charlesworth, Lee Martin McDonald and Blake A. Jurgens (London and New York: Bloomsbury T&T Clark, 2014), 137–51; 149–50 (from περὶ δὲ τοῦ πῶς λέγεται αὐτῷ to τὰ πάντα ἐπιλύοντος); Simon Gathercole, "Named Testimonia to the Gospel of Thomas: An Expanded Inventory and Analysis," *HTR* 105 (2012): 79; Gathecole, *The Gospel of Thomas. Introduction and Commentary*, Texts and Editions for New Testament Study 11 (Leiden-Boston: Brill, 2014), 55–56 (from περὶ δὲ τοῦ πῶς λέγεται αὐτῷ to τὰ πάντα ἐπιλύοντος).

19. I would like to thank Brigitte Mondrain (Paris) and Thomas S. Schmidt (Fribourg, Switzerland) for their revision of this translation. I am pleased to offer this paper as a modest tribute to my colleague and friend Peter Widdicombe, who is very familiar with Origen's *ComJn*; see his important monograph on *The Fatherhood of God from Origen to Athanasius* (Oxford: Oxford University Press, 1994). For more on the fatherhood of God in Origen and on Origen's treatment of Rom 8:15, see Miriam De Cock's contribution in this volume.

τοιαῦτα ἂν λεχθείη, ὅτι τῶν μὲν ἀξιωθησομένων ὑπὸ τοῦ σωτῆρος μείζονος θεωρίας περὶ τῆς ἐν τῷ ὄρει μεταμορφώσεως αὐτοῦ καὶ τῶν ὀφθέντων ἐν δόξῃ Μωσέως καὶ Ἡλίου τὰ ὀνόματα μετεποίησεν. τῶν δὲ λοιπῶν διὰ τοῦτο τὰ ὀνόματα οὐ μετεποίησεν, ἐπεὶ καὶ αὐτάρκη καὶ καθ' ἑαυτὰ ἦν παραστῆσαι τὸ ἑκάστου ἦθος. περὶ μὲν οὖν τῶν λοιπῶν ἀποστόλων οὐ νῦν πρόκειται λέγειν, περὶ δὲ τοῦ Θωμᾶ, ὃς ἑρμηνεύεται Δίδυμος, διὰ τοῦτο, ἐπεὶ δίδυμός τις τὸν λόγον ἦν ἀπογραφόμενος τὰ θεῖα δισσῶς καὶ μιμητὴς Χριστοῦ τοῖς μὲν ἔξω ἐν παραβολαῖς λαλοῦντος, κατ' ἰδίαν δὲ τοῖς ἰδίοις μαθηταῖς τὰ πάντα ἐπιλύοντος. καὶ οὐκ ἄτοπόν γε φάσκειν τοὺς γνησίους Χριστοῦ μαθητὰς κατορθοῦν διττὸν τοῦτο τῆς ἐν λόγῳ παρασκευῆς, ὅπερ ἤδη τάχα καὶ ἐξαιρέτως εἶχεν ἔκτοτε ὁ Θωμᾶς. εἴποι δ' ἄν τις καὶ διὰ τοῦτο τὴν ἑρμηνείαν μόνου τούτου ἀναγεγράφθαι, τῷ βεβουλῆσθαι τὸν εὐαγγελιστὴν Ἕλληνας ἐντυγχάνοντας τῷ εὐαγγελίῳ ἐπιστῆσαι τῇ ἰδιότητι τῆς ἑρμηνείας τοῦ ὀνόματος κατ' ἐξοχὴν μόνον ἑρμηνευθέντος ἐπὶ τῷ εὑρεῖν τὴν αἰτίαν τοῦ καὶ Ἑλληνιστὶ ἐκκεῖσθαι τὸ ὄνομα αὐτοῦ.

him: "Do not be unbelieving but believing" (Jn 20:27), and with regard to the name of Thomas, it could be said that, on the one hand, (Jesus)[20] changed the names of those who would be judged worthy by the Savior of a greater vision, that of the transfiguration on the mountain and that of Moses and Elijah appearing in glory (cf. Lk 9:30), and that, on the other hand, because of this, he did not change the names of the others since (their names) were sufficient in themselves to show the character of each one. So it is not about the other apostles that we should talk now, but about Thomas, which translates as "twin," because of this: since he was in a certain way a twin in speech, recording the divine (words) in two ways, and an imitator of Christ, who, on the one hand, expressed himself in parables for people outside, and, on the other hand, explained everything to his own disciples in private (cf. Mk 4:34). And it is certainly not out of place to assert that the authentic disciples of Christ succeeded in this double aspect of preparation regarding the discourse, precisely that which Thomas from then on immediately, quickly, and remarkably possessed. It could be said that, for this reason too, the translation of this name alone (cf. Jn 11:16; 20:24; 21:2) was inscribed because the Evangelist wanted the Greeks reading the Gospel to fix their attention on the singularity of the translation of the name, the only one to have actually been translated, in order to find the reason why its name was also translated into Greek.

---

20. I consider that the subject of τὰ ὀνόματα μετεποίησεν, "he changed the names," is Jesus and not the author of the Fourth Gospel, as does Gathercole. See his studies: Gathercole, "Named Testimonia," (2012):79 and Gathercole, *The Gospel of Thomas* (2014), 55.

The starting point of the fragment is the condition laid down by Thomas for believing in the resurrection of Jesus in Jn 20:25: "Unless I see in his hands the mark of the nails, and place my finger into the mark of the nails, and place my hand into his side, I will not believe." Thomas' objection is described by the fragment as something ἀκριβὲς καὶ ἐξητασμένον, "meticulous and inquisitive," which seems to be taken in a positive sense since it is seen not as an expression of incredulity but of prudence. Somewhat unexpectedly, the fragment then moves from Thomas' disbelief to the meaning of his name. As we can see afterwards, it is a question of explaining why he has a double name.

The author compares the case of Thomas with that of three other apostles to whom Jesus gave a new name, or rather, added a second name to their names. The first case is that of Simon (Peter) to whom Jesus gives the name of Cephas (Κηφᾶς), in Jn 1:42. The second is that of the sons of Zebedee, John and James, to whom Jesus gives the name of Boanerges, that is, "Sons of Thunder," in Mk 3:17. The primary reason for this change of name, explains the author, is that Peter, John and James—Andrew is left out—were destined to be witnesses to an exceptional vision, that of the transfiguration of Jesus on the mountain and the appearance at his side of Moses and Elijah. If the names of the other apostles have not been changed, continues the author, it was because they were not going to be the witnesses of the transfiguration, but also because their original names were considered significant enough in themselves. If we stick to this principle, there would be no reason to discuss the case of Thomas since he is one of the "other disciples" whose name Jesus did not change. But the author is nevertheless anxious to give an account of the surname of "twin" that the Gospel of John gives to Thomas.

As is well known, Thomas' name appears in two forms, a simple one (Θωμᾶς) in the synoptic Gospels, John and Acts (cf. Mt 10:3; Mk 3:18; Lk 6:15; Jn 14:5; 20:26.27.28; Acts 1:13), and a double one (Θωμᾶς ὁ λεγόμενος Δίδυμος) only in Jn (cf. 11:16; 20:24; 21:2). Most scholars see the Greek name Θωμᾶς as the transcription of a semitic name, in this case Aramaic תאומא, *te'ōm*, which means "twin."[21] The form of the Johannine gloss: A ὁ λεγόμενος B, "A, which is said to be B," is not the most common one for a double name. Apart from

---

21. Heinz Wuthnow, *Die semitischen Menschennamen in griechischen Inschriften und Papyri des vorderen Orients*, Studien zur Epigraphik und Papyruskunde ¼ (Leipzig: Dieterich, 1930), 55; Friedrich Blass, Albert Debrunner and Friedrich Rehkopf, *Grammatik des neutestamentlichen Griechisch* (Göttingen: Vandenhoeck & Ruprecht, 1976) 42–43 (no. 53).

New Testament attestations (the three occurrences in John, plus Mt 27:17 ["Jesus called the Christ"] and Col 4:11 ["Jesus called Justus]"), Gregory H. R. Horsley points to a documentary example and a literary attestation in Flavius Josephus.[22] The etymology given by John (Θωμᾶς ὁ λεγόμενος Δίδυμος) is to be explained not only by the fact that the name Thomas is a transliteration of the Aramaic *te'ōm*, but also by the assonance between his name—in Aramaic *t'ōmā'*—and that of the twin, a principle on which most etymologies found in the Hebrew Bible[23] or in Philo of Alexandria are based.[24]

Returning to fragment 106, the author justifies the double name of Thomas by the fact that the apostle is "an imitator of Christ, who, on the one hand, expressed himself in parables for people outside, and, on the other hand, explained everything to his own disciples in private." Like his master, Thomas was "in a certain way a twin in speech, recording the divine (words) in two ways" (δίδυμός τις τὸν λόγον ἦν ἀπογραφόμενος τὰ θεῖα δισσῶς). One would look in vain in the Fourth Gospel or in the Synoptics for a passage that would justify such an assertion. That is why Stephen Carlson proposed to read fragment 106 in the light of the beginning of the *Gospel according to Thomas*.[25] I think this is indeed the only way to account for the sibylline remark of fragment 106 about Thomas' double recording of the "divine words," obviously the words of Jesus of which he was to be the privileged interpreter after having been their listener.

The incipit and first logion of the *Gospel according to Thomas* read as follows: "These are the secret sayings which the living Jesus spoke and which Didymus Judas Thomas wrote down. And he said, 'Whoever finds the interpretation of these sayings will not experience death'"—ⲛⲁⲉⲓ ⲛⲉ ⲛ̄ϣⲁϫⲉ ⲉⲑⲏⲡ` ⲉⲛⲧⲁ ⲓ̅ⲥ̅ ⲉⲧⲟⲛϩ ϫⲟⲟⲩ ⲁⲩⲱ ⲁϥⲥϩⲁⲓ̈ⲥⲟⲩ ⲛ̄ϭⲓ ⲇⲓⲇⲩⲙⲟⲥ ⲓ̈ⲟⲩⲇⲁⲥ ⲑⲱⲙⲁⲥ. ⲁⲩⲱ ⲡⲉϫⲁϥ ϫⲉ ⲡⲉⲧⲁϩⲉ ⲉⲑⲉⲣⲙⲏⲛⲉⲓⲁ ⲛ̄ⲛⲉⲉⲓϣⲁϫⲉ ⲛ̄ϥⲛⲁϫⲓ †ⲡⲉ ⲁⲛ ⲙ̄ⲡⲙⲟⲩ`.[26] According to the *Gospel*, the words of Jesus are to be understood on a double

<hr>

22. Gregory Horsley, "Names, Double," in *The Anchor Bible Dictionary*, vol. 4, ed. David Noel Freedman (New York: Doubleday, 1992) 1011–17; 1013.

23. Cf. Johannes Fichtner, "Die etymologische Ätiologie in den Namengebungen der geschichtlichen Bücher des Alten Testaments," in *VT* 6 (1956): 372–96.

24. Cf. Lester L. Grabbe, *Etymology in Early Jewish Interpretation. The Hebrew Names in Philo*, BJS 115 (Atlanta: Scholars Press, 1988).

25. Cf. Carlson, *Origen's Use of the Gospel of Thomas*, 150–51.

26. Ed. and trans. Koester, Layton, Lambdin, and Attridge, "Tractate 2: The Gospel According to Thomas," 52–53.

level, that of elocution and that of interpretation. The connection between the beginning of the *Gospel* and the scribal activity attributed to Thomas by the fragment is reinforced if we consider that the subject of "he says" (ⲡⲉϫⲁϥ), usually considered as Jesus by the commentators of the *Gospel*, could just as well be Thomas, according to the sheer *prima facie* logic of the statement. Indeed, the nearest referent for the anaphoric pronoun "he" is Thomas and not Jesus. Therefore, Thomas is really writing down Jesus' words δισσῶς, "twice" or "doubly," "in two ways,"[27] for their outside reader or auditor and for those who discover their secret meaning.

The rest of the fragment asserts that access to the double meaning of Jesus' words was not reserved to Thomas alone, but that "the authentic disciples of Christ" (τοῖς ἰδίοις μαθηταῖς) had access to it. In fact, the author uses a somewhat convoluted expression here, whose interpretation and translation are far from assured. He writes that "the authentic disciples of Christ (κατορθοῦν διττὸν τοῦτο τῆς ἐν λόγῳ παρασκευῆς)," that is, if the proposed translation holds up, "succeeded in this double aspect of preparation regarding the discourse." I understand that the "double aspect of preparation" refers, on the one hand, to the discourse of Jesus aimed at the mass of listeners (τοῖς μὲν ἔξω), and, on the other hand, to its interpretation intended for insiders (κατ' ἰδίαν δὲ τοῖς ἰδίοις μαθηταῖς). If all the authentic followers of Jesus were able to grasp the double meaning of his words, Thomas distinguished himself by his immediate apprehension (ἤδη τάχα καὶ ἐξαιρέτως) of Jesus' life-giving message. Whether the fragment is by Origen or not, the idea of a *double entendre* of Jesus' words is decidedly Origenian!

Conclusion

In conclusion, the author of fragment 106 affirms that the evangelist wanted to draw the attention of Greek readers of the Fourth Gospel to the name of Thomas and the singularity of its translation. It is interesting to note that he considers the nickname Thomas to be a Greek translation (ἑρμήνεια) of his name, "the only one to have actually been translated." Despite its allusive

---

27. The expression δισσῶς ἀπογράφειν is used by Clement of Alexandria, *Stromata* II, 45, 3, in a variant form of Prv 22:20–21: "Write the commandments doubly (ἀπογράψαι δισσῶς) in counsel and knowledge that you may answer the words of truth to those who ask you."

character, this fragment of Origen, or of a Pseudo-Origen, bears witness to the fascination that the double name of Thomas exerted on the ancient readers of the Fourth Gospel and to their determination to account for it at all costs. It is also an interesting, though discreet, testimony to the *Gospel according to Thomas*, whose reception in the ancient Church has always been ambiguous. While condemning it as counterfeit, Clement of Alexandria and Origen, to mention but a few, did not hesitate to quote from it if only so as not to "appear ignorant of anything, because of those people who think they know something if they have examined these gospels."[28]

Bibliography

Attridge, Harold W. *The Acts of Thomas*, ECA 3. Salem, Oregon: Polebridge Publishers, 2010.

Blanc, Cécile. *Origène. Commentaire sur saint Jean. Tome V (Livres XXVIII et XXXII)*, SC 385. Paris: Cerf, 1992.

Blass, Friedrich, Albert Debrunner and Friedrich Rehkopf. *Grammatik des neutestamentlichen Griechisch*. Göttingen: Vandenhoeck & Ruprecht, 1976.

Brooke, Alan England. 1896. *The Commentary of Origen on S. John's Gospel*. Vol. II. Cambridge: Cambridge University Press, 1896.

Carlson, Stephen C. "Origen's Use of the *Gospel of Thomas*." Paper presented at the Annual Meeting of the Society of Biblical Literature. New Orleans, November 24, 2009.

Carlson, Stephen C. "Origen's Use of the *Gospel of Thomas*," in *Sacra Scriptura. How "Non-Canonical" Texts Functioned in Early Judaism and Early Christianity*, JCTCRS 20, edited by James H. Charlesworth, Lee Martin McDonald and Blake A. Jurgens, 137–51. London and New York: Bloomsbury T&T Clark, 2014.

Cordier, Balthasar. *Catena Patrum Graecorum in Sanctum Johannem*. Antwerp: Officina Plantiniana, Balthasar Moretus Pub., 1630.

Devreesse, Robert. "Notes sur les chaînes grecques de saint Jean," *Revue biblique* 36 (1927): 192–215.

Drijvers, Han J. W. "The Acts of Thomas," in *New Testament Apocrypha*. Revised Edition and trans. R. McL. Wilson. II. *Writings Relating to the Apostles, Apocalypses and Related Subjects*, edited by Werner Schneemelcher, 322–411. Cambridge/Louisville: James Clarke/Westminster-John Knox, 1992. See AATh 3, ed. M. Bonnet, Acta Apostolorum; transl. by Han J.W. Drijvers, ‚The Acts of Thomas', in Wilhelm Schneemelcher (ed.), New Testament Apocrypha, vol. II (Cambridge-Louisville: WJK, 1992), pp. 322–411.

---

28. Origen, *HomLc* 1, 2, trans. Joseph T. Lienhard (Washington D.C.: Catholic University of America Press, 1996), 6.

Fichtner, Johannes. "Die etymologische Ätiologie in den Namengebungen der geschichtlichen Bücher des Alten Testaments," *VT* 6 (1956): 372–96.

Gathercole, Simon J. "Named Testimonia to the *Gospel of Thomas*: An Expanded Inventory and Analysis," *HTR* 105 (2012): 53–89.

Gathercole, Simon J. *The Gospel of Thomas. Introduction and Commentary*, Texts and Editions for New Testament Study 11. Leiden-Boston: Brill, 2014.

Geerard, Maurits. *Clavis Patrum Graecorum. Volumen I. Patres Antenicaeni*, Corpus Christianorum. Turnhout: Brepols, 1983.

Geerard, Maurits. *Clavis Apocryphorum Novi Testamenti*, Corpus Christianorum. Turnhout: Brepols, 1992.

Geerard, Maurits and Jacques Noret. *Clavis Patrum Graecorum. Volumen IV. Concilia. Catenae*, Corpus Christianorum. Turnhout: Brepols, 2018.

Gögler, Rolf. *Origenes. Das Evangelium nach Johannes*, Menschen der Kirche in Zeugnis und Urkunde 4. Zurich: Benziger, 1959.

Grabbe, Lester L. *Etymology in Early Jewish Interpretation. The Hebrew Names in Philo*, BJS 115. Atlanta: Scholars Press, 1988.

Heine, Ronald E. "Can the Catena Fragments of Origen's Commentary on John Be Trusted?," *VC* 40 (1986): 118–34.

Heitlinger, Albert. "Der 'Codex Cusanus 18.' Die Vorlagehandschrift der 'Corderius-Katene' zum Johannesevangelium," *Biblica* 42 (1961): 443–54.

Holste, J. D and J.E. Spittler. "The Acts of Thomas and His Wonderworking Skin," in *New Testament Apocrypha. More Noncanonical Scriptures*, Volume 2, edited by Tony Burke, 316–39. Grand Rapid, MI: Eerdmans, 2020.

Horsley, Gregory H. R.. "Names, Double," in *The Anchor Bible Dictionary, Volume 4*, edited by David Noel Freedman, 1011–17. New York, Doubleday, 1992.

Koester, Helmut, Bentley Layton, Thomas Oden Lambdin and Harold W. Attridge. "Tractate 2: The Gospel According to Thomas," in *Nag Hammadi Codex II,2–7 together with XIII,2*, Brit. Lib. Or. 4926 (1), and P. Oxy. 1, 654, xs655. Volume One*, NHS 20, edited by Bentley Layton, 37–125. Leiden: Brill, 1989.

Nag Hammadi Codex II,2–7; together with XIII,2, Brit. Lib. OR.4926(1), and P.Oxy. 1, 654, 655*, ed. Bentley Layton, 2 vols., NHS 20. Leiden: E. J. Brill, 1989.

Lienhard, Joseph T. *Origen. Homilies on Luke. Fragments on Luke*, The Fathers of the Church 94. Washington, DC: The Catholic University of America Press, 1996.

Preuschen, Erwin. *Origenes Werke. Volume 4: Der Johanneskommentar*. GCS, 40. Leipzig: J. C. Hinrichs, 1903.

Reuss, Joseph. *Matthäus-, Markus- und Johannes-Katenen nach den handschriftlichen Quellen untersucht*, Neutestamentliche Abhandlungen 18, 4–5. Münster: Aschendorff, 1941.

Turner, John D. and Bentley Layton. "Tractate 7: The Book of Thomas the Contender Writing to the Perfect," in *Nag Hammadi Codex II,2–7 together with XIII, 2*, Brit. Lib. Or. 4926 (1), and P. Oxy. 1, 654, 655. Volume Two*, NHS 21. Leiden, E.J. Brill, 1989: 171–205.

Uro, Risto. *Thomas: Seeking the Historical Context of the Gospel of Thomas,* London and New York: T&T Clark, 2003.

Widdicombe, Peter. *The Fatherhood of God from Origen to Athanasius,* OTM. Oxford: Clarendon Press, 1994.

Wuthnow, Heinz. *Die semitischen Menschennamen in griechischen Inschriften und Papyri des vorderen* Orients, Studien zur Epigraphik und Papyruskunde 1/4. Leipzig: Dieterich, 1930.

14. VISIONARY EXEGESIS

Interpreting Scripture in Hildegard
of Bingen's *Scivias*

For scholars who work on the history of women's interpretation of the Bible, genre matters. If we limit our definition of scriptural interpretation to particular literary genres, such as the commentary or expository homily, then we radically alter our picture of women's contributions, since it was exceedingly rare for women before the early modern period to write in such genres—and highly controversial when they did.[1] To take a particularly famous example, Teresa of Avila was ordered by her confessor, Diego de Yangues, to burn her *Meditaciones sobre los Cantares* (*Commentary on the Song of Songs*), because "it was not fitting for a woman to comment on Scripture."[2] If it was a tenuous proposition for a pre-modern woman to write at all, it was an even graver risk to take up a literary form that was increasingly being claimed as the sole province of theologians and university masters.

1. Christiana DeGroot and Marion Ann Taylor remind us that it was uncommon for women to write in technical, academic interpretive genres well into the twentieth century, in their essay, "Recovering Women's Voices in the History of Interpretation," in *Recovering Nineteenth-Century Women Interpreters of the Bible* (eds. Christiana DeGroot and Marion Ann Taylor; Atlanta: SBL Press, 2007), 10. But, as they note for their subjects—which I would argue is also true of many pre-modern women—this does not mean that they were not "following developments in the fields of theology and biblical studies."

2. Cited in McGinn, "Women Reading the Song of Songs in the Christian Tradition," in *Scriptural Exegesis: The Shapes of Culture and the Religious Imagination: Essays in Honor of Michael Fishbane*, (eds. Deborah A. Green and Laura Lieber; New York, Oxford University Press, 2009), 281.

And yet, even among sympathetic historians and theologians, there remains a tendency to privilege biblical commentary as the highest interpretive form. The renowned historian of Christian mysticism Bernard McGinn inadvertently demonstrates this point in an otherwise characteristically illuminating essay on female interpreters of the Song of Songs. He begins with the twelfth-century Benedictine nun and *magistra* Hildegard of Bingen, one of the widest-ranging and most prolific writers of her century—male or female. She is the first female writer (of those whose writings have survived) to have interpreted the Song, and so she is a natural starting-point for McGinn's inquiry. But though McGinn will credit her as the "first major female exegete in the history of Christianity," there is a reservation in this claim.[3] As a woman not formally trained in the practice of exegesis, and who was forbidden by Church teaching from expressing opinions on her own authority, her theological works were based on visions and interpretations of these same visions that she claimed to receive directly from God. McGinn argues that since she incorporated scriptural texts in her visions to show their "conformity" with earlier authorities, she became a biblical commentator "through the back door."[4] Thus even though her visions are saturated with language and imagery drawn from the pages of scripture, her lack of systematic attention to these texts—and her jumbling them up with her own revelations—makes her identity as an interpreter incidental, rather than central, to her work.

A similar logic is operative in the work of Beverley Mayne Kienzle, who has done more than any other scholar to recover Hildegard as a preacher and biblical interpreter, through her editions, translations, and recent magisterial monograph, *Hildegard of Bingen and Her Gospel Homilies: Speaking New Mysteries*. Kienzle, an expert on medieval sermons, goes even further than McGinn, identifying Hildegard not simply as the first, but as the "only known systematic female exegete of the Middle Ages"—a designation she earns from her composition of fifty-eight homilies on the Gospels, the *Expositiones evangeliorum*.[5] While Kienzle notes that Hildegard's three most substantial works—her visionary trilogy consisting of *Scivias* (1151), *Liber vite meritorum* (1163), and *Liber divinorum operum* (1173)—"contain substantial passages of

---

3. McGinn, "Women Reading the Song of Songs," 284.

4. McGinn, "Women Reading the Song of Songs," 284.

5. Kienzle, *Hildegard of Bingen and Her Gospel Homilies: Speaking New Mysteries* (Turnhout: Brepols, 2009), 2.

exegesis," it is her use of the technical exegetical genre of the *expositio* that distinguishes her from her medieval female contemporaries and establishes her as a biblical interpreter of note. The focus on the *Expositiones evangeliorum* is undoubtedly a gift to scholarship. These homilies are massively understudied in comparison with more famous works, such as *Scivias*. The first critical edition, prepared by Kienzle herself, appeared only in 2007, and the first translation, again by Kienzle, followed only in 2011.[6] The homilies are, moreover, thoroughly allegorical and their meaning often obscure—something noted by Johannes Trithemius, a late medieval promoter of Hildegard's cult.[7] Kienzle compellingly situates the *expositiones* within Hildegard's oeuvre, offers a careful account of their method and sources, and presents her reader with "an extraordinary testimony to a medieval woman instructing her community on the Scriptures for the liturgical year."[8] And yet, Kienzle's rhetoric still demonstrates a privileging of the systematic, sequential exposition of discrete passages of scriptural texts over other forms of exegesis. *Scivias* contains exegesis; the *Expositiones* are exegesis.

In this essay, I wish to contest the idea that *Scivias* merely *contains* exegesis, which limits the practice of interpretation to those specific moments when Hildegard introduces a discrete passage of text and then offers a gloss on it. Rather, I wish to frame her entire visionary project as a distinct genre of interpretation, which I am here choosing to call "visionary exegesis." Visionary exegesis resists any firm demarcation between the biblical text and the content of the visions, treating commentary not as derivative of a firm and fixed primary source, but as a creative enterprise in its own right. This creative tension arises from the fact that both the biblical material and the visions are treated as direct revelations from God.

Hildegard's visionary works are particularly well-suited to analysis from this perspective, because they themselves are structured by a distinction between revealed images and the interpretation of those images—both of which derive, in their entirety, from divine revelation, and hence form a singular vision. *Scivias*, for example, is divided into three books, each of which in turn consists of multiple visions. And each vision begins in precisely the same manner: a vivid

---

6. The critical edition is published in CCCM 226, 135–333. The translation is Hildegard of Bingen, *Homilies on the Gospels* (Collegeville, MN: Cistercian Publications, 2011).

7. On which, see Kienzle, *Speaking New Mysteries*, 2.

8. Kienzle, *Speaking New Mysteries*, 2.

description of an image, or short series of images, that Hildegard receives from God, followed by lengthy commentary on each aspect of the vision, which she claims that God subsequently delivered to her. The format very much resembles that of a lemmatic commentary, with the images treated as the primary source material, which are initially described in full, and are then broken down, lemma by lemma, for exposition.[9] Indeed, the key distinction in *Scivias* is not between biblical sources and Hildegard's revelations, but between image and commentary. In the *Riesenkodex*, the giant manuscript that contains nearly all of her extant works and whose production she likely oversaw during the final years of her life, there are marginal notations that demarcate those passages where the image is being described.[10] These marginal notations occur not only at the beginning of each vision when the image is initially described, but they also occur every time that Hildegard's text refers back to the image by quoting a lemma from it.[11] No similar marginal notations appear when biblical texts are quoted, though the abbreviated title of the biblical book is usually inserted into the margin.[12] Hildegard, moreover, seems not only to have captured these images in words, but also completed sketches or drawings of them that were incorporated into the manuscript tradition.[13]

Biblical texts, language, and imagery play a foundational role in Hildegard's theological imagination. The editors of *Scivias* identified more than one thousand allusions to or citations of Scripture, including over one hundred passages that Hildegard glosses at length.[14] It is thus tempting for the student

9. I am grateful to Willemien Otten for first suggesting to me the idea that Hildegard was seeking to write her own scripture, in her comments on a different paper I delivered at the University of Chicago in June 2019.

10. Michael Embach, *Conspectus der Handschriften Hildegards von Bingen* (Münster: Aschendorff Verlag, 2013) is now the definitive resource for descriptions of Hildegard's extant manuscripts.

11. Wiesbaden HS 2 3v and *pass.*

12. See, e.g., Wiesbaden HS 2 5r, 6v and *pass.*

13. Although there has been considerable prevarication on the question of whether Hildegard was herself responsible for the illustrations in Rupertsberg *Scivias*, which sadly now survives only in a modern copy, I am generally convinced by the arguments of Madeline Caviness that Hildegard did oversee their production. She has made these arguments in several different essays and helpfully sums them up in "Hildegard as Designer of the Illustrations to her Works," in *Hildegard of Bingen: The Context of her Thought and Art* (ed. Charles Burnett and Peter Dronke; London: The Warburg Institute, 1998), 29–62. As will become apparent below, the illustrations often depict many details and flourishes not included in the text. Although the Rupertsberg *Scivias* was lost after it was moved to Dresden during the second World War, there is a black-and-white photographic copy (incomplete negatives at the Rheinisches Bildarchiv in Cologne and a complete printed copy at Eibingen Abbey) and a stunning replica completed by the sisters at Eibingen Abbey in the 1930s. On which, see Caviness, "Hildegard as Designer," 30, n. 8.

14. CCCM 43A, 639–52.

of Hildegard's exegesis to abstract these moments of explicit biblical interpretation and mine them for methods and sources. And there is certainly nothing methodologically suspect about a diachronic study of Hildegard's interpretation of a particular passage or book of the Bible.[15] But such abstraction does not allow us to fully appreciate the exegetical nature of Hildegard's visionary works themselves and perhaps even misses something fundamental to her thought and writing. One particularly striking feature of *Scivias* is that the images she describes contain virtually no scriptural language, even as they might be mapped onto various biblical texts or tropes; it is only in the lengthy "commentaries" that scriptural language appears. I would suggest that this allows for a kind of mutual interplay between image and scriptural text—the latter is invoked to explain some feature of the image, but is then itself thrown into an entirely new relief by the unlocking of the image's meaning(s).

I will thus offer a sketch of what Hildegard's "visionary exegesis" looks like in practice, through a close analysis of the second vision of the first book of *Scivias*. I have selected this particular vision because it is one of the few in *Scivias* that is closely connected with a specific biblical text—in this instance, Genesis 1–3. It is thus, I believe, a helpful site for exploring both Hildegard's close engagement with scripture, on the one hand, and her creative integration of scripture within a broader visionary account that itself becomes subject to systematic interpretation, on the other. Barred by her sex from establishing herself as an interpreter of the scriptures, she subversively (yet productively) subjects her own visionary source material to systematic and critical scrutiny.

It should not surprise the reader of *Scivias* that Hildegard, having begun her work with a brief vision of "the strength and stability of the eternal Kingdom of God" and admonishing the reader to seek the knowledge of God,[16] should then turn to a vision of "the Fall"—both of Lucifer and of the first two humans, events which are intimately and intricately connected in her telling. And, of course, the narrative of the Fall is thoroughly grounded in the opening chapters of Genesis, even as it came to incorporate an ever-growing

15. I have even undertaken this very approach in my forthcoming essay, "Singing the Song Anew: Hildegard of Bingen as Interpreter of the Song of Songs," in *Let Me Hear Your Voice: Women and the Song of Songs.* (no bibliographic data yet)

16. *Scivias* 1.1.1 (CCCM 43, 8). Translations of *Scivias* are my own, though I have benefited from engaging with the translation by Columba Hart and Jane Bishop in the CWS, Hildegard of Bingen, *Scivias* (New York: Paulist Press, 1990).

array of intertextual and extra-canonical sources and traditions as it developed across Late Antiquity. However, even as the image and its exposition are indebted to a particularly Western (Augustinian) interpretation of Gen 1–3, and the characters of Adam, Eve, and the serpent feature prominently, there are no explicit citations of this passage in the entire vision.[17] We are instead offered a re-narration of the events described therein. Hildegard does gloss six biblical texts, but they are drawn from the books of Job (cf. 21:17–18; cf. 1.2.4); Ezekiel (cf. 18:30; c.f. 1.2.8); 1 Corinthians (cf. 11:12; cf. 1.2.12); Wisdom of Solomon (cf. 3:1; 1.2.15); Hosea (cf. 5:4; 1.2.23); and the Apocalypse of John (cf. 3:20; 1.2.25). And these glosses, in each instance, take the form of "God" re-phrasing the text, rather than establishing its grammatical sense, its *historia*, or the identification of particular levels of allegorical meaning. There is a dissolution of firm boundaries between the scriptural text and the visionary voice, both deriving from the same divine source, both working together to produce a harmonious vision for the reader.

It seems sensible to begin with the image she describes, before turning to the lengthy commentary on the image, which spans twenty-four pages in the critical edition. In the text, Hildegard first draws our attention to a "great multitude of living lamps, which give off great brightness (*maximam multitudinem viventium lampadarum multam claritatem*)."[18] But this awe-inspiring image is jarringly interrupted by the appearance of a terrifying rupture: "But look, a hollow (*lacus*) of great width and depth appeared, having an opening as though it were an opening of a pit (*os velut os putei habens*), and sending forth fiery smoke with a terrible smell, out of which a hideous cloud extending itself touched a deceitful form taking the shape of a vein (*se extendens quasi venam visum deceptibilem habentem tetigit*)."[19] This terrible vein-like form then blows upon a "bright white cloud (*candidam nubem*)" that is coming out of a "beautiful form of a human (*pulchra forma hominis*)" and which has within it "many, many stars (*plurimas plurmiasque stellas*)," and this cloud and the human are then "cast out (*eiecit*)" from the "brilliant place (*clara regione*)" where

---

17. By Augustinian account, I am referring primarily to the identification of pride as the vice shared both by the fallen angels and the first humans that drives them from paradise. The key Augustinian texts are *civ. Dei* XII and *Gn. litt.* XI (cf. also, importantly, Gregory the Great, *Moralia in Job*, 27.39.65); see now the helpful discussion in Elizabeth Klein, *Augustine's Theology of Angels* (Cambridge: Cambridge University Press, 2018), 45–50.

18. *Scivias* 1.2.praef (CCCM 43, 13).

19. *Scivias* 1.2.praef (CCCM 43, 13).

they had previously been. The vision ends by noting that as a result of this ca-
lamity, "all the elements of the world (*omnia elementa mundi*)" were thrown
into "very great disturbance (*maximam inquietudinem*)."[20]

Already it would be difficult for the reader to miss clear allusions to the
narrative of the Fall, even as familiar language and images from Genesis are
avoided. The fiery hollow is undoubtedly to be identified as a hellish pit, the
vein-like form that blows humanity out of its home in the brilliant region
codes as the devil, and the disturbance that afflicts the world can be understood as the terrible consequences of this expulsion. Moreover, the visual representation of this image in the Rupertsberg Codex, which may reasonably be
traced in some form to Hildegard's own hand, draws out the connections even
more clearly.[21] The rectangular frame is divided into two registers; in the upper register are the lamps, separated from the lower register, in which all the
action takes place, by lines that could represent the firmament. The vein-like
creature has a recognizably serpentine form. In the bottom right of the frame
the illustrator has drawn two trees, which are never mentioned in the text of
the vision, but which might suggest a connection with the tree of life and the
tree of the knowledge of good and evil. But where the illustration adds the
most theological and exegetical depth is in its representation of the human
figure and the cloud. The starry cloud is coming out of the side of the human,
who is lying in a prone position, so that the human figure is coded as Adam,
the bright white cloud as Eve, and the stars as the human race that will descend
from her (undoubtedly influenced by God's proclamation to Abraham in Gn
15:5 that his descendants will be as numerous as the stars, *stellas*). The stars
in the cloud, moreover, look nearly identical to the brilliantly shining white
lamps at the top of the frame. An astute observer might connect these star-like
lamps (as Hildegard will in her commentary) with angelic beings, who share
some kinship with the nascent human race. But the illustration's greatest surprise lies with the Adam figure, whose left hand is curiously raised while his
right hand cradles his head. But if the image is rotated to its right, the reason
for the raised arm becomes clear: viewed from a vertical, rather than horizon-
tal, perspective, Adam's position (save for his right arm) mimics the posture of

20. *Scivias* 1.2.praef (CCCM 43, 13).
21. The following analysis is based on the black-and-white photographic reproduction of *Scivias*
preserved in the Rheinisches Bildarchiv, Cologne. This plate is reproduced in Caviness, "Hildegard as
Designer," 48, Fig. 6.

the crucified Christ, with both legs bent to the left at nearly ninety degree angles, as they appear in contemporary visual depictions of the crucifixion.

What sort of interpretive work might this image (especially in its visual, but also in its textualized, form) be doing? Perhaps most strikingly, this image collapses different moments of time into a single event, including those that occur before and after the Fall. The sleeping, pre-lapsarian Adam, out of whose side the cloud-like "Eve" emerges, is, at the same time, the crucified Christ, from whose side wound the Church processes. This suggests the cosmic pre-ordination not only of the Incarnation, but also of the crucifixion. Moreover, "Eve" in the very moment of her emergence from Adam, is attacked by the devil, her offspring alienated from their *patria*—although, of course, never abandoned, since the redemptive act of the crucifixion is already anticipated. Finally, we might dwell for a moment on this representation of Eve, not as a human, but as an ethereal vessel bearing the entirety of humanity within her. Adam, the androgynous first human, had presumably at the moment of its creation been the one bearing all humanity within itself, but now, with the emergence of Eve (and of gendered humanity), it is the woman who carries the multitudes *in potentia*.

Already in these few short lines of text and single illustration we are able to observe a stunningly complex and layered interpretation of the Genesis narrative, displaying subtle intertextual connection, careful engagement with earlier tradition, especially the theology of the Augustinian tradition, and vibrant authorial creativity. When we turn to the lengthy commentary, we encounter more explicit exegesis—both of scriptural texts and of the image itself. And this exegesis is rigidly systematic, proceeding in an orderly fashion to consider each lemma of the image's textual description (no explicit references to accompanying illustrations are ever made). Hildegard immediately introduces the first lemma of the image's description—the "great multitude of very bright living lamps"—and identifies the lamps as the "huge army of heavenly spirits (*plurimus exercitus supernorum spirituum*)" who have spent a blessed existence with God from the moment of creation.[22] Their receiving "fiery brightness (*igneum fulgorem*)" is attributed to their display of faithfulness to God "when Lucifer with his [angels] tried to revolt against the heavenly creator (*cum Lucifer cum suis superno creatori rebellare conaretur*)."[23]

22. *Scivias* 1.2.1 (CCCM 43, 14).
23. *Scivias* 1.2.1 (CCCM 43, 14).

Although this vision ostensibly begins with the creation of the angelic hosts, it pertains entirely to the narrative of the Fall, because the fiery brilliance of the angels is due to their faithfulness in the face of Lucifer's rebellion. And the next eight sections of the text deal at length with the nature and consequence of this rebellion. Hildegard emphasizes that it is Lucifer's "pride (*superbiam*)" that is responsible for his "being ejected (*eiectus est*)" from his heavenly home—pride he experienced because "he did not perceive any lack either in his beauty or in his strength (*nullum defectum nec in decore nec in fortitudine sua sensit*)."[24] The reader may be struck by the speculative nature of Hildegard's exegesis of her own image. This entire lengthy excursus on the devil—who appears only in the guise of the vein-like form—is meant to explain the fiery appearance of the angelic lamps. It is not, perhaps, entirely different from Augustine's self-consciously speculative attempts to discern the creation and fall of the angels from an oblique reference to "light" and "darkness," "day" and "night" in Genesis 1.[25] Hildegard's "lamps" likewise contain multitudes.

Intertextual exegesis—the juxtaposing of different texts based on a thematic or linguistic similarity or connection—is a strategy commonly employed by patristic and medieval biblical interpreters, and Hildegard utilizes this strategy in the interpretation of her image, quoting a text from Job that she then proceeds to gloss, which also contains the word "lamp:" "The lamp of the wicked ones (*lucerna impiorum*) will be extinguished, and an overflowing will come upon them, and [God] will divide the afflictions of his wrath."[26] Thus while the lamps may remind the reader/viewer of the "light (*lux*)" of Gn 1:3–5, which had been associated in Christian interpretation with the angels since Augustine, Hildegard connects her image with a less expected text from Job that also draws attention to how God will dim the brightness of the wicked and cast them into a place of punishment. Hildegard does not claim that the text from Job allegorically contains the story of the fall of Lucifer and the angels, but that it conveys the broader moral point that God "removes from the sight of his brightness all those who try to oppose themselves to Him."[27] Indeed, this fits well the unfolding of the *Scivias* commentary, which treats the

---

24. *Scivias* 1.2.2 (CCCM 43, 15).

25. *Civ. Dei* 11.7, 12.15; *Gn. Litt.* 11.17; cf. Klein, *Augustine's Theology of Angels*, 26–45.

26. Job 21:17 cited in *Scivias* 1.2.4 (CCCM 43, 15). Note that the text from Job uses the synonym *lucerna*, rather than *lampas*.

27. *Scivias* 1.2.3 (CCCM 43, 15).

fall of Lucifer and the angels as paradigmatic for the fall of humanity. Hildegard's interpretation of the Job passage, to which she devotes only a few sentences, takes the form of a paraphrase that emphasizes the terrors of God's wrath and the supreme emptiness of alienation from God. Unlike the careful exposition she gives of each word or clause of her image, her interpretation of Job 21:17 provides a simple expansion of the identified theme of God's just punishment of the wicked.

Following this excursus, she returns again to the image, identifying the "hollow of great width and depth" as "hell/the nether regions (*infernus*)," which possesses a "width of vices (*latitudinem vitiorum*) and a depth of ruins (*profunditatem perditionum.*)"[28] Arising from this hollow is fire and billowing black smoke, which are tortures prepared "for the devil and those who follow him, who have turned themselves from the highest good (*diabolo et eum sequentibus quo se de summo bono averterunt*)."[29] Hildegard again emphasizes at length, in keeping with the long Augustinian tradition, that the angels' fall is due to pride, which leads them to despise the good and set themselves up as gods in the place of God: "They have been cast out from every good, not because they were ignorant of that good, but because in their great pride (*in magna superbia*) they disdained it."[30] She refers to the devil as "the proud angel (*superbus angelus*)"—who sets himself up "as a snake (*ut coluber*)," anticipating the vein-like form of the next clause—and also as someone bound up in "proud presumption (*superbam praesumptionem*)," who needed to be cast down and punished lest there be "two gods in heaven (*in caelo duo dii*)."[31]

The devil's rebellion provides the paradigm for all human rebellion against God: "Thus also those humans (*homines isti*) who, by their actions, imitate them [Lucifer and the fallen angels], become sharers of their punishments (*participes poenarum eorum*), each according to their merits."[32] But despite the fact that human sin in every case follows the pattern of this primal disobedience, human fate does not necessarily follow the trajectory of the fallen angels. Some, according to Hildegard, "having the full measure of damnation (*cumulum damnationis habentes*)," are indeed condemned to an eternity

28. *Scivias* 1.2.5 (CCCM 43, 16).
29. *Scivias* 1.2.5 (CCCM 43, 16).
30. *Scivias* 1.2.5 (CCCM 43, 16).
31. *Scivias* 1.2.6 (CCCM 43, 17).
32. *Scivias* 1.2.6 (CCCM 43, 17).

in hell "without consolation (*sine consolatione*),"[33] but others, who "are not in a state of forgetfulness of God (*in oblivione Dei non exsistentes*)," merely experience a "purgation of their sins (*purgationem peccatorum suorum*)."[34] For Hildegard, the narrative of the fallen angels provides not only an etiology of human sin, but also a cautionary tale, as their fate can be avoided.

Notably, any Augustinian account of grace is lacking from Hildegard, who focuses entirely on the human capacity to avert themselves from sin. This is made especially clear in the second intertext that Hildegard introduces, from Ezekiel: "Be converted and perform penance for all your iniquities, and iniquity will not be ruin for you."[35] Hildegard's exegetical strategy with this passage is quite different from what we saw with her approach to Job. Here she assumes what Kienzle has called the *vox dramatis personae*—the adoption of the voice of the biblical speaker, in this case, Ezekiel (who is in turn speaking with the voice of God).[36] Thus her prose turns to vocatives and imperatives: "O you humans (*o vos homines*), who to this point have laid low in your sins, remember your name 'Christian' (*recordamini christiani nominis vestri*), turning yourselves to the way of salvation (*convertentes vos ad viam salutis*), and do other works in the font of penitence, you who earlier did many wicked things in uncountable vices."[37] Those who have successfully "cast away (*abiecistis*)" their iniquity will be rejoiced over by the angels "because withdrawn from the devil and run towards God, knowing (*cognoscentes*) him thus better through your good actions than you earlier knew (*sciretis*) him when you were in the mockery of the ancient seducer (*cum in irrisione antique seductoris fuistis*)."[38] The emphasis here lies entirely on the capacity of human agents to practice penitence and hence avert themselves from utter damnation and join the company of the angels.

Once again, Hildegard absorbs the intertext into the narrative shape of her vision. Of course, Hildegard's rephrasing of the passage employs the main verbs from the biblical text—*convertamini* and *agite penitentiam*—but her goal is not to interpret the Ezekiel passage on its own terms; rather, she uses it

---

33. *Scivias* 1.2.7 (CCCM 43, 17).
34. *Scivias* 1.2.7 (CCCM 43, 17).
35. Ez 18:30; *Scivias* 1.1.8 (CCCM 43, 17).
36. Kienzle, *Speaking New Mysteries*, 132.
37. *Scivias* 1.2.8 (CCCM 43, 17),
38. *Scivias* 1.2.8 (CCCM 43, 18).

to expand upon her earlier discourse of penance, showing the coherence of her vision with the totality of the scriptural revelation. It is worth noting that this does not necessarily distinguish Hildegard from other patristic and medieval interpreters of the Bible. Intertextual exegesis, almost by definition, collapses temporal, generic, thematic, and authorial distinctions between different biblical texts, demonstrating how they point to a singular meaning or *skopos* underlying the whole, which has, in its entirety, been authored by God.[39] Where Hildegard does differ is in foregrounding her own vision as part and parcel of this divine revelation; she is not simply an invisible interpreter drawing out the hidden meanings of long-established texts, but an active and productive agent in her own right. Perhaps ironically, the limits placed on her on account of her gender opened up a form of interpretive creativity to her that would not have existed for a male theologian or abbot.

Her commentary continues with an exposition of the "hideous cloud" and vein-like form, which turns into a lengthy discussion of marriage, sexuality, and gender that truly reveals Hildegard's creative engagement with scriptural texts and traditions. This part of the image, which describes how the "devil's fraud, flowing outwards, entered into the poisonous serpent (*diabolica fraus emanans serpentem virulentum … invasit*)," brings the reader into the narrative of Genesis 2–3 and allows Hildegard to introduce the figures of Adam and Eve, to whose primal sin she had earlier alluded.[40] In her telling, the devil is driven by jealousy at the sight of humans in the garden, and she has him cry out "with great dread (*cum magno horrore*):" "O who is this who touches me in the dwelling of true blessedness?" The devil then resolves to corrupt their "youthful innocence (*puerili innocentia*)," opting to possess the serpent because he knew that the "serpent was more like him than any other animal (*serpentem magis sibi assimilari quam aliud animal*)."[41] Hildegard here begins to offer an imaginative interpretation of the garden narrative, one that is rooted not in the exegesis of individual words or phrases, but rather through a re-telling of specific moments within that story, which is meant to elucidate motives, methods, and implications not stated in the text itself.

But these interjections and additions are narratively sparse. She is not

---

39. On this theme, see Frances M. Young, *Biblical Exegesis and the Formation of Christian Culture* (Cambridge: Cambridge University Press, 1997).

40. *Scivias* 1.2.9 (CCCM 43, 18).

41. *Scivias* 1.2.9 (CCCM 43, 18).

interested in a re-narration of the entire garden scene, but of very precise moments that are germane to her purposes in the vision. This is especially clear when she comes to the next lemma of her image, in which is described the white cloud coming from the human form. Here the focus lies entirely on why the devil chooses Eve, rather than Adam, to tempt and mislead, and she collapses the events that follow their eating of the forbidden fruit into a single sentence: "That same ancient seducer, expelling Eve and Adam from the seat of blessedness, sent them into the gloom of destruction."[42] There is no narration of what the serpent said to Eve, or what Eve said to Adam, or what God said to both of them following their disobedience. Rather, Hildegard asserts that the blame lies entirely with Eve, whom the devil chose because "he knew that the softness of woman (*mulieris mollitiem*) was more easily overcome than the strength of man (*viri fortitudinem*)."[43] Adam is here held nearly blameless, a victim of the "affectionate love (*caritas*)" that he held for his partner.[44] Indeed, Hildegard here draws the lesson that "woman rather quickly brings down man when he, not holding her in abhorrence, easily receives her words."[45]

Though it may seem that Hildegard is here replicating the misogynist reading of Genesis 2–3 first introduced in 1 Tim 2:14 and which reaches its apotheosis in Tertullian's *De cultu feminarum*, in which women are excoriated as the "devil's gateway,"[46] a very different aim quickly emerges. This aim is first evident in her assertion that the devil chose woman because of her "softness (*mollities*)." Although the devil exploits this softness, Hildegard does not conceive of it as a weakness, but as an essential part of femaleness, which in turn has much broader, cosmic significance.[47] In the next paragraph, Hildegard speaks of the complementarity of husband and wife: "For the husband is the producer [of the seed] (*seminator*), the wife is the receiver (*susceptrix*) of the seed. Whence also the wife remains under the man's power (*potestate*), since

42. *Scivias* 1.2.10 (CCCM 43, 19).

43. *Scivias* 1.2.10 (CCCM 43, 19).

44. Contrast this with *Scivias* 2.1.8, in which Adam alone, without mention of Eve, is held responsible for disobeying the "divine command (*divinum praeceptum*)."

45. *Scivias* 1.2.10 (CCCM 43, 19).

46. *Cult. fem.* 1.

47. An excellent account of Hildegard's view of femaleness can be found in Judith Newman, *Sister of Wisdom: St. Hildegard's Theology of the Feminine Divine* (Berkeley: University of California Press, 1987), 121–55.

just as the hardness of stone is to the tenderness of the earth, thus also is the strength (*fortitudo*) of the husband to the softness (*mollitiem*) of the wife."[48] The metaphor of "sowing" to describe coitus and child-bearing can be traced back to antiquity, and feminists may rightly object to the reduction of female identity to procreation, but Hildegard, for her part, conceives of this complementary "softness" as placing women on equal footing with men.

Hildegard presents Adam and Eve as embodying a genuine mutuality, a "perfect love (*perfecta caritas*)," whose end is the "increasing of the human race (*multiplicandum genus humanum*)."[49] Adam's (imagined) refusal to blame Eve for being cast out of the garden is not for Hildegard, as it is for Tertullian, a lesson about the moral superiority of men, but an act of kindness and love that both marital partners should seek to emulate. And this leads to what is perhaps the most revealing biblical gloss in the entire vision. To demonstrate the "pure love (*pura dilectione*)" that husbands and wives should have for one another, Hildegard quotes Paul's first letter to the Corinthians: "Just as woman from man thus also man through woman, but all things (are) from God" (1 Cor 11:12).[50] So far, so Pauline. But Hildegard's gloss swerves sharply in another direction. She continues, "What does this mean? Woman was created for man's sake, and man was made for woman's sake (*mulier propter virum creata est, et vir propter mulierem factus est*)."[51] The astute reader will recognize in these words a mangled echo of 1 Cor 11:9, which quite literally conveys the opposite meaning to the one Paul clearly makes: "For the man was *not* created for woman's sake, but woman for man's."[52] Hildegard is here not so much actively misquoting Paul as she is explicitly contesting him, in the divine voice.

Hildegard's modern readers have been divided in their handling of this passage. The *Scivias* editors have printed *mulier propter virum* in italics (as is their practice with direct biblical quotations), to reflect Hildegard's direct verbal dependence on the passage, and they add "cf. *ib.* 11,9" in the apparatus criticus. But this practice could give the misleading impression that this is a straightforward allusion, as though Hildegard is closely following Paul here. Scholars who work with patristic and medieval exegesis are used to biblical

---

48. *Scivias* 1.2.11 (CCCM 43, 20).
49. *Scivias* 1.2.11 (CCCM 43, 20).
50. *Scivias* 1.2.12 (CCCM 43, 21).
51. *Scivias* 1.2.12 (CCCM 43, 21).
52. *Scivias* 1.2.12 (CCCM 43, 21).

passages being quoted out of context, and for different ends than a contextu-
alized reading may suggest, but it is very uncommon to see an exegete partially citing a verse in order to clearly subvert its meaning. By contrast, the *Scivias* translators don't signal any relationship to 1 Cor 11:9, which is also deeply
problematic, since Hildegard is directly engaging with that passage.

How to resolve this quandary? We can rule out the possibility that Hildegard is somehow working with a different reading of 1 Cor 11:9, since none is
attested, and in nearly every other instance her wording of biblical intertexts
very closely follow that of the Vulgate. It is also a very strange passage since her
glosses (which are introduced with a phrase like *quod dicitur*, as in this case)
almost never involve the direct citation of other biblical texts. I propose that
Hildegard is here interpreting Paul against Paul, attempting to resolve what
she perceives to be a contradiction in a text—a necessity, since authoritative
writers can never internally contradict themselves—by taking 1 Cor 11:12 as
controlling the meaning of the entire unit. She does this, as pre-modern editors often would, by re-writing or excising the offending portion of text. Thus
Hildegard very clearly engages in a re-writing of 1 Cor 11:9; her choice to rep-
licate the specific wording of a portion of that verse, so that a reader or hearer would be unable to miss the intertext, suggests that she was being deliber-
ate and explicit in correcting Paul. At the same time, her visionary exegetical
method allows her to side-step the difficult questions that would have to be
answered if she were to do a similar thing in a commentary on 1 Corinthians.
Speaking in the voice of God affords her the freedom to subvert the words of
the Apostle, without acknowledging that she is doing so. Whatever gendered
inequality in the Church Hildegard is happy to support and even promote,
Paul's radical subordination of women in 1 Corinthians 11 is clearly a bridge
too far for Hildegard.

Mutuality is central to Hildegard's account of rightly-ordered love and
sexuality. Although she herself practiced lifelong celibacy and argued that
those who did so were following a more virtuous way of life,[53] she makes clear
that rightly-ordered sexuality was part of God's original plan for humanity.
She writes that after the humans were driven from the garden for their act of
disobedience, they "turn[ed] my right order into the lust of sin (*rectam con-
stitutionem meam in libidinem peccati vertentes*), although they ought to have

---

53. See especially *Letter* 52r.

known that the motion in their veins was not to facilitate the sweetness of sin but the love of children (*cum commotionem venarum suarum non in dulcedine peccati sed in amore filiorum*)."[54] Which is to say that, in an Augustinian vein, she imagines the possibility in the Edenic paradise of a lustless intercourse whose aim is procreative, although the fall has tainted intercourse so that it tends towards the satisfaction of illicit desire. Nevertheless, Hildegard maintains that conception of children remains a sacred duty and something that can be accomplished virtuously; thus she goes on at length about prohibitions on polygamy (1.2.13), incest (1.2.16), marrying someone who is too young (1.2.19), and intercourse when a woman is having her menses or is pregnant (1.2.20, 22). Although she will describe virginity as "the most beautiful fruit among all the fruits of the valley (*pulcherrimum pomum inter omnia poma convallium*)," which echoes the language of Sg 6:10, in this vision, she emphasizes the continuing goodness of sexual intercourse, when it is rightly practiced: "However, let man seek, according to that which human nature teaches him, the right way with his wife in the strength of his heat and the energy of his seed, and let him do this according to the human science for the sake of zeal for children."[55] Procreative sex remains a fundamental good for Hildegard, since it is the highest expression of the primal mutuality that God intended humanity to practice.

This "commentary" on the human form and the star-filled cloud emanating from it takes up the vast majority of the second vision. Although Hildegard identifies Eve as the primary agent responsible for humanity's fall into sin, her main concern is to demonstrate the mutuality that ought to exist between men and women, which is expressed through their co-operation in their shared task of procreation. This is not quite equality, since Hildegard says that "a wife is subject to her husband in whom he sows his seed (*mulier viro subiecta est in qua ipse semen suum seminet*)."[56] But she nevertheless imagines a world in which women retain their fundamental dignity—and it is not entirely clear that she sees this subordination as part of the right order of things.

Christ's sacrificial death on the cross plays a surprisingly small role in this vision, as Hildegard emphasizes the need for humans to practice penitence

---

54. *Scivias* 1.2.15 (CCCM 43, 24).
55. *Scivias* 1.2.20 (CCCM 43, 27).
56. *Scivias* 1.2.22 (CCCM 43, 29).

and self-control, especially in matters related to sexuality, which she seems to envision as the primary field of vice and temptation. The crucifixion is only introduced near the end of the vision, as the antidote to lust: "For my Son endured many sufferings in his body and submitted to the cross's death, and so you too will suffer many distresses for love of him, when you overcome in yourselves what was sown in the lust of sin from the taste of the fruit."[57] In this particular account, Hildegard emphasizes the mimetic character of the crucifixion, with Christ's death foreshadowing and providing the pattern for the suffering that will be experienced by those fallen souls fighting against the devil and his temptations. The "battles (*proelia*)" that humans wage against temptation have "great beauty and much fruit, brighter than the sun and sweeter than the love of spices (*mago decore et multo fuctu clariora super solem et dulciora super amorem aromatum*)" and the angels "admire (*admirantur*)" the conquest of death wrought by this "contest (*certamen*)."[58] Hildegard speaks repeatedly of conquering the *libido*, which primarily aims at sexual desire, but also includes "anger, pride, petulance and the other vices of this sort (*iram, superbiam, petulantiam et ceter huiusmodi vitia*)."[59]

After this lengthy excursus, she reaches the final lemma of the image, in which the world has been thrown into great instability. For Hildegard, humanity's primal sin of "disobedience (*inoboedientia*)" has turned nature into a prison of sorts, with humanity "confined by it (*per illam coercetur*)."[60] But Hildegard is also clear that all of this happened within the providence of God, who "foresaw all these things (*haec omnia praevidit*)" and thus planned from the first to send "his Only-begotten to die on behalf of the people, so that humanity might be freed from the devil's power."[61] But far from making an anticipatory move to redeem humanity to its original status, God has exalted humanity higher than they would have been previously, since the incarnation—the Son of God putting on flesh—would not have happened apart from this primal sin.[62]

The interpretive vision of Genesis 1–3 that Hildegard offers in the second vision of the first part of *Scivias* is one of a cosmos that is always tending towards

---

57. *Scivias* 1.2.24 (CCCM 43, 30).
58. *Scivias* 1.2.24 (CCCM 43, 31).
59. *Scivias* 1.2.24 (CCCM 43, 30).
60. *Scivias* 1.2.27 (CCCM 43, 32).
61. *Scivias* 1.2.30 (CCCM 43, 33).
62. *Scivias* 1.2.31 (CCCM 43, 34).

mutuality and union. But the totality of this vision only becomes clear by "reading" the image and commentary in tandem, as essential parts of a whole. The image is marked by terrible visuals—a dark hole breaking up the ground, belching out black smoke and unleashing a conniving serpent on an unsuspecting, innocent humanity. The fall of Lucifer and his angelic comrades seems to present an irruption in the good plans of God. But this irruption—this bursting forth of pride—that unleashes chaos on the world, opens the possibility of an even greater union with God than would have been available without it.

Too often, studies in the history of biblical interpretation are insufficiently concerned with the social and cultural dimensions—the structuring systems, to borrow a phrase from Bourdieu—in which the exposition of biblical texts take place. Not all aspiring exegetes had the same options available to them. Part of this, of course, is related to access to education, to leisure time, and to resources (scribes, libraries, and the like). But there is also the matter that not all voices were held to be equal. The biblical commentary was simply not a viable form for Hildegard to pursue in any substantial way. Hildegard's responsibilities as *magistra* of her two communities required her to expound the gospels regularly for her nuns, and there seems to have been an eager audience for her short bursts of (divinely-inspired) insight on these pericopes. And her status as a prophet encouraged her many devotees to seek her interpretations on difficult questions that could be resolved by the spiritual vision she possessed, as did the monks of Villiers. But her legacy could never have been secured by writing primarily in genres—the expository homily or the biblical commentary—that were associated with the male privileges of public preaching and scholastic study. But we can nonetheless see her inclination towards the exegetical and the expository in her writing visionary treatises that explicitly adopt the commentary genre.

And, thus, in a paradoxical way, those strict limitations that had restricted Hildegard from authoritatively interpreting the scriptures offered her the freedom to privilege her own, creative visions of the divine. Forbidden from composing lengthy biblical commentaries, she generated her own visionary sources to exposit—and, most notably, received ecclesial support and recognition for doing so. Thus to think of Hildegard as a Christian thinker who arrived at biblical exegesis through the "back door" is to limit our own vision of what counts (and what doesn't) as interpretation of the Scriptures. In this essay, I have shown how she engages in re-tellings of scriptural narratives, practices intertextual exegesis, and engages critically and creatively with earlier traditions of interpretation—all of these practices that occur in the structure of a lemmatic commentary. And beyond transgressing the line between biblical text and commentary, she also transgresses the boundary between image and text. There has been a growing interest among scholars of the history of interpretation in visual interpretations of the Bible, and Robin Jensen has been the field's leading figure in this regard.[63] But Hildegard offers something almost entirely unique, combining visual representation and textual exposition in a single work. And, as we have seen, Hildegard's images are conveyed in writing as well as in sketches (which are not extant in all manuscripts), further contesting this line between image and text. By taking a more capacious view of what constitutes a legitimate genre of biblical interpretation, we not only enrich and diversify the lineage of scriptural exegetes, but we also radically expand our understanding of how biblical texts, traditions, and images shaped the imaginations of readers and hearers across the centuries, especially among those from more marginalized classes who were prevented, for one reason or another, from composing commentaries on these texts.

Bibliography

Primary Sources

Hildegard of Bingen. *Scivias*, translated by Jane Bishop and Columba Hart. New York: Paulist Press, 1990.

Hildegard of Bingen. *Scivias. Corpus Christianorum Continuatio Medievalis*. XLIII/XLIIIA. Turnhout: Brepols, 1978.

Secondary Sources

Caviness, Madeline. "Hildegard as Designer of the Illustrations to her Works." In *Hildegard of Bingen: The Context of her Thought and Art*, edited by Charles Burnett and Peter Dronke, 29–62. London: The Warburg Institute, 1998.

DeGroot, Christina and Marion Ann Taylor. "Recovering Women's Voices in the History of Interpretation." In *Recovering Nineteenth-Century Women Interpreters of the Bible*, edited by Christina DeGroot and Marion Ann Taylor, 1–19. Atlanta: SBL Press, 2007.

Embach, Michael. *Conspectus der Handschriften Hildegards von Bingen*. Münster: Aschendorff Verlag, 2013.

63. Of particular note are her books *Understanding Early Christian Art* (London: Routledge, 2000) and *The Cross: History, Art, and Controversy* (Cambridge, MA: Harvard University Press, 2017).

Jensen, Robin. *Understanding Early Christian Art*. London: Routledge, 2000.

———. *The Cross: History, Art, and Controversy*. Cambridge, MA: Harvard University Press, 2017.

Kienzle, Beverly Mayne. *Hildegard of Bingen and Her Gospel Homilies: Speaking New Mysteries*. Turnhout: Brepols, 2009.

Klein, Elizabeth. *Augustine's Theology of Angels*. Cambridge: Cambridge University Press, 2018.

McGinn, Bernard. "Women Reading the Song of Songs in the Christian Tradition." In *Scriptural Exegesis: The Shapes of Culture and the Religious Imagination: Essays in Honor of Michael Fishbane*, edited by Deborah A. Green and Laura Lieber, 281–92. New York, Oxford University Press, 2009.

Newman, Judith. *Sister of Wisdom: St. Hildegard's Theology of the Feminine Divine*. Berkeley: University of California Press, 1987.

Young, Frances M. *Biblical Exegesis and the Formation of Christian Culture*. Cambridge: Cambridge University Press, 1997.

GENERAL INDEX